Bioreactors: Animal Cell Culture Control for Bioprocess Engineering

Bioreactors: Animal Cell Culture Control for Bioprocess Engineering

Editor

Luigi Salvay

scitus academics

Bioreactors: Animal Cell Culture Control for Bioprocess Engineering
Edited by **Luigi Salvay**

ISBN: 978-1-68117-695-6
Library of Congress Control Number: 2016958852

www.scitusacademics.com

Notice

Printed in United States of America on Acid Free Paper

Preface

Bioreactor is a key device during in vitro animal cell culture. There are several types of bioreactors, including stirred-tank, airlift, hollow-fiber, and Rotary Cell Culture System (RCCS) designs. The stirred-tank bioreactor is one of the most commonly used types, and is used both for industrial applications and laboratory research. The RCCS, invented by NASA, is increasingly used in the area of tissue engineering for medical purposes. Important improvements have been made in the design of traditional bioreactors, and new types of bioreactor are also being developed such as Couette-Taylor bioreactor, multifunctional-membrane bioreactor, and shaking bioreactor. It provides an appropriate growth environment for the cells, enabling them to proliferate and become the final bio-product. Since animal cells are different from microbial cells in morphology, culture skill needed, and mechanical stimulation needed, the traditional microbial bioreactors are not suitable for the large-scale animal cell culture any more, and many new bioreactors are developed.

Bioreactors play a key role in the field of biologics, where they are used for the production of recombinant therapeutic proteins by large-scale cultivation of animal cells. Work is also progressing on techniques to improve the performance of bioreactors, including perfusion culture, the use of microcarriers, and methods of suppressing apoptosis and of monitoring cell growth in real time. Given the demand for the production by animal cells for use in the growing number of clinical applications, further advances in bioreactor technology can be expected during the next few years. *Bioreactors: Animal Cell Culture Control for Bioprocess Engineering* presents the design, fabrication, and control of a new type of bioreactor meant especially for animal cell line culture. It reviews the bioreactors particularly designed for the animal cell culture, and addresses the mechanical loads on the cultured cells.

Animal cell processes are primarily used for the production of proteins and viral vaccines of relatively high value. Recent advancements in animal cell bioreactor are reviewed. Most previous concerns about the potential difficulties in scaling-up animal cell processes have been alleviated by the developments in bioreactors.

Table of Contents

Chapter 1

Membrane Bioreactor (MBR) Technology for Wastewater Treatment and Reclamation: Membrane Fouling

Oliver Terna Iorhemen *, Rania Ahmed Hamza and Joo Hwa Tay

Department of Civil Engineering, University of Calgary, Calgary, AB T2N 1N4, Canada

ABSTRACT

The membrane bioreactor (MBR) has emerged as an efficient compact technology for municipal and industrial wastewater treatment. The major drawback impeding wider application of MBRs is membrane fouling, which significantly reduces membrane performance and lifespan, resulting in a significant increase in maintenance and operating costs. Finding sustainable membrane fouling mitigation strategies in MBRs has been one of the main concerns over the last two decades. This paper provides an overview of membrane fouling and studies conducted to identify mitigating strategies for fouling in MBRs. Classes of foulants, including biofoulants, organic foulants and inorganic foulants, as well as factors influencing membrane fouling are outlined. Recent research attempts on fouling control, including addition of coagulants and adsorbents, combination of aerobic granulation with MBRs, introduction of granular materials with air scouring in the MBR tank, and quorum quenching are presented. The addition of coagulants and adsorbents shows a significant membrane fouling reduction, but further research is needed to establish optimum dosages of the various coagulants/adsorbents. Similarly, the integration of aerobic granulation with MBRs, which targets biofoulants and organic foulants, shows outstanding filtration performance and a significant reduction in fouling rate, as well as excellent nutrients removal. However, further research is needed on the enhancement of long-term granule integrity. Quorum quenching also offers a strong potential for fouling control, but pilot-scale testing is required to explore the feasibility of full-scale application.

Keywords: aerobic granulation; extracellular polymeric substances (EPS); membrane bioreactor (MBR); membrane fouling; quorum quenching; soluble microbial products (SMPs); wastewater treatment

1. INTRODUCTION

Membrane bioreactor (MBR) technology has emerged as a wastewater treatment technology of choice over the activated sludge process (ASP), which has been the conventional municipal wastewater technology over the last century. MBR is, in fact, one of the most important innovations in wastewater treatment [1,2,3,4], as it overcomes the drawbacks of the conventional ASP, including large space requirement for secondary clarifiers, liquid–solid separation issues, production of excess sludge, and limitations with removal of recalcitrants [5]. MBRs have been used for both municipal and industrial wastewater treatment and reclamation [6,7,8,9,10]. An MBR is a hybrid of a conventional biological treatment system and physical liquid–solid separation using membrane filtration [11,12,13] in one system. The MBR technology provides the following advantages over ASP: High-quality effluent, higher volumetric loading rates, shorter hydraulic retention times (HRT), longer solid retention times (SRT), less sludge production, and potential for simultaneous nitrification/denitrification in long SRTs [2,5,13,14,15,16]. The inclusion of membranes in the system eliminates the need for secondary clarifiers. The elimination of secondary clarifiers and operation of MBR at a shorter HRT results in significantly reduced plant area requirements. However, the use of MBR technology has disadvantages, including higher energy costs, the need to control membrane fouling problems, and potential high costs of periodic membrane replacement [17].

Membrane fouling remains a major drawback of MBR [2,18,19], as it significantly reduces membrane performances and membrane lifespan, leading to an increase in maintenance and operating costs [12,20]. Membrane fouling in MBRs is attributable to suspended particulates (microorganisms and cell debris), colloids, solutes, and sludge flocs [2]. These materials deposit onto the membrane surface and into the membrane pores, clogging the pores, and leading to a decline in the permeability of the membrane [11]. The heterogeneous nature of suspended solids and active microorganisms in mixed liquor suspended solids (MLSS) makes membrane fouling an inevitable challenge that is difficult to control in long-term MBR applications [12]. Membrane fouling mitigation in MBRs has been one of the key areas of extensive research in order to enhance the wider application of the MBR technology in wastewater engineering.

This paper provides an overview of the fundamentals of membrane fouling and advances in fouling mitigation strategies in MBRs, based on the recent and relevant publications on membrane fouling. The review covers background information on membrane fouling, classes of membrane foulants in MBRs, and a discussion on the factors affecting membrane fouling in MBRs. This is followed by a comprehensive review of the current research trends for membrane fouling control in MBR.

2. MEMBRANE FOULING IN MBR

According to the International Union of Pure and Applied Chemistry (IUPAC) Working Party on Membrane Nomenclatures, membrane fouling is "the process resulting in loss of performance of a membrane due to the deposition of suspended or dissolved substances on its external surfaces, at its pore openings, or within its pores" [21]. These foulants can be suspended particulates (microorganisms and cell debris), colloids, and solutes in the MLSS [2,14,18]. The physico-chemical interactions that take place between the foulants and the membrane material result in membrane fouling. Failure to appropriately control membrane fouling in MBRs may, in some cases, lead to failure to treat the required design flows [13].

Fouling in MBRs occurs in different forms, namely, pore narrowing, pore clogging and, cake formation. Pore clogging refers to the blocking of membrane micro pores by foulants. Pore clogging depends, to a large extent, on the size of the particle and the membrane pore size. The attachment of the materials in the pores is aided by sticky substances in the solution. Cake formation, on the other hand, results from the continuous accumulation of bacteria clusters, biopolymers and inorganic matter, which form a layer (biocake) on the membrane [22]. The cake layer increases membrane filtration resistance. Membrane fouling mechanisms in MBRs are schematically illustrated in Figure 1.

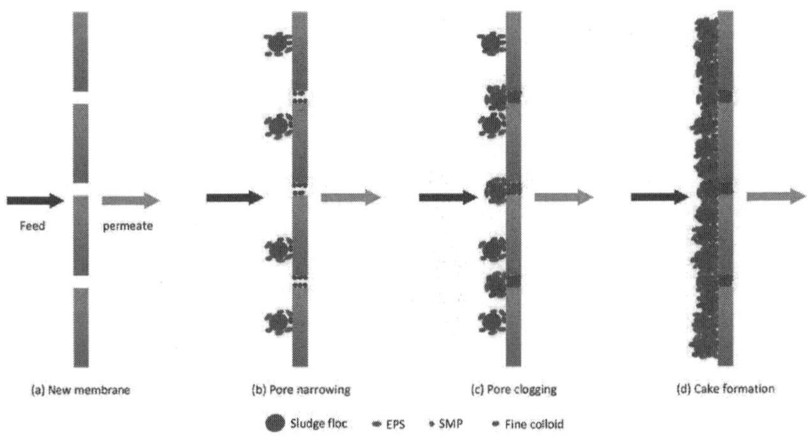

Figure 1. Mechanisms of membrane fouling in membrane bioreactors (MBR).

In operational terms, membrane fouling decreases the permeate flux when the MBR is operated at constant transmembrane pressure (TMP), and results in the increase of TMP when the MBR is operated at constant permeate flux. At constant flux operation, a sharp increase in TMP indicates severe membrane fouling. This sudden TMP increase is called a "TMP jump". TMP jump has been described as a three-stage process [1,23]: Stage 1—an initial "conditioning" fouling, which is caused by initial pore blocking and solutes adsorption; stage 2—linear or weakly exponential gradual rise in TMP due to biofilm formation and further membrane pore blocking;

and stage 3—a sudden rapid increase in the rate of TMP rise (dTMP/dt) [3]. Stage 3 is thought to be the consequence of severe membrane fouling, and is believed to be due to successive closure of pores and changes to the local flux resulting from fouling, which causes local fluxes to exceed the critical value, hence, acceleration of particle deposition [24,25] and sudden changes of the cake layer structure [23]. Bacteria in the inner biofilms tend to die due to oxygen limitations, thereby releasing more EPS [26]. Once stage 3 occurs, membrane cleaning is required. The practical implication of this is that a delay in stage 3 will allow for a reduction in membrane cleaning frequency, which will ultimately result in MBR operational cost savings. Thus, one key objective of fouling control is to retard TMP jump through modification of sludge characteristics (MLSS, floc size, EPS content, and apparent viscosity) or lowering of operational flux [2].

2.1. Classification of Foulants

Membrane foulants in MBR can be grouped into biofoulants, organic foulants and inorganic foulants based on their biological and chemical characteristics [27].

2.1.1. Biofoulants

Biofoulants refer to the bacteria or flocs whose deposition, growth and metabolism on the membrane results in fouling [2]. For a start, one bacteria cell may attach to the membrane surface or inside its pores and, after some time, the cell multiplies into a cluster of cells, leading to the formation of biocake, and hence reduced permeability. The bacteria (biofoulants) and their metabolic products contribute to fouling [28]. Essentially, membrane biofouling is a two-step process, starting with early bacterial attachment, followed by multiplication of bacteria on the membrane surface [29]. Some publications expand the definition of biofoulants to include the metabolic products of these clusters of bacteria cells [28]. However, in this paper, the organic substances produced by microorganisms are considered organic foulants (Section 2.1.2.) for the purpose of research on their mitigation strategies. Membrane biofouling is one of the most important operational problems in membrane-based systems [30].

2.1.2. Organic Foulants

Organic foulants in MBRs refer to biopolymers, e.g., polysaccharides and proteins, of which deposition on the membrane results in a decline of membrane permeability. These foulants are found in metabolic products of bacteria, which are collectively called EPS. Compared to large particles, such as sludge floc, the deposition of organic foulants on the membrane surface is more difficult to remove [5]. In an experiment to investigate membrane fouling under various operational conditions using a laboratory-scale submerged MBR with a hollow-fibre membrane module, Wang and Li [31] reported that biopolymers are important foulants and have a significant impact on membrane fouling. Findings from their experiment further revealed that the rate of membrane fouling in the reactor correlated with the biopolymer concentration in the sludge suspension under different conditions.

In addition to EPS, research has indicated that MBR sludge also contains a pool of large-sized free organic solutes called biopolymer clusters (BPC) [32]. BPCs result from the clustering of loose EPS and soluble microbial products (SMPs) in the sludge cake [33]. BPCs are much bigger than SMPs and are composed primarily of biopolymers and with few microorganisms [33,34]. The few microorganisms in BPCs make them different from bacterial flocs. Due to the bigger size of BPCs, they are retained by the membrane in MBRs and are thus, not found in the MBR effluent. The large membrane surface in an MBR provides a conducive environment for BPC formation and growth; and, the formation and accumulation of BPCs in MBR causes serious membrane fouling [34]. In an experiment to investigate the fouling propensity of MBR sludge, Sun *et al.* [35] reported that increasing the concentration of BPCs by 20% and 60% from about 3.5 mg/L in the mixed sludge liquor remarkably raised the rate of fouling by 120% and 300%, respectively. This indicates that BPCs in the MBR suspension have a significant effect on the fouling potential of the sludge. Research has also been conducted to find ways of mitigating membrane fouling due to BPCs. It has been reported that the ozonation of BPCs can reduce the negative role of BPCs in membrane fouling [35]. In this experiment, 0.03 mg O_3/mg total organic carbon (TOC) of BPCs reduced the mean BPC size from 38 to 27 μm and increasing the dosage to 0.3 mg O_3/mg TOC of BPCs further reduced the size to 12 μm. It was further reported that ozonation also modified BPCs surface properties, leading to an increase in the filterable fraction and a reduction in the viscosity of the mixed liquor.

2.1.3. Inorganic Foulants

Inorganic foulants are a group of inorganic substances that precipitate onto the membrane surface or into the membrane pores, resulting in membrane fouling. Examples of such substances include cations and anions such as Ca^{2+}, Mg^{2+}, Fe^{3+}, Al^{3+}, SO_4^{2-}, PO_4^{3-}, CO_3^{2-}, OH^-, *etc.* [36,37]. These species precipitate onto the membrane surface due to hydrolysis which leads to pH change, and oxidation [31]. Essentially, inorganic fouling is produced from the chemical precipitation of inorganic species and/or biological precipitation of inorganic-organic complexes [36]. While moderate amounts of metal ions, such as Ca^{2+} (up to 280 mg/L), can be beneficial in controlling and improving biofouling due to binding and bridging EPS (hence, enhanced bioflocculation), high concentrations (above 800 mg/L) have been shown to significantly increase inorganic fouling due to high inorganic precipitate content of the MBR mixed liquor [38]. Inorganic fouling is also termed "mineral scale" in order to differentiate it from biofouling and organic fouling [39]. Crystallization and particulate fouling are the two key mechanisms that play critical roles during inorganic membrane fouling in MBR. In crystallization, precipitation of ions is the pathway to deposition at the membrane surface; while particulate fouling is the deposition following convective transportation of colloidal particulate matter in the solution to the membrane surface [40]. To remove inorganic precipitation from the membrane surface, chemical cleaning is usually the adopted procedure, as it is more effective than physical cleaning [2].

3. FACTORS AFFECTING MEMBRANE FOULING IN MBR

Various factors affect membrane fouling in MBRs. These factors can be grouped into three categories, namely: membrane characteristics, operating conditions, and feed and biomass characteristics. Figure 2, below, is an illustration of the different factors, followed by their discussion in the subsections that follow.

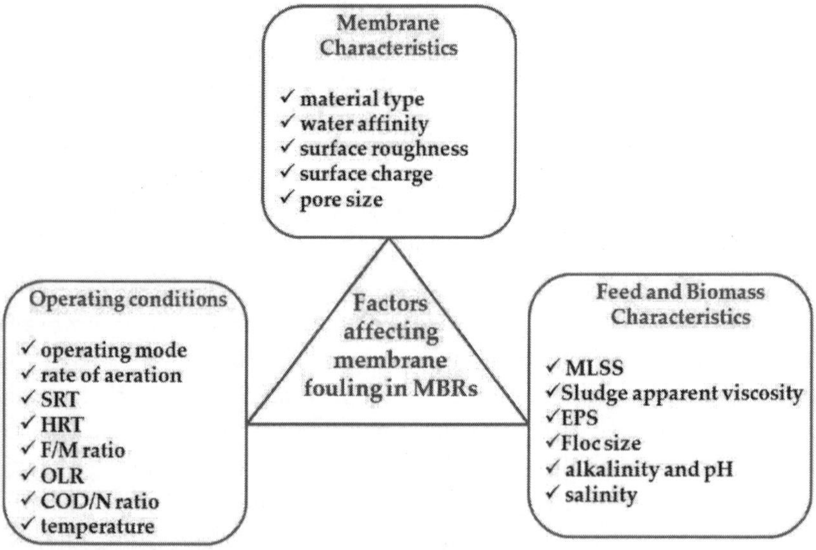

Figure 2. Factors affecting membrane fouling in MBRs.

3.1. Membrane Characteristics

3.1.1. Membrane Material

The material the membrane is made of has an impact on its fouling propensity in MBRs. Based on the membrane material, membranes can be classified into: ceramic membranes, polymeric membranes, and composite membranes. Ceramic membranes exhibit good filtration performance due to their high chemical resistance, integrity, inert nature and ease of cleaning leading to low operating costs [13,41,42]. Ceramic membranes are also highly hydrophilic [5], which makes them more fouling resistant. However, their high cost of fabrication and fragile nature [41] make them economically unfeasible for use in MBR applications. Polymeric membranes are the most common membrane types available. Polymeric membranes have good physical and chemical resistance but are mostly hydrophobic [5]. Examples of polymeric membrane materials include polyvinylidene fluoride (PVDF), polyethersulfone (PES), polyacrylonitrile (PAN), polysulfone (PS), polyethylene (PE), polyvinyl butyral (PVB), cellulose acetate (CA), polypropylene (PP), polytetrafluoroethylene (PTFE), *etc*. Due to their hydrophobic nature, polymeric membranes tend to foul easily, but they tend to be widely used now due to the ease of fabrication of the pore sizes. Composite membranes are membranes produced from two or more materials to combine the strengths of the constituent materials in the final product. Typically, one material constitutes the active surface and another forms the support layer [13]. In composite membrane applications, hydrophobic membranes are coated with hydrophilic polymer to overcome the fouling shortcoming.

The implication of this is that membrane properties can be modified as a fouling abatement measure. Hence, recent research has focused on modifying membrane materials to mitigate fouling in MBRs. Yu *et al.* [43] modified a PP membrane surface using air plasma treatment, and used the modified membrane to investigate the antifouling characteristics in a submerged MBR. The findings showed that flux recovery following water and caustic cleaning was 35% higher than that of the unmodified membrane [43]. Another investigation has been conducted on the modification of PES ultrafiltration (UF) membranes using different forms of nanosilver [44]. Findings from this research revealed that the modified membranes fouled less than the control. Another innovative membrane modification for fouling mitigation is the production of photocatalytic nanocomposite membranes. In this regard, Moghadam *et al.* [45] evaluated the flux performances and antifouling properties of PVDF-TiO_2 nanocomposite membranes, with and without UV irradiation. The authors found that the composite membranes (compared to unmodified PVDF membranes) reached flux stabilisation very rapidly both in darkness and under UV conditions; in addition, the PVDF-TiO_2 nanocomposite membranes presented the best flux recovery ratio when filtration was combined with UV irradiation at 365 nm. Lower membrane cleaning frequency was also reported for the PVDF-TiO_2 nanocomposite membrane compared to the unmodified PVDF membrane.

However, the long term effects of the modified membranes need further investigation especially for membranes modified with nano-particles as these nano-particles can have human health and ecotoxicological impacts [46].

3.1.2. Water Affinity

The water affinity (hydrophilicity or hydrophobicity) property of the membrane material affects fouling in MBRs. The water affinity behaviour of a membrane material is determined by measuring the contact angle of a water drop on its surface [47]. Smaller angles indicate hydrophilicity, whereas larger angles indicate hydrophobicity. Due to the hydrophobic interactions occurring between the membrane material, microbial cell and solutes, membrane fouling is more severe in hydrophobic membranes compared to hydrophilic membranes [1]. This is because the more hydrophilic a membrane material is, the less the adsorption of macrosolutes in the wastewater, such as proteins, there are. Hydrophobic materials, on the other hand, tend to adsorb hydrophobic substances in the wastewater, resulting in fouling. To strike a balance, composite membranes are produced by coating hydrophobic membranes with a thin layer of hydrophilic material to combine the sturdiness of the former and the low fouling propensity of the latter [47].

3.1.3. Membrane Surface Roughness

The surface roughness of the membrane material also has some influence on membrane fouling in MBRs. Membranes with homogeneous surfaces are less subject to be fouled than those with uneven surfaces [47]. Research findings have indicated that membranes with higher surface roughness foul faster [48]. This is because the rough membrane surface provides a valley for the colloidal particles in the wastewater to accumulate on [49], leading to the blocking of the valleys thus increasing the severity of fouling for rougher membrane surfaces [50]. However, a study conducted to investigate the relationship between surface roughness and membrane fouling in MBRs found that membranes having higher projections on their outer surface exhibited a higher antifouling property, with the recovery of permeability after backwashing following the same trend [51]. This is attributable to the accumulation of foulants in the valley between the projections. Therefore, although rough surfaces increase the propensity for fouling, rougher surfaces with protruding projections may trap the foulants in their valleys whilst still functioning normally.

3.1.4. Membrane Surface Charge

The membrane surface charge is another property of importance in relation to membrane fouling especially if there are charged particles in the feed. It has been indicated that most membrane materials are negatively charged under normal conditions [47]. This is partly attributable to the colloidal particles that deposit on the membrane surface [49]. Some cations in the MLSS like Ca^{2+} and Al^{3+} will react with the negatively charged membranes surfaces, leading to inorganic fouling.

3.1.5. Membrane Pore Size

Generally, membranes used in wastewater treatment are broadly grouped into two: porous membranes and non-porous membranes. Porous membranes employ straining, sieving, or size exclusion to separate particles, e.g., microfiltration (MF), ultrafiltration (UF), and loose end nanofiltration (NF) membranes [39]. Non-porous membranes, on the other hand, make use of the differences in diffusivity or solubility between the solvent and the solute in the membranes for separation [52], as cited by Shirazi *et al.* [39]. Examples of non-porous membranes include tight end (NF) and reverse osmosis (RO) membranes. Because the separation mechanism required in MBRs is sieving (size exclusion), MF and UF membranes are typically used [5], thus allowing the complete physical retention of bacterial flocs and virtually all suspended solids within the bioreactor [1].

The pore size of the membranes in relation to the sizes of the particles in the wastewater feed stream in MBRs can have an effect on membrane fouling. Pore blocking mechanism tends to increase with increasing membrane pore size [47]. This is because, it is easier for fine particles (smaller than the membrane pore size) to enter the membrane pores and get trapped in them, resulting in pore blocking [53]. With smaller pores, large particles rapidly form a top layer on the membrane and collect the smaller particles. The resulting layer formed on the membrane surface can be easily removed by air scouring or the turbulence resulting from cross-flow filtration. This is schematically illustrated in Figure 3 below. Generally, the effects of membrane pore size on fouling depend greatly on the composition of the feed stream, particularly the particle size distribution.

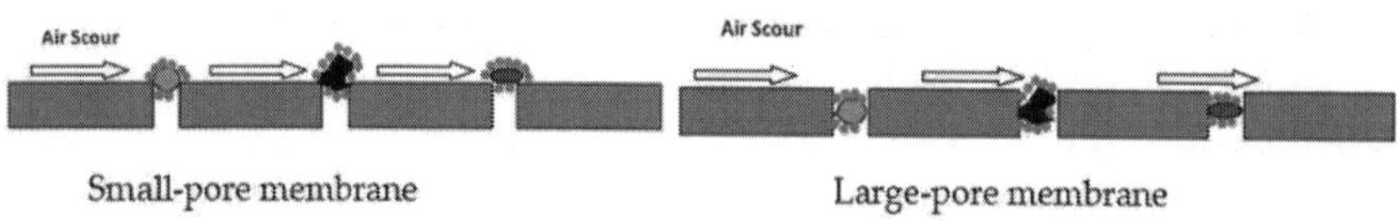

Figure 3. Schematic of pore blocking on small-pore and large-pore membranes.

Miyoshi *et al.* [54] investigated the effect of different polymeric membrane materials on the relationship between membrane pore size and fouling in an MBR using cellulose acetate butyrate (CAB), PVB, and PVDF membranes. Their result revealed that membrane fouling decreased with increasing membrane pore size for PVDF membranes; but CAB membranes exhibited an opposite trend with smaller pores showing less fouling tendency than those with larger pores [54]. This indicates that the best membrane pore size to abate membrane fouling in MBR differs for different polymeric materials. Hence, MBR operating parameters ought to be carefully selected for different polymeric membrane materials.

3.2. Operating Conditions

3.2.1. Operating Mode

Two operating modes are typically used in MBRs namely, constant TMP with variable permeate flux and constant permeate flux (L/m^2 h) with variable TMP. The latter is the preferred mode in MBRs as it can readily handle fluctuations in influent hydraulic loading [47]. When operating at constant permeate flux, membrane fouling is observed by TMP jump. The critical flux needs to be determined in constant flux operation, because it is an important parameter in MBR operation [5]. The determination of critical flux is presented by Diez *et al.* [55]. The critical flux is a quantitative parameter for the filterability of different membranes and/or different activated sludge mixed liquors [56]. Critical flux is the flux above which the deposition of solids on the membrane surface becomes evident (cake or gel formation) [55]. In practical terms, however, critical flux is not attainable in MBR. The tendency, therefore, is to operate at the sustainable flux rather than the critical flux. Sustainable flux refers to the flux above which membrane fouling rate is economically and environmentally unsustainable [57] or the flux for which there is gradual increase in TMP at an acceptable rate, such that chemical cleaning is unnecessary [1]. In essence, the sustainable flux, which is less than the critical flux, provides an acceptable rise in TMP. This operational flux plays a key role in MBR fouling. For a given MBR system, operating at a flux below the critical flux prevents excessive deposition of biomass on the membrane surface [2,44,58].

3.2.2. Rate of Aeration

Aeration plays a dual role in aerobic MBRs. It supplies oxygen for the biological processes and serves as a way of dislodging the cake layer formed on the membrane surface (air scouring). The oxygen supplied via aeration facilitates the biodegradability and cell synthesis of the biomass [12]. Research has shown that increasing the rate of aeration in an MBR leads to a reduction in membrane fouling [59,60]. In a study to investigate the impact of aeration velocity on membrane fouling in a pilot-scale submerged MBR, Yigit *et al.* [61] reported that increase in aeration velocity positively impacted fouling control. However, the degree of such a positive effect was substantially reduced as MLSS increased. This is attributable to increased viscosity resulting from elevated levels of MLSS. Air scouring rates in the literature range from 3 L air/min m^2 to 12 L air/min m^2 [17].

While a high rate of aeration can minimise membrane fouling through the scouring action, it also has an impact on biomass characteristics. High aeration intensities have been associated with the breakage of sludge flocs and subsequent production of SMPs [2]. Higher aeration rates also increase the energy consumption leading to an increase in operating costs [62,63]. Thus, an optimum aeration intensity needs to be found which strikes a balance between these. It has been indicated that going beyond the critical aeration intensity increases membrane fouling as the shear breaks up large flocs [64]. In this regards, Nywening and Zhou [63] studied the effectiveness of membrane fouling and scouring aeration in three pilot-scale submerged MBRs operated at a series of permeate fluxes, scouring aeration intensities and cyclic aeration frequencies to treat municipal wastewater. They developed a very useful empirical relationship relating the stable reversible fouling resistance to sustainable permeate fluxes and scouring aeration intensities, which is shown in Equation (1).

$$R_{f(i)} = R_{O(ref)}\left[\frac{-1}{\left(\frac{J_C}{J_{O(ref)}}-1\right)}\left(\frac{J_i}{J_{O(ref)}}-1\right)+1\right]\left(\frac{Q_{(i)}}{Q_{O(ref)}}\right)^{l} \quad (1)$$

where:

- $R_{f(i)}$ is the fouling resistance at operating conditions *i*, m^{-1};
- $R_{O(ref)}$ is the fouling resistance at reference point *O*, m^{-1};
- J_C is the critical flux, L/m^2 h;
- $J_{O(ref)}$ is the reference permeate flux at point *O*, L/m^2 h;
- J_i is the permeate flux at operating condition *i*, L/m^2 h;
- $Q_{(i)}$ is the scouring aeration intensity at operating condition *i*, m^3/h;

- $Q_{O(ref)}$ is the scouring aeration intensity at reference operating condition O, m^3/h;
- I is the scouring aeration intensity exponent, which is approximately −2.

3.2.3. Solids Retention Time (SRT)

The SRT is a very important factor affecting membrane fouling in MBRs [13]. The SRT varies with the formation of EPS. A majority of studies indicate that increasing the SRT results in a decrease in the concentration of EPS as the biomass stays longer in the system, and lowering the SRT increases the amount of EPS [65,66,67,68]. High SRTs produce starvation conditions in the bioreactor creating an enabling environment for reduced formation of EPS, low sludge production and nitrification [5,69]. However, extremely high SRTs are not desirable as they rather increase membrane fouling due to the accumulation of matters (high MLSS accumulation) and increasing sludge viscosity [66]. Excessively high SRTs can also lead to high biomass concentrations resulting in reduced aeration efficiency [53]. In an experiment to investigate the effect of SRT on membrane fouling in MBR, Van den Broeck *et al.* [53] reported lower membrane fouling rates at 30 days and 50 days SRTs compared to 10 days SRT. It has been indicated that operating above 50 days tends to increase fouling [13].

Similarly, operating at very low SRTs (down to two days) significantly increases membrane fouling [1]. This has been attributed to increased EPS (bound and soluble) concentration at these low SRTs [2]. Extremely low SRTs also result in a reduction in MBR performance as a result of low biomass concentration [70].

3.2.4. Hydraulic Retention Time (HRT)

The HRT has indirect effect on membrane fouling as it determines, with other operating parameters, the sludge characteristics. Most researchers agree that as HRT decreases, the rate of membrane fouling in MBRs increases [71,72] due to an increase in sludge viscosity and EPS concentrations [2]. The decrease in HRT stimulates the release of EPS from bacterial cells, causes overgrowth of filamentous bacteria, and the formation of irregular large flocs. Additionally, the decrease in HRT causes an increase in MLSS concentration and sludge viscosity which are predominant factors that affect hydrodynamic conditions of MBR systems [30,70]. Isma *et al.* [73] investigated the influence of HRT and SRT on membrane fouling using synthetic wastewater. Their study, which used SRTs of 4, 15 and 30 days at HRTs of 4, 8 and 12 h, respectively, found that lower membrane fouling and slower rise in TMP were observed at the longest SRT (30 days) and longest HRT (12 h). Similarly, a study of the effect of microbial activity and fouling potential in submerged anaerobic MBRs operated at HRTs of 14, 16, and 20 days found that decreasing the HRT from 20 to 14 days resulted in increased EPS (bound EPS and SMPs) production, and hence severe fouling [74].

3.2.5. Food–Microorganisms (F/M) Ratio

The F/M ratio is an important operational parameter in biological wastewater treatment systems. In order to determine the influence of F/M ratio on membrane fouling, Kimura *et al.* [19] investigated fouling in three identical pilot-scale MBRs using real municipal wastewater under different operating conditions. Their results indicated that the F/M ratio influences the nature of the foulants as high F/M correlated with higher proteinaceous foulant [19]. Similarly, Trussell *et al.* [75] reported that the rate of membrane fouling in MBRs increases with increasing F/M ratios. High values of the F/M ratio can also elevate EPS levels due to high food utilisation by biomass [70]. Another study also reported that decreasing F/M ratios resulted in a reduction in the concentration of EPS [76]. It is therefore desirable to operate at lower F/M ratio values.

3.2.6. Organic Loading Rate (OLR)

The OLR is one of the most important parameters affecting the operation of biological wastewater treatment systems [77]. In MBR, Zhang *et al.* [78] investigated the effect of constant and variable influent OLR on membrane fouling using two identical laboratory-scale submerged MBRs operated for 162 days at an SRT of 30 days;

the influent OLR was kept constant in one MBR and varied in the other. They reported that membrane fouling during start-up period in the MBR fed with variable OLR was more significant than the MBR fed with constant OLR. However, at the MBR stable state (when the MBR systems gradually stabilised in terms of biomass concentration and TOC removal), the fouling tendency was clearly reversed with less membrane fouling observed for variable feed OLR. In another study, Johir *et al.* [79] investigated the effect of OLR on membrane fouling in MBRs operated at six different OLRs ranging from 0.5 to 3.0 kg COD/m^3 day (COD = chemical oxygen demand) at constant HRT and SRT of 8 h and 40 days, respectively. Findings from their study revealed that higher fouling rates were observed at higher OLRs (2.75–3.0 kg COD/m^3 day) with more hydrophilic substances at higher OLRs.

3.2.7. Chemical Oxygen Demand/Nitrogen (COD/N) Ratio

The COD/N ratio is one of the most important parameters for the growth of microorganisms. It also plays a key role in nutrients' removal (particularly nitrification and denitrification) [80]. This operating parameter has also been reported to correlate well with membrane fouling in MBRs. Feng *et al.* [81] studied the effect of COD/N ratio on membrane fouling in two identical submerged MBRs operated in parallel at COD/N ratios of 10:1 and 5:1, respectively. They reported that operation at COD/N ratio of 10:1 remarkably reduced membrane fouling rate through the slower rise in TMP compared to the MBR operated at COD/N ratios of 5:1. They further found that the duration of stage 2 of the TMP jump was twice (over 30 days) as long in the COD/N ratio of 10:1 compared 5:1. Similarly, Hao *et al.* [82] investigated the effect of COD/N ratio on membrane fouling in MBRs operated at three different ratios (100:5, 100:2.5, and 100:1.8) for over a year. Findings from their research showed that increasing the COD:N ratio from 100:5 to 100:1.8 resulted in an improved membrane performance and a longer operation period before membrane cleaning; and, the bound EPS/SMP composition, such as protein to carbohydrate ratio, played a more significant role in controlling fouling than the total amount of bound EPS and SMP produced.

However, there is inconsistency on the effect of COD/N ratio on membrane fouling in the literature. Han *et al.* [83] compared membrane filtration performance in anoxic/oxic MBRs with COD/N ratios of 9.9 and 5.5. They reported more membrane fouling at high COD/N ratio as the increase in COD/N ratio led to an elevated production of humic acids in SMPs and carbohydrates, proteins, and humic acids in LB-EPS. Similarly, Gasmi *et al.* [84] found lower specific resistance to filtration and membrane fouling rate at low COD/N ratios (2.3 and 1.5). Yang *et al.* [85] also reported that low COD/N ratio of 3.5 greatly facilitated membrane fouling control by a simple aeration and backflushing strategy.

3.2.8. Temperature

Temperature is known to influence the rate of biodegradation. In MBRs, temperature impacts membrane fouling by altering the MLSS characteristics. It has been reported that decreasing operational temperature causes the bacteria to release more EPS [86]. Very low temperatures are associated with an increased occurrence of filamentous bacteria, which produce more SMPs in the MLSS [30], hence more propensity for membrane fouling. Deflocculation, diffusitivity, biodegradation, and adsorption in the MBR have also been indicated to depend on temperature [3]. Generally, four phenomena have been put forward to explain the increased membrane fouling at lower temperatures in MBRs: (a) increased viscosity which reduces the shear stress generated by aeration; (b) intensified deflocculation which reduces the size of biomass floc and releases EPS and submicron particles into the MLSS; (c) reduced back transport velocity; and (d) lower biodegradation of organic matter (COD) [87]. Ma *et al.* [86] investigated the effect of temperature on membrane fouling in a pilot-scale submerged MBR and reported much higher concentration of EPS (bound EPS and SMPs) under low temperature, with SMPs decreasing from 28.1 mg/g-MLSS at 8.7 °C, to 2.2 mg/g-MLSS at 19.7 °C with a difference of 25.9 mg/g-MLSS. Furthermore, sudden changes in temperature have been reported to cause spontaneous release of SMPs and increased fouling rates [88]. Deflocculation of sludge flocs have been reported to occur following a temperature increase from 30 °C to 45 °C which led to turbidity increase and increase in SMPs concentration [89]. Sudden temperature increase has also been indicated to deteriorate biomass and decrease proteins in EPS [30]. To overcome these problems, it is suggested to operate MBRs at ambient temperature and avoid sudden temperature changes (increase or decrease). If low temperatures are inevitable, aeration needs to be intensified to overcome the increased viscosity.

3.3. Feed and Biomass Characteristics

The feed (wastewater) and biomass characteristics play key roles in membrane fouling in MBRs. The complex interactions amongst the constituents of biomass and the membrane material affect membrane fouling in MBRs.

3.3.1. Mixed Liquor Suspended Solids (MLSS)

The MLSS contains bacteria flocs, EPS, colloids, microsolutes and macrosolutes. MBRs are operated at MLSS concentrations much higher than ASP. However, the higher concentration of MLSS in MBRs accelerates membrane fouling as a result of high suspended solids [90]. Research findings have indicated that membrane permeability decreases with increasing MLSS concentrations [60]. Wu and Huang [91] reported that operating at MLSS concentrations above 10,000 mg/L greatly increased the viscosity, which, in turn, affected the filterability. Yigit *et al.* [61] studied the impact of operational conditions and biomass characteristics on membrane fouling in a submerged MBR and reported that the concentrations of both polysaccharides and proteins fractions of EPS increase with increasing MLSS concentration. The study further found that the increase in MLSS resulted in a significant decrease in membrane permeability and increased fouling rate at each flux tested. These findings indicate that membrane fouling increases with increasing MLSS concentrations. Similarly, if there is a dominance of filamentous bacteria in the MLSS, there is a tendency for filamentous bulking to occur. Filamentous bulking can significantly increase the production of SMPs which in turn substantially increase the fouling of membranes [68].

However, reports about the effects of MLSS on membrane fouling in MBRs are not consistent in the literature. For example, Rosenberger *et al.* [92] reported reduced membrane fouling as MLSS concentration increased until 15 g/L when the trend reversed and the fouling rate increased at concentrations above 15 g/L. This can be explained in terms of remarkable changes to the sludge rheology. Other studies report no (or little) effect of MLSS concentration on membrane fouling in MBR including Rosenberger *et al.* [93] (MLSS = 9–14 g/L: no effect), Le-Clech *et al.* [94] (MLSS = 4.4–11.6 g/L: No impact between 4 and 8 g/L, but slightly less fouling at 12 g/L), and Brookes *et al.* [95] (MLSS = 6–18: Similar rate of fouling for flux below 10 L/m^2 h and slightly lower fouling rates for higher fluxes). Thus, there is no clear correlation between MLSS concentration and membrane fouling.

3.3.2. Sludge Apparent Viscosity

Viscosity is the measure of a fluid's resistance to gradual deformation by shear or tensile stress. Since MBRs are operated at high MLSS, the total suspended solids content is also very high and this results in higher viscosity values [96]. The high viscosity in MBRs can limit oxygen transfer leading to higher energy consumption for aeration. Trussell *et al.* [60] reported that increasing the viscosity results in membrane permeability decline. Typically, there is a critical MLSS concentration below which sludge viscosity stays low and increases only slowly with increasing concentration [1]. Operating above the critical MLSS concentration results in viscosity increasing exponentially with MLSS concentration [97]. Depending on the operating conditions, the critical MLSS value has been observed to range from 10,000 to 17,000 mg MLSS/L [1]. With higher MLSS viscosity, there is increased rate of membrane fouling in MBR.

3.3.3. Extracellular Polymeric Substances (EPS)

Extracellular polymeric substances (EPS) are waste products of bacteria originating from microbial metabolites, cell lysis, or unmetabolised wastewater components [3]. EPS are known to significantly affect the physico-chemical properties of microbial aggregates such as surface charge, structure, settling properties, flocculation, adsorption ability, *etc.* [98]. They primarily comprise proteins, polysaccharides (carbohydrates), humic acids, nucleic acids, lipids and uronic acids [68,99,100]. Proteins and polysaccharides are the major components of EPS [98] and are the components typically measured as an indication of the amount of EPS. In terms of fouling, proteins exhibit hydrophobic properties while polysaccharides are hydrophilic in nature and this implies that the polysaccharides fractions of EPS have a higher propensity for fouling than protein fractions [61,101], given that hydrophilic membranes are used. EPS are divided into two, namely bound EPS and soluble EPS (also referred to as SMPs) [100]. Bound EPS are further split into loosely bound EPS (LB-EPS) and tightly bound EPS (TB-EPS) [102]. SMPs and bound EPS are considered the major foulants in MBRs [2,36,103,104] as they have multiple interactions with all other foulants [100]. The aggregation of biomass can happen by participation of bound EPS and SMPs, which provides a highly hydrated gel matrix [12,104]. These substances act as a "glue" to keep the microbial aggregates together.

Bound EPS are characterised by adhesion to sludge flocs [99,100]. They are located at or outside the cell surface. Bound EPS facilitate the aggregation of biomass to form microbial aggregates, which alters the flocculation ability, surface charge, hydrophobicity, and sludge viscosity [13]. This alteration affects membrane fouling. TB-EPS provide the inner layer, while LB-EPS are distributed on outer surface of the microbial aggregates. Bound EPS are construction materials for microbial aggregates like sludge flocs and biofilms. In these microbial aggregates, EPS have many charged groups, such as hydroxyl, carboxyl, sulfhydryl, phosphoric and phenolic groups; and polar groups, such as hydrophobic regions in carbohydrates, aliphatics in proteins and aromatics [30]. The presence of both hydrophobic and hydrophilic groups in EPS implies that they are amphoteric in nature. Since the hydrophilic fraction is known to foul the membrane (hydrophilic membrane) more than the hydrophobic fraction, the proportion of hydrophobic to hydrophilic organics plays an important role in the formation of fouling [105]. Thus, the ratio of proteins (hydrophobic) to polysaccharides (hydrophilic) in EPS governs membrane fouling in MBRs, especially cake layer formation [12].

SMPs are the organic compounds released into solution from substrate metabolism and biomass decay [5,106]. SMPs released from substrate metabolism are referred to as substrate utilisation-associated products (UAP) and those resulting from biomass decay are termed biomass-associated products (BAP) [107]. SMPs composition is dominated by polysaccharides, proteins and humic acids [68]. It has been reported that SMPs contribute more to membrane fouling than colloids in MBRs [91]. Another study found that MLSS and bound EPS are not major contributors to fouling when compared to SMPs [99]. The effect of SMPs on membrane fouling in MBRs depends on their concentration, membrane materials, and mode of operation [13]. This implies that the control of SMPs concentration in MBRs is a key factor in controlling fouling. Research indicates that SMPs concentration decreases with increasing SRT, and higher SMPs concentrations are observed at lower dissolved oxygen (DO) concentrations [2]. In contrast to bound EPS, SMPs more easily penetrate into sludge flocs spaces and the membrane pores, and hence there is more fouling.

3.3.4. Floc Size

Microorganisms tend to aggregate and form flocs in biological wastewater treatment systems. The size of the flocs formed aids the liquid-solids separation of the treated water from the MLSS. In MBRs, a wide range of sizes for these flocs have been reported in the literature with size ranging from 5 to 240 μm [1,108]. In a recent study, Shen *et al.* [109] investigated the impact of floc size on membrane fouling in a submerged MBR treating synthetic wastewater. Findings from their study, which had sludge floc size above 1 μm, revealed that a decrease in floc size slightly increased the specific energy barrier but greatly increased the attractive specific interaction energy [109]. This implies an increase in adhesion ability of small flocs to the membrane surface, hence more fouling. The practical implication of this is that the larger the floc size, the better it is for fouling reduction. Current research has thus focused on increasing the floc size using aerobic granulation [11,110,111,112,113], activated carbon addition [114], or zeolite addition [115]. The increment in floc size improves filtration by reducing fouling.

3.3.5. Alkalinity and pH

Alkalinity and pH are important parameters in biodegradation. In relation to MBR, these two factors affect the rate of membrane fouling. It has been reported that low pH values result in increased adsorption of MBR-originated EPS onto the membrane [116]. Another study found the highest EPS flocculation tendency at pH 4.8 [117]. Zhang *et al.* [118] also reported that a repulsive energy barrier exists between sludge flocs and the membrane surface; and, this repulsive energy barrier decreases with decreasing pH which in turn facilitates the attachment of foulants to the membrane. Similarly, Sanguanpak *et al.* [119] reported more severe fouling at low pH (5.5) due to more EPS formation in an MBR treating landfill leachate. All these studies agree that a decrease in the pH of the mixed liquor increases the rate of membrane fouling in MBR. Within the bioreactor, nitrification process generates acid which would lower the pH [120]. To keep the bioreactor at an optimum pH range, alkalinity is required in the feed to buffer the H^+ generated in the nitrification process. If alkalinity is low in the feed, the deficiency would need to be accounted for by adding extra alkalinity.

It should be noted that since inorganic fouling results from chemical precipitation and biological precipitation, pH can affect chemical precipitation. It has been indicated that high pH (8–9) increases the precipitation of $CaCO_3$ [2]. However, moderate amounts of calcium precipitates can be beneficial in controlling biofouling due to binding and bridging EPS (hence, enhanced bioflocculation). Arabi and Nakhla [38] reported that calcium concentration of 280 mg/L improved membrane permeability, while higher concentrations of 830 mg/L resulted in significant membrane inorganic fouling.

3.3.6. Salinity

Salinity is known to have adverse effects on biological systems. In MBRs, it has been demonstrated that the presence of salts in the MLSS cause chemical precipitation and electrostatic attraction towards the surface of the membrane [48]. High salinity also modifies biomass characteristics in the system. Reid *et al.* [121] studied the impact of high salinity (up to 5000 mg/L) on activated sludge characteristics and membrane permeability in a submerged

MBR. Findings from their research revealed that high salinity greatly affected the physical and biochemical properties of activated sludge by increasing bound EPS and SMPs concentrations, and decreasing membrane permeability (increasing membrane fouling) [121]. Similarly, Jang*et al.* [122] investigated the effects of salinity on membrane filtration in MBRs with high salt loadings and reported that high salt concentrations accelerated membrane fouling through increased pore blockings. This implies high salinity altered biomass characteristics like EPS, floc size and zeta potential, which eventually resulted in increased membrane fouling. In another study, Di Bella *et al.* [123] reported that the MBR plant exhibited high biomass respiratory activity and high removal efficiencies at normal salinity content. However, as salinity increased, a decrease of respiration rates was observed alongside increased fouling (cake deposition) attributable to the deterioration of high EPS concentration.

In addition, the ionic composition of the wastewater also plays a role in floc formation. It has been indicated that floc structure and strength strongly depend on the ionic composition and concentration [124]. High concentrations of multivalent cations, e.g., Mg^{2+} and Ca^{2+}, are known to form strong and compact flocs [125,126]. This can be explained by the divalent bridging model where Ca^{2+} and other divalent ions bridge the EPS negatively charged sites, thereby forming a matrix of EPS and single cells. Monovalent cations, on the otherhand, lower floc strength rather [127]. Hence, the presence of polyvalent cations in relation to monovalent cations, in spite of high salinity, can aid the formation of strong bioflocs which would aid membrane filtration.

A summary of the different factors affecting membrane fouling in MBRs and their respective effects are presented inTable 1 below.

Table 1. Factors affecting membrane fouling in membrane bioreactors (MBR).

Factor	Effect on Membrane Fouling	Reference
Membrane Characteristics		
Membrane Material	Ceramic membranes are hydrophilic, hence they foul less. Polymeric membranes are mostly hydrophobic and exhibit more fouling	[5,13,41,42]
Water affinity	Increasing hydrophilicity indicates less membrane fouling propensity while hydrophobicity correlates well with increase propensity for membrane fouling	[47]

4. CURRENT RESEARCH TRENDS FOR MEMBRANE FOULING ABATEMENT IN MBR

4.1. Coagulant Addition

The addition of coagulants to water and wastewater treatment systems facilitates the formation of large flocs from fine particulates in solution. In MBRs, the coagulants help the formation of larger size sludge flocs which enhance membrane filtration. Alum [$Al_2(SO_4)_3$] and ferric chloride ($FeCl_3$) were reported to enhance filterability of MBR mixed liquor and ultimately controlled membrane fouling [128,129]. Wu *et al.* [130] studied the effects of polymeric coagulants on membrane fouling in MBRs using three coagulants: polymeric ferric sulphate (PFS), polymeric aluminium chloride (PACl), and polymeric aluminium ferric chloride (PAFC). They reported that the addition of these coagulants resulted in membrane fouling control through the reduction of the initial TMP and the rate of TMP increase. This was attributed to the ability of the coagulants to restrain the formation of gel layer, decelerate foulants development, and remove stable foulants from the surface of the membrane. PFS was found to be the most effective in controlling membrane fouling with an optimum dose of 1.05 mM Fe. The reduction of initial TMP and delayed rate of TMP increase when coagulants were added can be explained in terms of charge neutralisation and bridging of the SMPs. Coagulation could also minimise membrane fouling due to the flocculation of the particulates (colloids) in the MBR reactor brought about by coagulant addition. Wu *et al.* [131] further investigated the effect of PFS on membrane fouling characteristics and performance in a long-term (60 days) MBR operation. Findings from their study indicated that the addition of PFS efficiently impeded membrane fouling in long-term MBR operation; and, the optimum PFS dosage and dosing interval were 1.0 mM Fe and 15 to 30 days at an MLSS 7–10 g/L. Additionally, PFS increased the flocs size through the supply of positive charges for organic particles, hence enhanced charge neutralization.

In another study, Zhang *et al.* [132] investigated the ability of $FeCl_3$ to retard membrane fouling in MBR. They reported that an optimum dose of 1.2 mM Fe(III) remarkably improved the filterability of the MBR mixed liquor; which, they attributed to the fact that Fe(III) supplied positive charges for soluble macromolecular substances and sludge flocs, and enhanced the function of charge neutralisation. The added Fe(III) interacted with the negatively charged EPS groups and enhanced the bioflocculation of small particles.

Furthermore, Mishima and Nakajima [133] investigated the mitigation of membrane fouling in MBR by coagulant addition in laboratory-scale batch and MBR experiments. They reported that ferric chloride performed slightly better than aluminium sulphate. Thus, using ferric chloride in the MBR process, they reported that during the 40-day MBR experiment, the reference MBR tank (without coagulant addition) was cleaned 18 times; the tank with 2.26 g/L coagulant addition was cleaned nine times; and the MBR tank with 4.52 g/L addition was cleaned only five times [133]. This indicates that, with coagulant addition, the fouling rate reduced appreciably. It has also been found that the addition of a very low-dose of green bioflocculant could achieve significant membrane fouling mitigation after 70 days of operation (TMP development of 2.5 kPa only) with less backwash frequency [134].

However, the addition of coagulants to the MBR mixed liquor can decrease the pH. The decrease in pH may affect the bioactivities of the MBR mixed liquor. In addition, coagulant overdosage can result in the deposition of the excess coagulant on the membrane surface. Research is, thus, needed on finding sustainable dosages that mitigate membrane fouling without lowering the pH.

4.2. Adsorbent Addition

Adsorbents provide a large surface area for the adsorption of materials in water and wastewater. In MBR, adsorbents offer the potential to adsorb dissolved organic polymers, notably SMPs, hence reducing membrane fouling propensity. Powdered activated carbon (PAC) is typically applied in MBRs for the purpose of reducing organic fouling and biofouling. PAC also serves as media for bacterial attachment and subsequent growth [5], hence, reducing their attachment onto the membrane surface and pores.

Ying and Ping [135] studied the effect of PAC dosage on membrane fouling using PAC dosages of 0, 0.75, and 1.5 g/L of wastewater, respectively. They reported that PAC application was effective in reducing the amount of EPS inside the microbial floc at PAC dosage of 0.75 g/L; and, the addition of PAC decreased the EPS deposited on the membrane. The cake resistance decreased as the PAC dosage increased. The optimum PAC dosage for organics removal and filtration flux was found to be 0.75 g/L. Similarly, Satyawali and Balakrishnan [136] studied the effect of PAC addition on sludge properties in MBR treating high-strength wastewater from an alcohol distillery in long-term operation (over 180 days). They reported that PAC addition decreased the SVI (sludge volume index) which improved sludge dewaterability. They further found that PAC addition did not substantially affect total EPS concentration; however, the composition of the SMPs in terms of proteins/polysaccharides ratio was altered resulting in a high proteins/polysaccharides ratio.

In another study, Remy *et al.* [114] investigated the effect of PAC on membrane fouling in two pilot-scale MBRs treating municipal wastewater. Findings from their research revealed that low PAC dosage (500 mg/L of sludge) combined with a relatively long SRT (50 days) resulted in about 10% improvement of the critical flux and a strong filtration period increment without significant fouling at high fluxes (50–70 L/m^2 h). Other positives reported from their research include: Easier removal of gels deposited on the membrane at high fluxes; a reduction in the deposition of gel on the membrane surface after a long period of filtration; and a slight increase in the permeate quality. Torretta *et al.* [137] investigated the optimum dose of PAC in an MBR pilot plant by using low PAC doses: 0, 2, 5, 10 and 20 mg/L. Findings from this study showed that PAC addition was effective at the low doses (2 and 5 mg/L) by reducing the permeate flux loss (from 16% up to 27%, respectively). Rezaei and Mehrnia [116] found that the addition of the zeolite (clinoptilolite) resulted in significant improvement of sludge properties including 22.5% increase in MLSS, more accumulation of large particles (7%), 50% reduction in SMPs, and 66% reduction in TMP. The increase in flocs size, reduction in SMPs and TMP translate to remarkable membrane fouling abatement. Similarly, another study found that MBR with PAC in the mixed liquor exhibited low fouling tendency and prolonged filtration as compared to conventional MBR [138]. The authors further indicated that PAC stabilised the biomass in form of biological activated carbon with porous cake structure that prolonged filtration.

It has been indicated that higher concentration of fresh PAC in submerged MBR would offer enhanced simultaneous adsorption and biodegradation effects for the reduction of EPS, fine colloids and planktonic cells in MBR mixed liquor supernatant [139]. Membrane fouling abatement in MBRs through the addition of PAC has been attributed to the combined action of flocculation and adsorption [138]. The adsorption opportunity provided by PAC in MBRs is expected to enhance organics removal. In general, PAC addition to MBR acts as mobile carriers for active biomass, reduces membrane cake layer formation, and retains microorganisms by making the MBR both attached growth and suspended growth [140]. An additional advantage offered by enhancing MBRs with adsorbents (particularly PAC) is the removal of recalcitrant pollutants from wastewater [141].

Furthermore, Deng *et al.* [142] reported that the addition of sponge to the MBR resulted in lower biomass growth, less filamentous bacteria, reduced sludge viscosity, larger sludge flocs, and lower concentration of EPS and SMPs, leading to lower pore blocking resistance and lower cake formation when compared to conventional MBR [142]. This clearly shows that sponge addition can significantly alleviate membrane fouling in MBRs.

While the addition of adsorbents mitigates membrane fouling in MBR, further research is needed to establish optimum dosages of the various adsorbents. Operating above the optimum dosage can be counterproductive as it may rather increase sludge apparent viscosity, aggravate fouling through deflocculation, reduce mass transfer and sludge dewaterability [141]. It has also been indicated that overdose of adsorbents (especially PAC) may increase membrane fouling due to their potential to become foulants themselves through cake layer formation over the membrane and/or by blocking the membrane pores [135,143]. It is necessary to determine the optimum dosage in batch experiments for any wastewater. Low PAC dosages (in the neighbourhood of 0.5 g/L) coupled with short SRTs have been recommended for membrane fouling mitigation in MBRs [144]. The optimum dosage of the adsorbents will also allow the striking of a balance between the cost savings arising from membrane fouling abatement and the cost of the additives and handling of the resulting sludge.

4.3. Use of Granular Biomass (Aerobic Granulation)

As indicated in Section 3.3.3, EPS are the construction materials for microbial aggregates. As such, recent research has focused on incorporating biotechnological processes that can use up these foulants. A key innovation in this regard is the integration of aerobic granulation biotechnology with MBR to develop the aerobic granulation membrane bioreactor (AGMBR) as a novel approach to control membrane fouling. Aerobic granulation refers to the process of microbe-to-microbe self-immobilisation without any biocarriers [145,146,147,148]. The resulting granular biomass are dense microbial consortia packed with different microbial species that can collectively degrade wastewater pollutants [77,149]. Compared to the ASP, aerobic granulation technology offers the following advantages: excellent settling properties, smaller footprints, strong microbial structure, higher biomass retention, less sludge production, high resilience to toxic chemicals, and good ability to handle high organic and shock loading rates [77,111,149,150,151,152]. AGMBR offers a distinctive advantage of utilising EPS for granule formation and offering the large size and rigid structure of the granules for bacteria to attach to rather than the membrane surface. The large size and rigid structure of the granules is expected to reduce cake-layer formation, pore blocking and surface deposition on the membrane surface.

The integration of aerobic granulation and MBR was first reported by Li *et al.* [112]. Findings from their study showed that membrane permeability in the AGMBR system was over 50% higher when compared to conventional MBR. Following this was a four-months bench-scale study by Tay *et al.* [11] who compared the processes and performances of AGMBR and submerged MBR. They found that while AGMBR and submerged MBR showed similar treatment efficiencies, the AGMBR showed much better filtration characteristics with the membrane permeability loss (34.5%) in AGMBR being twice as low as that of submerged MBR at constant pressure testing. Constant flux testing also showed that, increasing the flux threefold resulted in membrane permeability loss of 2.4% with the AGMBR mixed liquor (*i.e.*, 21 times lower than that of the MBR). In continuous operational mode, the TMP increment in the AGMBR was negligible (3–6 kPa) and the membrane required no physical cleaning; whereas, the TMP increment in the submerged MBR was significant (50–60 kPa) and regular physical cleaning of the membrane module was required. Similarly, in a long-term study (10 months), Tu *et al.* [18] reported a higher removal efficiency of pollutants, as well as improved membrane performance (fouling rate was maintained below 0.1 kPa/day at MLSS > 18,000 mg/L) when aerobic granules were formed in MBR. They indicated that the granule size change and improved settling ability were responsible for maintaining membrane permeability.

Another study by Juang *et al.* [105] investigated membrane fouling in AGMBR and reported that most bacteria cells were retained by the granules thus preventing their penetration through the membrane pores and the chance to cause internal fouling layer. The combination of aerobic granulation and MBR has also been reported to enhance good filtration performance and lower propensity for membrane fouling [115]. Other reported findings on AGMBR include: stable operation at 20 L/m^2 h for 61 days with significant filtration improvement [153]; extension of filtration period by 78 days without physical cleaning [111]; and excellent fouling control [154].

Regarding treatment performance, aerobic granulation offers diverse microbial aggregates that exhibit superior treatment efficiency when compared to floccular sludge. This is attributable to the strong microbial structure of aerobic granule as well as their high biomass retention and high resilience to toxic chemicals. Tu *et al.* [18] reported a higher removal efficiency of pollutants when aerobic granules were formed in MBR. Aerobic granules exhibit a layered structure with an oxic zone near the granule surface, an anoxic zone in the middle layer, and an anaerobic core at the granule centre [155,156]. This layered structure is suitable for simultaneous organics, nitrogen, and phosphorus removal. A study conducted to determine the removal of nitrogen in AGMBR reported about 60% total nitrogen removal in the AGMBR [111]. Another study to determine the performance of AGMBR reported the removal of COD, total phosphorus, nitrate-nitrogen and total nitrogen as 93.17%, 90.42%, 95% and 95%, respectively [157].

However, the major technical problem of AGMBR is the long-term system operation instability of aerobic granulation and granule disintegration problems [151,158]. Aerobic granules have been observed to disintegrate after prolonged operation [149,159,160,161]. The deterioration in granule stability over time impacts the efficiency of wastewater treatment and is a major issue affecting the effectiveness of aerobic granulation in full-scale operations. As applied to AGMBR, the granule disintegration increases the concentration of soluble EPS, consequently increasing the membrane fouling propensity [154]. Hence, the production of granules with sustainable long-term structural integrity is a key area requiring further research.

4.4. Use of Granular Materials with Aeration

To enhance the detachment of foulants from the membrane in MBR, research has focused on using granular materials with air scouring to provide continuous mechanical cleaning. In this regard, Siembida *et al.* [162] reported that the abrasion produced by granular materials introduced into the MBR tank significantly reduced cake layer formation on the membranes. The study further found that this method resulted in a successful long-term operation (more than 600 days) at permeate flux of 40 L/m^2 h without membrane chemical cleaning. The introduction of the granular materials also allowed MBR operation at a higher permeate flux (more than 20% higher) compared to the conventional MBR. Similarly, Kurita *et al.* [163] found that the introduction of granular materials (made of polyethylene glycol) into a submerged MBR increased the critical flux by more than 40%; allowed for the stable operation of MBR despite the reduction of aeration by 50%. The reduction of aeration would remarkably reduce MBR operational and maintenance cost. Johir *et al.* [164] studied the effect of different particle sizes of granular activated carbon (GAC) on submerged MBR operated at a filtration flux of 20 L/m^2 h. Three size ranges of GAC were used in the study: 150–300, 300–600 and 600–1200 µm. The authors reported that GAC size played a significant role in membrane fouling abatement as the total membrane resistance reduced by 60% with GAC particle sizes of 300–600 µm. In addition, organics removal was up to 95% with the addition GAC.

Furthermore, Pradhan *et al.* [165] found that the addition of granular media in the MBR reactor resulted in the same TMP reduction as doubling the aeration intensity (from 600 to 1200 L/h/m^2). A recent study also found that the rate of aeration in MBR can be reduced by over 50% with the introduction of granular materials [166]. In the same regard, Krause *et al.*[167] investigated the removal of the membrane fouling layer by continuous physical abrasion by adding granular materials to the activated sludge. They reported no membrane permeability decline throughout the over eight months of operation at fluxes of up to 40 L/m^2 h.

The effectiveness of using granular material as a fouling control mechanism in anaerobic fluidised membrane bioreactor (AFMBR) has also been reported in the literature. Kim *at al.* [168] examined the effect of placing GAC directly in contact with membranes in an AFMBR in a 120-day continuous-feed experiment using two-stage anaerobic treatment system: first stage consisting of a fluidised-bed bioreactor without membranes followed by an AFMBR. The fluidised GAC produced scouring action on the membrane surface which reduced membrane fouling evidenced by the cleaning of the membrane only twice during the 120 days of operation. The authors reported an energy requirement of 0.028 kWh/m^3, which is remarkably low compared to the values reported for anaerobic membrane bioreactors using gas sparging for membrane fouling control. Similarly, Aslam *et al.* [169] studied the effectiveness of using GAC and non-adsorbing silica and polyethylene terephthalate (PET) beads as fluidised media in an AFMBR in reducing membrane fouling and for energy requirement for fluidisation. Findings of their study indicated that GAC can reduce membrane fouling both by adsorption of foulants and scouring action along membrane surfaces. Smaller particles demonstrated higher sorption capacity and less energy requirement for fluidisation until sorption capacity was exhausted. Afterwards, membrane scouring became the dominant mechanism; and, fouling reduction was a function of energy expenditure, with larger GAC particles that required more energy for fluidisation providing the best fouling reduction. In addition, increasing the packing ratio of GAC particles from 10% to 50% increased the energy required for fluidisation and also lowered the membrane fouling rate. Non-adsorbing silica particles and PET beads demonstrated similar results to pre-adsorbed GAC, lower fouling was accomplished by the larger media that had a higher energy requirement for fluidisation. Fouling reduction was also somewhat better at a given energy expenditure with lower specific gravity PET beads than with denser and smaller pre-adsorbed GAC particles. Additionally, recently, Kim *et al.* [170] used GAC as the fluidised particles for scouring the membrane and as a support for bacterial growth. They found that membrane fouling was successfully controlled by GAC fluidisation as the TMP was low, and could be maintained below 0.12 bar by a daily removal of excess solids. With the scouring action of the GAC and daily withdrawal of solids, membrane cleaning was not required. These results open up a new possibility of using this method to make chemical cleaning of the membrane a seldom activity in MBR operation. However, granular materials have a tendency to damage the membrane material. Further research is needed to find the optimum aeration intensity and the right granular material that would not cause damage to the membranes.

4.5. Quorum Quenching

Another innovative approach to membrane fouling control in MBRs is the use of quorum quenching. The regulation of microbial group behaviours by cell-to-cell communication (quorum sensing) is involved in biofilm formation [171]. Bacteria produce autoinducers, which are used in intercellular communication [172]. When the concentration of autoinducer attains a threshold level, it combines with the receptor protein and activates the transcription of specific genes to induce group behaviours such as biofilm formation and EPS production [171,173]. On this basis, the concept of quorum quenching was introduced in MBR for biofouling control through quorum sensing (QS) control by the blocking intercellular communications.

Yeon *et al.* [174] utilised acylase attached to magnetic carrier to inhibit QS in MBR; and, they reported reduced biofouling and enhanced the membrane permeability. Another study found that disrupting the energy metabolism and subsequently producing QS signaling molecules effectively controlled biofouling [175]. Similarly, Jahangir *et al.* [176] and Oh *et al.* [177] investigated membrane biofouling control by encapsulating quorum quenching bacteria into a hollow fiber membrane. Findings from these two separate studies showed that membrane biofouling was successfully inhibited. The study of Jahangir *et al.* [176] further found that as the recirculation rate (of the mixed liquor between the bioreactor and the membrane tank) increased, the biofouling inhibition (quorum quenching effect) increased. This was attributed to the facilitated transport of signal molecules from the biofilm into the bulk mixed liquor, and then to the microbial-vessel.

Kim *et al.* [178] immobilised acylase onto the membrane surface and reported that the MBR system showed mitigation of membrane biofouling. Similarly, Jiang *et al.* [173] immobilised acylase into sodium alginate capsules for enzymatic quorum quenching in MBRs. They reported that quorum quenching influenced sludge characteristics and membrane biofouling through better sludge settleability, smaller sludge particle size, less production of EPS and SMPs, lower apparent viscosity and higher zeta potential of mixed liquor. Quorum quenching further altered the characteristics, behaviour and function of EPS and SMPs, ultimately weakened biofilm formation ability but enhanced membrane filterability.

Another quorum quenching approach reported in the literature is the use of free-moving beads entrapped with quorum quenching bacteria [179]. The cell entrapping beads (CEBs) were prepared by entrapping quorum quenching bacteria (*Rhodococcus* sp. BH4) into alginate beads. The introduction of CEBs in the MBR significantly delayed the TMP rise (the time to reach a TMP of 70 kPa was 10 times longer than the control MBR). This membrane biofouling mitigation was attributed to both physical (abrasion) and biological (quorum quenching) effects of CEBs. The explanation is that microbial cells in the biofilm produced fewer EPS and thus formed a loosely bound biofilm due to the quorum quenching effect of CEBs. This enabled the biofilm to slough off easily from the membrane surface from the abrasion of the CEBs.

Additionally, recently, Wood *et al.* [180] engineered a beneficial biofilm that mitigates biofouling (through limiting its own thickness) by sensing the number of its cells that are present via a QS circuit. This was based on the secretion and uptake of a communication signal; hence, biofilm formation was limited by self-monitoring and selective dispersal. The beneficial biofilm prevented the formation of biofilm by deleterious bacteria through the secretion of nitric oxide, a general biofilm dispersal agent. The engineered beneficial biofilm further removed the environmental pollutant, epichlorohydrin, through the production of epoxide hydrolase. Thus, the engineered beneficial biofilm plays two significant roles: mitigation of membrane biofouling and provision of a platform for biodegradation of recalcitrant organic pollutants.

However, practical issues on the cost and stability of enzymes that are used in QS are yet to be determined. The use of free-moving beads entrapped with quorum quenching bacteria can open the door to practical application but this quorum quenching method needs pilot-scale testing. Engineered living biofouling-resistant membrane system needs further testing at pilot-scale.

5. CONCLUSIONS

In this paper, fundamentals of membrane fouling and advances in fouling mitigation strategies in MBRs are reviewed. Membrane fouling in MBRs can be classified into biofoulants, organic foulants and inorganic foulants based on their biological and chemical characteristics. Of these, biofoulants and organic foulants are the major contributors to membrane fouling in MBRs. Most research on membrane fouling targets these foulants. There are different factors that influence membrane fouling in MBRs. These factors include: membrane characteristics (material type, water affinity, surface roughness, surface charge, and pore size), operating conditions (operating mode, rate of aeration, SRT, HRT, F/M ratio, OLR, COD/N ratio, and temperature), and feed and biomass characteristics (MLSS, sludge apparent viscosity, EPS, floc size, alkalinity, pH and salinity). EPS, in particular, are major contributors to membrane fouling.

Current research trends for membrane fouling mitigation in MBR have been presented; namely, the addition of coagulants and adsorbents, use of granular biomass, use of granular materials with air scouring, and quorum quenching. The addition of coagulants and adsorbents shows significant membrane fouling reduction but further research is needed to establish optimum dosages of the various coagulants and adsorbents in order to strike a balance between cost savings arising from fouling abatement and the cost of the additives and handling of the resulting sludge. Aerobic granulation is a promising biotechnology that targets biofouling and organic fouling. Early results of integrating aerobic granulation with MBRs show significant reduction in membrane fouling as well as enhanced organics and nutrients removal. However, AGMBR is still in the development phase. Further research is needed to establish the EPS-membrane fouling relationship in AGMBR and optimum operating conditions on real wastewater applications. Granule stability and disintegration in long-term operation is a major shortcoming of the granulation technology, which brings forth an area for further research. The introduction of granular materials with aeration in the MBR tank to provide continuous mechanical cleaning significantly reduces the cake layer formation, resulting in successful long-term operation. Quorum quenching also offers a strong potential for fouling control but pilot-scale testing is required to explore the feasibility of full-scale application.

AUTHOR CONTRIBUTIONS

Oliver Terna Iorhemen and Rania Ahmed Hamza wrote the first draft; Joo Hwa Tay provided scientific input. All authors read and approved the final manuscript.

CONFLICTS OF INTEREST

The authors declare no conflict of interest.

REFERENCES

1. Le-Clech, P.; Chen, V.; Fane, T.A.G. Fouling in membrane bioreactors used in wastewater treatment. J. Membr. Sci.2006, 284, 17–53.

2. Meng, F.; Chae, S.-R.; Drews, A.; Kraume, M.; Shin, H.-S.; Yang, F. Recent advances in membrane bioreactors (MBRs): Membrane fouling and membrane material. Water Res. 2009, 43, 1489–1512.

3. Drews, A. Membrane fouling in membrane bioreactors—Characterisation, contradictions, cause and cures. J. Membr. Sci. 2010, 363, 1–28.

4. Lin, H.; Gao, W.; Meng, F.; Liao, B.Q.; Leung, K.T.; Zhao, L.; Chen, J.; Hong, H. Membrane bioreactors for industrial wastewater treatment: A critical review. Crit. Rev. Environ. Sci. Technol. 2012, 42, 677–740.

5. Mutamim, N.S.A.; Noor, Z.Z.; Hassan, M.A.A.; Yuniarto, A.; Olsson, G. Membrane bioreactor: Applications and limitations in treating high strength industrial wastewater. Chem. Eng. J. 2013, 225, 109–119.

6. Brindle, K.; Stephenson, T. The application of membrane biological reactors for the treatment of wastewaters.Biotechnol. Bioeng. 1996, 49, 601–610.

7. van Dijk, L.; Roncken, G.C.G. Membrane bioreactors for wastewater treatment: The state of the art and new developments. Water Sci. Technol. 1997, 35, 35–41.

8. Friha, I.; Karray, F.; Feki, F.; Jlaiel, L.; Sayadi, S. Treatment of cosmetic industry wastewater by submerged MBR with consideration of microbial community dynamics. Int. Biodeterior. Biodegrad. 2014, 88, 125–133.

9. Chu, L.; Zhang, X.; Yang, F.; Li, X. Treatment of domestic wastewater by using a microaerobic membrane bioreactor.Desalination 2006, 189, 181–192.

10. Ueda, T.; Hata, K. Domestic wastewater treatment by a submerged membrane bioreactor with gravitational filtration.Water Res. 1999, 33, 2888–2892.

11. Tay, J.H.; Yang, P.; Zhuang, W.Q.; Tay, S.T.L.; Pan, Z.H. Reactor performance and membrane filtration in aerobic granular sludge MBR. J. Membr. Sci. 2007, 304, 24–32.

12. Chang, I.; Le Clech, P.; Jefferson, B.; Judd, S. Membrane fouling in membrane bioreactors for wastewater treatment. J. Environ. Eng. 2002, 128, 1018–1029.

13. Water Environment Federation. Membrane Bioreactors: Water Environment Federation (WEF) Manual of Practice No. 36; McGraw-Hill: New York, NY, USA, 2011.

14. Vargas, A.; Moreno-Andrade, I.; Buitrón, G. Controlled backwashing in a membrane sequencing batch reactor used for toxic wastewater treatment. J. Membr. Sci. 2008, 320, 185–190.

15. Wang, Z.; Wu, Z.; Mai, S.; Yang, C.; Wang, X.; An, Y.; Zhou, Z. Research and applications of membrane bioreactors in China: Progress and prospect. Sep. Purif. Technol. 2008, 62, 249–263.

16. Judd, S. The status of membrane bioreactor technology. Trends Biotechnol. 2008, 26, 109–116.

17. Metcalf & Eddy Inc.; Tchobanoglous, G.; Stensel, H.D.; Tsuchihashi, R.; Burton, F.L.; Abu-Orf, M.; Bowden, G.; Pfrang, W. Wastewater Engineering: Treatment & Resource Recovery, 5th ed.; McGraw Hill: New York, NY, USA, 2014.

18. Tu, X.; Zhang, S.; Xu, L.; Zhang, M.; Zhu, J. Performance and fouling characteristics in a membrane sequence batch reactor (MSBR) system coupled with aerobic granular sludge. Desalination 2010, 261, 191–196.

19. Kimura, K.; Yamato, N.; Yamamura, H.; Watanabe, Y. Membrane Fouling in pilot-scale Membrane Bioreactors

(MBRs) treating municipal wastewater. Environ. Sci. Tech. 2005, 39, 6293–6299.

20. Wei, Y.; Li, G.; Wang, B. Application of granular sludge MBR in the treatment of wastewater. Proced. Environ. Sci.2011, 10, 108–111.

21. Koros, W.J.; Ma, Y.H.; Shimidzu, T. Terminology for membranes and membrane processes (IUPAC Recommendations 1996). Pure Appl. Chem. 1996, 68, 1479–1489.

22. Meng, F.; Zhang, H.; Yang, F.; Liu, L. Characterization of cake layer in submerged membrane bioreactor. Environ. Sci. Technol. 2007, 41, 4065–4070.

23. Zhang, J.; Chua, H.C.; Zhou, J.; Fane, A.G. Factors affecting the membrane performance in submerged membrane bioreactors. J. Membr. Sci. 2006, 284, 54–66.

24. Ye, Y.; Clech, P.L.; Chen, V.; Fane, A.G. Evolution of fouling during crossflow filtration of model EPS solutions. J. Membr. Sci. 2005, 264, 190–199.

25. Ognier, S.; Wisniewski, C.; Grasmick, A. Membrane bioreactor fouling in sub-critical filtration conditions: A local critical flux concept. J. Membr. Sci. 2004, 229, 171–177.

26. Hwang, B.-K.; Lee, W.-N.; Yeon, K.-M.; Park, P.-K.; Lee, C.-H.; Chang, I.-S.; Drews, A.; Kraume, M. Correlating TMP increases with microbial characteristics in the bio-cake on the membrane surface in a membrane bioreactor. Environ. Sci. Technol. 2008, 42, 3963–3968.

27. Spettmann, D.; Eppmann, S.; Flemming, H.-C.; Wingender, J. Simultaneous visualisation of biofouling, organic and inorganic particle fouling on separation membranes. Water Sci. Technol. 2007, 55, 207–210.

28. Malaeb, L.; Le-Clech, P.; Vrouwenvelder, J.S.; Ayoub, G.M.; Saikaly, P.E. Do biological-based strategies hold

promise to biofouling control in MBRs? Water Res. 2013, 47, 5447–5463.

29. Vanysacker, L.; Declerck, P.; Bilad, M.R.; Vankelecom, I.F.J. Biofouling on microfiltration membranes in MBRs: Role of membrane type and microbial community. J. Membr. Sci. 2014, 453, 394–401.

30. Guo, W.; Ngo, H.-H.; Li, J. A mini-review on membrane fouling. Bioresour. Technol. 2012, 122, 27–34.

31. Wang, X.-M.; Li, X.-Y. Accumulation of biopolymer clusters in a submerged membrane bioreactor and its effect on membrane fouling. Water Res. 2008, 42, 855–862.

32. Lin, H.J.; Xie, K.; Mahendran, B.; Bagley, D.M.; Leung, K.T.; Liss, S.N.; Liao, B.Q. Sludge properties and their effects on membrane fouling in submerged anaerobic membrane bioreactors (SAnMBRs). Water Res. 2009, 43, 3827–3837.

33. Wang, X.-M.; Sun, F.-Y.; Li, X.-Y. Investigation of the role of biopolymer clusters in MBR membrane fouling using flash freezing and environmental scanning electron microscopy. Chemosphere 2011, 85, 1154–1159.

34. Sun, F.-Y.; Wang, X.-M.; Li, X.-Y. Change in the fouling propensity of sludge in membrane bioreactors (MBR) in relation to the accumulation of biopolymer clusters. Bioresour. Technol. 2011, 102, 4718–4725.

35. Sun, F.-Y.; Wang, X.-M.; Li, X.-Y. Effect of biopolymer clusters on the fouling property of sludge from a membrane bioreactor (MBR) and its control by ozonation. Process Biochem. 2011, 46, 162–167.

36. Wang, Z.; Ma, J.; Tang, C.Y.; Kimura, K.; Wang, Q.; Han, X. Membrane cleaning in membrane bioreactors: A review. J. Membr. Sci. 2014, 468, 276–307.

37. Wang, Z.; Wu, Z.; Yin, X.; Tian, L. Membrane fouling in a submerged membrane bioreactor (MBR) under sub-

critical flux operation: Membrane foulant and gel layer characterization. J. Membr. Sci. 2008, 325, 238–244.

38. Arabi, S.; Nakhla, G. Impact of calcium on the membrane fouling in membrane bioreactors. J. Membr. Sci. 2008, 314, 134–142.

39. Shirazi, S.; Lin, C.-J.; Chen, D. Inorganic fouling of pressure-driven membrane processes—A critical review.Desalination 2010, 250, 236–248.

40. Lee, S.; Lee, C.-H. Effect of operating conditions on CaSO4 scale formation mechanism in nanofiltration for water softening. Water Res. 2000, 34, 3854–3866.

41. Hofs, B.; Ogier, J.; Vries, D.; Beerendonk, E.F.; Cornelissen, E.R. Comparison of ceramic and polymeric membrane permeability and fouling using surface water. Sep. Purif. Technol. 2011, 79, 365–374.

42. Jin, L.; Ong, S.L.; Ng, H.Y. Comparison of fouling characteristics in different pore-sized submerged ceramic membrane bioreactors. Water Res. 2010, 44, 5907–5918.

43. Yu, H.-Y.; Liu, L.-Q.; Tang, Z.-Q.; Yan, M.-G.; Gu, J.-S.; Wei, X.-W. Surface modification of polypropylene microporous membrane to improve its antifouling characteristics in an SMBR: Air plasma treatment. J. Membr. Sci. 2008, 311, 216–224.

44. Dolina, J.; Dlask, O.; Lederer, T.; Dvořák, L. Mitigation of membrane biofouling through surface modification with different forms of nanosilver. Chem. Eng. J. 2015, 275, 125–133.

45. Moghadam, M.T.; Lesage, G.; Mohammadi, T.; Mericq, J.-P.; Mendret, J.; Heran, M.; Faur, C.; Brosillon, S.; Hemmati, M.; Naeimpoor, F. Improved antifouling properties of TiO2/PVDF nanocomposite membranes in UV-coupled ultrafiltration. J. Appl. Polym. Sci. 2015, 132.

46. Hamza, R.A.; Iorhemen, O.T.; Tay, J.H. Occurrence, impacts and removal of emerging substances of concern from wastewater. Environ. Technol. Innov. 2016, 5, 161–175.

47. Guglielmi, G.; Andreottola, G. Selection and Design of Membrane Bior, Handbook of Environmental Engineeringeactors in Environmental Bioengineering, in Environmental Biotechnology; Wang, L.K., Ivanov, V., Tay, J.-H., Hung, Y.-T., Eds.; Humana Press: New York, NY, USA, 2010; Volume 10, pp. 439–514.

48. Elimelech, M.; Xiaohua, Z.; Childress, A.E.; Seungkwan, H. Role of membrane surface morphology in colloidal fouling of cellulose acetate and composite aromatic polyamide reverse osmosis membranes. J. Membr. Sci. 1997, 127, 101–109.

49. Rana, D.; Matsuura, T. Surface modifications for antifouling membranes. Chem. Rev. 2010, 110, 2448–2471.

50. Vrijenhoek, E.M.; Hong, S.; Elimelech, M. Influence of membrane surface properties on initial rate of colloidal fouling of reverse osmosis and nanofiltration membranes. J. Membr. Sci. 2001, 188, 115–128.

51. Hashino, M.; Katagiri, T.; Kubota, N.; Ohmukai, Y.; Maruyama, T.; Matsuyama, H. Effect of surface roughness of hollow fiber membranes with gear-shaped structure on membrane fouling by sodium alginate. J. Membr. Sci. 2011,366, 389–397.

52. Crittenden, J.C.; Trussell, R.R.; Hand, D.W.; Howe, K.J.; Tchobanoglous, G. Water Treatment: Principles and Design, MWH, 2nd ed.; John Wiley and Sons: Hoboken, NJ, USA, 2005.

53. Van den Broeck, R.; van Dierdonck, J.; Nijskens, P.; Dotremont, C.; Krzeminski, P.; van der Graaf, J.H.J.M.; van Lier, J.B.; van Impe, J.F.M.; Smets, I.Y. The influence of solids retention time on activated sludge

bioflocculation and membrane fouling in a membrane bioreactor (MBR). J. Membr. Sci. 2012, 401, 48–55.

54. Miyoshi, T.; Yuasa, K.; Ishigami, T.; Rajabzadeh, S.; Kamio, E.; Ohmukai, Y.; Saeki, D.; Ni, J.; Matsuyama, H. Effect of membrane polymeric materials on relationship between surface pore size and membrane fouling in membrane bioreactors. Appl. Surf. Sci. 2015, 330, 351–357.

55. Diez, V.; Ezquerra, D.; Cabezas, J.L.; García, A.; Ramos, C. A modified method for evaluation of critical flux, fouling rate and in situ determination of resistance and compressibility in MBR under different fouling conditions. J. Membr. Sci. 2014, 453, 1–11.

56. Van der Marel, P.; Zwijnenburg, A.; Kemperman, A.; Wessling, M.; Temmink, H.; van der Meer, W. An improved flux-step method to determine the critical flux and the critical flux for irreversibility in a membrane bioreactor. J. Membr. Sci. 2009, 332, 24–29.

57. Bacchin, P.; Aimar, P.; Field, R.W. Critical and sustainable fluxes: theory, experiments and applications. J. Membr. Sci.2006, 281, 42–69.

58. Kimura, K.; Ogyu, R.; Miyoshi, T.; Watanabe, Y. Transition of major components in irreversible fouling of MBRs treating municipal wastewater. Sep. Purif. Technol. 2015, 142, 326–331.

59. Ji, L.; Zhou, J. Influence of aeration on microbial polymers and membrane fouling in submerged MBRs. J. Membr. Sci.2006, 276, 168–177.

60. Trussell, R.S.; Merlo, R.P.; Hermanowicz, S.W.; Jenkins, D. Influence of mixed liquor properties and aeration intensity on membrane fouling in a submerged MBR at high mixed liquor suspended solids concentrations. Water Res. 2007,41, 947–958.

61. Yigit, N.O.; Harman, I.; Civelekoglu, G.; Koseoglu, H.; Cicek, N.; Kitis, M. Membrane fouling in a pilot-scale

submerged membrane bioreactor operated under various conditions. Desalination 2008, 231, 124–132.

62. Verrecht, B.; Judd, S.; Guglielmi, G.; Brepols, C.; Mulder, J.W. An aeration energy model for an immersed membrane bioreactor. Water Res. 2008, 42, 4761–4770.

63. Nywening, J.-P.; Zhou, H. Influence of filtration conditions on membrane fouling and scouring aeration effectiveness in submerged membrane bioreactors to treat municipal wastewater. Water Res. 2009, 43, 3548–3558.

64. Chua, H.; Arnot, T.; Howell, J. Controlling fouling in membrane bioreactors operated with a variable throughput.Desalination 2002, 149, 225–229.

65. Ahmed, Z.; Cho, J.; Lim, B.-R.; Song, K.-G.; Ahn, K.-H. Effects of sludge retention time on membrane fouling and microbial community structure in a membrane bioreactor. J. Membr. Sci. 2007, 287, 211–218.

66. Jiang, T.; Myngheer, S.; De Pauw, D.J.W.; Spanjers, H.; Nopens, I.; Kennedy, M.D.; Amy, G.; Vanrolleghem, P.A. Modelling the production and degradation of soluble microbial products (SMP) in membrane bioreactors (MBR).Water Res. 2008, 42, 4955–4964.

67. Liang, S.; Liu, C.; Song, L. Soluble microbial products in membrane bioreactor operation: Behaviors, characteristics; fouling potential. Water Res. 2007, 41, 95–101.

68. Pan, J.R.; Su, Y.; Huang, C. Characteristics of soluble microbial products in membrane bioreactor and its effect on membrane fouling. Desalination 2010, 250, 778–780.

69. Judd, S.; Judd, C. The MBR Book: Principles and Applications of Membrane Bioreactors in Water and Wastewater Treatment; Elsevier: Amsterdam, The Netherlands, 2006.

70. Meng, F.; Yang, F. Fouling mechanisms of deflocculated sludge, normal sludge; bulking sludge in membrane bioreactor. J. Membr. Sci. 2007, 305, 48–56.

71. Fallah, N.; Bonakdarpour, B.; Nasernejad, B.; Alavi Moghadam, M.R. Long-term operation of submerged MBR for the treatment of synthetic wastewater containing styrene as volatile organic compound (VOC): Effect of HRT. J. Hazard. Mater. 2010, 178, 718–724.

72. Shariati, S.R.; Bonakdarpour, B.; Zare, N.; Ashtiani, F.Z. The effect of HRT on the performance and fouling characteristics of membrane sequencing batch reactors used for the treatment of synthetic petroleum refinery wastewater. Bioresour. Technol. 2011, 102, 7692–7699.

73. Isma, M.I.A.; Idris, A.; Omar, R.; Razreena, A.R.P. Effects of SRT and HRT on treatment performance of MBR and membrane fouling. Int. J. Chem. Mol. Nucl. Mater. Metall. Eng. 2014, 8, 485–489.

74. Jeong, E.; Kim, H.-W.; Nam, J.-Y.; Ahn, Y.-T.; Shin, H.-S. Effects of the hydraulic retention time on the fouling characteristics of an anaerobic membrane bioreactor for treating acidified wastewater. Desalin. Water Treat. 2010, 18, 251–256.

75. Trussell, R.S.; Merlo, R.P.; Hermanowicz, S.W.; Jenkins, D. The effect of organic loading on process performance and membrane fouling in a submerged MBR treating municipal wastewater. Water Res. 2006, 40, 2675–2683.

76. Dvořák, L.; Gómez, M.; Dvořáková, M.; Růžičková, I.; Wanner, J. The impact of different operating conditions on membrane fouling and EPS production. Bioresour. Technol. 2011, 102, 6870–6875.

77. Tay, J.-H.; Liu, Y.; Tay, S.-L.; Hung, Y.-T. Aerobic granulation technology. In Advanced Biological Treatment Processes; Wang, L.K., Shammas, N.K., Hung,

Y.-T., Eds.; Humana Press: New York, NY, USA, 2009; pp. 109–128.

78. Zhang, J.; Zhou, J.; Liu, Y.; Fane, A.G. A comparison of membrane fouling under constant and variable organic loadings in submerge membrane bioreactors. Water Res. 2010, 44, 5407–5413.

79. Johir, M.A.H.; Vigneswaran, S.; Sathasivan, A.; Kandasamy, J.; Chang, C.Y. Effect of organic loading rate on organic matter and foulant characteristics in membrane bio-reactor. Bioresour. Technol. 2012, 113, 154–160.

80. Meng, Q.; Yang, F.; Liu, L.; Meng, F. Effects of COD/N ratio and DO concentration on simultaneous nitrification and denitrification in an airlift internal circulation membrane bioreactor. J. Environ. Sci. 2008, 20, 933–939.

81. Feng, S.; Zhang, N.; Liu, H.; Du, X.; Liu, Y.; Lin, H. The effect of COD/N ratio on process performance and membrane fouling in a submerged bioreactor. Desalination 2012, 285, 232–238.

82. Hao, L.; Liss, S.N.; Liao, B.Q. Influence of COD:N ratio on sludge properties and their role in membrane fouling of a submerged membrane bioreactor. Water Res. 2016, 89, 132–141.

83. Han, X.; Wang, Z.; Ma, J.; Zhu, C.; Li, Y.; Wu, Z. Membrane bioreactors fed with different COD/N ratio wastewater: impacts on microbial community, microbial products; membrane fouling. Environ. Sci. Pollut. Res. 2015, 22, 11436–11445.

84. Gasmi, A.; Heran, M.; Hannachi, A.; Grasmick, A. Fouling analysis and biomass distribution on a membrane bioreactor under low ratio COD/N. Membr. Water Treat. 2015, 6, 263–276.

85. Yang, Y.; Lesage, G.; Barret, M.; Bernet, N.; Grasmick, A.; Hamelin, J.; Heran, M. New urban wastewater

treatment with autotrophic membrane bioreactor at low chemical oxygen demand/N substrate ratio. Water Sci. Technol. 2014,69, 960–965.

86. Ma, Z.; Wen, X.; Zhao, F.; Xia, Y.; Huang, X.; Waite, D.; Guan, J. Effect of temperature variation on membrane fouling and microbial community structure in membrane bioreactor. Bioresour. Technol. 2013, 133, 462–468.

87. Van den Brink, P.; Satpradit, O.-A.; van Bentem, A.; Zwijnenburg, A.; Temmink, H.; van Loosdrecht, M. Effect of temperature shocks on membrane fouling in membrane bioreactors. Water Res. 2011, 45, 4491–4500.

88. Drews, A.; Mante, J.; Iversen, V.; Vocks, M.; Lesjean, B.; Kraume, M. Impact of ambient conditions on SMP elimination and rejection in MBRs. Water Res. 2007, 41, 3850–3858.

89. Morgan-Sagastume, F.; Grant Allen, D. Activated sludge deflocculation under temperature upshifts from 30 to 45 °C.Water Res. 2005, 39, 1061–1074.

90. Bottino, A.; Capannelli, G.; Comite, A.; Mangano, R. Critical flux in submerged membrane bioreactors for municipal wastewater treatment. Desalination 2009, 245, 748–753.

91. Wu, J.; Huang, X. Effect of mixed liquor properties on fouling propensity in membrane bioreactors. J. Membr. Sci.2009, 342, 88–96.

92. Rosenberger, S.; Evenblij, H.; Te Poele, S.; Wintgens, T.; Laabs, C. The importance of liquid phase analyses to understand fouling in membrane assisted activated sludge processes—Six case studies of different European research groups. J. Membr. Sci. 2005, 263, 113–126.

93. Rosenberger, S.; Laabs, C.; Lesjean, B.; Gnirss, R.; Amy, G.; Jekel, M.; Schrotter, J.C. Impact of colloidal and

soluble organic material on membrane performance in membrane bioreactors for municipal wastewater treatment. Water Res. 2006, 40, 710–720.

94. Le-Clech, P.; Jefferson, B.; Judd, S.J. Impact of aeration, solids concentration and membrane characteristics on the hydraulic performance of a membrane bioreactor. J. Membr. Sci. 2003, 218, 117–129.

95. Brookes, A.; Jefferson, B.; Guglielmi, G.; Judd, S.J. Sustainable Flux Fouling in a Membrane Bioreactor: Impact of Flux and MLSS. Sep. Sci. Technol. 2006, 41, 1279–1291.

96. Moreau, A.A.; Ratkovich, N.; Nopens, I.; van der Graaf, J.H.J.M. The (in)significance of apparent viscosity in full-scale municipal membrane bioreactors. J. Membr. Sci. 2009, 340, 249–256.

97. Itonaga, T.; Kimura, K.; Watanabe, Y. Influence of suspension viscosity and colloidal particles on permeability of membrane used in membrane bioreactor (MBR). Water Sci. Technol. 2004, 50, 301–309. [PubMed]

98. Sheng, G.-P.; Yu, H.-Q.; Li, X.-Y. Extracellular polymeric substances (EPS) of microbial aggregates in biological wastewater treatment systems: A review. Biotechnol. Adv. 2010, 28, 882–894.

99. Ng, K.-K.; Lin, C.-F.; Lateef, S.K.; Panchangam, S.C.; Hong, P.-K.A.; Yang, P.-Y. The effect of soluble microbial products on membrane fouling in a fixed carrier biological system. Sep. Purif. Technol. 2010, 72, 98–104.

100. Lin, H.; Zhang, M.; Wang, F.; Meng, F.; Liao, B.-Q.; Hong, H.; Chen, J.; Gao, W. A critical review of EPSs in MBRs: Characteristics, roles in membrane fouling & control strategies. J. Memb. Sci. 2014, 460, 110–125.

101. Li, J.; Yang, F.; Liu, Y.; Song, H.; Li, D.; Cheng, F. Microbial community and biomass characteristics associated severe membrane fouling during start-up of a hybrid

anoxic–oxic membrane bioreactor. Bioresour. Technol. 2012, 103, 43–47.

102. Liu, X.-M.; Sheng, G.-P.; Luo, H.-W.; Zhang, F.; Yuan, S.-J.; Xu, J.; Zeng, R.J.; Wu, J.-G.; Yu, H.-Q. Contribution of Extracellular Polymeric Substances (EPS) to the sludge AGGREGATION. Environ. Sci. Technol. 2010, 44, 4355–4360.

103. Chang, I.-S.; Lee, C.-H. Membrane filtration characteristics in membrane-coupled activated sludge system —The effect of physiological states of activated sludge on membrane fouling. Desalination 1998, 120, 221–233.

104. Jang, N.; Shon, H.; Ren, X.; Vigneswaran, S.; Kim, I.S. Characteristics of bio-foulants in the membrane bioreactor.Desalination 2006, 200, 201–202.

105. Juang, Y.-C.; Su, A.; Fang, L.-H.; Lee, D.-J.; Lai, J.-Y. Fouling with aerobic granule membrane bioreactor. Water Sci. Technol. 2011, 64, 1870–1875.

106. Barker, D.J.; Stuckey, D.C. A review of soluble microbial products (SMP) in wastewater treatment systems. Water Res.1999, 33, 3063–3082.

107. Laspidou, C.S.; Rittmann, B.E. A unified theory for extracellular polymeric substances, soluble microbial products; active and inert biomass. Water Res. 2002, 36, 2711–2720.

108. Lee, W.; Kang, S.; Shin, H. Sludge characteristics and their contribution to microfiltration in submerged membrane bioreactors. J. Membr. Sci. 2003, 216, 217–227.

109. Shen, L.-G.; Lei, Q.; Chen, J.-R.; Hong, H.-C.; He, Y.-M.; Lin, H.-J. Membrane fouling in a submerged membrane bioreactor: Impacts of floc size. Chem. Eng. J. 2015, 269, 328–334.

110. Zhao, X.; Chen, Z.-L.; Wang, X.-C.; Shen, J.-M.; Xu, H. PPCPs removal by aerobic granular sludge membrane bioreactor. Appl. Microbiol. Biotechnol. 2014, 98, 9843–9848.

111. Thanh, B.X.; Visvanathan, C.; Ben Aim, R. Fouling characterization and nitrogen removal in a batch granulation membrane bioreactor. Int. Biodeterior. Biodegrad. 2013, 85, 491–498.

112. Li, X.; Gao, F.; Hua, Z.; Du, G.; Chen, J. Treatment of synthetic wastewater by a novel MBR with granular sludge developed for controlling membrane fouling. Sep. Purif. Tech. 2005, 46, 19–25.

113. Li, W.-W.; Wang, Y.-K.; Sheng, G.-P.; Gui, Y.-X.; Yu, L.; Xie, T.-Q.; Yu, H.-Q. Integration of aerobic granular sludge and mesh filter MBR for cost-effective wastewater treatment. Bioresour. Technol. 2012, 122, 22–26.

114. Remy, M.; van der Marel, P.; Zwijnenburg, A.; Rulkens, W.; Temmink, H. Low dose powdered activated carbon addition at high sludge retention times to reduce fouling in membrane bioreactors. Water Res. 2009, 43, 345–350.

115. Rezaei, M.; Mehrnia, M.R. The influence of zeolite (clinoptilolite) on the performance of a hybrid membrane bioreactor. Bioresour. Technol. 2014, 158, 25–31.

116. Sweity, A.; Ying, W.; Belfer, S.; Oron, G.; Herzberg, M. pH effects on the adherence and fouling propensity of extracellular polymeric substances in a membrane bioreactor. J. Membr. Sci. 2011, 378, 186–193.

117. Wang, L.-L.; Wang, L.-F.; Ren, X.-M.; Ye, X.-D.; Li, W.-W.; Yuan, S.-J.; Sun, M.; Sheng, G.-P.; Yu, H.-Q.; Wang, X.-K. pH Dependence of Structure and Surface Properties of Microbial EPS. Environ. Sci. Technol. 2012, 46, 737–744.

118. Zhang, Y.; Zhang, M.; Wang, F.; Hong, H.; Wang, A.; Wang, J.; Weng, X.; Lin, H. Membrane fouling in a submerged membrane bioreactor: Effect of pH and its implications. Bioresour. Technol. 2014, 152, 7–14.

119. Sanguanpak, S.; Chiemchaisri, C.; Chiemchaisri, W.; Yamamoto, K. Influence of operating pH on biodegradation performance and fouling propensity in membrane bioreactors for landfill leachate treatment. Int. Biodeterior. Biodegrad. 2015, 102, 64–72.

120. Hu, D.; Zhou, Z.; Shen, X.; Wei, H.; Jiang, L.-M.; Lv, Y. Effects of alkalinity on membrane bioreactors for reject water treatment: Performance improvement, fouling mitigation and microbial structures. Bioresour. Technol. 2015, 197, 217–226.

121. Reid, E.; Liu, X.; Judd, S.J. Effect of high salinity on activated sludge characteristics and membrane permeability in an immersed membrane bioreactor. J. Membr. Sci. 2006, 283, 164–171.

122. Jang, D.; Hwang, Y.; Shin, H.; Lee, W. Effects of salinity on the characteristics of biomass and membrane fouling in membrane bioreactors. Bioresour. Technol. 2013, 141, 50–56.

123. Di Bella, G.; Di Trapani, D.; Torregrossa, M.; Viviani, G. Performance of a MBR pilot plant treating high strength wastewater subject to salinity increase: Analysis of biomass activity and fouling behaviour. Bioresour. Technol. 2013,147, 614–618.

124. Christensen, M.L.; Keiding, K.; Nielsen, P.H.; Jørgensen, M.K. Dewatering in biological wastewater treatment: A review. Water Res. 2015, 82, 14–24.

125. Larsen, P.; Nielsen, J.L.; Svendsen, T.C.; Nielsen, P.H. Adhesion characteristics of nitrifying bacteria in activated sludge. Water Res. 2008, 42, 2814–2826.

126. Higgins, M.J.; Tom, L.A.; Sobeck, D.C. Case study I: Application of the divalent cation bridging theory to

improve biofloc properties and industrial activated sludge system performance—Direct addition of divalent cations. Water Environ. Res. 2004, 76, 344–352.

127. Biggs, C.; Ford, A.; Lant, P. Activated sludge flocculation: direct determination of the effect of calcium ions. Water Sci. Technol. 2001, 43, 75–82. [PubMed]

128. Zhang, Y.; Bu, D.; Liu, C.; Luo, X.; Gu, P. Study on retarding membrane fouling by ferric salts dosing in membrane bioreactors. In Proceedings of the IWA Specialty Conference on Water Environment Membrane Technology WEMT2004, Seoul, Korea, 7–10 June 2004.

129. Lee, J.; Kim, J.; Kang, I.; Cho, M.; Park, P.; Lee, C. Potential and limitations of alum or zeolite addition to improve the performance of a submerged membrane bioreactor. Water Sci. Technol. 2001, 43, 59–66. [PubMed]

130. Wu, J.; Chen, F.; Huang, X.; Geng, W.; Wen, X. Using inorganic coagulants to control membrane fouling in a submerged membrane bioreactor. Desalination 2006, 197, 124–136.

131. Wu, J.; Huang, X. Effect of dosing polymeric ferric sulfate on fouling characteristics, mixed liquor properties and performance in a long-term running membrane bioreactor. Sep. Purif. Technol. 2008, 63, 45–52.

132. Zhang, H.-F.; Sun, B.-S.; Zhao, X.-H.; Gao, Z.-H. Effect of ferric chloride on fouling in membrane bioreactor. Sep. Purif. Technol. 2008, 63, 341–347.

133. Mishima, I.; Nakajima, J. Control of membrane fouling in membrane bioreactor process by coagulant addition. Water Sci. Technol. 2009, 57, 1255–1262.

134. Ngo, H.-H.; Guo, W. Membrane fouling control and enhanced phosphorus removal in an aerated submerged membrane bioreactor using modified green

bioflocculant. Bioresour. Technol. 2009, 100, 4289–4291.

135. Ying, Z.; Ping, G. Effect of powdered activated carbon dosage on retarding membrane fouling in MBR. Sep. Purif. Technol. 2006, 52, 154–160.

136. Satyawali, Y.; Balakrishnan, M. Effect of PAC addition on sludge properties in an MBR treating high strength wastewater. Water Res. 2009, 43, 1577–1588.

137. Torretta, V.; Urbini, G.; Raboni, M.; Copelli, S.; Viotti, P.; Luciano, A.; Mancini, G. Effect of powdered activated carbon to reduce fouling in membrane bioreactors: A sustainable solution. case study. Sustainability 2013, 5, 1501–1509.

138. Jamal Khan, S.; Visvanathan, C.; Jegatheesan, V. Effect of powdered activated carbon (PAC) and cationic polymer on biofouling mitigation in hybrid MBRs. Bioresour. Technol. 2012, 113, 165–168.

139. Ng, C.A.; Sun, D.; Bashir, M.J.K.; Wai, S.H.; Wong, L.Y.; Nisar, H.; Wu, B.; Fane, A.G. Optimization of membrane bioreactors by the addition of powdered activated carbon. Bioresour. Technol. 2013, 138, 38–47.

140. Ngo, H.-H.; Guo, W.; Xing, W. Evaluation of a novel sponge-submerged membrane bioreactor (SSMBR) for sustainable water reclamation. Bioresour. Technol. 2008, 99, 2429–2435.

141. Skouteris, G.; Saroj, D.; Melidis, P.; Hai, F.I.; Ouki, S. The effect of activated carbon addition on membrane bioreactor processes for wastewater treatment and reclamation—A critical review. Bioresour. Technol. 2015, 185, 399–410.

142. Deng, L.; Guo, W.; Ngo, H.H.; Zhang, J.; Liang, S.; Xia, S.; Zhang, Z.; Li, J. A comparison study on membrane fouling in a sponge-submerged membrane bioreactor and a conventional membrane bioreactor. Bioresour. Technol. 2014, 165, 69–74.

143. Yang, J.; Spanjers, H.; van Lier, J.B. Non-feasibility of magnetic adsorbents for fouling control in anaerobic membrane bioreactors. Desalination 2012, 292, 124–128.

144. Remy, M.; Potier, V.; Temmink, H.; Rulkens, W. Why low powdered activated carbon addition reduces membrane fouling in MBRs. Water Res. 2010, 44, 861–867.

145. Beun, J.J.; Hendriks, A.; van Loosdrecht, M.C.M.; Morgenroth, E.; Wilderer, P.A.; Heijnen, J.J. Aerobic granulation in a sequencing batch reactor. Water Res. 1999, 33, 2283–2290.

146. Tay, J.-H.; Liu, Q.-S.; Liu, Y. Microscopic observation of aerobic granulationin sequential aerobic sludge blanket reactor. J. Appl. Microbiol. 2001, 91, 168–175.

147. Adav, S.S.; Lee, D.-J.; Show, K.-Y.; Tay, J.-H. Aerobic granular sludge: Recent advances. Biotechnol. Adv. 2008, 26, 411–423.

148. Wang, Z.-W.; Liu, Y.; Tay, J.-H. Biodegradability of extracellular polymeric substances produced by aerobic granules.Appl. Microbiol. Biotechnol. 2007, 74, 462–466.

149. Liu, Y.; Tay, J.-H. State of the art of biogranulation technology for wastewater treatment. Biotechnol. Adv. 2004, 22, 533–563.

150. Thanh, B.X.; Visvanathan, C.; Spérandio, M.; Aim, R.B. Fouling characterization in aerobic granulation coupled baffled membrane separation unit. J. Membr. Sci. 2008, 318, 334–339.

151. Show, K.-Y.; Lee, D.-J.; Tay, J.-H. Aerobic Granulation: Advances and Challenges. Appl. Biochem. Biotechnol. 2012, 167, 1622–1640.

152. Kong, Y.; Liu, Y.-Q.; Tay, J.-H.; Wong, F.-S.; Zhu, J. Aerobic granulation in sequencing batch reactors with

different reactor height/diameter ratios. Enzyme Microb. Technol. 2009, 45, 379–383.

153. Wang, Y.; Zhong, C.; Huang, D.; Wang, Y.; Zhu, J. The membrane fouling characteristics of MBRs with different aerobic granular sludges at high flux. Bioresour. Technol. 2013, 136, 488–495.

154. Vijayalayan, P.; Thanh, B.X.; Visvanathan, C. Simultaneous nitrification denitrification in a Batch Granulation Membrane Airlift Bioreactor. Int. Biodeterior. Biodegrad. 2014, 95, 139–143.

155. Yilmaz, G.; Lemaire, R.; Keller, J.; Yuan, Z. Simultaneous nitrification, denitrification; phosphorus removal from nutrient-rich industrial wastewater using granular sludge. Biotechnol. Bioeng. 2008, 100, 529–541.

156. Wang, J.; Wang, X.; Zhao, Z.; Li, J. Organics and nitrogen removal and sludge stability in aerobic granular sludge membrane bioreactor. Appl. Microbiol. Biotechnol. 2008, 79, 679–685.

157. Zhao, X.; Chen, Z.; Shen, J.; Wang, X. Performance of aerobic granular sludge in different bioreactors. Environ. Technol. 2013, 35, 938–944.

158. Khan, M.Z.; Mondal, P.K.; Sabir, S. Aerobic granulation for wastewater bioremediation: A review. Can. J. Chem. Eng.2013, 91, 1045–1058.

159. Moy, B.Y.P.; Tay, J.H.; Toh, S.K.; Liu, Y.; Tay, S.T.L. High organic loading influences the physical characteristics of aerobic sludge granules. Lett. Appl. Microbiol. 2002, 34, 407–412.

160. Tay, S.T.L.; Ivanov, V.; Yi, S.; Zhuang, W.Q.; Tay, J.H. Presence of Anaerobic Bacteroides in Aerobically Grown Microbial Granules. Microb. Ecol. 2002, 44, 278–285.

161. Adav, S.S.; Lee, D.-J.; Tay, J.-H. Extracellular polymeric substances and structural stability of aerobic granule. Water Res. 2008, 42, 1644–1650.

162. Siembida, B.; Cornel, P.; Krause, S.; Zimmermann, B. Effect of mechanical cleaning with granular material on the permeability of submerged membranes in the MBR process. Water Res. 2010, 44, 4037–4046.

163. Kurita, T.; Kimura, K.; Watanabe, Y. The influence of granular materials on the operation and membrane fouling characteristics of submerged MBRs. J. Membr. Sci. 2014, 469, 292–299.

164. Johir, M.A.; Shanmuganathan, S.; Vigneswaran, S.; Kandasamy, J. Performance of submerged membrane bioreactor (SMBR) with and without the addition of the different particle sizes of GAC as suspended medium. Bioresour. Technol. 2013, 141, 13–18.

165. Pradhan, M.; Vigneswaran, S.; Kandasamy, J.; Aim, R.B. Combined effect of air and mechanical scouring of membranes for fouling reduction in submerged membrane reactor. Desalination 2012, 288, 58–65.

166. Kurita, T.; Kimura, K.; Watanabe, Y. Energy saving in the operation of submerged MBRs by the insertion of baffles and the introduction of granular materials. Sep. Purif. Technol. 2015, 141, 207–213.

167. Krause, S.; Zimmermann, B.; Meyer-Blumenroth, U.; Lamparter, W.; Siembida, B.; Cornel, P. Enhanced membrane bioreactor process without chemical cleaning. Water Sci. Technol. 2010, 61, 2575–2580.

168. Kim, J.; Kim, K.; Ye, H.; Lee, E.; Shin, C.; McCarty, P.L.; Bae, J. Anaerobic fluidized bed membrane bioreactor for wastewater treatment. Environ. Sci. Technol. 2011, 45, 576–581.

169. Aslam, M.; McCarty, P.L.; Bae, J.; Kim, J. The effect of fluidized media characteristics on membrane fouling and energy consumption in anaerobic fluidized membrane bioreactors. Sep. Purif. Technol. 2014, 132, 10–15.

170. Kim, K.-Y.; Yang, W.; Ye, Y.; LaBarge, N.; Logan, B.E. Performance of anaerobic fluidized membrane bioreactors using effluents of microbial fuel cells treating domestic wastewater. Bioresour. Technol. 2016, 208, 58–63.

171. Davies, D.G.; Parsek, M.R.; Pearson, J.P.; Iglewski, B.H.; Costerton, J.T.; Greenberg, E. The involvement of cell-to-cell signals in the development of a bacterial biofilm. Science 1998, 280, 295–298.

172. Yeon, K.-M.; Cheong, W.-S.; Oh, H.-S.; Lee, W.-N.; Hwang, B.-K.; Lee, C.-H.; Beyenal, H.; Lewandowski, Z. Quorum Sensing: A New Biofouling Control Paradigm in a Membrane Bioreactor for Advanced Wastewater Treatment.Environ. Sci. Technol. 2009, 43, 380–385.

173. Jiang, W.; Xia, S.; Liang, J.; Zhang, Z.; Hermanowicz, S.W. Effect of quorum quenching on the reactor performance, biofouling and biomass characteristics in membrane bioreactors. Water Res. 2013, 47, 187–196.

174. Yeon, K.-M.; Lee, C.-H.; Kim, J. Magnetic enzyme carrier for effective biofouling control in the membrane bioreactor based on enzymatic quorum quenching. Environ. Sci. Technol. 2009, 43, 7403–7409.

175. Xu, H.; Liu, Y. Control and cleaning of membrane biofouling by energy uncoupling and cellular communication.Environ. Sci. Technol. 2010, 45, 595–601.

176. Jahangir, D.; Oh, H.-S.; Kim, S.-R.; Park, P.-K.; Lee, C.-H.; Lee, J.-K. Specific location of encapsulated quorum quenching bacteria for biofouling control in an external submerged membrane bioreactor. J. Membr. Sci. 2012, 411, 130–136.

177. Oh, H.-S.; Yeon, K.-M.; Yang, C.-S.; Kim, S.-R.; Lee, C.-H.; Park, S.Y.; Han, J.Y.; Lee, J.-K. Control of membrane biofouling in MBR for wastewater treatment by quorum

quenching bacteria encapsulated in microporous membrane. Environ. Sci. Technol. 2012, 46, 4877–4884.

178. Kim, J.-H.; Choi, D.-C.; Yeon, K.-M.; Kim, S.-R.; Lee, C.-H. Enzyme-immobilized nanofiltration membrane to mitigate biofouling based on quorum quenching. Environ. Sci. Technol. 2011, 45, 1601–1607.

179. Kim, S.-R.; Oh, H.-S.; Jo, S.-J.; Yeon, K.-M.; Lee, C.-H.; Lim, D.-J.; Lee, C.-H.; Lee, J.-K. Biofouling control with bead-entrapped quorum quenching bacteria in membrane bioreactors: Physical and biological effects. Environ. Sci. Technol.2013, 47, 836–842.

180. Wood, T.L.; Guha, R.; Tang, L.; Geitner, M.; Kumar, M.; Wood, T.K. Living biofouling-resistant membranes as a model for the beneficial use of engineered biofilms. Proc. Natl. Acad. Sci. USA 2016, 113, E2802–E2811.

Chapter 2

Anaerobic Membrane Bioreactors (AnMBR) for Wastewater Treatment

Sheng Chang

School of Engineering, University of Guelph, Guelph, Canada

ABSTRACT

This paper focuses on the recent research in the development of anaerobic membrane bioreactors in wastewater treatment. Anaerobic wastewater treatment technology is gaining increasing attention due to its capacity to convert wastewater BODs to usable biogas with relatively low energy consumption. The anaerobic membrane bioreactor (AnMBR), which is a combination of the anaerobic biological wastewater treatment process and membrane filtration, represents a recent development in the high-rate anaerobic bioreactors. This paper reviews applications and performances of AnMBR and the membrane filtration behaviour in AnMBRs.

Keywords: Anaerobic Membrane Bioreactor; Wastewater Treatment; Membrane Fouling; Energy Recovery; Membrane Bioreactor

1. INTRODUCTION

Environmental sustainability is one of the most critical challenges that we are currently facing. To maintain a sustainable environment requires effective and advanced waste and wastewater management technologies which should not only remove the contaminants, but also be of high energy efficiency with the capacity to recover useful resources from waste and wastewater. One of the technologies to meet such requirements is the anaerobic digestion which can convert the waste BOD to usable biogas, reserve useful nitrogen and phosphorus for further recovery, and require minimum energy to operate. However, the efficiency of anaerobic digestion has been largely limited by the intrinsic slow growth rate of the anaerobic microorganisms, which results in a large reactor volume necessary for wastewater treatment by anaerobic digestion. One of the advanced solutions to improve the efficiency of anaerobic treatment is to integrate anaerobic wastewater treatment reactor with membrane filtration process to form an anaerobic membrane bioreactor system. In this system, the membrane filtration process can separate the treated wastewater from the anaerobic biomass and, at the same time, concentrate the biomass concentration in the anaerobic bioreactor to a desired level.

Although the concept of AnMBR was developed in 1980s [1], applications of the anaerobic membrane technology have been limited by concerns on the membrane fouling in the anaerobic environment, the energy consumption of the membrane processes, and the pre-matured large-scale wastewater treatment membrane filtration technology. However, with the success of MBR technology in recent years, the large-scale membrane filtration systems have become a proved technology with effective strategies for the membrane process design, operation, and maintenance developed for the biological wastewater treatment applications. These progresses and the potential of the AnMBR as an energy recovery technology have stimulated increased research interests in AnMBRs. This paper reviews the current status and recent development.

2. ANMBR SYSTEMS

The anaerobic membrane bioreactor is an integrated system of the anaerobic bioreactor and the low pressure ultrafiltration or microfiltration membrane filtration. Since MF/UF membranes can physically retain suspended solids, including suspended biomass and inert solids, the AnMBR can achieve complete separation of the solid retention time from the hydraulic retention time, independent of the wastewater characteristics, biological process conditions, and the sludge properties. As shown in Figure 1, the membrane filtration can be integrated with anaerobic bioreactors in three different forms: the internal submerged membrane filtration (A), the external submerged membrane filtration (B), and the external crossflow membrane filtration (C). The anaerobic bioreactor can be the complete mix [2], the up-flow anaerobic sludge blank (UASB) [3], the expanded granular sludge bed (EGSB) [4], the fluidized anaerobic bed reactors [5], and other type of anaerobic reactors. The complete mix anaerobic bioreactor is a conventional anaerobic bioreactor. Without coupling with the membrane filtration, the complete mix bioreactor may only be suitable for the solid or sludge digestion or for the small-scale wastewater treatment because its low organic loading capacity could result in a large reactor volume for the treatment of a large wastewater flow, which becomes economically unfeasible. The UASB and EGSB can decouple the HRT from SRT through growing dense biomass to avoid the biomass wash-out under a short HRT condition, while the fluidized bed biofilm reactors through attached growth to retain the biomass in the bioreactor system. The current commercial high rate anaerobic bioreactor systems include Biothane UASB and EGSB, ADI hybrid bioreactor, BioPaQ$^{\grave{O}}$ UASB, PAQ IC, etc. with the main market segments covering brewery, potato, pulp & paper, dairy, vegetable, etc. [6]. According to Kassam et al. [6], the current commercial high rate anaerobic reactors have successfully treated high strength wastewaters with COD up to 60,000 mg/L and achieved a COD removal higher than 85% in a HRT range less than 5 days. The biogas production rates of commercial full-scale anaerobic systems are usually around 500 L/kg COD. Integrating the high rate anaerobic bioreactors with the membrane filtration could further improve the effluent quality and operation stability.

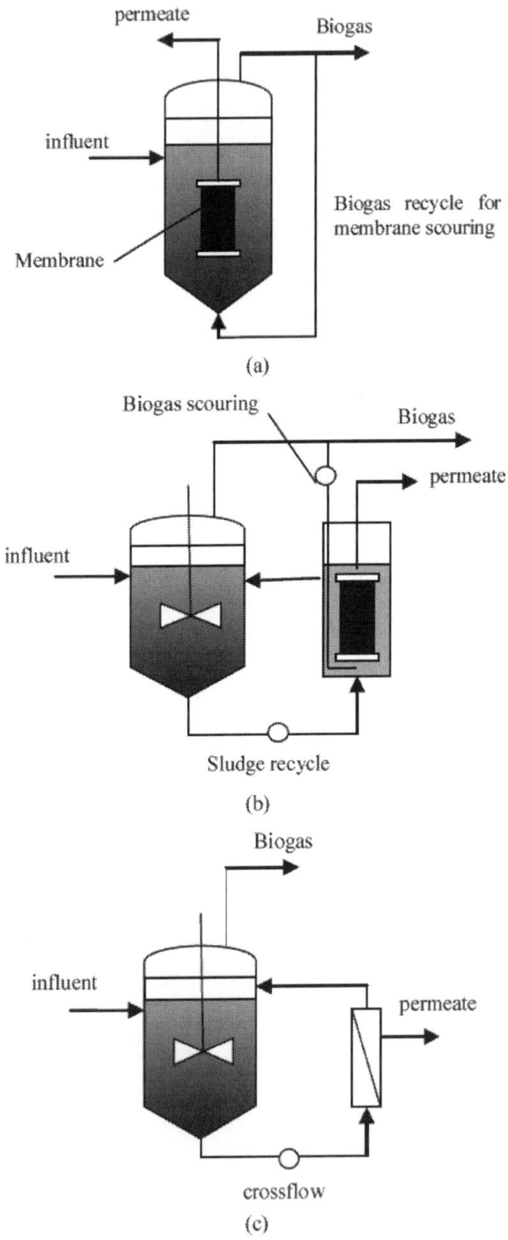

Figure 1. Different AnMBR system configurations. (a) Submerged membrane AnMBR; (b) AnMBR with external submerged hollow fiber membrane; (c) AnMBR with external crossflow membrane.

One of the key components of an AnMBR system is the membrane filtration system. As shown inFigure 1, two different membrane filtration modules, the crossflow pressurised membrane modules and the submerged membrane filtration, can be used in AnMBRs: the external crossflow membrane filtration usually uses the conventional plate & frame or the cylindrical hollow fiber cartridge configurations. In such system, the liquid crossflow is used to generate the surface shear to control the membrane fouling. The permeate flow is driven by the crossflow generated pressure or obtained by pump suction. The immersed or submerged membrane modules have been widely used in the aerobic membrane processes. The immersed membrane modules include the submerged flat sheet membrane modules and the submerged hollow fibre membrane modules. Figure 2(a) shows a schematic of the submerged flat sheet membrane panels which are usually arranged at a gap of around 8 to 12 mm with gas injected into these gaps to prevent the sludge accumulation and membrane fouling. For a fullscale module, up to 100 panels can be connected to a common manifold to form a filtration unit. Figure 2(b) shows a typical design of a submerged hollow fibre membrane module. The submerged hollow fibre membrane module consists of the module headers and fibre bundles. Most of the hollow fibre membranes used in MBRs are polyvinylidene fluoride (PVDF) hollow fibres with OD/ID range of 1 - 2/0.65 - 1 (mm/mm) [7] and the fibre bundle can be packed into a curtain or cylindrical configuration. The current commercial submerged hollow fiber membrane modules can achieve a packing density around 160 m^2/m^3 tank volume, which can provide a total production capacity of 800 m^3/day at an average day design flux of 22 L/m^2/day [8].

3. APPLICATIONS OF ANMBRS IN WASTEWATER TREATMENT

AnMBRs have been tested for the treatment of a wide range of wastewaters and high solid content wastes, which include food processing wastewater, pulp and paper, landfill, municipal wastewater, etc. Table 1 summarises some reported results on the treatment of high strength wastewater of different sources by AnMBRs. In general, it has been showed that AnMBRs can achieve around 90% or higher COD

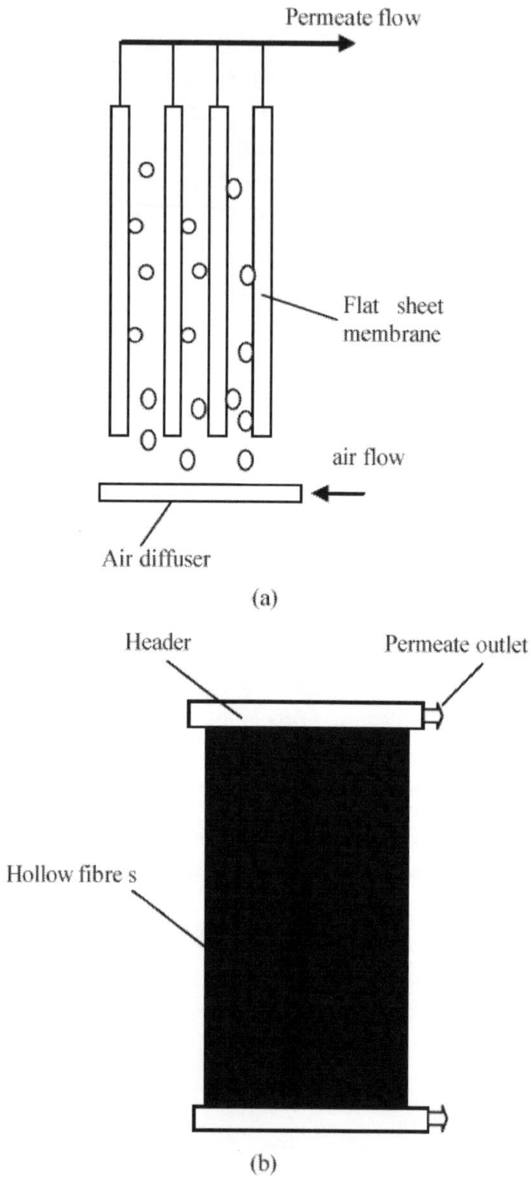

Figure 2. Schematics of submerged membrane modules. (a) Submerged flat sheet membrane modules; (b) Submerged d hollow fiber membrane modules.

removal and a methane production of 0.25 to 0.35 m^3 CH_4/kg COD. The organic loadings of AnMBRs ranged from 5 to 30 g COD/L/day, MLSS concentration from 15 to 30 g/L or higher, HRT from 1 to 25 days, and the membrane filtration flux from 5 to 10 LMH, were reported.

Recently, there is an increasing interest in the application of AnMBRs to municipal wastewater treatment [14-16]. Table 2 summarised some of the reported results on the applications of AnMBR in municipal wastewater treatment. Many studies showed that AnMBR can achieve efficient COD removal at temperature ranging from 20˚C to 30˚C in the treatment of municipal wastewater with a HRT from 24 to 6 hours tested. Most of studies showed that a long-term sustainable flux around 5 to 10 LMH was achievable for the municipal wastewater treatment AnMBRs. Lin et al. [14] conducted a feasibility evaluation of submerged anaerobic membrane bioreactor for municipal secondary wastewater treatment. A cost analysis based on their lab-scale test showed that the operational cost of an AnMBR could be only 1/3 of the aerobic treatment process and the energy generated from methane production can theoretically balance the energy required for the membrane biogas scouring [16]. Although it is feasible to treat municipal wastewater using AnMBR in terms of theoretical energy balance calculation, the full-scale commercial applications is still be limited by concerns of the stability of the treatment performance under ambient temperature; the effluent

Table 1. Treatment performances and process conditions of AnMBR used in high strength wastewater treatment.

	Anderson *et al.* [9]	Choo & Lee [10]	Xie, *et al.* [11]	Van Zyl, *et al.* [12]	Zayen *et al.* [13]
Wastewater	Brewery	Distillery	Kraft evaporator condensate	Coal industria WW	Landfill
WW COD (g/L)	80 to 90	22.6	10	19.1	41
Temperature (˚C)	35 to 37	53 to 55	36 to 38	37	37
OLR (kg COD/m^3/day)	Above 30	1.5	22.5	Up to 25	6.27
HRT (day)	2.5 to 4.2	15	-	1.3	7
MLSS concentration (g/L)	Up to 51	-	8 to 12	36	-
COD removal (%)	99%	97%	93% to 99%	96.8%	90.7%
Gas production (m^3 CH_4/kgCOD)	0.28	0.26	0.35	-	0.48

Table 2. Treatment performances and process conditions of AnMBR used in low strength municipal wastewater treatment.

	Lew, *et al.* [14]	Martinez-Sosa [15]	Lin, *et al.* [16]
WW COD (g/L)	0.54	0.6*	0.342 - 0.527 (SCOD)
Temperature (°C)	25	20	30
Reactor type	Complete mix	Complete mix	UASB
Reactor volume (m^3)	0.18	0.35	0.06
Membrane location	Side stream	Submerged	Submerged
module type	Hollow fiber (dead end)	Flat-sheet	Flat sheet
Membrane area (M^2)	4	3.5	0.6
OLR (kg COD/m^3/day)	2.16*	0.4 - 0.9	1
HRT (day)	0.25	1.5 - 0.67	0.42
COD removal	88%	84 - 94	90
Gas yield (m^3 CH_4/kgCOD)	-	0.24	0.24
Membrane flux (LMH)	7.5	7	12

quality; and the energy recovery efficient under low influent COD conditions. The current experimental results showed that the temperature range for the effective anaerobic treatment of municipal wastewater is around 20°C to 30°C, so the anaerobic treatment of municipal wastewater may be still a challenge for places with cold winter since it is not economic feasible to heat large amount of wastewater flow. Martinez-Sosa reported that the methane production reduced from 0.27 L/gCOD to 0.24 L/gCOD when the temperature is reduced from 35°C to 20°C. Baek et al., [17], reported that no methane production was detected when treating municipal water with soluble COD ranging from 38 to 131 mg/L although 72% COD removal was observed. Dissolution of the methane in the treated effluent will also affect the energy recovery and increase the green house gas emission from the discharged effluent.

4. MEMBRANE FILTRATION PERFORMANCE IN ANMBR

One of the key design and operation parameters of the membrane filtration is the operation flux, which directly affects the capital and operation costs of AnMBRs. The membrane process design flux determines the membrane surface area or the number of the membrane modules required to treat a certain wastewater flow. The number of the membrane modules installed will further affect the size of the membrane tank, piping, and the consumption of the chemicals used for the membrane cleaning. The design flux of AnMBRs, at which a stable operation is supposed to be attained, should be determined based on relatively long term testing. Some of the main observations on the membrane filtration operation in AnMBRs are summarised as below:

- Fluxes ranging from 6.7 to 10 LMH were achievable for the treatment of the different wastewaters [18]. Based on the concept of the critical flux, controlling the operation flux is still the most critical strategies to achieve long-term stable operation.

- Intermittent permeation is important to achieve the long-term stable operation. The typical operation cycles could include 10 to 15 minutes permeation and 10 to 60 seconds relaxing. No obvious advantage of the membrane backwash over relaxing was observed.

- Many studies showed that the membrane filtration in AnMBRs could tolerate much higher suspended solid concentrations than the aerobic MBR systems, where the high MLSS concentration can considerably reduce the oxygen transfer efficiency, resulting in a drastic change in the filterability of the mixed liquor.

The membrane fouling is still the major factors limiting the efficiency of the AnMBR. For the sub-critical flux operation, rapid particle deposition on the membrane surface can be avoided and the membrane fouling is mainly caused by the graduate accumulation of colloidal or soluble SMP in the mixed liquor. Although many studies have showed that the SMPs mainly consist of protein and polysaccharides, little insights into the colloidal properties of the SMPs have been developed so far. Hence, the interaction mechanisms between the SMPs and the membrane surface are still unclear. In addition to the membrane fouling caused by the SMPs, the inorganic compounds can also play an important role in the membrane fouling in AnMBR. Herrera-Robledo et al. [19] reported that the cake layer was mainly composed of volatile solids (85%) and the rest were related to mineral matter, with the presence of inorganic salts containing Ca, Mg, Fe, P and Si. Studies showed that metal complexation could play an important role in the development of the irreversible membrane fouling. Lyko et al. [20] demonstrated that a significant amount of extracellular polymeric substances (EPS) could be released by treating the fouled membrane samples with Ca^{2+} selective cation exchange resin (CER). Iron has also been detected on the fouled membrane surface. Choo and Lee [10] suggested that the precipitation of the struvite ($MgNH_4PO_4{\cdot}6H_2O$) might play an important role in the inorganic membrane fouling in AnMBRs.

The main strategies to control membrane fouling in AnMBR include the crossflow for the external membrane filtration and the biogas scouring for the submerged membrane filtration system. The membrane gas scouring technology has been well developed through the aerobic MBR development. The energy efficient membrane filtration gas scouring technologies include intermittent gas scouring [8] and, recently, the pulse gas scouring [21]. Other techniques tested for the membrane fouling control include using ultrasonic techniques [22], vibrating membranes [23], and adding chemicals or adsorbents, such as powder activated carbon, to improve the filterability of the mixed liquor or reduce the concentration of the soluble membrane foulants [24]. Recently, Kim et al. [5] tested directly immersing the hollow fiber membrane in a fluidized granular activated carbon (GAC) anaerobic biofilm reactor and reported that the fluidized GAC particle could be utilized for the membrane fouling control.

5. CONCLUSION

AnMBR concept was developed about three decades ago, but its commercial applications have been largely limited by the efficiency of the membrane filtration. Recent development in the large-scale wastewater treatment MBR has largely increased the potential of the anaerobic membrane technology as a practical, advanced full-scale wastewater treatment technology. The current research demonstrated that the AnMBR technology can be used for the treatment of a wide range of wastewaters with a great potential to recover energy and resources from both high strength wastewaters.

REFERENCES

1. B. Q. Liao, J. T. Kraemer and D. M. Bagley, "Anaerobic Membrane Bioreactors: Applications and Research Directions," Critical Review in Environmental Science and Technology, Vol. 36, No. 6, 2006, pp. 489-530.

2. D. Martinez-Sosa, B. Helmreich, T. Netter, S. Paris, F. Bischof and H. Horn, "Anaerobic Submerged Membrane Bioreactor (AnSMBR) for Municipal Wastewater Treatment under Mesophilic and Psychrophilic Temperature Conditions," Bioresource Technology, Vol. 102, No. 22, pp. 10377-10385.

3. M. L. Salazar-Pelaez, J. M. Morgan-Sagastume and A. Noyola, "Influence of Hydraulic Retention Time on Fouling in a UASB Coupled with an External Ultrafiltration Membrane Treating Synthetic Municipal Wastewater," Desalination, Vol. 277, No. 1, 2011, pp. 164-170.

4. L. B. Chu, F. L. Yang and F. L. Zhang, "Anaerobic Treatment of Domestic Wastewater in a Membrane-Coupled Expended Granular Sludge Bed (EGSB) Reactor under Moderate to Low Temperature," Process Biochemistry, Vol. 40, No. 3, 2005, pp. 1063-1070.

5. J. Kim, K. Kim, H. Young, H. Ye, E. Lee, C. Shin, P. Mccarty and J. Bae, "Anaerobic Fluidized Bed Membrane Bioreactor for Wastewater Treatment," Environmental Science & Technology Letters, Vol. 45, No. 17, 2011, pp. 576-581. [Paper reference:2]

6. Z. A. Kassam, L. Yerushalmi and S. Guiot, "A Market Study on the Anaerobic Wastewater Treatment Systems," Water, Air, and Soil Pollution, Vol. 143, No. 1-4, 2003, pp. 179-192.

7. S. Chang, "Application of Submerged Hollow Fibre Membrane in Membrane Bioreactors: Filtration Principles, Operation, and Membrane Fouling," Desalination, Vol. 283, 2011, pp. 31-39.

8. T. Bure and J. Cumin, "MBR Module Design and Operation," Desalination, Vol. 250, No. 3, 2010, pp. 1073- 1077.

9. G. K. Anderson, B. Kasapgil and O. Ince, "Microbial Kinetics of a Membrane Anaerobic Reactor," Environmental Technology, Vol. 17, No. 5, 1996, p. 449.

10. K. H. Choo and C. H. Lee, "Membrane Fouling Mechanisms in the Membrane-Coupled Anaerobic Bioreactor," Water Research, Vol. 30, No. 8, 1996, pp. 1771-1780.

11. K. Xie, H. J. Lin, B. Mahendran, D. M. Bagle, K. T. Leung, S. N. Liss and B. Q. Liao, "Performance and Fouling Characteristics of a Subme Rged Anaerobic Membrane Bioreactor for Kraft Evaporator Condensate Treatment," Environmental Technology, Vol. 31, No. 5, 2010, pp. 511-521.

12. P. J. Van Zyl, M. C. Wentzel, G. A. Ekama and K. J. Riedel, "Design and Start-Up of a High Rate Anaerobic Membrane Bioreactor for the Treatment of a Low pH, High Strength, Dissolved Organic Waste Water," Water Science Technology, Vol. 57, No. 2, 2008, pp. 291-295.

13. A. Zayen, S. Mnif, F. Aloui, F. Fki, S. Loukil, M. Bouaziz and S. Sayadi, "Anaerobic Membrane Bioreactor for the Treatment of Leachates from Jebel Chakir Discharge in Tunisia," Journal of Hazardous Materials, Vol. 177, No. 1-3, 2010, pp. 918-923.

14. B. Lew, S. Tarre, M. Beliavski, C. Dosoretz and M. Green, "Anaerobic Membrane Bioreactor (AnMBR) for Domestic Wastewater Treatment," Desalination, Vol. 243, No. 1-3, 2009, pp. 251-257.

15. D. Martinez-Sosa, B. Helmreich, T. Netter, S. Paris and F. bischof, "Anaerobic Submerged Membrane Bioreactor (AnSMBR) for Municipal Wastewater Treatment under Mesophilic and Psychrophilic Temperature Conditions," Bioresource Technology, Vol. 102, No. 22, 2011, pp. 10377-10385.

16. H. Lin, J. Chen, F. Wang, L. Ding and H. Hong, "Feasibility Evaluation of Submerged Anaerobic Membrane Bioreactor for Municipal Secondary Wastewater Treatment," Desalination, Vol. 280, 2011, pp. 120-126.

17. S. H. Baek, K. R. Pagilla and H. J. Kim, "Lab-Scale Study of an Anaerobic Membrane Bioreactor (AnMBR) for Dilute Municipal

Wastewater Treatment," Biotechnology and Bioprocess Engineering, Vol. 15, No. 4, 2010, pp. 704-708.

18. S. Kirmura, "Japans Aqua Renaissance'90 Project," Water Science & Technology, Vol. 23, No. 7-9, 1991, pp. 1573-1592.

19. H. Herrera-Robledo, J. M. Morgan-Sagastume and A. Noyola, "Biofouling and Pollutant Removal during LongTerm Operation of an Anaerobic Membrane Bioreactor Treating Municipal Wastewater," Biofouling, Vol. 26, No. 1, 2010, pp. 23-30. S. Lyko, D. Al-Halbouni, T. Wintgens, A. Janot, J. Hollender, W. Dott and T. Melin, "Polymeric Compounds in Activated Sludge Supernatant—Characterisation and Retention Mechanisms at a Full-Scale Municipal Membrane Bioreactor," Water Research, Vol. 41, No. 17, 2007, pp. 3894-3902.

20. M. Kondo, J. Cumin, Y. Hong, R. Bayly, M. Gao and R. Rubin, "Reexamination of the Gas Sparging Mechanism for Membrane Fouling Control," Proceedings of the Water Environment Federation, WEFTEC 2010, New Orleans, pp. 6986-7007. [Paper reference:1]

21. P. Sui, X. Wen and X. Huang, "Feasibility of Employing Ultrasound for On-Line Membrane, Fouling Control in an Anaerobic Membrane Bioreactor," Desalination, Vol. 219, No. 1, 2008, pp. 203-213.

22. A. Kola, Y. Ye, A. Ho, P. Le-Clech and V. Chen, "Application of Low Frequency Transverse Vibration on Fouling Limitation in Submerged Hollow Fibre Membranes," Journal of Membrane Science, Vol. 409-410, 2012, pp. 54-65.

23. H. Park, K. H. Choo and C. H. Lee, "Flux Enhancement with Powder Activated Carbon Addition in the Membrane Anaerobic Bioreactor," Separation Science and Technology, Vol. 34, No. 14, 1999, pp. 2781-2792.

Chapter 3

The Potential for Microalgae as Bioreactors to Produce Pharmaceuticals

Na Yan [1,2], Chengming Fan [1], Yuhong Chen [1] and Zanmin Hu [1,*]

[1]*Institute of Genetics and Developmental Biology, Chinese Academy of Sciences, Beijing 100101, China*

[2]*University of Chinese Academy of Sciences, Beijing 100049, China*

ABSTRACT

As photosynthetic organisms, microalgae can efficiently convert solar energy into biomass. Microalgae are currently used as an important source of valuable natural biologically active molecules, such as carotenoids, chlorophyll, long-chain polyunsaturated fatty acids, phycobiliproteins, carotenoids and enzymes. Significant advances have been achieved in microalgae biotechnology over the last decade, and the use of microalgae as bioreactors for expressing recombinant proteins is receiving increased interest. Compared with the bioreactor systems that are currently in use, microalgae may be an attractive alternative for the production of pharmaceuticals, recombinant proteins and other valuable products. Products synthesized via the genetic engineering of microalgae include vaccines, antibodies, enzymes, blood-clotting factors, immune regulators, growth factors, hormones, and other valuable products, such as the anticancer agent Taxol. In this paper, we briefly compare the currently used bioreactor systems, summarize the progress in genetic engineering of microalgae, and discuss the potential for microalgae as bioreactors to produce pharmaceuticals.

Keywords: microalgae; bioreactor; pharmaceuticals; recombinant proteins

1. INTRODUCTION

The demand for recombinant proteins is growing globally because of their great application values in industry, diagnosis and therapy. The bioreactor systems that are used to produce recombinant proteins are becoming more important for producing large quantities of proteins, particularly those that have associated limitations due to cost or traditional source availability. Based on different types of organisms, several novel bioreactor systems were recently developed due to the advance in biotechniques. In general, a particular bioreactor system may be selected for a specific protein production based on costs as well as the integrity, purity and expression level of the protein.

Currently, recombinant proteins can be expressed in bacteria, yeasts, mammalian cell lines, transgenic animals and plants, and each of these bioreactor systems has specific advantages and limitations [1,2,3]. As a source of natural products, bacteria and yeasts have long been employed in the production of small and simple recombination proteins at a relatively low cost [1,4]. However, bacteria have no post-transcriptional and post-translational modifications, such as intron splicing, multimeric protein assembly, glycosylation and disulfide bond formation, and processes that are essential for generating functional eukaryotic proteins [5,6]. Furthermore, heterologous proteins, expressed in intracellular with high levels, readily aggregate and form insoluble inclusion bodies that require expensive downstream processing [1,2,3]. Despite the ability of yeasts to carry out post-translational modifications, the protein glycosylation pattern usually involves hyperglycosylation, which does not reflect what occurs in higher organisms [7].

Mammalian cell lines are frequently used to produce proteins for therapeutic use; indeed, the USA has approved many different therapeutic and diagnostic proteins that are produced in mammalian cell lines [8,9]. However, oxygen deficiency, the accumulation of waste product or sensitivity to stirring forces can result in instability of mammalian cells, making it difficult to culture these cells in large volumes [9,10,11]. In addition, high levels of complex proteins can be obtained from the milk of transgenic animals [12]. Regardless, the greatest disadvantage of mammalian bioreactor systems is contamination of agents and oncogenic sequences, which can cause diseases [13].

Compared with the above-mentioned expression systems, transgenic plants provide numerous advantages, including the capacity to produce functional recombinant proteins at high levels in an inexpensive and safe manner. Furthermore, the scaling-up process for plants can more easily meet demands by utilizing existing agricultural processes ("molecular farming"), and the input is lower in contrast with other systems [14]. As eukaryotes, plants are able to perform post-translational modifications; similar to animal cells, plant cells have pathways for protein synthesis and folding, and protein secretion and modification, which are required for pharmaceutical protein bioactivity [15]. More importantly, plants cannot be infected by the major human pathogens, which may contaminate the systems of bacterial and mammalian [16]. The expression levels of total soluble proteins (TSPs) obtained from transgenic plants range from 0.001% to 46.1% [17,18], and the most of plants-produced human therapeutic proteins display structural, biochemical and functional properties that are very similar to proteins in humans and animal cell culture-produced proteins [19,20].

Plants produce many types of proteins, including enzymes [21], hormones [22], functional vaccines [17,23], antibodies [24,25], and a variety of other therapeutic proteins [26]. Examples of pharmaceutical proteins that are being expressed in plants include human growth hormone, human serum albumin, interferons, and erythropoietin [27]. Several recent reviews describe the significant advances in this field [28,29,30,31,32]. The first Food and Drug Administration (FDA)-approved plant-made biopharmaceutical (PMB) is glucocerebrosidase; this injectable product produced in carrot cells is used to treat a genetic/metabolic disorder [33]. Another major advancement is the application of chloroplast-generated biopharmaceuticals for toxic antibody suppression [29]. Chan and Daniell noted the challenges of plant cells-produced vaccine antigens toward clinical development, though these oral vaccines may be quite attractive for both human and veterinary purposes [31,34].

Nonetheless, several disadvantages have hindered the use of plants as successful recombinant protein-producing system. Firstly, plants have different types of glycosylation patterns compared with animal cells, which may alter the function of the recombinant protein or even decrease immunogenicity; The second problem includes the controversial issues of regulations and safety, especially with regard to the risk of gene flow via transgenic pollen. Studies on gene flow between transgenic plants and native races have been reported, such as genes that encode *Bacillus thuringiensis* proteins in corn [35] and herbicide resistance genes in canola [36]; Third, much time is required from the transformation step to the acquisition of a purified protein. Moreover, the purification of proteins from plants is inconvenient because they cannot be secreted [37].

Microalgae are a diverse photosynthetic group, consisting of eukaryotic organisms and prokaryotic cyanobacteria. Microalgae have unique advantages, including a high growth rate, ease of cultivation, low growth costs and metabolic pathways that are similar to those of higher plants, leading to the same post-transcriptional and post-translational modifications that occur in higher plants [38,39]. Indeed, as photoautotrophic sunlight-driven cell factories, microalgae provide an efficient means of converting solar energy into biomass, producing fatty acids, lipids, vitamins, carbohydrates, antibiotics, antioxidants and proteins [40,41].

Moreover, microalgae are valuable sources of novel biologically active products, and because their growth requires only inexpensive substrates, these cells can serve as economical and effective bioreactors for obtaining high added-value compounds for healthy food [42,43,44]. Microalgae, such as *Spirulina maxima*, *Synechococcus* sp., *Scenedesmus obliquus*,*Porphyridium cruentum*, *Dunaliella salina*, *Chlorella vulgaris*, *Chlamydomonas reinhardtii*, and *Anabaena cylindrica* contain valuable nutrient compounds. However, microalgal cultivation began only several decades ago [45,46].

In addition to naturally produced compounds, microalgae are also a promising platform for producing recombinant proteins and other valuable natural products, such as cosmetics, pharmaceuticals, biofuels and health supplements [47,48,49,50], providing an attractive alternative to the current bioreactor systems. Compounds that are synthesized by microalgae include growth and blood-clotting factors, immune regulators, hormones, enzymes, monoclonal antibodies, viral vaccines, and other natural products, such as the anticancer agent Taxol. Table 1 roughly summarizes the advantages and disadvantages of bacteria, yeasts, cultured mammalian cells, animals, plants and microalgae for production purposes. This paper reviews the status of microalgae as bioreactors that produce pharmaceuticals.

Table 1. Rough comparison among different expression platforms to produce pharmaceuticals (modified from [51,52]).

Expression Systems	Bacteria	Yeasts	Cultured Mammalian Cells	Animals	Plants	Microalgae
Protein folding accuracy	Low	Medium	High	High	High	High
Glycosylation	None	Incorrect	Correct	Correct	Minor Differences	Minor Differences
Product quality	Low	Medium	High	High	High	High
Protein yield	Medium	High	High	High	High	High
Production scale	Limited	Limited	Limited	Limited	Worldwide	High
Production time	Short	Medium	Long	Long	Long	Short
Scale-up cost	High	High	High	High	Medium	Low
Overall cost	Medium	Medium	High	High	Low	Low
Contamination risk	Endotoxins	Low	High	High	Low	Low
Safety	Low	Unknown	High	High	High	High
Storage cost	Moderate	Moderate	Expensive	Expensive	Inexpensive	Low
Distribution	Medium	Medium	Difficult	Difficult	Easy	Very easy
Reproduction	Easy	Easy	Difficult	Medium	Easy	Very easy

2. BRIEF INTRODUCTION TO MICROALGAE

Algae include the microscopic (microalgae) and macroscopic forms (macroalgae) forms, with the latter largely consisting of seaweed. It has been estimated that there are one to ten million algae species, most of which are microalgae [53]. Culturable microalgae can be classified into four categories: cyanobacteria, green algae, chrysophyte and red algae. Cyanobacteria, also known as blue-green algae, are distinguished from other bacteria because they perform oxygenic photosynthesis.

2.1. Growth Characteristics

An obvious and tangible diversity can be observed among microalgae. Their growth modes include phototrophy, photoheterotrophy, and heterotrophy, and each growth mode can be either obligate or facultative [54].

Compared with plants traditionally used for production, microalgae have several advantages with respect to their growth characteristics. Microalgae do not require fertile soil; because microalgae can use nutrients quite efficiently, a medium that only contains essential nutrients can be used, thus avoiding water pollution due to unused fertilizers. Furthermore, some microalgae can grow in brackish water, saline water or seawater, which can help to conserve limited freshwater resources.

Microalgae photosynthesize under conditions of high light and low temperature. However, lack of essential nutrients, such as nitrogen, can result in starvation conditions, and nitrogen starvation leads to the cessation or slowing down of cell division, which then results in reduced utilization of photosynthetic products [55,56,57]. Based on this, nitrogen starvation had been employed to manipulate the mass-cultivated microalgal metabolism to obtain lipids or carbohydrates-rich biomass [58].

2.2. Nutrient Value

Microalgae can improve the nutritive value of conventional food and animal feed and can effectively improve the health of humans and animals [59]. As sources of protein, various microalgae are unconventional and contain a high protein content [60]. The patterns of amino acids have advantages over that of other food proteins [61]. Carbohydrates in microalgae exist in the forms of sugars, starch, glucose, and other polysaccharides, which are very easy to digest.

Thus, whole dried microalgae can be used as supplements in food or feed with no limitations [62].

The lipid content in some microalgae can account for 90% of the dry weight under certain conditions, with an average lipid content of 1% to 70% [63]. As an essential component of lipids, fatty acids of the ω3 and ω6 families in microalgae are of special interest. Microalgae contain nearly all essential vitamins, such as nicotinate, biotin, folic acid and pantothenic acid [64,65,66,67]. Moreover, there are large amounts of pigments, such as chloroiphyll, phycobiliproteins and carotenoids, in microalgae cells.

The production of nutritional supplements from microalgae has been a major research area in microalgal biotechnology for many years. Products generated from dried biomass or cell extracts of *Chlorella*, *Dunaliella* and *Spirulina* are marketed as nutraceuticals or health food and are sold for many hundreds of thousands of dollars [68,69].

2.3. Genetic Research on Microalgae

Genetic research on microalgae has achieved great progress to date. The Calvin cycle was discovered through *Chlorella*research in 1948 [70]. The genome sequences ofseveral microalgae including *Cyanobacteria* [71,72], *Cyanidioschyzon merolae*[73], *Thalassiosira pseudonana* [74], and *C. reinhardtii* [75] are publicly available. In addition, the genome sequence and genetic transformation of *Chlorella pyrenoidosa* [76] and the oleaginous alga *Nannochloropsis gaditana* [77], were reported.

C. reinhardtii is a model organism in microalgal genetics research, and much progress has been achieved using this organism in recent years. Fu *et al.* found that N^6-methyldeoxyadenosine, a DNA modification, is an active transcriptional start sites in the genome of *Chlamydomonas* [78]. Li *et al.* established an indexed, mapped *C. reinhardtii* mutant library that enables reverse genetic studies of biological processes in this species [79]. Yang *et al.* described the disruption of *C. reinhardtii* ferredoxin-5 (FDX5) can lead to a dark growth deficiency and influence the membrane ultrastructure and membrane lipids [80], and Dejtisakdi and Miller found that overexpression of *C. reinhardtii* fructose 1,6-bisphosphatase (CrFBPase) has a negative effect on growth [81]. A mutation of starch deficiency in *Dunaliella tertiolecta* resulted in increased triacylglycerol content in the cells [82], and the genomic basis for the Starch-to-Lipid Switch has been investigated in *Chlorella* [76]. A new nuclear transformation method by microparticle bombardment was developed in*Phaeodactylum tricornutum* using PCR-amplified DNA fragments [83]. In addition, Ferreira-Camargo *et al.* found that selenocystamine can improve accumulation of disulfide bonds-contained proteins in green algal chloroplasts [84].

These studies helped to lay the foundation for research on microalgal applications, including genetic engineering.

3. GENETIC ENGINEERING AND PRODUCTION OF PHARMACEUTICALS AND RECOMBINANT PROTEINS

3.1. Microalgal Transformation

As a platform for producing recombinant protein, the effective utilization of transgenic microalgae relies on stable transformation systems, including vector construction and transformation methods. Recombinant proteins are typically expressed by the genome of nucleus or chloroplast, which have important differences (see Table 2). In the past 20 years, many species of microalgae were successfully transformed, most of which have been achieved via nuclear transformation [85].

Table 2. Differences between the genome engineering of the nucleus and chloroplast.

Genome Engineering	Nucleus	Chloroplast
Gene expression machinery	Eukaryotic	Prokaryotic
Protein localization	Cytoplasm, nucleus, chloroplast, ER, mitochondria, secretion	Chloroplast
Modifications	Phosphorylation, glycosylation, disulfide bond	Phosphorylation, disulfide bond
Accumulation levels	Low	High
Transformation methods	Electroporation, biolistic, glass beads, silicon whiskers	Biolistic
Integration mode	Non-homologous end joining	Homologous recombination

Typical methods for microalgal transformation are based on transient permeabilization of the cell membrane, which enables plasmid DNA to pass through the membrane and enter the cell. There are many methods for cell permeabilization. One method is to vortex the cells with the DNA, polyethylene glycol (PEG) and glass beads [86]; this is simple, efficient, and suitable for transforming wild-type *Chlamydomonas* after enzyme-mediated cell wall degradation. Another method of*Chlamydomonas* transformation employs silicon carbide (SiC) whiskers, an approach that does not require removal of the cell wall [87] and has been used to manipulate several microalgae, such as *Symbiodinium* and *Amphidinium* [88]. However, SiC whiskers are harmful to human health and should not be the first choice. Electroporation was introduced for transferring genes into many types of cells and organisms, such as thin-walled cells, cell wall-reduced mutants, protoplasts, and naked cells, and is used to obtain stable *Chlamydomonas* transformants with high efficiency [89,90]. In this method, the lipid bilayer is temporarily disrupted by an electronic pulse and DNA molecules are allowed to pass into the cell. Using this technique, the transformation of *C. reinhardtii*, *D. salina*, *C. vulgaris*, *Ostreococcus tauri*, and the red algae *Cyanidioschyzon merolae* has been successfully achieved. Microparticle bombardment is the preferred method of transformation for previously untransformed species of microalgae. Viruses, which infect brown algae and Chlorella-like algae, can also be used in microalgal transformation [91,92], but this approach requires more investigation. In addition, the use of artificial transposons has expanded to the application of genetic transformation. Artificial mini-transposons contain elements of natural transposons that are essential for transposition, and a mini-transposon-transposase complex has been introduced into *Cyanobacterium spirulina* [93]. Although eukaryotic microalgal transformation has not been reported to date using this method, the transposon approach may also be suitable for eukaryotic microalgae when no host factor is required. Particle bombardment is the most frequently used method for transformation of plant tissues and cells as well as prokaryotes; regarding microalgae, it has been successfully used in diatoms [94,95,96,97]. Organelles can also been transformed using this method, such as chloroplasts and mitochondria [98,99,100,101].

Chloroplast transformation has also been reported in the unicellular red algae *Porphyridium* sp. [98]. The chloroplast transformation system of *Chlamydommonas* is the first and best studied in green algae [86,102,103]. *Chlamydommonas* is an excellent model system for research because its genome has been sequenced [104]. Many microalgal species have been stably transformed to date. A luciferase (Luc) and a homologous nitrate reductase gene have been transformed into*Chlorella* [105]. Five heterololgous genes were transformed into the chloroplast of *D. tertiolecta*, and the recombinant enzymes were produced in a stable manner [106]. Other economically valued chlorophytes, such as *Haematococcus pluvialis*, have been stably transformed through the development of a novel chloroplast expression vector [107]. A food source in aquaculture, diatoms with silica-based cell walls, can also be used to produce therapeutic proteins, and six species,*Phaeodactylum tricornutum* [94], *Cyclotella cryptica* [95], *Navicula saprophila* (pennate diatoms) [95], *Cylindrotheca fusiformis*[108], *Thalassiosira weissflogii* [96] and *Thalassiosira pseudonana* [109], as well as *Chaetoceros* sp. (centric diatoms) [110], have been transformed using the microparticle bombardment. Dinoflagellates, an important phytoplankton, are unicellular eukaryotic alveolar algae and some species have typical prokaryote characteristics and eukaryotic features. Among this group, *Amphidinium* and *Symbiodinium* have been successfully transformed [88].

The application of selectable markers is essential for efficient transformation of microalgae. Several dominant and recessive markers have been investigated. Recessive markers have been chosen by functional complementation of the corresponding endogenous genes and mutants [111]. Among these, nitrate reductase has been employed in *C. reinhardtii*[112], *Volvox carteri* [113], *Chlorella sorokiniana* [105], and *Dunaliella viridis* [114]. Dominant markers are the most widely used selectable markers that confer resistance to antibiotics or herbicides. In *Chlamydomonas*, *aadA* is used for resistance to spectinomycin and streptomycin [115], *aphA*6 for resistance to kanamycin, *aph*7 for resistance to hygromycin B, the *aphVIII*for resistance to paromomycin [116], *ble* for resistance to zeomycin and phleomycin [117], the 16S ribosomal gene for resistance to spectinomycin; a mutated *als* gene also confers resistance to sulfonylurea herbicides [118]. All of these markers provide effective, stable antibiotic resistance. In addition to *Chlamydomonas*, the *ble* gene can also be used in *Volvox carteri*[119], *Phaeodactylum tricornutum* [94,96], and *Cylindrotheca fusiformis* [108]. Additionally, the *nptII* gene can be used in*Navicula saprophila*, *Cyclotella cryptica* [95], in the dinoflagellates *Amphidinium* sp. and *Symbiodinium microadriaticum* [88], in*Chlorella* [76,120,121] and in the diatoms *Phaeodactylum tricornutum* [97]. Different microalgal species exhibit diverse antibiotic sensitivities due to the presence of different marker genes [96,97].

The promoter is an important aspect of successful microalgal transformation. For nuclear transformation in *P. tricornutum*, likely promoter choices are those of *fcpB* encoding chlorophyll a/c binding protein B of fucoxanthin [94,97,122], and nitrate reductase, which is activated when nitrate is the nitrogen source in the medium [123,124,125,126,127]. The CaMV35S promoter is also efficient in microalgae, such as *C. ellipsoidea* [128,129,130], *C. vulgaris* [131], *Haematococcus pluvialis* [132], *D. salina* [133,134,135] and *C. reinhardtii*. However, the expression level in *C. reinhardtii* is low. The RbcS2 promoter of *C. reinhardtii* has successfully been used in *C. ellipsoidea* for transient expression of the resistance gene or recombinant protein [128,131]. The maize *Ubiquitin* (*Ubi*1) gene promoter can be used for stable expression of NP-1, an α-defensin encoded by a rabbit gene, in *C. ellipsoidea* [120]. The tobacco mosaic virus (TMV) promoter enhances translation efficiency [130], and in *D. salina* the ubiquitin-Ω promoter successfully drives expression of hepatitis B surface antigen [133]. With regard to chloroplast transgenes, the *psbA*, *psbD* and *rbcL* promoters are typically used in *C. reinhardtii*. Recently, Seo *et al.* indicated that the EF2 promoter of *P. tricornutum* can be utilized for the expression of target gene in *P. tricornutum*and *C. reinhardtii* [136].

Many species of microalgae had been successfully transformed; however, stable *Chlorella* transformants are lacking for a long time. *Chlorella* is an important genus in which a few species of microalgae can be used for industrial production, and genetic transformation of this group has important significance for employing *Chlorella* as a biological reactor. Although foreign gene transient expression has been successfully achieved in *Chlorella*, *C. sorokiniana* and *C. vulgaris*, none was able to produce target product [129,131,137]. Flounder growth hormone (fGH) was produced in protoplasts of *C. ellipsoidea*, and it was accumulated to 400 mg/L estimated by ELISA [128]. In our previous work, NP-1 was successfully expressed in *Chlorella*[130], but the lines stably expressing NP-1 were not obtained because when the selection antibiotic G418 was removed, the NP-1-expressing cells were lost [138]. Nonetheless, stable expression of foreign genes in transgenic *Chlorella* was achieved with technique improvement. For example, as stated above, a luciferase (Luc) gene and homologous nitrate reductase gene have been stably transformed into *Chlorella* [105,129,139]. Defensin NP-1 can be produced in *C. ellipsoidea* [120], and expression of GmDof4 in *C. ellipsoidea* can significantly increase the total lipid content. In *Chlorella pyrenoidosa*, overexpression of an *Arabidopsis thaliana* nicotinamide adenine dinucleotide (NAD(H)) kinase increased the lipid content of cells by 110.4% without effects on the growth rate [76]. Recently, a new inducible expression system has also been developed for *Chlorella vulgaris* [140].

Nuclear transgenic expression in microalgae is occasionally inefficient, possibly due to gene silencing [141,142,143]. Furthermore, exogenous genes might not be expressed properly if the transgenic clones are not maintained under constant selection [144]. With regard to the general feasibility of expressing foreign proteins in microalgae, it appears that despite the considerable body of knowledge accumulated, inducing high expression of transgenes is difficult, possibly due to epigenetic mechanisms [144]. Other reasons for transient expression may include the following: (1) the heterologous genes might be not actually inserted into the genome, which can be detected by Southern hybridization, and Southern hybridization results were not provided in most of the papers reporting the transient expression of foreign genes in microalgae [129,145,146]; (2) the selected transgenic colony contained non-transgenic cells, and without constant selection, the number of transgenic cells may have decreased or these cells may have disappeared. In our work on NP-1 expression in*C. ellipsoidea*, at least five rounds of continuous selection were performed to obtain stable transgenic lines [120]. Therefore, to obtain stable transgenic *Chlorella*, a long period of continuous selection of individual clone is necessary.

3.2. Genetically Engineered Microalgae

Microalgal biotechnology has achieved important advances in recent years due to the development of new technologies [147], and several examples in biotechnological applications of engineered microalgae have shown significant promise. In diatoms, Genetic engineering is an important approach of microalgae to produce particular lipids and bio-diesel [148]. In*C. ellipsoidea*, overexpression of GmDof4, a soybean transcription factor, significantly increased the lipid content by 46.4% to 52.9% [121]. In addition, researchers found that the expression of a foreign metallothionein gene can enhance the binding capacity to metals and the moth bean pyrroline-5-carboxylate synthetase (P5CS) gene expression can result in the accumulation of free proline in microalgae [149,150].

Most of the advances in genetic engineering of microalgae have been realized in *C. reinhardtii* through the use of both nuclear and chloroplast transformation. *C. reinhardtii* is a good bioreactor for the production of many important recombinant proteins, including antibodies, protein therapeutics, vaccines, enzymes and additives, such as anti-CD22-gelonin single chain, viral protein 28 (VP28), erythropoietin, phytase (see Table 3). A summary of information on the production of recombination proteins in *C. reinhardtii* and several other important microalgae is provided in Table 3.

In addition to *C. reinhardtii*, several other microalgae have been studied and are considered more robust and more productive or are generally recognized and certified as safe, including species of *Chlorella*, *Scenedesmus* and *Dunaliella*. Although information about recombinant protein production in these species is lacking, in some cases, they can produce recombinant proteins at the same levels as *C. reinhardtii*. For example, five chloroplast industrial enzymes were produced in*D. tertiolecta*, accumulating in the same amounts as in *C. reinhardtii* [106], and recombinant protein expression in*Scenedesmus dimorphus* has achieved the same results [179]. Thus, other species of microalgae also have the ability to

Table 3. Summary information of recombinant proteins manufactured in several important microalgae.

Microalgae	Transformation Method	Expressed Genes	Promoters	Selective Marker Genes	Products	Expression Location (Chloroplast/Nucleus)	Product Content or Activity	References
Amphidinium sp.	SiC whiskers	*Gus*	CaMV 35S	*nptII* gene (neomycin resistance), *hpt* gene (hygromycin resistance)	β-glucuronidase	Nucleus	–	[88]
C. reinhardtii	Particle bombardment	*lsc*	atpA or rbcL	a 16S ribosomal gene (spectinomycin resistance)	Anti-HSV glycoprotein D lsc	Chloroplast	>1% of TSP	[151]
C. reinhardtii	Particle bombardment	*gelonin*	psbA	*aphA6* (kanamycin resistance)	Anti-CD22-gelonin sc	Chloroplast	0.1%–0.2% of TSP	[152]
C. reinhardtii	Particle bombardment	*Exotoxin A*	psbA	*aphA6*	Anti-CD22-ETA sc	Chloroplast	0.2%–0.3% of TSP	[153]
C. reinhardtii	Particle bombardment	*VP1, CTB*	atpA	*aadA* (spectinomycin resistance)	VP1-CTB	Chloroplast	3% of TSP	[154]
C. reinhardtii	Glass beads method	*E7GGG*	psbD	*aadA*	E7GGG	Chloroplast	0.12% of TSP	[155]
C. reinhardtii	Particle bombardment	*VEGF*	psbA	*aphA6*	VEGF	Chloroplast	2% of TSP	[156]
C. reinhardtii	Particle bombardment	*HMGB1*	psbA	*aphA6*	HMGB1	Chloroplast	2.5% of TSP	[156]
C. reinhardtii	Particle bombardment	*14FN3*	psbA	*aphA6*	14FN3	Chloroplast	3% of TSP	[156]
C. reinhardtii	Particle bombardment	*metallothionein-2*	psbA	*aadA*	Metallothionein-2	Chloroplast	–	[157]
C. reinhardtii	Particle bombardment	*Strail*	atpA	*aadA*	TRAIL	Chloroplast	0.43%–0.67% of TSP	[158]
C. reinhardtii	Particle bombardment	*apcA* and *apcB*	psbA	*aadA*	Allophycocyanin	Chloroplast	2%–3% of TSP	[159]
C. reinhardtii	–	IgG1 *lc, hc*	psbA	*aadA*	Anti-PA 83 anthrax IgG1	Chloroplast	100 μg/g of dry algal biomass	[160]
C. reinhardtii	Glass beads method	*crEpo*	HSP70A/RBCS2	*ARG7*	Erythropoietin	Nucleus	100 μg/L	[161]
C. ellipsoidea	Electroporation	*mNP-1*	Ubi1	*Npt*II and *NR* genes	mNP-1	Nucleus	11.42 mg/L	[120]
C. reinhardtii	Particle Bombardment	*m-saa*	psbA	–	M-SAA (bovine mammary-associated serum amyloid)	Chloroplast	5% of TSP	[162]
Microalgae	**Transformation Method**	**Expressed Genes**	**Promoters**	**Selective Marker Genes**	**Products**	**Expression Location (Chloroplast/Nucleus)**	**Product Content or Activity**	**References**
C. reinhardtii	Particle bombardment	*E2*	atpA	*aadA*	Swine fever virus (CSFV) structural protein	Chloroplast	1.5%–2% of TSP	[163]
C. reinhardtii	Particle bombardment	*VP28*	psbA	*aadA*	VP28	Chloroplast	21% of TCP (about 42% of TSP)	[164]
C. reinhardtii	Particle bombardment	*hGAD65*	rbcL	a 16S ribosomal gene	hGAD65	Chloroplast	0.3% of TSP	[165]
C. reinhardtii	Particle bombardment	*CTB, D2*	rbcL	aadA	CTB-D2	Chloroplast	0.7% of TSP	[166]
C. reinhardtii	Glass beads method	*PfMSP*$_{1-19}$	HSP70A/RbcS2	*AphVIII* gene (paromomycin resistance)	GBSS-PfMSP$_{1-19}$	Nucleus	–	[167]
C. reinhardtii	Glass beads method	*PbAMA*$_{1-C}$	HSP70A/RbcS2	*AphVIII* gene	GBSS-PbAMA$_{1-C}$	Nucleus	–	[167]
C. reinhardtii	Particle bombardment	*Pfs25*	psbA	*kanR* (a kanamycin resistance cassette)	Pfs25	Chloroplast	–	[168]
C. reinhardtii	Particle bombardment	*Pfs28*	psbA	*kanR*	Pfs28	Chloroplast	–	[168]
C. reinhardtii	Particle bombardment	*c.r.pfs48/45*	psbA/psbD	–	c.r.Pfs48/45	Chloroplast	–	[169]
C. reinhardtii	Particle bombardment	*Cr.ctxB-pfs25*	psbA	*kanR*	Cr.CtxB-Pfs25	Chloroplast	–	[170]
C. reinhardtii	Particle bombardment	*appA*	atpA	–	AppA phytase	Chloroplast	–	[171]
C. reinhardtii	Electroporation	*xyn1*	PAR4 (hsp70A and the rbcs2)	*aph7* gene (hygromycin B resistance), *sh-ble* gene (zeocin resistance)	β-1,4-endoxylanase	Nucleus	–	[172]
C. reinhardtii	LiAc/PEG	*fGH*	CaMV 35S	*Sh ble* gene (phleomycin resistance)	Flounder growth hormone	Nucleus	420 μg of fGH protein per liter of culture	[128]
C. reinhardtii	Glass beads method	*human Sep15*	Hsp70-RBCS2	*ble* gene (zeocin resistance)	Human Sep15 protein	Nucleus	–	[173]
D. salina	Electroporation	*HBsAg*	ubiquitin-Ω	*CAT* gene (chloramphenicol resistance)	HBsAg	Nucleus	1.6–3.1 ng/mg	[133]
D. salina	Glass beads method	*VP28*	Ubi1-Ω	–	VP28	Nucleus	3 ng/mg	[174]
D. tertiolecta	Particle bombardment	*xylanase/ α-galactosidase/ phytase*	psbD	Erythromycin esterase (erythromycin resistance)	Xylanase/α-galactosidase/phytase	Chloroplast	–	[106]
L. amoebiformis	Particle bombardment	*RbcS*	LarbcS1 promoter	–	Rubisco small subunit (RbcS) protein	Nucleus	–	[175]
Porphyridium sp.	Particle bombardment	*AHAS (W492S)*	Endogenous AHAS promoter	*AHAS*	acetohydroxyacid synthase	Chloroplast	–	[98]
P. tricornutum	Particle bombardment	IgG *LC, HC*	Nitrate reductase promoter	–	Monoclonal human IgG antibody against HBsAg	Chloroplast	8.7% of TSP, 21 mg/g of dry algal biomass	[123]
S. microadriaticum	SiC whiskers	*Gus*	CaMV 35S	*nptII* gene, *hpt* gene	β-glucuronidase	Nucleus	–	[88]
C. reinhardtii	Agrobacterium	*HBcAgII*	CaMV 35S	*NptII* (kanamycin resistance)	HBcAg-GS-AgII-GS-HBcAg	Chloroplast	0.02%–0.05% of TSP	[176]
C. reinhardtii	Glass beads method	*P24*	*PSAD* promoter	*aphVIII* gene (paromomycin resistance)	subunit of HIV-1 viral particles	Nucleus	0.25% of the total cellular protein	[177]
C. reinhardtii	Particle bombardment	*CTB.p210*	*atpA*	*aadA* gene (spectinomycin resistance)	the p210 epitope from ApoB100	Chloroplast	up to 60 μg/g of fresh weight biomass	[178]

C. reinhardtii represents *Chlamydomonas reinhardtii*; *C. ellipsoidea* represents *Chlorella ellipsoidea*; *D. salina* represents *Dunaliella salina*; *S. microadriaticum* represents *Symbiodinium microadriaticum*; *L. amoebiformis* represents *Lotharella amoebiformis*; *P. tricornutum* represents *Phaeodactylum tricornutum*; TSP represents total soluble proteins.

produce recombinant proteins [179]. For instance, a monoclonal human IgG antibody against hepatitis B has been expressed in the diatom *P. tricornutum* [123,126]. Because the codon usage of *P. tricornutum* is similar to that of humans [180], this species could be beneficial for the production of biopharmaceuticals.

Additionally, successful *Porphytridium* spp., *Euglena gracilis* and *Haematococcus pluvialis* chloroplast transformation has also been reported [98,100,107].

3.3. Production of Pharmaceuticals and Therapeutic Proteins

3.3.1. Subunit Vaccines

As a platform for the production of subunit vaccines, transgenic microalgae have attracted considerable attention [181]. Potential vaccine candidates have been produced against viruses and bacteria as well as malaria and other communicable diseases or have been investigated for non-viral diseases.

The E2 protein, which constitutes an antigen for vaccines against classical swine fever virus (CSFV), can be produced in*Chlamydomonas* chloroplast. The E2 protein can accumulate to 1.5%–2% of TSP [163], and crude extracts of E2-transformed algae have been administered via subcutaneous injection and orally immunization in mice; the former resulted in a significant level of serum antibody against CSFV, whereas the later caused no immune response to E2.

Foot-and-mouth disease virus (FMDV) is an important virus that affects livestock. To produce a vaccine against FMDV in*C. reinhardtii*, the VP1 protein was fused with a potent mucosal adjuvant, cholera toxin B subunit (CTB). VP1-CTB can accumulate to 3% of TSP [154] and exhibited binding affinity towards GM1-ganglioside, separately acting as an antigen for FMDV VP1 and CTB proteins, separately.

The gene that encodes the hepatitis B virus surface antigen (HBsAg) was successfully transformed into the green alga *D. salina* by electroporation, and stable nuclear transformants were obtained [133]. Western blot analysis demonstrated HBsAg production, with levels of 1.6–3.1 ng/mg of total protein in different transformants with different insertion sites.

White Spot Syndrome Virus (WSSV) causes severe damage to shrimp farms worldwide. The main viral envelop protein of WSSV, Viral protein 28 (VP28), is a target for subunit vaccines [182]. The gene encoding the VP28 protein was successfully transformed into the nuclear genome of *D. salina* and the chloroplast of *C. reinhardtii* [164,174], with an output of 21% of total protein in the former case [164], and approximately 3 ng/mg of total protein in the latter [174]. Under the challenge of WSSV, the survival rate of Ds-VP28-vaccinated crayfish was 41%, much higher than the control group, which had a mortality rate of 100%. This indicated that oral administration of VP28-transformed algae can protect crayfish against viral pathogens.

Staphylococcus aureus is a bacterium that can cause skin infections, respiratory diseases and food poisoning. The fused protein of D2 fibronectin-binding domain of *S. aureus* and the CTB mucosal adjuvant was stably expressed in the chloroplast of *Chlamydomonas* [166]. The fused D2-CTB protein was accumulated to 0.7% of TSP, and oral administration to mice caused both systemic IgG and mucosal IgA responses. Oral vaccination of mice with D2-CTB protected against a lethal dose of *S. aureus*, which is the first demonstration of the efficacy of an oral vaccine produced in algae.

Vaccines have been developed to prevent or treat cancers. The FDA has approved Gardasil and Cervarix as cancer vaccines to protect against human papillomavirus (HPV) types 16 and 18, which is the arch-criminal of about 70% of cervical cancer cases. A transgene encoding the E7 oncoprotein of HPV-16 was transformed to *C. reinhardtii* and accumulated to 0.12% of TSP [155]. The experiment of subcutaneous injections showed that protection with high levels were achieved after the E7 protein expressed in a tumour cell line, which indicated that green microalgae can be used as a viable platform to produce cancer vaccines.

Glutamic acid decarboxylase-65 (GAD65) is a major autoantigen for human type 1 diabetes, which is an autoimmune disease resulting from the destruction of insulin-producing beta cells in the pancreas.

By immunizing non-obese diabetic (NOD) mice, studies on type 1 diabetes found that GAD65 can prevent or delay diabetes onset [183]. The expression level of human GAD65 in the chloroplasts of *C. reinhardtii* can reach 0.25% to 0.3% of TSP [165], and the algal-derived hGAD65 reacts with diabetic sera and has the ability to induce the proliferation of spleen lymphocytes from NOD mice.

Many other vaccines have been expressed in microalgae, such as *C. reinhardtii*-produced malaria vaccines [167,169] that fuse the algal starch matrix protein called granule-bound starch synthase (GBSS) with apical major antigen (AMA1) and major surface protein (MSP1), two clinically relevant malaria antigens, separately. Experiments showed a significant reduction in parasitemia and an increased life span, and the immune sera from GBSS-MSP1 immunized mice resulted in strongly protection against malarial infection [167].

One strategy for malaria eradication includes the combination of transmission blocking vaccines (TBVs) for preventing the disease spread with drug-based therapies. As potential TBVs, Pfs48/45, Pfs25, and Pfs28, which are difficult to produce in traditional expression systems, were transformed into *Chlamydomonas* [168,169]. The transmission of *Plasmodium* oocytes can be completely blocked by antibodies against algal-expressed Pfs25. Mice fed freeze-dried Pfs25-CTB produced in algae displayed a mucosal IgA response to Pfs25 and CTB, and elicited serum IgG antibodies against CTB. Because no IgG antibodies of Pfs25 were elicited, malaria transmission couldn't be blocked. However, this study does support that the transgenic algae are promising to produce oral vaccines against mucosal infections [170,179].

Immunotherapy is a promising alternative to conventional drug therapy for hypertension. A chimeric protein, angiotensin II fused with a nucleocapsid antigen of hepatitis B virus (HBcAg) was produced in *C. reinhardtii*. The expression levels of this fused protein reached 0.05% of TSP in several transgenic lines; but the immunogenic properties of antigen derived from the HBcAgII algae still need to be assessed [176].

By modifying gene codons, HIV antigen P24 was expressed in *Chlamydomonas*, with the level of recombinant protein accounting for up to 0.25% of the total cellular protein [177]. In addition, a new recombinant protein that is a chimaera fused the CTB mucosal adjuvant with the p210 epitope of ApoB100 (CTB:p210) was expressed in the chloroplasts of *C. reinhardtii* as an approach to create an oral vaccine against atherosclerosis. The production of this fusion protein can reach 60 μg/g of fresh algae weight. The immunogenic activity was tested by orally administration in BALB/c mice, and elicited anti-p210 serum antibodies, which can last for at least 80 days [178].

3.3.2. Antibodies, Immunotoxins, Antimicrobial Agents and Others

Monoclonal antibody is an effective therapy for the treatment of various human diseases. The first mammalian protein produced in the chloroplast of microalgae was a monoclonal antibody protecting human against glycoprotein D of herpes simplex virus (HSV). This large single-chain (lsc) antibody, which is a fusion protein of the entire IgA heavy chain and the light chain variable region via a flexible linker, was expressed in *C. reinhardtii* chloroplast [151].

Immunotoxins, consisting of a toxin molecule and an antibody domain, can bind to target cells and inhibit its proliferation, thus can be used to kill cancer cells in anti-cancer therapies. Using a single-chain antibody fragment targeting a B-cell surface epitope CD22, fused with exotoxin A enzymatic domain from *Pseudomonas aeruginosa*, Tran *et al.* found that both the monovalent and divalent immunotoxins can be produced and assembled in chloroplast of microalgae [153]. Furthermore, both immunotoxin molecules can significantly inhibit tumour growth in animal experiments, improving mouse survival rate in the assay of tumour-challenge [153]. Similar results were observed when gelonin, a different eukaryotic toxin from *Gelonium multiflorum*, was fused to monovalent and divalent anti-CD22 single-chain antibodies [152].

Defensins, a kind of small cationic peptides, can be used as promising alternative to antibiotics. For example, mature rabbit neutrophil peptide 1 (NP-1), an α-defensin with a broad anti-microbial activity that can defend against gram-negative or positive bacteria, certain viruses, and pathogenic fungi, has been successfully transformed into *C. ellipsoidea*[120].

Flounder growth hormone (fGH) can be expressed in *C. ellipsoidea* and accumulate to approximately 400 μg per liter. Flounder fry fed transgenic *Chlorella* increased by 25% in length and width within 30 days [128].

Several types of enzymes have been successfully produced in microalgae. A gene from *E. coli* encoding a bioactive phytase enzyme (AppA) was expressed in *C. reinhardtii*, and AppA algae can significantly reduce the phytate content and increase the content of inorganic phosphate in chick manure when used as a direct food additive [171]. Moreover, bioactive xylanase and two α-galactosidases have been expressed in the chloroplasts of *C. reinhardtii* and *D. tertiolecta* [106]. In particular, *C. reinhardtii* nuclear genome transformation resulted in more than 100-fold the xylanase activity when xylanase was fused to a secretion signal, self-processing viral peptide (2A), and the selection marker gene *ble* [172].

We summarized the potential pharmaceuticals and recombinant proteins that were produced from microalgae and tested in animal experiments in Table 4.

4. DISCUSSIONS AND CONCLUSIONS

Microalgae are important natural resources that contain valuable proteins, oils, fatty acids, polysaccharides and other bioactive proteins that are currently commercially available. Moreover, as a new type of bioreactor, microalgae can produce recombinant pharmaceutical proteins, such as vaccines and antibodies. In this review, we outlined significant potential avenues for microalgal production of pharmaceuticals.

Table 4. Preclinical trials of recombinant proteins expressed in microalgae.

Recombinant Proteins	Preclinical Trials	Activity Analysis	References
Anti-CD22-ETA sc	Compared with mice treated with the antibody deficient immune toxin, mice treated with immunotoxin produced by algae can significantly inhibit the propagation of tumor, suggesting immunotoxins expressed in algae significantly affect tumor progression in animal experiments.	-	[153]
VP1-CTB	The CTB-VP1, fusion protein expressed in *C. reinhardtii* chloroplast, exhibited significant binding affinity to GM1-ganglioside.	Southern blot, Western blot, ELISA	[154]
E7GGG	E7GGG expressed in *Chlamydomonas* elicited tumor protection in 60% of mice. Mice vaccinated with the purified E7GGG-FLAG protein were 100% tumor-free after 9 weeks.	Western blot, ELISA	[155]
E2	Responsing against CSFV, E2 can induce significant serum antibody by subcutaneous immunization, but oral immunization resulted in no detectable serum response.	Southern blot, Western blot	[163]
hGAD65	Algal-derived hGAD65 had higher binding capacity to diabetic serum samples and can stimulate proliferation of splenic T cells from NOD mice *in vitro*, demonstrating its antigenic and immunogenic characteristics.	Western blot	[165]
CTB-D2	Oral vaccination of CTB-D2 to mice induced responses of specific systemic and mucosal immune against *S. aureus*.	-	[166]
GBSS-pfMSP$_{1\text{-}19}$ GBSS-pfAMA$_{1\text{-}C}$	The starch antigens accumulated in the chloroplast can protect against lethal *P. berghei* infection in mice.	Western blot	[167]
Cr.CtxB-Pfs25	Oral vaccination of Cr.CtxB-Pfs25-producing algae to mice elicited IgG and IgA antibodies to CTB, and IgG antibodies to Pfs25.	ELISA	[170]
AppA phytase	AppA-producing algae can significantly reduce the phytate content and increase the content of inorganic phosphate content in chick manure.	-	[171]
fGH	Flounder fry fed with transgenic *Chlorella* increased by 25% within 30 days in length and width.	Southern blot, immunoblot	[128]
VP28	Survival rates of crayfish vaccinated by Ds-VP28 were significantly higher (59% mortality) than the positive control groups and Ds empty control (100% mortality).	Western blot, ELISA	[174]
p210 epitope from ApoB100	The immunogenic activity was tested by orally administration in BALB/c mice, and elicited anti-p210 serum antibodies, which can last for at least 80 days.	Western blot, ELISA	[178]

Subunit vaccines are mainly produced and delivered from expensive injection administration of purified protein. In the microalgal production of pharmaceuticals, the use of microalgae to produce oral vaccines could be highly promising. It had been proved that several vaccine antigens can accumulate and correctly fold in microalgae, and some fusion proteins with increased antigenicity can be effectively delivered orally. These give a potential alternative way to produce subunit vaccines by making oral tablet of microalgae inexpensively with systemic and mucosa immune reactivities [181]. A better acknowledgement of the immune responses of adjuvants and orally proteins will promote the development of oral vaccines significantly [184].

According to advances in microalgal research, it appears that *C. reinhardtii* is the most promising microalgae for producing pharmaceuticals. In addition to *C. reinhardtii*, other microalgae have been preliminarily considered as bioreactors for pharmaceutical production, but some species, such as *Chlorella spp.* and *Phaeodactylum tricornutum*, may be more promising due to recent significant achievements in research of their genomes [83,146,185,186]. Indeed, these microalgae have advantages compared with *C. reinhardtii*, such as ease of cultivation, edibility (*Chlorella*), rapid growth, and ease of industrialized production. Nevertheless, *Chlorella* is small in size and possesses a resilient cell wall; thus, utilization of *Chlorella* for recombinant protein expression is hampered by a lack of genetic tools. Although several reports have shown stable expression of transgenes in *Chlorella* [76,120,129,139], achieving stable transformation in *Chlorella* is still difficult compared to many other microalgae due to unstable nuclear integration, position effects, inefficient selection of transgenic cells, inefficient transcription of heterologous genes, inaccurate RNA processing, and the bias of codon usage. In addition, transformed strains are easily lost during passaging once the selective pressure has been removed [187]. Therefore, the development of sophisticated genetic tools such as a powerful expression box would be helpful for nuclear and chloroplast transformations in *Chlorella* genetic engineering.

With regard to plants, after decades of work, the first biopharmaceutical-taliglucerase alfa, which was produced in cultured carrot cells, was approved by the FDA of the United States for treatment with Gaucher's Disease in 2012 [188,189,190,191,192]. Several plant-based oral vaccines have been assessed in clinical trials to determine their safety and immunogenicity [193,194,195,196]. Despite the many advantages for pharmaceutical production and the significant advances, especially for *C. reinhardtii*, the microalgal approach for bioreactors is still in its infancy. To date, no pharmaceuticals produced from microalgae have obtained approval for commercial production or are under clinical trial, and only a few subunit vaccines/recombinant proteins were tested in animal experiments (see Table 4). Therefore, extensive work remains to be performed before microalgae can be used for large-scale production of pharmaceuticals for commercial use.

The following aspects should be given more attention in future work: (1) transgenic microalgal safety evaluations according to the regulations of different countries; (2) production standards for recombinant pharmaceutical proteins under GMP conditions, including transgenic algal culture at a large scale, algal cell processing, protein purification, structural and function characterizations and product quality control; (3) preclinical trials to verify product safety and efficiency; and (4) clinical trials.

"The application of algal systems to edible vaccines is increasingly gaining interest", comments from Christoph Griesbeck. "Aside from biopharmaceuticals, an additional application of algae for pharmaceutical products could involve novel metabolites improved by metabolic engineering" [197]. With the development of new techniques for molecular manipulation and metabolic engineering, advances in microalgal approaches will inevitably be achieved, and the significant potential of these organisms as routine expression systems for the manufacture of pharmaceuticals will be realized in the near future.

ACKNOWLEDGMENTS

This work was supported by projects (31570365, 21306222) from National Natural Science Foundation of China and a project (2016ZX08009-003) from Agriculture Ministry of China.

AUTHOR CONTRIBUTIONS

Na Yan and Zanmin Hu wrote the paper; Chengming Fan and Yuhong Chen analyzed the references and wrote comments on microalgal transformation.

CONFLICTS OF INTEREST

The authors declare no conflict of interest.

REFERENCES

1. Demain, A.L.; Vaishnav, P. Production of recombinant proteins by microbes and higher organisms. Biotechnol. Adv.2009, 27, 297–306.

2. Ferrer-Miralles, N.; Domingo-Espín, J.; Corchero, J.L.; Vázquez, E.; Villaverde, A. Microbial factories for recombinant pharmaceuticals. Microb. Cell Fact. 2009, 8, 17.

3. Corchero, J.L.; Gasser, B.; Resina, D.; Smith, W.; Parrilli, E.; Vázquez, F.; Abasolo, I.; Giuliani, M.; Jäntti, J.; Ferrer, P. Unconventional microbial systems for the cost-efficient production of high-quality protein therapeutics. Biotechnol. Adv. 2013, 31, 140–153.

4. Sanchez, S.; Demain, A.L. Enzymes and bioconversions of industrial, pharmaceutical, and biotechnological significance. Org. Process Res. Dev. 2010, 15, 224–230.

5. Cereghino, G.P.L.; Cregg, J.M. Applications of yeast in biotechnology: Protein production and genetic analysis. Curr. Opin. Biotechnol. 1999, 10, 422–427.

6. Swartz, J.R. Advances in Escherichia coli production of therapeutic proteins. Curr. Opin. Biotechnol. 2001, 12, 195–201.

7. Fischer, R.; Liao, Y.-C.; Hoffmann, K.; Schillberg, S.; Emans, N. Molecular farming of recombinant antibodies in plants. Biol. Chem. 1999, 380, 825–839.

8. Kelley, B. Biochemical engineering: Bioprocessing of therapeutic proteins. Curr. Opin. Biotechnol. 2001, 12, 173–174.

9. Chu, L.; Robinson, D.K. Industrial choices for protein production by large-scale cell culture. Curr. Opin. Biotechnol.2001, 12, 180–187.

10. Jänne, J.; Alhonen, L.; Hyttinen, J.-M.; Peura, T.; Tolvanen, M.; Korhonen, V.-P. Transgenic bioreactors. Biotechnol. Ann. Rev. 1998, 4, 55–74.

11. Giddings, G.; Allison, G.; Brooks, D.; Carter, A. Transgenic plants as factories for biopharmaceuticals. Nat. Biotechnol.2000, 18, 1151–1155.

12. Echelard, Y. Recombinant protein production in transgenic animals. Curr. Opin. Biotechnol. 1996, 7, 536–540.

13. Scott, M.R.; Will, R.; Ironside, J.; Nguyen, H.-O.B.; Tremblay, P.; DeArmond, S.J.; Prusiner, S.B. Compelling transgenetic evidence for transmission of bovine spongiform encephalopathy prions to humans. Proc. Natl. Acad. Sci. USA 1999, 96, 15137–15142.

14. Mason, H.S.; Arntzen, C.J. Transgenic plants as vaccine production systems. Trends Biotechnol. 1995, 13, 388–392.

15. Cabanes-Macheteau, M.; Fitchette-Lainé, A.-C.; Loutelier-Bourhis, C.; Lange, C.; Vine, N.D.; Ma, J.K.; Lerouge, P.; Faye, L. N-Glycosylation of a mouse IgG expressed in transgenic tobacco plants. Glycobiology 1999, 9, 365–372.

16. Herbers, K.; Sonnewald, U. Production of new/modified proteins in transgenic plants. Curr. Opin. Biotechnol. 1999, 10, 163–168.

17. Mason, H.S.; Lam, D.; Arntzen, C.J. Expression of hepatitis B surface antigen in transgenic plants. Proc. Natl. Acad. Sci. USA 1992, 89, 11745–11749.

18. De Cosa, B.; Moar, W.; Lee, S.-B.; Miller, M.; Daniell, H. Overexpression of the Bt CRY2Aa2 operon in chloroplasts leads to formation of insecticidal crystals. Nat. Biotechnol. 2001, 19, 71–74.

19. Sijmons, P.C.; Dekker, B.M.; Schrammeijer, B.; Verwoerd, T.C.; van den Elzen, P.J.; Hoekema, A. Production of correctly processed human serum albumin in transgenic plants. Nat. Biotechnol. 1990, 8, 217–221.

20. Cramer, C.; Boothe, J.; Oishi, K. Transgenic plants for therapeutic proteins: Linking upstream and downstream strategies. Plant Biotechnol. 2000, 95–118.

21. Mor, T.S.; Sternfeld, M.; Soreq, H.; Arntzen, C.J.; Mason, H.S. Expression of recombinant human acetylcholinesterase in transgenic tomato plants. Biotechnol. Bioeng. 2001, 75, 259–266.

22. Sheldrake, A. The production of hormones in higher plants. Biol. Rev. 1973, 48, 509–559.

23. Streatfield, S.J.; Lane, J.R.; Brooks, C.A.; Barker, D.K.; Poage, M.L.; Mayor, J.M.; Lamphear, B.J.; Drees, C.F.; Jilka, J.M.; Hood, E.E. Corn as a production system for human and animal vaccines. Vaccine 2003, 21, 812–815.

24. Hiatt, A.; Caffferkey, R.; Bowdish, K. Production of antibodies in transgenic plants. Nature 1989, 342, 76–78.

25. Ram, N.; Ayala, M.; Lorenzo, D.; Palenzuela, D.; Herrera, L.; Doreste, V.; Pérez, M.; Gavilondo, J.V.; Oramas, P. Expression of a single-chain Fv antibody fragment specific for the hepatitis B surface antigen in transgenic tobacco plants. Transgenic Res. 2002, 11, 61–64.

26. Borisjuk, N.V.; Borisjuk, L.G.; Logendra, S.; Petersen, F.; Gleba, Y.; Raskin, I. Production of recombinant proteins in plant root exudates. Nat. Biotechnol. 1999, 17, 466–469.

27. Fischer, R.; Emans, N. Molecular farming of pharmaceutical proteins. Transgenic Res. 2000, 9, 279–299.

28. Arntzen, C. Plant-made pharmaceuticals: From 'Edible Vaccines' to Ebola therapeutics. Plant Biotechnol. J. 2015, 13, 1013–1016.

29. Jin, S.; Zhu, L.; Sherman, A.; Wang, X.; Lin, S.; Kamesh, A.; Norikane, J.H.; Streatfield, S.J.; Herzog, R.W.; Daniell, H. Low cost industrial production of coagulation factor IX bioencapsulated in lettuce cells for oral tolerance induction in hemophilia B. Biomaterials 2015, 70, 84–93.

30. Su, J.; Sherman, A.; Doerfler, P.A.; Byrne, B.J.; Herzog, R.W.; Daniell, H. Oral delivery of Acid Alpha Glucosidase epitopes expressed in plant chloroplasts suppresses antibody formation in treatment of Pompe mice. Plant Biotechnol. J. 2015, 13, 1023–1032.

31. Chan, H.T.; Daniell, H. Plant-made oral vaccines against human infectious diseases—Are we there yet? Plant Biotechnol. J. 2015, 13, 1056–1070.

32. Takaiwa, F.; Wakasa, Y.; Takagi, H.; Hiroi, T. Rice seed for delivery of vaccines to gut mucosal immune tissues. Plant Biotechnol. J. 2015, 13, 1–15.

33. Fox, J.L. First plant-made biologic approved. Nat. Biotechnol. 2012, 30, 472.

34. Daniell, H.; Streatfield, S.J.; Rybicki, E.P. Advances in molecular farming: Key technologies, scaled up production and lead targets. Plant Biotechnol. J. 2015, 13, 1011–1012.

35. Quist, D.; Chapela, I.H. Transgenic DNA introgressed into traditional maize landraces in Oaxaca, Mexico. Nature2001, 414, 541–543.

36. Rieger, M.A.; Lamond, M.; Preston, C.; Powles, S.B.; Roush, R.T. Pollen-mediated movement of herbicide resistance between commercial canola fields. Science 2002, 296, 2386–2388.

37. Griesbeck, C.; Kobl, I.; Heitzer, M. Chlamydomonas reinhardtii: A protein expression system for pharmaceutical and biotechnological proteins. Mol. Biotechnol. 2006, 34, 213–223.

38. Potvin, G.; Zhang, Z. Strategies for high-level recombinant protein expression in transgenic microalgae: A review.Biotechnol. Adv. 2010, 28, 910–918.

39. Wang, S.-K.; Hu, Y.-R.; Wang, F.; Stiles, A.R.; Liu, C.-Z. Scale-up cultivation of Chlorella ellipsoidea from indoor to outdoor in bubble column bioreactors. Bioresour. Technol. 2014, 156, 117–122.

40. Clarke, A.R. Photosynthesis fifth edition: By D O Hall and K K Rao, pp 211. Cambridge University Press, Cambridge. 1994. £9.95/$14.95 ISBN 0-521-43622-2. Biochem. Educ. 1995, 23, 47.

41. Chisti, Y. Biodiesel from microalgae. Biotechnol. Adv. 2007, 25, 294–306.

42. Olaizola, M. Commercial development of microalgal biotechnology: From the test tube to the marketplace. Biomol. Eng. 2003, 20, 459–466.

43. Morris, H.J.; Almarales, A.; Carrillo, O.; Bermúdez, R.C. Utilisation of Chlorella vulgaris cell biomass for the production of enzymatic protein hydrolysates. Bioresour. Technol. 2008, 99, 7723–7729.

44. Shimizu, Y.; Li, B. Microalgae as a source of bioactive molecules: Special problems and methodology. In Frontiers in Marine Biotechnology; Proksch, P., Muller, W.E.G., Eds.; Horizon Biosciences: Wymondham, UK, 2006; pp. 145–174.

45. Borowitzka, M.A. Commercial production of microalgae: Ponds, tanks, tubes and fermenters. J. Biotechnol. 1999, 70, 313–321.

46. Kumar, R.R.; Rao, P.H.; Subramanian, V.V.; Sivasubramanian, V. Enzymatic and non-enzymatic antioxidant potentials of Chlorella vulgaris grown in effluent of a confectionery industry. J. Food Sci. Technol. 2011, 51, 322–328.

47. Chisti, Y. Microalgal Biotechnology: Potential and Production; Posten, C., Walter, C., Eds.; De Gruyter: Berlin, Germany, 2012.

48. Das, P.; Aziz, S.S.; Obbard, J.P. Two phase microalgae growth in the open system for enhanced lipid productivity.Renew. Energ. 2011, 36, 2524–2528.

49. Richmond, A. Handbook of Microalgal Culture: Biotechnology and Applied Phycology; Wiley-Blackwell: Oxford, UK, 2008.

50. Abreu, A.P.; Fernandes, B.; Vicente, A.A.; Teixeira, J.; Dragone, G. Mixotrophic cultivation of Chlorella vulgaris using industrial dairy waste as organic carbon source. Bioresour. Technol. 2012, 118, 61–66.

51. Basaran, P.; Rodríguez-Cerezo, E. Plant molecular farming: Opportunities and challenges. J. Serb. Chem. Soc. 2008, 28, 153–172.

52. Yao, J.; Weng, Y.; Dickey, A.; Wang, K.Y. Plants as factories for human pharmaceuticals: Applications and challenges.Int. J. Mol. Sci. 2015, 16, 28549–28565.

53. Chu, W.-L. Biotechnological applications of microalgae. IeJSME 2012, 6, S24–S37.

54. Kaplan, D.; Richmond, A.; Dubinsky, Z.; Aaronson, S. Algal nutrition. In Handbook of Microalgal Mass Culture; CRC Press: Boca Raton, FL, USA, 1986; pp. 147–198.

55. Cunningham, A.; Maas, P. Time lag and nutrient storage effects in the transient growth response of Chlamydomonas reinhardii in nitrogen-limited batch and continuous culture. Microbiology 1978, 104, 227–231.

56. Garcia-Ferris, C.; Rios, A.; Ascaso, C.; Moreno, J. Correlated biochemical and ultrastructural changes in nitrogen-starved Euglena gracilis. J. Phycol. 1996, 32, 953–963.

57. Přibyl, P.; Cepák, V.; Zachleder, V. Production of lipids in 10 strains of Chlorella and Parachlorella, and enhanced lipid productivity in Chlorella vulgaris. Appl. Microbiol. Biotechnol. 2012, 94, 549–561.

58. Zachleder, V.; Brányiková, I. Starch overproduction by means of algae. In Algal Biorefineries; Bajpai, R., Prokop, A., Zappi, M., Eds.; Springer: Dordrecht, The Netherlands, 2014; Volume 1, pp. 217–240.

59. Spolaore, P.; Joannis-Cassan, C.; Duran, E.; Isambert, A. Commercial applications of microalgae. J. Biosci. Bioeng.2006, 101, 87–96.

60. Soletto, D.; Binaghi, L.; Lodi, A.; Carvalho, J.; Converti, A. Batch and fed-batch cultivations of Spirulina platensis using ammonium sulphate and urea as nitrogen sources. Aquaculture 2005, 243, 217–224.

61. Guil-Guerrero, J.; Navarro-Juárez, R.; López-Martınez, J.; Campra-Madrid, P.; Rebolloso-Fuentes, M. Functional properties of the biomass of three microalgal species. J. Food Eng. 2004, 65, 511–517.

62. Becker, W.; Richmond, A. Microalgae in human and animal nutrition. In Handbook of Microalgal Culture: Biotechnology and Applied Phycology; Richmond, A., Ed.; Wiley-Blackwell: Oxford, UK, 2004; pp. 312–351.

63. Metting, F., Jr. Biodiversity and application of microalgae. J. Ind. Microbiol. 1996, 17, 477–489.

64. Borowitzka, M. Fats, oils and hydrocarbons. In Micro-Algal Biotechnology; Cambridge University Press: Cambridge, UK, 1988; pp. 257–287.

65. Brown, M.; Jeffrey, S.; Volkman, J.; Dunstan, G. Nutritional properties of microalgae for mariculture. Aquaculture1997, 151, 315–331.

66. Tonon, T.; Harvey, D.; Larson, T.R.; Graham, I.A. Long chain polyunsaturated fatty acid production and partitioning to triacylglycerols in four microalgae. Phytochemistry 2002, 61, 15–24.

67. Tzovenis, I.; de Pauw, N.; Sorgeloos, P. Optimisation of T-ISO biomass production rich in essential fatty acids: I. Effect of different light regimes on growth and biomass production. Aquaculture 2003, 216, 203–222.

68. Apt, K.E.; Behrens, P.W. Commercial developments in microalgal biotechnology. J. Phycol. 1999, 35, 215–226.

69. Rasoul-Amini, S.; Ghasemi, Y.; Morowvat, M.H.; Mohagheghzadeh, A. PCR amplification of 18S rRNA, single cell protein production and fatty acid evaluation of some naturally isolated microalgae. Food Chem. 2009, 116, 129–136.

70. Calvin, M.; Benson, A. The Path of Carbon in Photosynthesis; Ernest Orlando Lawrence Berkeley National Laboratory: Berkeley, CA, USA, 1948.

71. Hirose, Y.; Fujisawa, T.; Ohtsubo, Y.; Katayama, M.; Misawa, N.; Wakazuki, S.; Shimura, Y.; Nakamura, Y.; Kawachi, M.; Yoshikawa, H. Complete genome sequence of cyanobacterium Nostoc sp. NIES-3756, a potentially useful strain for

phytochrome-based bioengineering. J. Biotechnol. 2016, 218, 51–52.

72. Kaneko, T.; Tabata, S. Complete genome structure of the unicellular cyanobacterium Synechocystis sp. PCC6803. Plant Cell Physiol. 1997, 38, 1171–1176.

73. Matsuzaki, M.; Misumi, O.; Shin-i, T.; Maruyama, S.; Takahara, M.; Miyagishima, S.-Y.; Mori, T.; Nishida, K.; Yagisawa, F.; Nishida, K. Genome sequence of the ultrasmall unicellular red alga Cyanidioschyzon merolae 10D. Nature2004, 428, 653–657.

74. Armbrust, E.V.; Berges, J.A.; Bowler, C.; Green, B.R.; Martinez, D.; Putnam, N.H.; Zhou, S.; Allen, A.E.; Apt, K.E.; Bechner, M. The genome of the diatom Thalassiosira pseudonana: Ecology, evolution, and metabolism. Science 2004,306, 79–86.

75. Merchant, S.S.; Prochnik, S.E.; Vallon, O.; Harris, E.H.; Karpowicz, S.J.; Witman, G.B.; Terry, A.; Salamov, A.; Fritz-Laylin, L.K.; Maréchal-Drouard, L. The Chlamydomonas genome reveals the evolution of key animal and plant functions. Science 2007, 318, 245–250.

76. Fan, J.; Ning, K.; Zeng, X.; Luo, Y.; Wang, D.; Hu, J.; Li, J.; Xu, H.; Huang, J.; Wan, M. Genomic foundation of starch-to-lipid switch in oleaginous Chlorella spp. Plant Physiol. 2015, 169, 2444–2461.

77. Radakovits, R.; Jinkerson, R.E.; Fuerstenberg, S.I.; Tae, H.; Settlage, R.E.; Boore, J.L.; Posewitz, M.C. Draft genome sequence and genetic transformation of the oleaginous alga nannochloropsis gaditana. Nat. Commun. 2012, 3, 686.

78. Fu, Y.; Luo, G.Z.; Chen, K.; Deng, X.; Yu, M.; Han, D.; Hao, Z.; Liu, J.; Lu, X.; Doré, L. N6-Methyldeoxyadenosine marks active transcription start sites in Chlamydomonas. Cell 2015, 161, 879–892.

79. Li, X.; Zhang, R.; Patena, W.; Gang, S.S.; Blum, S.R.; Ivanova, N.; Yue, R.; Robertson, J.M.; Lefebvre, P.; Fitz-Gibbon, S.T. An indexed, mapped mutant library enables reverse genetics studies of biological processes in Chlamydomonas reinhardtii. Plant Cell 2016, 28, 367–387.

80. Yang, W.; Wittkopp, T.M.; Li, X.; Warakanont, J.; Dubini, A.; Catalanotti, C.; Kim, R.G.; Nowack, E.C.M.; Mackinder, L.C.M.; Aksoy, M. Critical role of Chlamydomonas reinhardtii ferredoxin-5 in maintaining membrane structure and dark metabolism. Proc. Natl. Acad. Sci. USA 2015, 112, 14978–14983.

81. Dejtisakdi, W.; Miller, S.M. Overexpression of calvin cycle enzyme fructose 1,6-bisphosphatase in Chlamydomonas reinhardtii has a detrimental effect on growth. Algal Res. 2016, 14, 116–126.

82. Sirikhachornkit, A.; Vuttipongchaikij, S.; Suttangkakul, A.; Yokthongwattana, K.; Juntawong, P.; Pokethitiyook, P.; Kangvansaichol, K.; Meetam, M. Increasing the triacylglycerol content in Dunaliella tertiolecta through isolation of starch-deficient mutants. J. Microbiol. Biotechnol. 2016, 28, 854–866.

83. Kira, N.; Ohnishi, K.; Miyagawa-Yamaguchi, A.; Kadono, T.; Adachi, M. Nuclear transformation of the diatomPhaeodactylum tricornutum using PCR-amplified DNA fragments by microparticle bombardment. Mar. Genom. 2016,25, 49–56.

84. Ferreira-Camargo, L.S.; Tran, M.; Beld, J.; Burkart, M.D.; Mayfield, S.P. Selenocystamine improves protein accumulation in chloroplasts of eukaryotic green algae. AMB Express 2015, 5, 1–11.

85. Gong, Y.; Hu, H.; Gao, Y.; Xu, X.; Gao, H. Microalgae as platforms for production of recombinant proteins and valuable compounds: Progress and prospects. J. Ind. Microbiol. Biotechnol. 2011, 38, 1879–1890.

86. Kindle, K. Nuclear transformation: Technology and applications. In The Molecular Biology of Chloroplasts and Mitochondria in Chlamydomonas; Rochaix, J.-D., Goldschmidt-Clermont, M., Merchant, S., Eds.; Springer: Dordrecht, The Netherlands, 2004; Volume 7, pp. 41–61.

87. Dunahay, T. Transformation of Chlamydomonas reinhardtii with silicon carbide whiskers. Biotechniques 1993, 15, 452–455, 457–458, 460.

88. Te, M.R.; Miller, D.J. Genetic transformation of dinoflagellates (Amphidinium and Symbiodinium): Expression of GUS in microalgae using heterologous promoter constructs. Plant J. 1998, 13, 427–435.

89. Shimogawara, K.; Fujiwara, S.; Grossman, A.; Usuda, H. High-efficiency transformation of Chlamydomonas reinhardtiiby electroporation. Genetics 1998, 148, 1821–1828.

90. Hayashi, M.; Hirono, M.; Kamiya, R. Recovery of flagellar dynein function in a Chlamydomonas actin/dynein-deficient mutant upon introduction of muscle actin by electroporation. Cell Motil. Cytoskelet. 2001, 49, 146–153.

91. Henry, E.C.; Meints, R.H. Recombinant viruses as transformation vectors of marine macroalgae. J. Appl. Phycol. 1994,6, 247–253.

92. Van Etten, J.L.; Meints, R.H. Giant viruses infecting algae. Annu. Rev. Microbiol. 1999, 53, 447–494.

93. Kojima, H.; Kawata, Y. A mini-transposon/transposase complex as a new tool for the genetic transformation of microalgae. In Photosynthetic Microorganisms in Environmental Biotechnology; Kojima, H., Lee, Y.K., Eds.; Springer Verlag: Berlin, Germany, 2001; pp. 41–61.

94. Apt, K.E.; Grossman, A.; Kroth-Pancic, P. Stable nuclear transformation of the diatom Phaeodactylum tricornutum. Mol. Gen. Genet. 1996, 252, 572–579.

95. Dunahay, T.G.; Jarvis, E.E.; Roessler, P.G. Genetic transformation of the diatoms Cyclotella cryptica and Navicula saprophila. J. Phycol. 1995, 31, 1004–1012.

96. Falciatore, A.; Casotti, R.; Leblanc, C.; Abrescia, C.; Bowler, C. Transformation of nonselectable reporter genes in marine diatoms. Mar. Biotechnol. 1999, 1, 239–251.

97. Zaslavskaia, L.A.; Lippmeier, J.C.; Kroth, P.G.; Grossman, A.R.; Apt, K.E. Transformation of the diatomPhaeodactylum tricornutum (bacillariophyceae) with a variety of selectable marker and reporter genes. J. Phycol. 2000,36, 379–386.

98. Lapidot, M.; Raveh, D.; Sivan, A.; Arad, S.M.; Shapira, M. Stable chloroplast transformation of the unicellular red alga Porphyridium species. Plant Physiol. 2002, 129, 7–12.

99. Boynton, J.E.; Gillham, N.W.; Harris, E.H.; Hosler, J.P.; Johnson, A.M.; Jones, A.R.; Randolph-Anderson, B.L.; Robertson, D.; Klein, T.M.; Shark, K.B. Chloroplast transformation in Chlamydomonas with high velocity microprojectiles. Science 1988, 240, 1534–1538.

100. Doetsch, N.A.; Favreau, M.R.; Kuscuoglu, N.; Thompson, M.D.; Hallick, R.B. Chloroplast transformation in Euglena gracilis: Splicing of a group III twintron transcribed from a transgenic psbK operon. Curr. Genet. 2001, 39, 49–60.

101. Randolph-Anderson, B.L.; Boynton, J.E.; Gillham, N.W.; Harris, E.H.; Johnson, A.M.; Dorthu, M.-P.; Matagne, R.F. Further characterization of the respiratory deficient dum-1 mutation of Chlamydomonas reinhardtii and its use as a recipient for mitochondrial transformation. Mol. Gen. Genet. 1993, 236, 235–244.

102. Fernández, E.; Schnell, R.; Ranum, L.; Hussey, S.C.; Silflow, C.D.; Lefebvre, P.A. Isolation and characterization of the nitrate reductase structural gene of Chlamydomonas reinhardtii. Proc. Natl. Acad. Sci. USA 1989, 86, 6449–6453.

103. Debuchy, R.; Purton, S.; Rochaix, J. The argininosuccinate lyase gene of Chlamydomonas reinhardtii: An important tool for nuclear transformation and for correlating the genetic and molecular maps of the ARG7 locus. EMBO J. 1989, 8, 2803–2809.

104. Shrager, J.; Hauser, C.; Chang, C.-W.; Harris, E.H.; Davies, J.; McDermott, J.; Tamse, R.; Zhang, Z.; Grossman, A.R.Chlamydomonas reinhardtii genome project. A guide to the generation and use of the cDNA information. Plant Physiol.2003, 131, 401–408.

105. Dawson, H.N.; Burlingame, R.; Cannons, A.C. Stable transformation of Chlorella: Rescue of nitrate reductase-

deficient mutants with the nitrate reductase gene. Curr. Microbiol. 1997, 35, 356–362.

106. Georgianna, D.R.; Hannon, M.J.; Marcuschi, M.; Wu, S.; Botsch, K.; Lewis, A.J.; Hyun, J.; Mendez, M.; Mayfield, S.P. Production of recombinant enzymes in the marine alga Dunaliella tertiolecta. Algal Res. 2013, 2, 2–9.

107. Gutierrez, C.L.; Gimpel, J.; Escobar, C.; Marshall, S.H.; Henríquez, V. Chloroplast genetic tool for the green microalgae Haematococcus pluvialis (chlorophyceae, volvocales). J. Phycol. 2012, 48, 976–983.

108. Fischer, H.; Robl, I.; Sumper, M.; Kröger, N. Targeting and covalent modification of cell wall and membrane proteins heterologously expressed in the diatom Cylindrotheca fusiformis (bacillariophyceae). J. Phycol. 1999, 35, 113–120.

109. Poulsen, N.; Chesley, P.M.; Kröger, N. Molecular genetic manipulation of the diatom Thalassiosira pseudonana(bacillariophyceae). J. Phycol. 2006, 42, 1059–1065.

110. Miyagawa-Yamaguchi, A.; Okami, T.; Kira, N.; Yamaguchi, H.; Ohnishi, K.; Adachi, M. Stable nuclear transformation of the diatom Chaetoceros sp. Phycol. Res. 2011, 59, 113–119.

111. Walker, T.L.; Purton, S.; Becker, D.K.; Collet, C. Microalgae as bioreactors. Plant Cell Rep. 2005, 24, 629–641.

112. Kindle, K.L.; Schnell, R.A.; Fernández, E.; Lefebvre, P.A. Stable nuclear transformation of Chlamydomonas using theChlamydomonas gene for nitrate reductase. J. Cell Biol. 1989, 109, 2589–2601.

113. Schiedlmeier, B.; Schmitt, R.; Müller, W.; Kirk, M.M.; Gruber, H.; Mages, W.; Kirk, D.L. Nuclear transformation ofVolvox carteri. Proc. Natl. Acad. Sci. USA 1994, 91, 5080–5084.

114. Sun, Y.; Gao, X.; Li, Q.; Zhang, Q.; Xu, Z. Functional complementation of a nitrate reductase defective mutant of a green alga Dunaliella viridis by introducing the nitrate reductase gene. Gene 2006, 377, 140–149.

115. Cerutti, H.; Johnson, A.M.; Gillham, N.W.; Boynton, J.E. A eubacterial gene conferring spectinomycin resistance onChlamydomonas reinhardtii: Integration into the nuclear genome and gene expression. Genetics 1997, 145, 97.

116. Sizova, I.; Fuhrmann, M.; Hegemann, P. A Streptomyces rimosus aphVIII gene coding for a new type phosphotransferase provides stable antibiotic resistance to Chlamydomonas reinhardtii. Gene 2001, 277, 221–229.

117. Stevens, D.R.; Purton, S.; Rochaix, J.-D. The bacterial phleomycin resistance gene ble as a dominant selectable marker in Chlamydomonas. Mol. Gen. Genet. 1996, 251, 23–30.

118. Kovar, J.L.; Zhang, J.; Funke, R.P.; Weeks, D.P. Molecular analysis of the acetolactate synthase gene of Chlamydomonas reinhardtii and development of a genetically engineered gene as a dominant selectable marker for genetic transformation. Plant J. 2002, 29, 109–117.

119. Hallmann, A.; Rappel, A. Genetic engineering of the multicellular green alga Volvox: A modified and multiplied bacterial antibiotic resistance gene as a dominant selectable marker. Plant J. 1999, 17, 99–109.

120. Bai, L.-L.; Yin, W.-B.; Chen, Y.-H.; Niu, L.-L.; Sun, Y.-R.; Zhao, S.-M.; Yang, F.; Wang, R.R.-C.; Wu, Q.; Zhang, X. A new strategy to produce a defensin: Stable production of mutated NP-1 in nitrate reductase-deficient Chlorella ellipsoidea. PLoS ONE 2013, 8, e54966.

121. Zhang, J.; Hao, Q.; Bai, L.; Xu, J.; Yin, W.; Song, L.; Xu, L.; Guo, X.; Fan, C.; Chen, Y. Overexpression of the soybean transcription factor GmDof4 significantly enhances the lipid content of Chlorella ellipsoidea. Biotechnol. Biofuels 2014, 7, 1–16.

122. Miyagawa, A.; Okami, T.; Kira, N.; Yamaguchi, H.; Ohnishi, K.; Adachi, M. High efficiency transformation of the diatom Phaeodactylum tricornutum with a promoter from the diatom Cylindrotheca fusiformis. Phycol. Res. 2009, 57, 142–146.

123. Hempel, F.; Lau, J.; Klingl, A.; Maier, U.G. Algae as protein factories: Expression of a human antibody and the respective

antigen in the diatom Phaeodactylum tricornutum. PLoS ONE 2011, 6, e28424.

124. Poulsen, N.; Kröger, N. A new molecular tool for transgenic diatoms. FEBS J. 2005, 272, 3413–3423.

125. Gonzalez, N.H.; Felsner, G.; Schramm, F.D.; Klingl, A.; Maier, U.-G.; Bolte, K. A single peroxisomal targeting signal mediates matrix protein import in diatoms. PLoS ONE 2011, 6, e25316.

126. Hempel, F.; Maier, U.G. An engineered diatom acting like a plasma cell secreting human IgG antibodies with high efficiency. Microb. Cell Fact. 2012, 11, 126.

127. Stork, S.; Moog, D.; Przyborski, J.M.; Wilhelmi, I.; Zauner, S.; Maier, U.G. Distribution of the selma translocon in secondary plastids of red algal origin and predicted uncoupling of ubiquitin-dependent translocation from degradation. Eukaryot. Cell 2012, 11, 1472–1481.

128. Kim, D.-H.; Kim, Y.T.; Cho, J.J.; Bae, J.-H.; Hur, S.-B.; Hwang, I.; Choi, T.-J. Stable integration and functional expression of flounder growth hormone gene in transformed microalga, Chlorella ellipsoidea. Mar. Biotechnol. 2002, 4, 63–73.

129. Jarvis, E.E.; Brown, L.M. Transient expression of firefly luciferase in protoplasts of the green alga Chlorella ellipsoidea.Curr. Genet. 1991, 19, 317–321.

130. Chen, Y.; Wang, Y.; Sun, Y.; Zhang, L.; Li, W. Highly efficient expression of rabbit neutrophil peptide-1 gene inChlorella ellipsoidea cells. Curr. Genet. 2001, 39, 365–370.

131. Hawkins, R.L.; Nakamura, M. Expression of human growth hormone by the eukaryotic alga, Chlorella. Curr. Microbiol. 1999, 38, 335–341.

132. Kathiresan, S.; Chandrashekar, A.; Ravishankar, G.; Sarada, R. Agrobacterium-mediated transformation in the green alga Haematococcus pluvialis (Chlorophyceae, Volvocales). J. Phycol. 2009, 45, 642–649.

133. Geng, D.; Wang, Y.; Wang, P.; Li, W.; Sun, Y. Stable expression of hepatitis B surface antigen gene in Dunaliella salina(chlorophyta). J. Appl. Phycol. 2003, 15, 451–456.

134. Feng, S.; Xue, L.; Liu, H.; Lu, P. Improvement of efficiency of genetic transformation for Dunaliella salina by glass beads method. Mol. Biol. Rep. 2009, 36, 1433–1439.

135. Chai, X.-J.; Chen, H.-X.; Xu, W.-Q.; Xu, Y.-W. Expression of soybean kunitz trypsin inhibitor gene SKTI in Dunaliella salina. J. Appl. Phycol. 2013, 25, 139–144.

136. Seo, S.; Jeon, H.; Hwang, S.; Jin, E.S.; Chang, K.S. Development of a new constitutive expression system for the transformation of the diatom Phaeodactylum tricornutum. Algal Res. 2015, 11, 50–54.

137. Maruyama, M.; Horáková, I.; Honda, H.; Xing, X.H.; Shiragami, N.; Unno, H. Introduction of foreign DNA intoChlorella saccharophila by electroporation. Biotechnol. Tech. 1994, 8, 821–826.

138. Yang, A.; Bai, L.; Chen, Y.; Hu, Z.; Institute of Genetics and Developmental Biology, Chinese Academy of Sciences, Beijing. The expression of NP-1 in Chlorella ellipsoidea. unpublished work. 2009.

139. Wang, Y.; Chen, Y.; Zhang, X.; Wang, P.; Geng, D.; Zhao, S.; Zhang, L.; Sun, Y. Isolation and characterization of a nitrate reductase deficient mutant of Chlorella ellipsoidea (Chlorophyta). J. Appl. Phycol. 2005, 17, 281–286.

140. Niu, Y.F.; Zhang, M.H.; Xie, W.H.; Li, J.N.; Gao, Y.F.; Yang, W.D.; Liu, J.S.; Li, H.Y. A new inducible expression system in a transformed green alga, Chlorella vulgaris. Genet. Mol. Res. 2011, 10, 3427–3434.

141. Cerutti, H.; Johnson, A.M.; Gillham, N.W.; Boynton, J.E. Epigenetic silencing of a foreign gene in nuclear transformants of Chlamydomonas. Plant Cell 1997, 9, 925–945.

142. Cerutti, H.; Ma, X.; Msanne, J.; Repas, T. RNA-mediated silencing in algae: Biological roles and tools for analysis of gene function. Eukaryot. Cell 2011, 10, 1164–1172.

143. Kim, E.J.; Ma, X.; Cerutti, H. Gene silencing in microalgae: Mechanisms and biological roles. Bioresour. Technol. 2015,184, 23–32.

144. Doron, L.; Segal, N.A.; Shapira, M.; Wilhelm, R.A.; Geisler, K. Transgene expression in microalgae—From tools to applications. Front. Plant Sci. 2016, 7, 505.

145. El-Sheekh, M. Stable transformation of the intact cells of Chlorella kessleri with high velocity microprojectiles. Biol. Plant. 1999, 42, 209–216.

146. Ahmed, E.G.; Sung Kwon, L.; Sang, M.S.; Seung, H.Y.; Gyuhwa, C. Development of stable marker-free nuclear transformation strategy in the green microalga Chlorella vulgaris. Afr. J. Biotechnol. 2015, 14, 2715–2723.

147. Pulz, O.; Scheibenbogen, K.; Groß, W. Biotechnology with cyanobacteria and microalgae. In Biotechnology Set, 2nd ed.; Rehm, H.-J., Reed, G., Eds.; Wiley-VCH Verlag GmbH: Weinheim, Germany, 2008; pp. 105–136.

148. Dunahay, T.G.; Jarvis, E.E.; Dais, S.S.; Roessler, P.G. Manipulation of microalgal lipid production using genetic engineering. Appl. Biochem. Biotechnol. 1996, 57, 223–231.

149. Cai, X.-H.; Brown, C.; Adhiya, J.; Traina, S.J.; Sayre, R.T. Growth and heavy metal binding properties of transgenicChlamydomonas expressing a foreign metallothionein gene. Int. J. Phytoremediat. 1999, 1, 53–65.

150. Siripornadulsil, S.; Traina, S.; Verma, D.P.S.; Sayre, R.T. Molecular mechanisms of proline-mediated tolerance to toxic heavy metals in transgenic microalgae. Plant Cell 2002, 14, 2837–2847.

151. Mayfield, S.P.; Franklin, S.E.; Lerner, R.A. Expression and assembly of a fully active antibody in algae. Proc. Natl. Acad. Sci. USA 2003, 100, 438–442.

152. Tran, M.; Henry, R.E.; Siefker, D.; Van, C.; Newkirk, G.; Kim, J.; Bui, J.; Mayfield, S.P. Production of anti-cancer immunotoxins in algae: Ribosome inactivating proteins as fusion partners. Biotechnol. Bioeng. 2013, 110, 2826–2835.

153. Tran, M.; Van, C.; Barrera, D.J.; Pettersson, P.L.; Peinado, C.D.; Bui, J.; Mayfield, S.P. Production of unique immunotoxin cancer therapeutics in algal chloroplasts. Proc. Natl. Acad. Sci. USA 2013, 110, E15–E22.

154. Sun, M.; Qian, K.; Su, N.; Chang, H.; Liu, J.; Shen, G. Foot-and-mouth disease virus VP1 protein fused with cholera toxin B subunit expressed in Chlamydomonas reinhardtii chloroplast. Biotechnol. Lett. 2003, 25, 1087–1092.

155. Demurtas, O.C.; Massa, S.; Ferrante, P.; Venuti, A.; Franconi, R.; Giuliano, G. A Chlamydomonas-derived human papillomavirus 16 E7 vaccine induces specific tumor protection. PLoS ONE 2013, 8, e61473.

156. Rasala, B.A.; Muto, M.; Lee, P.A.; Jager, M.; Cardoso, R.M.; Behnke, C.A.; Kirk, P.; Hokanson, C.A.; Crea, R.; Mendez, M. Production of therapeutic proteins in algae, analysis of expression of seven human proteins in the chloroplast ofChlamydomonas reinhardtii. Plant Biotechnol. J. 2010, 8, 719–733.

157. Zhang, Y.K.; Shen, G.F.; Ru, B.G. Survival of human metallothionein-2 transplastomic Chlamydomonas reinhardtii to ultraviolet B exposure. Acta Biochim. Biophys. Sin. 2006, 38, 187–193.

158. Yang, Z.; Chen, F.; Li, D.; Zhang, Z.; Liu, Y.; Zheng, D.; Wang, Y.; Shen, G. Expression of human soluble TRAIL inChlamydomonas reinhardtii chloroplast. Chin. Sci. Bull. 2006, 51, 1703–1709.

159. Su, Z.L.; Qian, K.X.; Tan, C.P.; Meng, C.X.; Qin, S. Recombination and heterologous expression of allophycocyanin gene in the chloroplast of Chlamydomonas reinhardtii. Acta Biochim. Biophys. Sin. 2005, 37, 709–712.

160. Tran, M.; Zhou, B.; Pettersson, P.L.; Gonzalez, M.J.; Mayfield, S.P. Synthesis and assembly of a full-length human monoclonal

antibody in algal chloroplasts. Biotechnol. Bioeng. 2009, 104, 663–673.

161. Eichler-Stahlberg, A.; Weisheit, W.; Ruecker, O.; Heitzer, M. Strategies to facilitate transgene expression inChlamydomonas reinhardtii. Planta 2009, 229, 873–883.

162. Manuell, A.L.; Beligni, M.V.; Elder, J.H.; Siefker, D.T.; Tran, M.; Weber, A.; McDonald, T.L.; Mayfield, S.P. Robust expression of a bioactive mammalian protein in Chlamydomonas chloroplast. Plant Biotechnol. J. 2007, 5, 402–412.

163. He, D.-M.; Qian, K.-X.; Shen, G.-F.; Zhang, Z.-F.; Yi-Nü, L.; Su, Z.-L.; Shao, H.-B. Recombination and expression of classical swine fever virus (CSFV) structural protein E2 gene in Chlamydomonas reinhardtii chroloplasts. Colloids Surf. B Biointerfaces 2007, 55, 26–30.

164. Surzycki, R.; Greenham, K.; Kitayama, K.; Dibal, F.; Wagner, R.; Rochaix, J.-D.; Ajam, T.; Surzycki, S. Factors effecting expression of vaccines in microalgae. Biologicals 2009, 37, 133–138.

165. Wang, X.; Brandsma, M.; Tremblay, R.; Maxwell, D.; Jevnikar, A.M.; Huner, N.; Ma, S. A novel expression platform for the production of diabetes-associated autoantigen human glutamic acid decarboxylase (hGAD65). BMC Biotechnol. 2008, 8, 87.

166. Dreesen, I.A.; Charpin-El Hamri, G.; Fussenegger, M. Heat-stable oral alga-based vaccine protects mice fromStaphylococcus aureus infection. J. Biotechnol. 2010, 145, 273–280.

167. Dauvillée, D.; Delhaye, S.; Gruyer, S.; Slomianny, C.; Moretz, S.E.; d'Hulst, C.; Long, C.A.; Ball, S.G.; Tomavo, S. Engineering the chloroplast targeted malarial vaccine antigens in Chlamydomonas starch granules. PLoS ONE 2010,5, e15424.

168. Gregory, J.A.; Li, F.; Tomosada, L.M.; Cox, C.J.; Topol, A.B.; Vinetz, J.M.; Mayfield, S. Algae-produced Pfs25 elicits antibodies that inhibit malaria transmission. PLoS ONE 2012, 7, e37179.

169. Jones, C.S.; Luong, T.; Hannon, M.; Tran, M.; Gregory, J.A.; Shen, Z.; Briggs, S.P.; Mayfield, S.P. Heterologous expression of the C-terminal antigenic domain of the malaria vaccine candidate

Pfs48/45 in the green algaeChlamydomonas reinhardtii. Appl. Microbiol. Biotechnol. 2013, 97, 1987–1995.

170. Gregory, J.A.; Topol, A.B.; Doerner, D.Z.; Mayfield, S. Alga-produced cholera toxin-Pfs25 fusion proteins as oral vaccines. Appl. Environ. Microbiol. 2013, 79, 3917–3925.

171. Yoon, S.-M.; Kim, S.Y.; Li, K.F.; Yoon, B.H.; Choe, S.; Kuo, M.M.-C. Transgenic microalgae expressing Escherichia coliAppA phytase as feed additive to reduce phytate excretion in the manure of young broiler chicks. Appl. Microbiol. Biotechnol. 2011, 91, 553–563.

172. Rasala, B.A.; Lee, P.A.; Shen, Z.; Briggs, S.P.; Mendez, M.; Mayfield, S.P. Robust expression and secretion of xylanase1 in Chlamydomonas reinhardtii by fusion to a selection gene and processing with the FMDV 2A peptide. PLoS ONE2012, 7, e43349.

173. Hou, Q.; Qiu, S.; Liu, Q.; Tian, J.; Hu, Z.; Ni, J. Selenoprotein-transgenic Chlamydomonas reinhardtii. Nutrients 2013, 5, 624–636.

174. Feng, S.; Feng, W.; Zhao, L.; Gu, H.; Li, Q.; Shi, K.; Guo, S.; Zhang, N. Preparation of transgenic Dunaliella salina for immunization against white spot syndrome virus in crayfish. Arch. Virol. 2014, 159, 519–525.

175. Hirakawa, Y.; Ishida, K.I. Internal plastid-targeting signal found in a RubisCO small subunit protein of a chlorarachniophyte alga. Plant J. 2010, 64, 402–410.

176. Soria-Guerra, R.E.; Ramírez-Alonso, J.I.; Ibáñez-Salazar, A.; Govea-Alonso, D.O.; Paz-Maldonado, L.M.T.; Bañuelos-Hernández, B.; Korban, S.S.; Rosales-Mendoza, S. Expression of an HBcAg-based antigen carrying angiotensin II inChlamydomonas reinhardtii as a candidate hypertension vaccine. Plant Cell Tissue Organ Cult. 2014, 116, 133–139.

177. Barahimipour, R.; Neupert, J.; Bock, R. Efficient expression of nuclear transgenes in the green alga Chlamydomonas: Synthesis of an HIV antigen and development of a new selectable marker. Plant Mol. Biol. 2016, 90, 403–418.

178. Beltrán-López, J.I.; Romero-Maldonado, A.; Monreal-Escalante, E.; Bañuelos-Hernández, B.; Paz-Maldonado, L.M.; Rosales-Mendoza, S. Chlamydomonas reinhardtii chloroplasts express an orally immunogenic protein targeting the p210 epitope implicated in atherosclerosis immunotherapies. Plant Cell Rep. 2016, 35, 1–9.

179. Rasala, B.A.; Mayfield, S.P. Photosynthetic biomanufacturing in green algae; production of recombinant proteins for industrial, nutritional, and medical uses. Photosynth. Res. 2014, 123, 227–239.

180. Heitzer, M.; Eckert, A.; Fuhrmann, M.; Griesbeck, C. Influence of codon bias on the expression of foreign genes in microalgae. Adv. Exp. Med. Biol. 2007, 616, 46–53.

181. Specht, E.A.; Mayfield, S.P. Algae-based oral recombinant vaccines. Front. Microbiol. 2014, 5, 60.

182. Van Hulten, M.C.; Witteveldt, J.; Peters, S.; Kloosterboer, N.; Tarchini, R.; Fiers, M.; Sandbrink, H.; Lankhorst, R.K.; Vlak, J.M. The white spot syndrome virus DNA genome sequence. Virology 2001, 286, 7–22.

183. Tisch, R.; Yang, X.-D.; Singer, S.M.; Liblau, R.S.; Fugger, L.; McDevitt, H.O. Immune response to glutamic acid decarboxylase correlates with insulitis in non-obese diabetic mice. Nature 1993, 366, 72–75.

184. Gregory, J.A.; Mayfield, S.P. Developing inexpensive malaria vaccines from plants and algae. Appl. Microbiol. Biotechnol. 2014, 98, 1–8.

185. Liu, J.; Sun, Z.; Gerken, H.; Huang, J.; Jiang, Y.; Chen, F. Genetic engineering of the green alga Chlorella zofingiensis: A modified norflurazon-resistant phytoene desaturase gene as a dominant selectable marker. Appl. Microbiol. Biotechnol.2014, 98, 5069–5079.

186. Miyahara, M.; Aoi, M.; Inoue-Kashino, N.; Kashino, Y.; Ifuku, K. Highly efficient transformation of the diatomPhaeodactylum tricornutum by multi-pulse electroporation. Biosci. Biotechnol. Biochem. 2013, 77, 874–876.

187. Liu, J.; Chen, F. Biology and industrial applications of Chlorella: Advances and prospects. Adv. Biochem. Eng. Biotechnol. 2016, 135, 1–35.

188. Shaaltiel, Y.; Bartfeld, D.; Hashmueli, S.; Baum, G.; Brill-Almon, E.; Galili, G.; Dym, O.; Boldin-Adamsky, S.A.; Silman, I.; Sussman, J.L. Production of glucocerebrosidase with terminal mannose glycans for enzyme replacement therapy of gaucher's disease using a plant cell system. Plant Biotechnol. J. 2007, 5, 579–590.

189. Hollak, C. An evidence-based review of the potential benefits of taliglucerase alfa in the treatment of patients with Gaucher disease. Core Evid. 2012, 7, 15–20.

190. Shaaltiel, Y.; Gingis-Velitski, S.; Tzaban, S.; Fiks, N.; Tekoah, Y.; Aviezer, D. Plant-based oral delivery of β-glucocerebrosidase as an enzyme replacement therapy for Gaucher's disease. Plant Biotechnol. J. 2015, 13, 1033–1040.

191. Rosalesmendoza, S.; Angulo, C.; Meza, B. Food-grade organisms as vaccine biofactories and oral delivery vehicles.Trends Biotechnol. 2015, 34, 124–136.

192. Santos, R.B.; Abranches, R.; Fischer, R.; Sack, M.; Holland, T. Putting the spotlight back on plant suspension cultures.Front. Plant Sci. 2016, 7, 297.

193. Tacket, C.O.; Mason, H.S.; Losonsky, G.; Estes, M.K.; Levine, M.M.; Arntzen, C.J. Human Immune Responses to a Novel Norwalk Virus Vaccine Delivered in Transgenic Potatoes. J. Infect. Dis. 2000, 182, 302–305.

194. Yusibov, V.; Hooper, D.; Spitsin, S.; Fleysh, N.; Kean, R.; Mikheeva, T.; Deka, D.; Karasev, A.; Cox, S.; Randall, J. Expression in plants and immunogenicity of plant virus-based experimental rabies vaccine. Vaccine 2002, 20, 3155–3164.

195. Thanavala, Y.; Mahoney, M.; Pal, S.; Scott, A.; Richter, L.; Natarajan, N.; Goodwin, P.; Arntzen, C.J.; Mason, H.S. Immunogenicity in humans of an edible vaccine for hepatitis B. Proc. Natl. Acad. Sci. USA 2005, 102, 3378–3382.

196. Hefferon, K. Clinical trials fuel the promise of plant-derived vaccines. Am. J. Clin. Med. 2010, 7, 30–37.

197. Heinzelmann, E. The management centre innsbruck keeping one step ahead with algae innovation. Chim. Int. J. Chem. 2015, 69, 362–364.

Chapter 4

Retention of Silica Nanoparticles in a Lab-Scale Membrane Bioreactor: Implications for Process Performance and Membrane Fouling

Mark Larracas Sibag [1], Soo Mi Lee [1], Hee Jun Kim [2] and Jinwoo Cho [1,*]

[1]*Department of Environment and Energy, Sejong University, 98 Gunja-dong, Gwangjin-gu, Seoul 143-747, Korea*

[2]*JIU Corporation, Yangcheon-ro, Gangseo-gu, Seoul 157-801, Korea*

ABSTRACT

In conventional activated sludge (CAS) involving aerobic biological processes, the retention of silica nanoparticles (SiO_2 NPs) has no detrimental effect on chemical oxygen demand (COD) and ammonia nitrogen (NH_3–N) removal. However, for the membrane bioreactor (MBR) system, which is also based on the activated sludge process in addition to the membrane separation process, it has implications not only on the process performance but also on membrane fouling. To investigate these two implications in lab-scale experiments, we continuously operated a control MBR and two experimental MBRs, in which the 28 nm SiO_2 NPs and 144 nm SiO_2 NPs were added separately to the influent at a final concentration of 100 mg/L. Although the retention of SiO_2 NPs in the MBR, as confirmed by dynamic light scattering (DLS) analysis, did not compromise the COD and NH_3–N removal, it resulted in substantial increases in the transmembrane pressure (TMP) suggesting the onset of membrane fouling. Analyses by batch-dead end filtration revealed the same fouling trend as observed during the continuous MBR experiments; membrane fouling is aggravated in the presence of SiO_2 NPs. This was evident from permeate flux decline of between 30% and 74% at very low TMP (5 kPa) and the further increases in the total resistance.

Keywords: silica nanoparticles; membrane bioreactor; membrane fouling; activated sludge respiration inhibition

1. INTRODUCTION

The presence of SiO_2 NPs in wastewater discharged from domestic and industrial sources raises two concerns for the biological wastewater treatment systems. One is their substantial stability in wastewater [1] that leads to the release of some of them into the effluent stream [2]. Another one is the potential impact of their consequent retention in activated sludge [3,4], which is the core of biological wastewater treatment processes.

Although the presence of SiO_2 NPs in wastewater recently has been considered in operational strategies [5,6,7] and performance evaluation [8] for biological wastewater treatment systems, many of the studies have focused on CAS systems. In a CAS, the presence of SiO_2 NPs has no detrimental effect on the aerobic removal of COD [2] and NH_3–N [8]. Hence, the greater concern for developing strategies is to improve their aggregation with, incorporation into and settling along with activated sludge [1,5] instead.

Additional efforts are also needed to extend this research to membrane bioreactor (MBR) systems, which are also based on the activated sludge process in addition to a membrane separation process that allows MBR operation at higher mixed liquor suspended solids (MLSS) and longer sludge retention time (SRT) [9]. Thus, one may expect that the biological response to SiO_2 in an MBR is similar to that observed in a CAS considering that the biological processes occurring in both systems are governed by activated sludge process. To demonstrate this, we performed continuous lab-scale MBR experiments under a constant flux and evaluated the response of activated sludge to SiO_2 NPs based on the activated sludge respiration inhibition test and measurement of the removal efficiency of COD and NH_3–N. As the particle size may influence SiO_2 NPs' colloidal stability in wastewater [1,2,3,4,5,6,7,8,9,10] and thus their retention in a MBR, we considered two types of SiO_2 NPs based on size range, assessed their retention by comparison of activated sludge biomass between a control and an experimental group and confirmed their retention in a series of batch filtration tests.

Unlike a CAS, an MBR is challenged by membrane fouling [9], which can be more seriously challenged with colloidal particles such as SiO_2 NPs present in the wastewater [11]. In a microfiltration process alone, colloidal particles can foul the membrane by their accumulation on the membrane surface resulting in the formation of a so-called cake layer and/or by plugging the membrane pores [12]. The extent of these two membrane fouling events is also influenced by the size of the particles relative to the membrane pores [13]. Similarly, in an MBR that integrates microfiltration, colloidal particles in the range of 10 nm to 100 nm are responsible for a major part of membrane fouling [14]. Thus, if SiO_2 NPs are present in wastewater entering an MBR, membrane fouling will be aggravated possibly due to interaction effect of SiO_2 NPs themselves and the assumed colloidal fraction of activated sludge. To investigate this, we monitored online the changes in the TMP of the MBRs from the same continuous lab-scale MBR experiments. We also performed a series of batch dead-end filtration tests to further investigate its effect on permeate flux and total resistance. This paper reports on our experimental investigation of the effects of SiO_2 NPs on an MBR. It describes the retention of SiO_2 NPs in an MBR and its implications for process performance and membrane fouling.

2. MATERIALS AND METHODS

2.1. Materials

SiO_2 NPs were purchased from Nissan Chemical Industries (Tokyo, Japan). Two types of SiO_2 NPs according to size were used, 10–15 nm (Snowtex® ST-30) and 70–100 nm (Snowtex® ST-ZL). Their hydrodynamic size in synthetic wastewater were 28 nm for

Snowtex® ST-30 and 144 nm for Snowtex® ST-ZL based on our evaluation by using DLS (PSS Nicomp, Santa Barbara, CA, USA) following the manufacturer's instructions.

Three lab-scale MBRs, which were made of acryl plastic (polymethylmethacrylate), were used. Installed in each MBR setup was a 0.1 m^2, flat sheet chlorinated-polyvinyl chloride (C-PVC) membrane module (240 mm × 340 mm × 7.5 mm) with a nominal pore size of 0.25 μm (GS Yuasa, Kyoto, Japan). Each MBR setup was connected to an air pump with continuous fine bubble diffused aeration that was controlled at 5 L/min by using an airflow meter (Dwyer, Michigan, IN, USA). The air diffuser was directly installed 5 mm beneath the membrane module. The activated sludge inoculum was obtained from an aerobic basin of a domestic wastewater treatment plant (Janghanpyeong, Seoul, South Korea).

The influent was a synthetic wastewater [15], whose composition includes 300 mg/L glucose ($C_6H_{12}O_6$), 260 mg/L ammonium sulfate [$(NH_4)_2SO_4$], 8.5 mg/L potassium dihydrogen phosphate (KH_2PO_4), 2.2 mg/L dipotassium hydrogen phosphate (K_2HPO_4), 4.5 mg/L disodium hydrogen phosphate dodecahydrate ($Na_2HPO_4 \cdot 12H_2O$), 9.4 mg/L manganese sulfate monohydrate ($MnSO_4 \cdot H_2O$), 0.25 mg/L ferric chloride hexahydrate ($FeCl_3 \cdot 6H_2O$), 23.3 mg/L calcium chloride ($CaCl_2$), 22.5 mg/L magnesium sulfate heptahydrate ($MgSO_4 \cdot 7H_2O$) and 670 mg/L sodium bicarbonate ($NaHCO_3$) (Daejung Chemical & Metal Co., Ltd., Shiheung, South Korea).

2.2. Continuous Lab-Scale MBR Experiments

2.2.1. Operating Conditions

Three lab-scale submerged MBRs (Figure 1) were set up, each having an effective reactor volume (*V*) of 6 L. One MBR setup served as the control setup, i.e., SiO_2 NPs were not added to the influent. The two other MBR setups served as the experimental setups, i.e., SiO_2 NPs were added to the influent. All the MBR setups were operated under the same conditions as follows: 6 h hydraulic retention time (HRT), 20 d solids retention time (SRT) and 10 $L/(m^2 \cdot h^{-1})$ influent/effluent flux. The average initial value of MLSS concentration of the three MBR

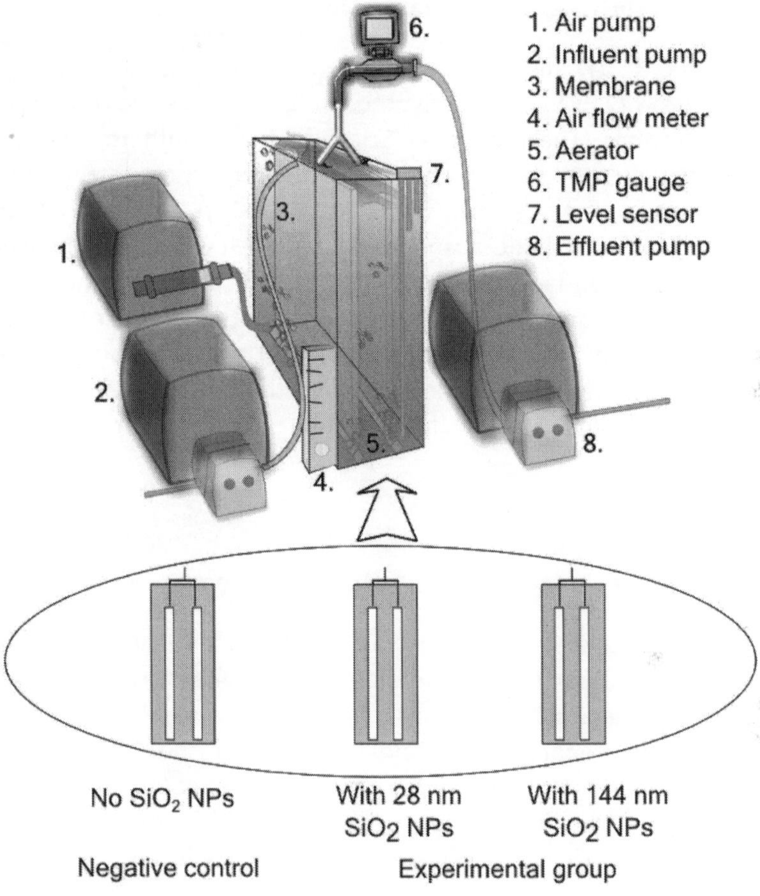

Figure 1. Schematic of the lab-scale membrane bioreactor (MBR) used in the continuous experiment.

setups was 4.2 g MLSS/L ± 0.46. The desired SRT was maintained by daily withdrawing 300 mL of activated sludge.

When the removal of COD and NH_3–N in all MBR setups had become stable (the values did not change over time), 28 nm and 144 nm SiO_2 NPs were separately added to the influent (on day 15) of each experimental MBR setup at a final concentration of 100 mg/L (SiO_2, 0.01 wt. %).

2.2.2. Characterization of Activated Sludge

The pH (7 ± 1), dissolved oxygen (DO) (7 ± 1 mg O_2/L) and temperature (22 ± 1 °C) of activated sludge were measured by using Thermo® probes (Thermo Fisher Scientific Inc., Waltham, MA, USA). Their values did not differ significantly between the control and the two experimental MBR setups [$F(2,21) = 0.53$, $p > 0.05$]. The MLSS and mixed liquor volatile suspended solids (MLVSS) were measured based on the Standard Methods [16]. Statistical significance of the difference between group means of data sets was determined by using one-way analysis of variance (ANOVA) and independent t-test (Origin Pro 8, OriginLab Corporation, Northampton, MA, USA). The same statistical analysis was done, where necessary, throughout the study.

2.2.3. Activated Sludge Respiration Inhibition Test

The oxygen uptake rate (OUR) was measured by using DO probes connected to a portable stand-alone data collection and analysis device (LabNavigator™, Forston Labs, Fort Collins, CO, USA). The samples were prepared as follows: 250 mL of the 300 mL waste sludge from each MBR setup was centrifuged at 4000 rpm and 4 °C for 15 min. The supernatant was discarded, the pellet was reconstituted with tap water and finally diluted to a final concentration of 3 g MLSS/L. From each dilution, 250 mL was obtained, mixed with 16 mL of Organization for Economic Cooperation and Development (OECD) 209 medium [17] and filled with tap water up to 500 mL.

The mixture containing activated sludge taken from the control MBR setup was designated as the control (RTB) mixture. The remaining two mixtures with activated sludge taken from the two experimental MBR setups were the test mixtures (RT). In addition, 500 mL of the following abiotic control (RTA) mixtures were also tested: OECD 209 medium, 100 mg/L of 28 nm SiO_2 NPs and 144 nm SiO_2 NPs. The procedures were based on the OECD 209 test guidelines [17] and the inhibition of total respiration (IT) was calculated using the equation:

$$I_T = \left[1 - \frac{R_T - R_{TA}}{R_{TB}}\right] \times 100\%. \quad (1)$$

2.2.4. Performance Evaluation

The concentrations of COD, NH_3–N, total nitrogen (TN) and total phosphorus (TP) of both influent and effluent were measured three times a week by using water quality test kits (C-MAC Co., Ltd., Daejeon, Korea). The removal efficiency (R)was calculated using the equation:

$$R = \frac{C_i - C_e}{C_i} \times 100\% \quad (2)$$

where Ci and Ce are concentrations of each parameter in the influent and effluent, respectively. All water quality measurements were performed using an Optizen UV-VIS spectrophotometer with pre-programmed water analysis methods (Mecasys Co., Ltd., Daejeon, Korea).

2.2.5. Transmembrane Pressure Monitoring

A pressure transmitter was installed in each MBR setup for on-line monitoring of the changes in the TMP. It converts the pressure, which is detected from the elastic deformation of the silicon diaphragm of the integrated sensor chip, into an electrical signal in the presence of an auxiliary electrical supply (Keller-Druck, Winterthur, Switzerland). The pressure transmitter was connected to a computer for continuous data collection through a LabVIEW program (National Instruments, Austin, TX, USA). The TMP profile of each MBR setup was compared based on the absolute value of the slope of the linear portion of TMP versus time plot, at select points in time, i.e., when the TMP of the two experimental MBRs increased relative to the control MBR.

2.3. Batch Experiments

2.3.1. Influence of SiO_2 NPs on MLSS Measurement

To evaluate the potential contribution of SiO_2 NPs to the increase in MLSS values of activated sludge (assuming that or if some of them remained in activated sludge), 50 mg/L, 100 mg/L, 250 mg/L, 500 mg/L and 1000 mg/L each of 28 nm and 144 nm SiO_2 NPs were subject to the same MLSS measurement as described on Section 2.2.2.

2.3.2. SiO_2 NPs Settling Experiments and Dead-End Filtration Tests

A total of 200 mL each of 28 nm SiO_2 NPs (1000 mg/L), 144 nm SiO_2 NPs (1000 mg/L) and activated sludge (3 g MLSS/L) was prepared in the same but fresh synthetic wastewater. This group of samples served as controls. The experimental group was two mixtures consisting of each SiO_2 NP plus activated sludge. The final concentrations of SiO_2 NPs and activated sludge in the two mixtures were the same as those in the control group.

A series of settling experiments were conducted to investigate the colloidal stability of SiO_2 NPs. The experimental and control groups were mixed by continuous magnetic stirring at 125 rpm (Daihan Scientific, Seoul, South Korea) for 30 min followed by gravitational settling for 3 h. DLS analysis of the decantate from each sample was done to determine the hydrodynamic size of the dispersed particles present as described in Section 2.1. A batch dead-end filtration test of each samples from the control group (except activated sludge) and experimental group was conducted at 5 kPa, and DLS analysis was done to confirm the presence of SiO_2 NPs in the permeate.

A series of batch dead-end filtration tests were also conducted as described elsewhere [18,19,20], but the applied pressure was increased in a step-wise fashion during each run of batch dead-end filtration test. A detailed and determinative investigation of membrane fouling was unnecessary since we only aimed at briefly comparing the fouling trend observed during the continuous MBR experiments to that during the batch dead-end filtration; thus only for relative comparison. The total resistance (RT) was determined from each constant pressure data using the expression:

$$J = \frac{\Delta P}{\mu R_T} \quad (3)$$

The effect of SiO_2 NPs on activated sludge microfiltration was investigated over a range of TMP (ΔP), from 5 kPa to 35 kPa at a 5-kPa interval. We used a 180-mL unstirred cell unit (Amicon 8200, Amicon™, Danvers, MA, USA) and a 28.7 cm^2 (A) C-PVC membrane that we cut from one whole sheet of the membrane. A new membrane was used in every batch dead-end filtration test and the permeate flux of deionized water (JCW) through the membrane at a given pressure was measured [21]. The values of permeate flux (J) obtained from all of samples were normalized by their respective JCWvalues. The filtrate viscosity (μ) was measured by using a DV-II+Pro viscometer (Brookfield AMETEK, Inc., Middleboro, MA, USA) following the manufacturer's instructions.

3. RESULTS AND DISCUSSION

3.1. Retention of SiO_2 NPs in MBR

The evolution of MLSS following the addition of SiO_2 NPs in the two experimental MBR setups (Figure 2a) indicates retention of SiO_2 NPs in the mixed liquor. Unlike that in the control MBR setup, the MLSS concentration in the experimental MBR setups was increased by 0.08 g MLSS/L/d (with 28 nm SiO_2 NPs) and 0.14 g MLSS/L/d (with 144 nm SiO_2 NPs). MLVSS measurements in both the control MBR and experimental MBR setups, which did not differ significantly from each other ($F(2,21) = 3, p > 0.05$), confirm that the increasing MLSS concentration is non-biomass-related and is due to the accumulation of SiO_2 NPs. Subsequent batch experiments with pure SiO_2 NPs further confirm the contribution of SiO_2NPs to MLSS measurement due to their accumulation; 1000 mg/L SiO_2 NPs contributed as much as 0.3 g/L and 0.7 g/L for 28 nm and 144 nm SiO_2 NPs, respectively (Figure 2b).

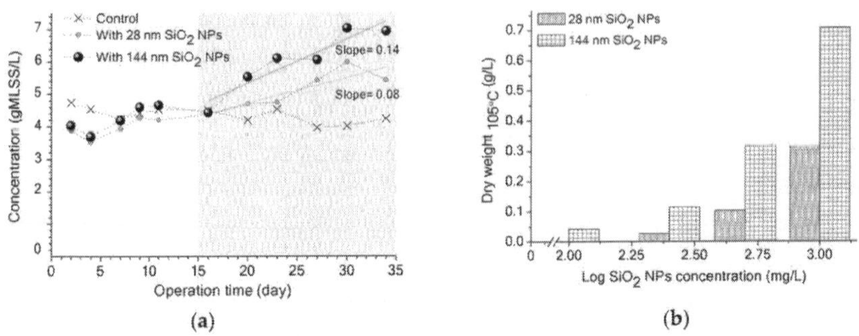

Figure 2. Effect of SiO_2 NPs on the evolution of MLSS during (**a**) a continuous experiment in a membrane bioreactor (MBR) and (**b**) batch experiment with pure SiO_2NPs. The shaded area indicates exposure to SiO_2 NPs.

At the end of the experiment, the final MLSS concentration in the experimental MBR setups relative to the control MBR setup (4.2 g MLSS/L) increased by 28% (with 28 nm SiO_2 NPs) and 64% (with 144 nm SiO_2 NPs). Converting these percentage increases in MLSS concentration to wt. % SiO_2 NPs, approximately 0.12 wt. % of 28 nm SiO_2 NPs and 0.27 wt. % of 144 nm SiO_2 NPs were present in the experimental MBR setups. Considering 29.38 g as the total input of SiO_2 NPs over the period of 15 days of operation (19.584 L/d × 15 d × 100 mg/L SiO_2 NPs), the estimated retention of 28 nm SiO_2 NPs and 144 nm SiO_2 NPs in the MLSS of MBR was 4% and 9%, respectively.

The results demonstrate that some of the SiO_2 NPs accumulate in the mixed liquor despite their size being smaller than the membrane pore size, thus confirming actual exposure of activated sludge to SiO_2 NPs. This is particularly important to subsequently evaluating the potential outcomes of the exposure of activated sludge to SiO_2 NPs in an MBR.

With the substantial stability of SiO_2 NPs due to their low point of zero charge in wastewater (pH < 3.5) [1], some are most likely retained in the mixed liquor. For instance, in the secondary treatment of a CAS that involves deliberate settling of activated sludge, poor aggregation/sedimentation of SiO_2 NPs was observed [2] and for that same reason may hold true in activated sludge of an MBR. We demonstrated this in a batch settling experiment followed by DLS analysis of the decantate, where particles with nearly 28 nm and 144 nm size distribution were detected, suggesting the retention of SiO_2NPs in the dispersion medium (synthetic wastewater and/or activated sludge) (Figure 3a–d). Meanwhile, particles of approximately between 100 nm to 400 nm were also present in the sample containing a mixture of 28 nm SiO_2 NPs and activated sludge (Figure 3b), suggesting that some colloidal particles from activated sludge remain dispersed along with SiO_2 NPs. These colloidal particles from activated sludge, however, are apparently not detectable in the sample containing a mixture of 144 nm SiO_2 NPs and activated sludge (Figure 3d) for some unknown reasons. We suspect that they may be present but overshadowed by the dominant presence of 144 nm SiO_2 NPs in the sample.

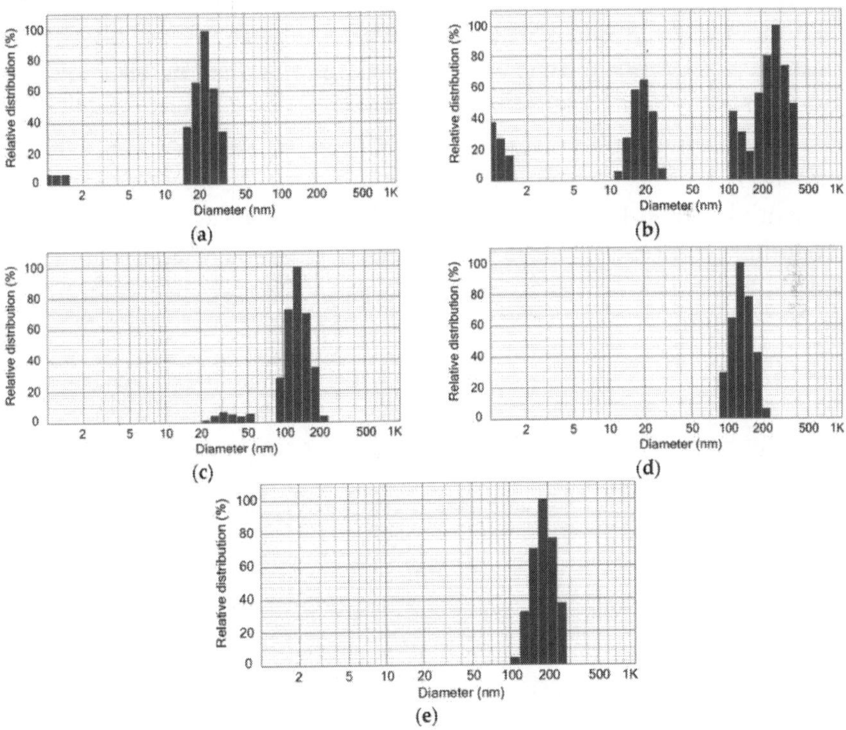

Figure 3. Particle size distribution of the decantate from batch settling experiments involving (**a**) 28 nm SiO_2 NPs; (**b**) 28 nm SiO_2 NPs + activated sludge; (**c**) 144 nm SiO_2NPs; (**d**) 144 nm SiO_2 NPs + activated sludge and (**e**) activated sludge only.

In an MBR, the estimated values for the retention of SiO_2 NPs may be expected to be lower than those reported in a CAS (35%) [2]. This is reasonable because of (1) the continuous aeration in an MBR that further keeps SiO_2 NPs dispersed in the mixed liquor, (2) the suction pressure that facilitates their discharge into the effluent stream and (3) the size of SiO_2 NPs being smaller relative to the membrane pore size that allows them to easily pass through the membrane. DLS analysis confirms the presence of 28 nm SiO_2 NPs and 144 nm SiO_2 NPs in the permeate (Figure 4). In addition, it is clear from DLS analysis that other than the SiO_2 NPs, some colloidal particles from activated sludge of approximately less than 100 nm can also pass through the membrane (Figure 4b). The mean floc size of activated sludge used in the dead-end filtration tests was 7.5 um (25% of distribution < 3.8 um, 50% of the distribution < 5.9 um). In an MBR system, the average size of activated sludge flocs can be as small as 5 um and as large as 240 um [9]. In the decantate (after allowing the activated sludge to settle), there remained particles with an average size of 191 nm (Figure 3e) while in the permeate (after filtration of activated sludge), 123 nm particles were detected (Figure 4e). Together, the results prove that some of the SiO_2 NPs remain in the mixed liquor of an MBR, thus allowing potential interaction with activated sludge.

3.2. Potential Biological Effect of SiO_2 NPs on Activated Sludge and MBR Performance

That the total respiration decreased in the two experimental MBR setups indicates the potential biological effect of activated sludge exposure to SiO_2 NPs. The maximum IT by SiO_2 NPs was as low as 5% (with 28 nm SiO_2 NPs) and as high as 60% (with 144 nm SiO_2 NPs) (Figure 5).

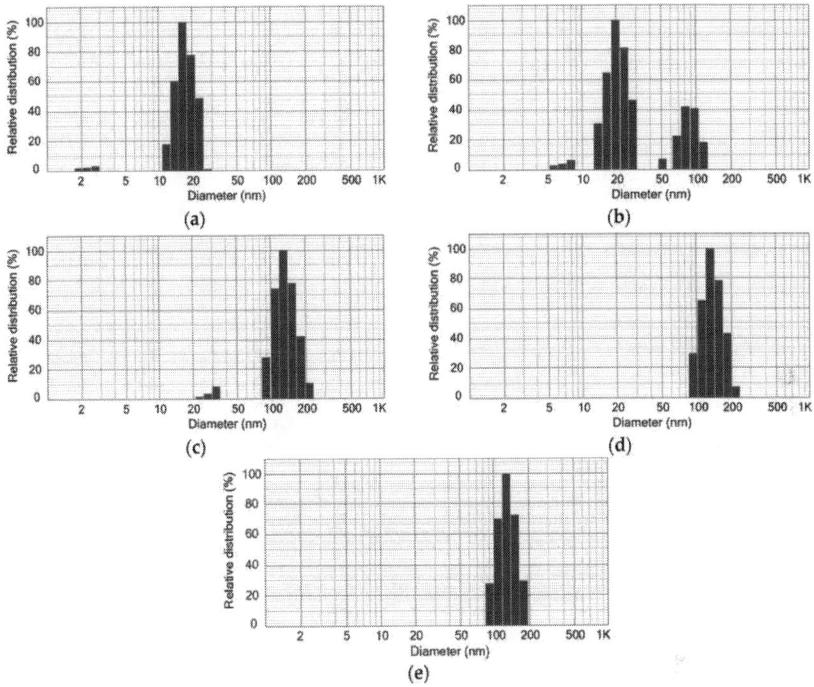

Figure 4. Particle size distribution of the permeate from dead-end filtration tests involving (**a**) 28 nm SiO_2 NPs; (**b**) 28 nm SiO_2 NPs + activated sludge; (**c**) 144 nm SiO_2NPs; (**d**) 144 nm SiO_2 NPs + activated sludge and (**e**) activated sludge only.

The lesser inhibitory effect of 28 nm SiO_2 NPs compared with that of 144 nm SiO_2 NPs may be due to the relatively lower retention of 28 nm SiO_2 NPs in an MBR. Despite the same initial concentration of SiO_2 NPs in the influent of the two experimental MBR setups, the estimated amount of SiO_2 NPs in the mixed liquor actually differed (Figure 2) as did the extent of activated sludge exposure to SiO_2 NPs.

The size-dependent toxicity of nanoparticles has been widely reported in literature, particularly in studies of nanoparticle toxicity in pure culture bacteria [22,23]. Previously, we have shown in batch experiments that smaller SiO_2NPs (~12 nm and ~151 nm) were more inhibitory than the larger SiO_2 NPs (442 nm and 683 nm) given that

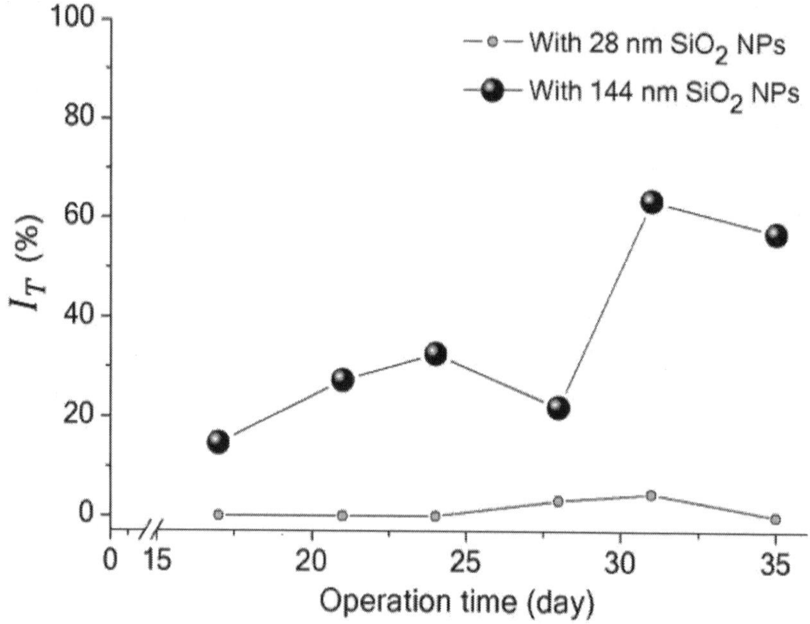

Figure 5. Inhibition of activated sludge total respiration (IT) in an MBR by SiO_2 NPs.

the concentration or dose did not change throughout the period of study [24]. The size-dependent toxicity of nanoparticles observed from these studies is most likely due to their greater surface area [25]. However, size-dependent toxicity was not observed in the present study. One reason is that despite the same initial SiO_2 NPs concentration, the exposure to 28 nm SiO_2 NPs and their respiration inhibitory effect are less than those of 144 nm SiO_2 NPs because the smaller SiO_2 NPs can easily pass through the membrane, thus having lower retention in MBR activated sludge. Lower retention could mean lower exposure of MBR-activated sludge to SiO_2 NPs.

Of the several possible mechanisms of nanoparticle-induced toxicity reviewed in the literature [26], oxidative stress, release of toxic cations and change in protein conformation mainly stand out [27]. However, there is no conclusive evidence for the mechanism of SiO_2 NPs inhibition of activated sludge total respiration although indirect evidence from fatty acid methyl ester (FAME) analysis of activated sludge suggests that SiO_2 NPs altered the composition of the microbial membrane lipids [24]. The potential biological effects of SiO_2 NPs on activated sludge warrants further investigations, especially because in nanotoxicity the key role of the interaction of nanoparticles (including SiO_2 NPs) with proteins, which are also a component of activated sludge extracellular polymeric substances (EPS), has been recognized recently [28,29,30].

Similar to that observed in a CAS for yet unclear reasons, activated sludge exposure to SiO_2 NPs [8] and their inhibitory effect on total respiration [24] were also not associated with low oxidation of COD and NH_3. Over a period of 20 days after the exposure of activated MBR to SiO_2 NPs, I_T in the presence of 144 nm SiO_2 NPs (M = 37, SD = 7) was higher than with 28 nm SiO_2 NPs (M = 8, SD = 9), $t(10) = -6$, $p < 0.05$. However, there was no statistically significant effect of exposure to both SiO_2 NPs on the removal of COD ($F(2,15) = 0.08$, $p > 0.05$) and NH_3–N ($F(2,13) = 0.003$, $p > 0.05$). The removal of TN ($F(2,24) = 0.32$, $p > 0.05$) and TP ($F(2,24) = 1$, $p > 0.05$) also did not statistically differ between the control and the experimental setups. The overall performance of the control and experimental setups based on the removal of organic matter and nutrients are summarized in Table 1. Although it may be disregarded as a potential threat to the process performance of an MBR, the retention of SiO_2 NPs in the mixed liquor may pose a risk of membrane fouling [31,32].

Table 1. Summary of the performance of MBR with and without exposure to SiO_2NPs.

Treatment	COD (SD) mg/L		Removal %	NH_3–N (SD) mg/L		Removal %	TN (SD) mg/L		Removal %	TP (SD) mg/L		Removal %
	Influent	Effluent		Influent	Effluent		Influent	Effluent		Influent	Effluent	
MBR control	279 (60)	10 (2)	96	39 (9)	< 0.02	99	50 (5)	47 (4)	6	11 (2)	9 (1)	18
MBR with 28 nm SiO_2 NPs	282 (54)	10 (2)	96	41 (7)	< 0.02	99	48 (5)	44 (3)	8	11 (1)	9 (1)	18
MBR with 144 nm SiO_2 NPs	284 (105)	11 (2)	96	40 (9)	< 0.02	99	48 (4)	45 (4)	6	11 (1)	9 (1)	18

3.3. Implications of SiO_2 NPs Retention for Membrane Fouling in an MBR

The slope of the linear portion of the TMP versus time plot of the two experimental MBR setups was relatively higher than that of the control MBR setup (Figure 6). This indicates an occurrence of membrane fouling that is apparently related to the relatively smaller

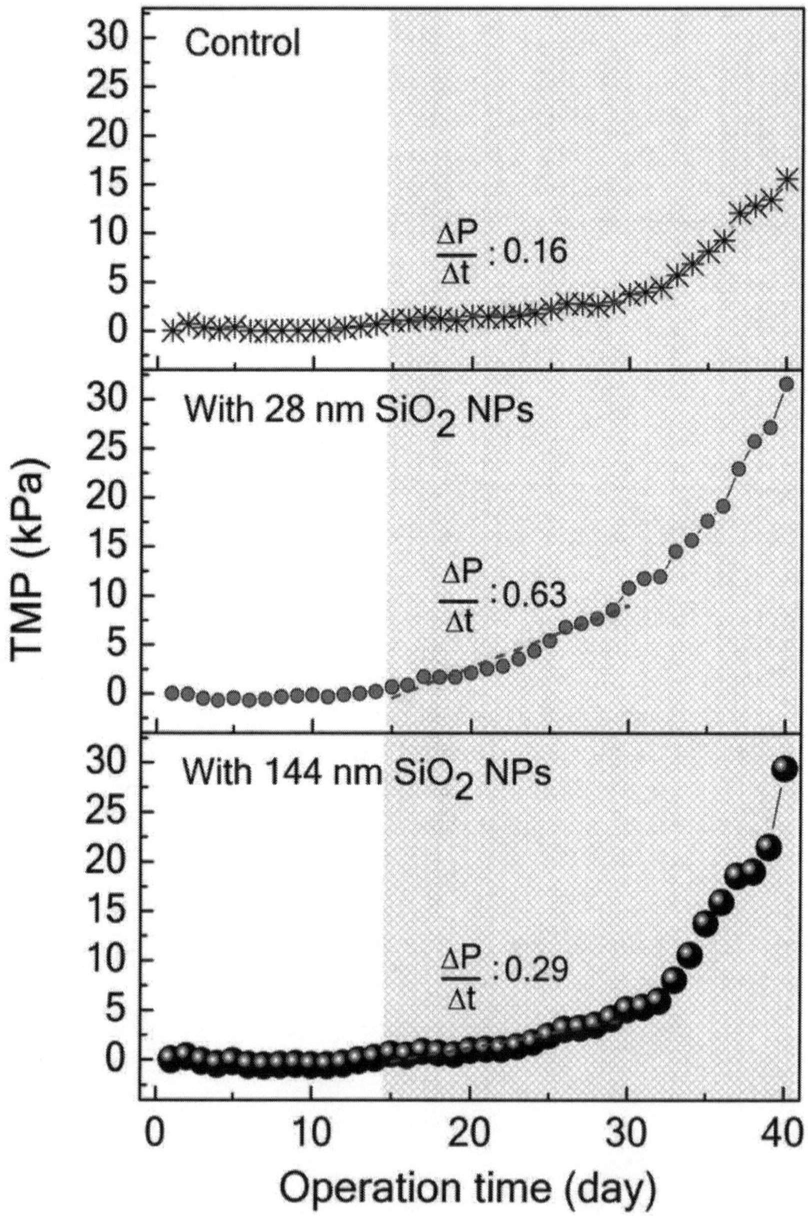

Figure 6. Effect of SiO_2 NPs on the evolution of transmembrane pressure (TMP) in an MBR. The shaded area indicates exposure to SiO_2 NPs.

SiO_2 NPs (28 nm). The difference in the TMP values between the control and the experimental setups (with 28 nm SiO_2 NPs and 144 nm SiO_2 NPs) was statistically significant (F (2,78) = 4, p = 0.03). The TMP monitoring data agree with the observations from previous studies regarding the effects of colloidal particles, having relatively smaller size than the membrane pores, on microfiltration. We could infer that the most likely nature of the observed membrane fouling in the experimental MBR is pore plugging [13], although particle accumulation on the membrane surface [12] could also be responsible for this.

The SiO_2 NPs, being in the "colloidal size range" between 1 nm and 1000 nm [33], are actually colloids [30]. Colloids are also implicated in membrane fouling, which we specifically refer to as colloidal fouling in the following discussion. Colloidal fouling is a phenomenon typical [31,34,35] but not exclusive to microfiltration processes [13,36,37]. It is influenced by some factors including colloidal particle size, applied pressure and the interaction with other colloidal particles that may be present in activated sludge [11,38,39].

However, the effect of each factor may differ depending on the extent of the other factor. We observed this during the comparative evaluation of permeate flux and total resistance of SiO_2 NPs only (28 nm and 144 nm) and a mixture of each SiO_2 NPs and activated sludge at increasing TMP during the dead-end filtration tests.

All samples exhibit an initially decreasing permeate flux that levels off towards the end of the range of TMP tested. Alone (as a dispersion) or when mixed with activated sludge, the 28 nm SiO_2 NPs exhibited a higher permeate flux than did the 144 nm SiO_2 NPs. However, in the experimental group, although the presence of both SiO_2 NPs in activated sludge decreases the permeate flux during the initial low-pressure stage, which can be as low as low as 30% (28 nm SiO_2 NPs) and as high as 74% (144 nm SiO_2 NPs), the permeate flux decline equalizes as TMP further increases from 10 kPa to 35 kPa (Figure 7). The results clearly show that SiO_2 NPs can reduce permeate flux during microfiltration of activated sludge.

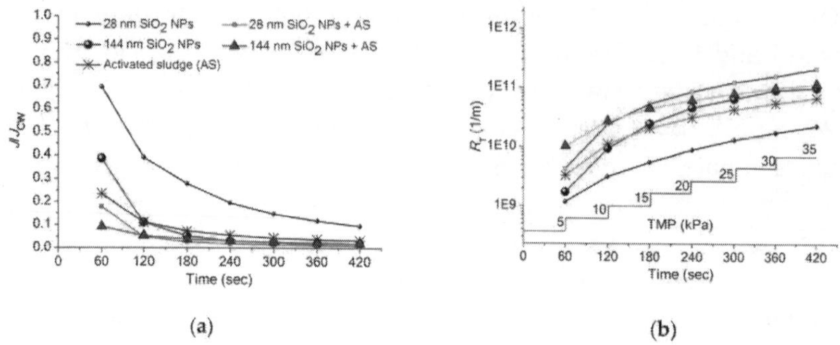

Figure 7. Membrane filtration characteristics in dead-end filtration of activated sludge with SiO_2 NPs. (**a**) normalized permeate flux and (**b**) total resistance.

All samples also show an increasing total resistance over the range of TMP tested. The experimental group generally exhibits a higher total resistance, suggesting that the presence of SiO_2 NPs can aggravate membrane fouling. Unlike the SiO_2 NPs alone, the 144 nm SiO_2 NPs when mixed with activated sludge, exhibit a higher total resistance only at the initial stage when the pressure is between 5 kPa and 10 kPa. The 28 nm SiO_2 NPs-activated sludge mixture increases further and surpasses the 144 nm SiO_2 NPs at much higher pressures (Figure 7).

In the experimental group, we suspect that the difference in the transport characteristics [36] of the two SiO_2 is responsible for the difference in their values of permeate flux decline and total resistance at the initial low-pressure stage. Unlike the 28 nm SiO_2 NPs, the 144 nm SiO_2 NPs are more easily retained in a cake layer along with other particles originating from activated sludge so they exert more hydraulic resistance and a corresponding permeate flux decline (Figure 7). However, as TMP further increases over time (Figure 6), SiO_2 NPs accumulate but the smaller particles form a more compact structure with less degree of porosity [11] as do the 28 nm SiO_2 NPs along with other particles originating from activated sludge. This likely explains the observed further decreases in permeate flux and an increasing total resistance in the mixture of 28 nm SiO_2 NPs and activated sludge. Although our results clearly demonstrate that SiO_2 NPs aggravate membrane fouling in an MBR, it is possible that other factors that were not examined in this study, for example, the size of activated sludge flocs after exposure to SiO_2 NPs, also contributed to membrane fouling. A recent study has shown that SiO_2 NPs at a final tested concentration of 100 mg/L improved flocculation ability of activated sludge after 24 h of exposure. The improved flocculation resulted from the decrease in the interaction barrier between activated sludge flocs as they were exposed to SiO_2 NPs [40]. The clear identification and differentiation of the mechanisms of membrane fouling observed in our study shall be considered for further investigations.

4. CONCLUSIONS

The retention of SiO_2 NPs in an MBR has no adverse effect on the removal of COD and NH_3–N despite the observable inhibition of total respiration in activated sludge. However, it contributes to membrane fouling that results in TMP increases for a given flux, or conversely it can considerably reduce the permeate flux at a given TMP. More specifically, the presence of smaller SiO_2 NPs in activated sludge, contrary to that of the larger counterparts, eventually exerts higher total resistance as the TMP increases, although a substantial flux decline can already be observed at low TMP. As our results, which are similar to those in a CAS, show no detrimental effect of SiO_2 NPs on the overall performance of an MBR, we anticipate that future studies will further investigate the interaction of SiO_2 NPs with activated sludge in an MBR, which is apparently where the challenge in fouling control lies.

ACKNOWLEDGMENTS

This research was supported by a grant from the Korean Ministry of Environment (MOE) as “The advancement of scientific research and technology development in environmental science program (2013001340004)”.

AUTHOR CONTRIBUTIONS

Mark Larracas Sibag and Jinwoo Cho conceived and designed the experiments; Mark Larracas Sibag and Soo Mi Lee performed the experiments; Mark Larracas Sibag and Soo Mi Lee analyzed the data; Jinwoo Cho and Hee Jun Kim contributed reagents/materials/analysis tools; Mark Larracas Sibag, Soo Mi Lee, Hee Jun Kim and Jinwoo Cho contributed to the writing of the manuscript.

CONFLICTS OF INTEREST

The authors declare no conflict of interest.

REFERENCES

1. Otero-González, L.; Barbero, I.; Field, J.A.; Shadman, F.; Sierra-Alvarez, R. Stability of alumina, ceria, and silica nanoparticles in municipal wastewater. Water Sci. Technol. 2014, 70, 1533–1539.

2. Otero-González, L.; Field, J.A.; Calderon, I.A.; Aspinwall, C.A.; Shadman, F.; Zeng, C.; Sierra-Alvarez, R. Fate of fluorescent core-shell silica nanoparticles during simulated secondary wastewater treatment. Water Res. 2015, 77, 170–178.

3. Brar, S.K.; Verma, M.; Tyagi, R.D.; Surampalli, R.Y. Engineered nanoparticles in wastewater and wastewater sludge—Evidence and impacts. Waste Manage. 2010, 30, 504–520.

4. Mohanty, A.; Wu, Y.; Cao, B. Impacts of engineered nanomaterials on microbial community structure and function in natural and engineered ecosystems. Applied Microbiol. Biot. 2014, 98, 8457–8468.

5. Kiser, M.A.; Ryu, H.; Jang, H.; Hristovski, K.; Westerhoff, P. Biosorption of nanoparticles to heterotrophic wastewater biomass. Water Res. 2010, 44, 4105–4114.

6. Park, H.J.; Kim, H.Y.; Cha, S.; Ahn, C.H.; Roh, J.; Park, S.; Kim, S.; Choi, K.; Yi, J.; Kim, Y.; Yoon, J. Removal characteristics of

engineered nanoparticles by activated sludge. Chemosphere 2013, 92, 524–528.

7. Rottman, J.; Shadman, F.; Sierra-Alvarez, R. Interactions of inorganic oxide nanoparticles with sewage biosolids.Water Sci. Technol. 2012, 66, 1821–1827.

8. Zheng, X.; Su, Y.; Chen, Y. Acute and chronic responses of activated sludge viability and performance to silica nanoparticles. Environ. Sci. Technol. 2012, 46, 7182–7188.

9. Judd, S. The MBR Book: Principles and Applications of Membrane Bioreactors for Water and Wastewater Treatment; Elsevier: Oxford, UK, 2010; pp. 174–176.

10. Auffan, M.; Rose, J.; Bottero, J.Y.; Lowry, G.V.; Jolivet, J.P.; Wiesner, M.R. Towards a definition of inorganic nanoparticles from an environmental, health and safety perspective. Nat. Nanotechnol. 2009, 4, 634–641.

11. Wang, F.; Tarabara, V.V. Pore blocking mechanisms during early stages of membrane fouling by colloids. J. Colloid Interf. Sci. 2008, 328, 464–469.

12. Belfort, G.; Davis, R.H.; Zydney, A.L. The behavior of suspensions and macromolecular solutions in crossflow microfiltration. J. Membrane Sci. 1994, 96, 1–58.

13. Zhu, X.; Elimelech, M. Colloidal fouling of reverse osmosis membranes: measurements and fouling mechanisms.Environ. Sci. Technol. 1997, 31, 3654–3662.

14. Allen, P.T.; Stephenson, G.M. Inter-group understanding and size of organisation. Brit. J. Ind. Relat. 1983, 21, 312–329.

15. Hur, J.; Shin, J.; Kang, M.; Cho, J. Tracking variations in fluorescent-dissolved organic matter in an aerobic submerged membrane bioreactor using excitation-emission matrix spectra combined with parallel factor analysis.Bioprocess. Biosyst. Eng. 2014, 37, 1487–1496.

16. Rice, E.W.; Baird, R.B.; Eaton, A.D.; Clesceri, L.S. Standard Methods for the Examination of Water and Wastewater;

American Public Health Association, American Water Works Association and Water Environment Federation: Washington, DC, USA, 2012.

17. Organization for Economic Co-operation and Development (OECD). OECD 209 Guideline for the Testing of Chemicals, Activated Sludge Respiration Inhibition Test; OECD: Paris, France, 1993.

18. Foley, G. Membrane Filtration: A Problem Solving Approach with MATLAB; Cambridge University Press: New York, NY, USA, 2013; pp. 16–45.

19. Cho, J.; Song, K.G.; Ahn, K.H. The activated sludge and microbial substances influences on membrane fouling in submerged membrane bioreactor: unstirred batch cell test. Desalination 2005, 183, 425–429.

20. Ahmed, Z.; Cho, J.; Lim, B.R.; Song, K.G.; Ahn, K.H. Effects of sludge retention time on membrane fouling and microbial community structure in a membrane bioreactor. J. Membrane Sci. 2007, 287, 211–218.

21. Munir, A. Dead end membrane filtration, laboratory feasibility studies in environmental engineering. Available online: http://www.egr.msu.edu/~hashsham/courses/ene806/docs/Membrane%20Filtration.pdf (accessed on 27 June 2016).

22. Simon-Deckers, A.; Loo, S.; Mayne-L'hermite, M.; Herlin-Boime, N.; Menguy, N.; Reynaud, C.; Gouget, B.; Cariere, M. Size-, composition-and shape-dependent toxicological impact of metal oxide nanoparticles and carbon nanotubes toward bacteria. Environ. Sci. Technol. 2009, 43, 8423–8429.

23. Hajipour, M.J.; Fromm, K.M.; Ashkarran, A.A.; de Aberasturi, D.J.; de Larramendi, I.R.; Rojo, T.; Serpooshan, V.; Parak, W.J.; Mahmoudi, M. Antibacterial properties of nanoparticles. Trends Biotechnol. 2010, 30, 499–511.

24. Sibag, M.; Choi, B.G.; Suh, C.; Lee, K.H.; Lee, J.W.; Maeng, S.K.; Cho, J. Inhibition of total oxygen uptake by silica nanoparticles in activated sludge. J. Haz. Mat. 2015, 283, 841–846.

25. Jiang, W.; Mashayekhi, H.; Xing, B. Bacterial toxicity comparison between nano-and micro-scaled oxide particles.Environ. Pollut. 2009, 157, 1619–1625.

26. Manke, A.; Wang, L.; Rojanasakul, Y. Mechanisms of nanoparticle-induced oxidative stress and toxicity. BioMed Res. Int. 2013, 2013, 942916.

27. Bottero, J.Y. Environmental risks of nanotechnology: A new challenge? In Nanosciences and Nanotechnology; Springer International Publishing: Cham, Switzerland, 2016; pp. 287–311.

28. Zanganeh, S.; Spitler, R.; Erfanzadeh, M.; Mahmoudi, M. Protein Corona: Opportunities and Challenges. Int. J. Biochem. Cell. Biol. 2016, 75, 143–147.

29. Saptarshi, S.R.; Duschl, A.; Lopata, A.L. Interaction of nanoparticles with proteins: relation to bio-reactivity of the nanoparticle. J. Nanobiotechnol. 2013, 11, 26.

30. Lynch, I.; Cedervall, T.; Lundqvist, M.; Cabaleiro-Lago, C.; Linse, S.; Dawson, K.A. The nanoparticle-protein complex as a biological entity; a complex fluids and surface science challenge for the 21st century. Adv. Colloid Interface Sci.2012, 134, 167–174.

31. Pan, J.R.; Huang, C.; Jiang, W.; Chen, C. Treatment of wastewater containing nano-scale silica particles by dead-end microfiltration: evaluation of pretreatment methods. Desalination 2005, 179, 31–40.

32. Singh, G.; Song, L. Quantifying the effect of ionic strength on colloidal fouling potential in membrane filtration. J. Colloid Interface Sci. 2005, 28, 630–638.

33. Kissa, E. Dispersions: Characterization, Testing, and Measurement; CRC Press: Boca Raton, FL, USA, 1999; Volume 84.

34. Trzaskus, K.W.; Zdeb, A.; de Vos, W.M.; Kemperman, A.; Nijmeijer, K. Fouling behavior during microfiltration of silica nanoparticles and polymeric stabilizers. J. Membrane Sci. 2016, 505, 205–215.

35. Guo, W.; Ngo, H.H.; Li, J. A mini-review on membrane fouling. Bioresour. Technol. 2012, 122, 27–34.

36. Boo, C.; Lee, S.; Elimelech, M.; Meng, Z.; Hong, S. Colloidal fouling in forward osmosis: Role of reverse salt diffusion.J. Membrane Sci. 2012, 390, 277–284.

37. Shirazi, S.; Lin, C.J.; Chen, D. Inorganic fouling of pressure-driven membrane processes—A critical review.Desalination 2010, 250, 236–248.

38. Rosenberger, S.; Laabs, C.; Lesjean, B.; Gnirss, R.; Amy, G.; Jekel, M.; Schrotter, J.C. Impact of colloidal and soluble organic material on membrane performance in membrane bioreactors for municipal wastewater treatment. Water Res. 2006, 40, 710–720.

39. Laabs, C.N.; Amy, G.L.; Jekel, M. Understanding the size and character of fouling-causing substances from effluent organic matter (EfOM) in low-pressure membrane filtration. Environ. Sci. Technol. 2006, 40, 4495–4499.

40. Xu, J.; Li, X.Y. Investigation of the effect of nanoparticle exposure on the flocculability of activated sludge using particle image volecimetry in combination with the extended DLVO analysis. Colloids Surf. B Biointerfaces. 2016, 143, 382–389.

Chapter 5

Development of a Comprehensive Fouling Model for a Rotating Membrane Bioreactor System Treating Wastewater

Parneet Paul * and Franck Anderson Jones

Water Sustainability Research Centre, Department of Mechanical, Aerospace, and Civil Engineering, Brunel University London, Uxbridge, Middlesex UB8 3PH, UK

ABSTRACT

Membrane bioreactors (MBRs) are now main stream wastewater treatment technologies. In recent times, novel pressure driven rotating membrane disc modules have been specially developed that induce high shear on the membrane surface, thereby reducing fouling. Previous research has produced dead-end filtration fouling model which combines all three classical mechanisms that was later used by another researcher as a starting point for a greatly refined model of a cross flow side-stream MBR that incorporated both hydrodynamics and soluble microbial products' (SMP) effects. In this study, a comprehensive fouling model was created based on this earlier work that incorporated all three classical fouling mechanisms for a rotating MBR system. It was tested and validated for best fit using appropriate data sets. The initial model fit appeared good for all simulations, although it still needs to be calibrated using further appropriate data sets.

Keywords: membrane bioreactor; rotating membranes; fouling; cake filtration; modeling

1. INTRODUCTION

Membrane bioreactors (MBRs) are now main stream wastewater treatment technologies used extensively for both municipal and industrial situations. In recent times pressure driven rotating membrane disc modules have been specially developed that have high shear effects on the membrane surface thereby reducing associated fouling whilst minimising energy usage. These systems have been shown to yield high permeate flux in the ultra-filtration range [1]. The reason for their good performance is the very high shear rate of approximately $2 \times 10^5\ s^{-1}$ which prevents cake formation and concentration polarisation [2]. However, this is not limited to rotating MBRs only. Vibration systems are known to also produce high shears with a maximum membrane shear rate of $1.4 \times 10^5\ s^{-1}$ for fluids having viscosities comparable to that of water [2,3]. The shear rate at the membrane in these vibratory systems is created by the inertia of the retentate which moves at 180 degrees out of phase with the membrane and is a sinusoidal time variant [2]. Rotary filtration systems come in many forms, some of which are bespoke where a rotating disc operates near a stationary circular membrane disc or systems where the membrane module rotates on a single shaft driven by a motor. Experimental studies reported so far include filtration of mineral suspension [4], black liquor [1] and skimmed milk [5]. Sarkar and Bhattacharjee [6] presented a semi analytical model based on the evaluation of back transport flux, which was later refined by Sarkar *et al.* [7]. Conversely the shear stresses occurring near the surface of a rotating disc located adjacent to a stationary circular membrane encased in a cylindrical housing was modelled by means of computational fluid dynamics by Torras *et al.* [8]. A similar study for a rotational cross-flow membrane bioreactor was undertaken by Bentzen *et al.* [9]. In a related study, Engler and Mark [10] investigated the fouling mechanism of a rotating membrane disc as a function of operating conditions. Finally, using rotating ceramic membrane discs which were fouled by sludge, Jørgensen *et al.* [11] showed the dependence of shear on fouling and ultimately presented a model that linked the shear rate to the limiting flux.

Unfortunately like any other system filtering activated sludge, a defining issue of rotating membrane systems is the decline of permeate flux with time. This is mostly attributed to the phenomenon known as concentration polarisation with associated fouling problems. The true origin of fouling has yet to be fully defined, although many researchers widely acknowledge that SMP (soluble microbial products) and EPS (extracellular polymeric substances) are the most likely fouling agents [12]. This is since the build-up of SMP and EPS can cause reduction in membrane permeability [13,14]. Additional factors affecting fouling mechanisms include; Scaling, biofilm formation, operating conditions such as pH, temperature and flow rates, solution properties such as particle size distribution [12]. Different approaches have also been developed for modelling the physical and biological aspects of membrane fouling in a normal non-rotating MBR system. A main one was developed by Hermia [15] where a power law model is used to distinguish between different fouling mechanisms, namely cake filtration, intermediate pore blockage, pore constriction and complete pore blockage. Meng *et al.*[16] established the fractal permeation model while Liu *et al.* [17] presented the empirical hydrodynamic model. Furthermore, Duclos-Orsello *et al.* [18] introduced a dead-end filtration fouling model that combined the first three classical fouling mechanisms mentioned by Hermia [15] that was later used by Paul [19] as a starting point for a greatly refined model for a cross flow side-stream MBR that incorporated both hydrodynamics and SMP effects.

Despite several experimental studies, modelling and simulation of a rotating membrane module is still a nascent topic to date. This is mainly attributed to the poor understanding and great complexity of the hydrodynamics involved. Since mathematical modelling can be used to simulate flux decline and thus potentially afford a greater understanding of the membrane fouling mechanisms involved, the aims of this research work was to create: (i) A fully comprehensive fouling model incorporating all three classical fouling mechanisms for a rotating MBR system; (ii) The model would also incorporate the rotational hydrodynamics and SMP effects; and (iii) Full data sets would be used to validate and calibrate it under short and medium term filtration conditions.

2. THEORETICAL MODELLING APPROACH

Using the power law for non-Newtonian fluids, such as activated sludge, the viscosity (Pa s) of mixed liquor suspended solids (MLSS) in a MBR is proportional to the shear rate as depicted in Equation (1) [9].

$$\mu = m\dot{\gamma}^{n-1} \tag{1}$$

To calculate the shear rate over the rotating membrane, consideration must be given to the type flow through the membrane module. The shear rate based on different flow regimes is computed using Equation (2) [20].

$$\text{if,}\begin{cases} Re_{NN} \leq 2\cdot 10^5, \text{laminar flow}, \dot{\gamma} = 1.81\cdot (k_\omega \cdot \omega)^{1.5}\cdot r_o \cdot \nu^{-0.5} \\ Re_{NN} \geq 2\cdot 10^5, \text{turbulent flow}, \dot{\gamma} = 0.057\cdot (k_\omega \cdot \omega)^{1.8}\cdot {r_o}^{1.6} \cdot \nu^{-0.8} \end{cases} \tag{2}$$

Firstly, it was assumed that the pores were cylindrical and uniformly distributed throughout the membrane, so that fluid flow could be described by Hagen-Poiseuille flow. Hence, pore constriction occurs through all open pores, and gradually the membrane surface becomes obstructed by aggregates forming a somewhat uneven blocked area. Once the pores are blocked by aggregates pore constriction is stopped. Consequently, a cake layer will form over any blocked area. The resistance of this deposit layer is time dependent with regions of greatest resistance delivering the smallest flux. However, in reality the actual membrane fouling process is extremely complex in nature with usually all effects simultaneously occurring. Nevertheless, to simplify the model the above assumptions are made as well as overlooking the effect of frictional forces and temperature. Figure 1 shows the combined fouling mechanisms in the model.

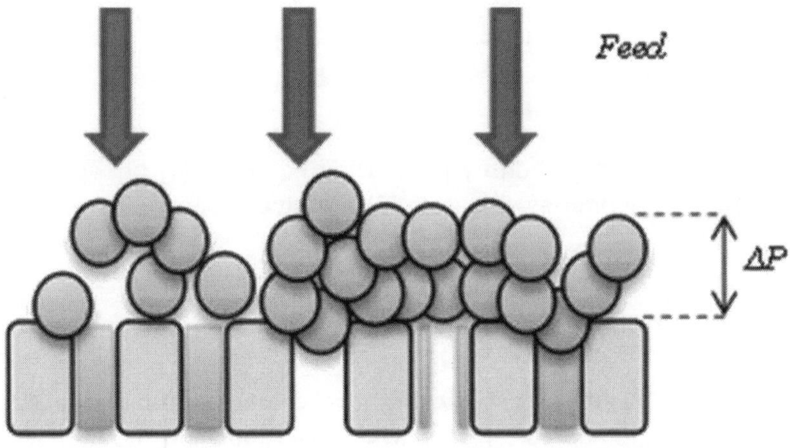

Figure 1. Diagram of the combined fouling mechanisms. Colloids or small particles constrict the pores while larger particles blocked them, forming a cake.

In a similar manner to the reformulation of the Duclos-Orsello *et al.* [18] model undertaken by Paul [19], the bulk concentration C_b (g/L) is replaced by the MLSS concentration, C_{MLSS} (g/L). Although in order to facilitate later model descriptions, the term C_b does still appear in later discussions.

Assuming the membrane rotates around a fixed axis (here defined as an imaginary straight line passing through the shaft) with angular velocity, ω, and using the pore constriction model, the unblocked flux, *Ju* (m s−1), is defined as a function of time within the unblocked area, Au (m^2), as shown in Equation (3) [18,19].

$$\frac{J_u(t)}{J_0} = \frac{1}{(1+\beta \cdot Q_0 \cdot C_{MLSS} \cdot t)^2}; \text{ where } \beta = \frac{\sigma_a}{\pi \cdot (r_p)^2 \cdot \delta_m}$$
$$\rightarrow \tag{3}$$
$$J_u(t) = \frac{r_0'.k_\omega.\omega}{(1+\beta \cdot Q_0 \cdot C_{MLSS} \cdot t)^2}; \text{ where } J_0 = r_0' \cdot k_\omega \cdot \omega$$

As the membrane fouls with time, the unblocked area also decreases at the same rate, and the rate of unblocked area reduction is given in Equation (4).

$$\frac{dA_u}{A_u} = \frac{-\alpha \cdot C_{MLSS} \cdot r_0' \cdot k_\omega \cdot \omega}{(1 + \beta \cdot Q_0 \cdot C_{MLSS} \cdot t)^2} dt \tag{4}$$

Assuming that at time $t = 0$, the initial unblocked area through the membrane is A_{u0} (m^2), then by integrating Equation (4) between the time filtration boundaries, Equation (5) is derived.

$$A_u(t) = A_{u_0} \cdot e^{\frac{\alpha \cdot r_0' \cdot k_\omega \cdot \omega}{\beta \cdot Q_0} \cdot \left(\frac{1}{1+\beta \cdot Q_0 \cdot C_{MLSS} \cdot t} - 1\right)} \tag{5}$$

By combining Equations (3) and (5), the volumetric flow rate (Q_u, m^3/s) through open pores can be calculated as shown in Equation (6).

$$Q_u(t) = A_u(t) \cdot J_u(t) = \frac{A_{u_0} \cdot r_0' \cdot k_\omega \cdot \omega}{(1 + \beta \cdot Q_0 \cdot C_{MLSS} \cdot t)^2} \cdot e^{\left\{\frac{\alpha \cdot r_0' \cdot k_\omega \cdot \omega}{\beta \cdot Q_0} \cdot \left(\frac{1}{1+\beta \cdot Q_0 \cdot C_{MLSS} \cdot t} - 1\right)\right\}} \tag{6}$$

The blocked flux, J_b ($m.s^{-1}$), can be calculated from Equation (7) using Darcy's law and a resistance in-series approach, whilst the trans-membrane pressure (TMP), can be expressed in terms of density and angular velocity in Equation (8) [20].

$$J_b = \frac{TMP}{\mu \cdot (R_{in,b} + R_b)} \tag{7}$$

$$TMP = -PT - \left(\frac{1}{4} \cdot \rho_f \cdot (k_\omega \cdot \omega \cdot r_o)^2\right) \tag{8}$$

Once the pore constriction stops at time, t_b, the time at which a pore was first blocked, $R_{in,b}$ can be calculated from Equation (9) [18].

$$R_{in,b} = R_m (1 + \beta \cdot Q_0 \cdot C_{MLSS} \cdot t_b)^2 \tag{9}$$

The resistance of the particles deposited increases with time due to the growth in mass (or thickness) of the cake layer, and within the cake filtration model, the resistance R_b is determined in Equation (10).

$$\frac{dR_b}{dt} = f' \cdot R' \cdot J_b \cdot C_{MLSS} \tag{10}$$

Assuming, no loss in area, the blocked area, A_b (m^2), is given by Equation (11), and is directly proportional to the unblocked area A_u (m^2) at time t_b.

$$\frac{dA_b}{dt_b} = -\frac{dA_u}{dt_b} \rightarrow A_b(t_b) = \int_0^t \left(\frac{A_{u0} \cdot \alpha \cdot C_{MLSS} \cdot r'_0 \cdot k_\omega \cdot \omega}{(1 + \beta \cdot Q_0 \cdot C_{MLSS} \cdot t_b)^2} \cdot e^{\left\{ \frac{\alpha . r'_0 . k_\omega . \omega}{\beta \cdot Q_0} \left(\frac{1}{1+\beta \cdot Q_0 \cdot C_{MLSS} \cdot t_b} - 1 \right) \right\}} \right) dt_b \tag{11}$$

At low rotational speeds, the flow is considered laminar and by combining Equations (1), (2), (7)–(9) and (11), the volumetric flow rate (Q_b, m^3/s) through the blocked pores is given by Equation (12).

$$Q_b(t) = \frac{-PT - \left(\frac{1}{4} \cdot \rho_f \cdot (k_\omega \cdot \omega \cdot r_o)^2 \right)}{m \cdot (1.81 \cdot (k_\omega \cdot \omega)^{1.5} \cdot r_o \cdot \nu^{-0.5})^{n-1} . (R_m (1 + \beta \cdot Q_0 \cdot C_{MLSS} \cdot t_b)^2 + R_b)} \cdot \int_0^t \left(\frac{A_{u0} \cdot \alpha \cdot C_{MLSS} \cdot r'_0 \cdot k_\omega \cdot \omega}{(1 + \beta \cdot Q_0 \cdot C_{MLSS} \cdot t_b)^2} \cdot e^{\left\{ \frac{\alpha \cdot r'_0 \cdot k_\omega \cdot \omega}{\beta \cdot Q_0} \left(\frac{1}{1+\beta \cdot Q_0 \cdot C_{MLSS} \cdot t_b} - 1 \right) \right\}} \right) dt_b \tag{12}$$

Hence the total volumetric flow rate through the membrane is expressed as the summation of the flow rate through the unblocked Q_u and blocked Q_b pores respectively as shown in Equation (13).

$$Q_t = \frac{A_{u_0} \cdot r'_0 \cdot k_\omega \cdot \omega}{(1 + \beta \cdot Q_0 \cdot C_{MLSS} \cdot t)^2} . e^{\left\{\frac{\alpha \cdot r'_0 \cdot k_\omega \cdot \omega}{\beta \cdot Q_0} . \left(\frac{1}{1+\beta \cdot Q_0 \cdot C_{MLSS} \cdot t} - 1\right)\right\}} + \frac{-PT - \left(\frac{1}{4} . \rho_f . (k_\omega . \omega . r_o)^2\right)}{m \cdot (1.81 \cdot (k_\omega \cdot \omega)^{1.5} \cdot r_o \cdot \nu^{-0.5})^{n-1} \cdot (R_m (1 + \beta \cdot Q_0 \cdot C_{MLSS} \cdot t_b)^2 + R_b)} . \int_0^t \left(\frac{A_{u0} \cdot \alpha \cdot C_{MLSS} \cdot r'_0 \cdot k_\omega \cdot \omega}{(1 + \beta \cdot Q_0 \cdot C_{MLSS} \cdot t_b)^2} . e^{\left\{\frac{\alpha \cdot r'_0 \cdot k_\omega \cdot \omega}{\beta \cdot Q_0} . \left(\frac{1}{1+\beta \cdot Q_0 \cdot C_{MLSS} \cdot t_b} - 1\right)\right\}} \right) dt_b \tag{13}$$

2.1. Hydrodynamic Regime

When describing the hydrodynamic regime in this model, the air scouring flux, J_{air} (m/s), is a key parameter for the management and prevention of membrane fouling in most submerged MBR systems. As such, cake layer growth rate depends on the scouring energy induced by the aeration. Furthermore, rotation in rotating MBRs produces a torque which induces additional shear effects to reduce fouling on the membrane surface. Rightfully so, since the rotating MBR has a very low rotational speed of 2.09 rad/s (or 20 revolutions per minute), the aforementioned scenario and ensuing equations will be correct. However, it is worth mentioning that at very high rotational speeds there is a high possibility that the air scouring effect will be significantly much less than that induce by rotation. The net total effect on the membrane responsible for reducing fouling can tentatively be calculated by the summation of the air scouring and rotational effects. However in hindsight, at some point during the filtration process, these two effects work in opposite directions. This fact alone ultimately poses a physical limitation to the model since a completely isolated hydrodynamic study of the shear stresses will be required, which is not the scope of this study. In the aforementioned scenario, the cake's resistance is consequently decreased to allow the system to gain flux due to these membrane cleaning effects. To account for these changes, an additional removal term was added to the rate of membrane blocked area as shown in Equation (14), and was defined as the flux induced by the air scouring flow combined with rotational effects. This additional removal term is also in-line with Liang *et al.* [21] cake's formulation equation which accounted for the change in reversible fouling due to cake build-up. An analogous reformulation is found in Equation (14) but includes air scouring and rotational effects.

$$\frac{dR_b}{dt} = f' \cdot R' \cdot J_b \cdot C_{MLSS} - g_o \cdot (\alpha_v \cdot J_{air} - k_\omega \cdot \omega \cdot r_o) \cdot \delta \cdot R_c \quad (14)$$

Subsequently, the blocked area, A_b (m^2), is mathematically given by Equation (15).

$$\frac{dA_b}{dt} = \alpha \cdot J_u \cdot A_u \cdot C_{MLSS} - k_{A_b} \cdot (\alpha_v \cdot J_{air} - k_\omega \cdot \omega \cdot r_o) \cdot \theta_c(t) \quad (15)$$

2.2. Soluble Microbial Products' (SMP) Inclusion

To account for variations in the sludge properties, it was assumed that the concentration of MLSS as C_{MLSS} was directly proportional to the concentration of SMPs, C_{SMP}, on the membrane surface. C_{SMP} (g/L) is calculated in accordance with the model of Giraldo and Le Chevallier [22] as shown in Equation (16).

$$C_{SMP} = C_b' \cdot e^{\frac{k_i \cdot \theta_c}{J_{mo}}} \quad (16)$$

Thus, differentiating Equation (3) yields the unblocked flux in Equation (17) with SMP effects included.

$$\frac{dJ_u}{dt} = -2 \cdot \beta \cdot Au_0 \cdot \left(\epsilon_{smp} \cdot C_b' \cdot e^{\frac{k_i.\theta_c}{J_{mo}}}\right).(r'_0 \cdot k_\omega \cdot \omega)^2 \cdot \frac{1}{\left(1 + \beta \cdot Q_0 \cdot \left(\epsilon_{smp} \cdot C_b' \cdot e^{\frac{k_i \cdot \theta_c}{J_{mo}}}\right) \cdot t\right)^3} \quad (17)$$

2.3. Constant Flow/Varying Trans-Membrane Pressure (TMP) Mode

As TMP increases, the total available area for permeate will decrease at a uniform rate such that there exists a time constant, t_c (s^{-1}) < $1/t$, that yields Equation (18) where the time constant is proportional to initial flux.

$$A = A_0(1 - t_c \cdot t) = A_0(1 - K_\alpha \cdot Jm_o \cdot t) \qquad (18)$$

Using a Taylor's expansion of order 1, Equation (18) reduces conveniently into Equation (19).

$$A = A_0 \cdot \ln\left(e \cdot (1 - K_\alpha \cdot Jm_o \cdot t)\right) \equiv A_0 \cdot e^{(-K_\alpha \cdot Jm_o \cdot t)} \qquad (19)$$

However, this reformulation has an extreme limitation in that simulated values will be under estimated after a certain period of time due to the truncation induced by the Taylor's expansion term. For the same *Kα*, both the reformulation and original area model will exhibit almost similar behaviour so long as the following is true: $0 < K_\alpha \cdot Jm_o \cdot t \leq 0.1 \rightarrow K_\alpha \leq \frac{0.1}{Jm_o \cdot t}$; Outside this range, it is expected that large errors of more than 10% would occur.

In this model and as experienced in practice, as the pore constriction continues, there is an exponential increase in TMP. Since total membrane resistance (*R*total) is the summation of cake's resistance and all other mechanisms, this is approximated in the model as a constant term known as ϕ as shown in Equation (20).

$$R_{total} = (R_{in,b} + \varphi R_c) \qquad (20)$$

Equation (21) is yielded by using Darcy's law and differentiating the TMP with respect to filtration time, *t*.

$$\frac{\mu}{A_0} \cdot \left(\lim_{\Delta t \to 0}\left(\frac{\Delta Q}{\Delta t}\right)\right) = \frac{A}{A_0} \cdot \left(\frac{d(TMP)}{dt} \cdot \left(\frac{1}{R_{total}}\right) + TMP. \frac{d\left(\frac{1}{R_{total}}\right)}{dt}\right) \qquad (21)$$

Since the flow, *Q* (m^3/s), is kept constant, d*Q*/d*t* = *0*, and thus combining Equations (19)–(21), yields the final and full model formulation shown in Equations (22) and (23). Equation (22) also includes the specific cake resistance (m^{-2}) formulation via the Carman–Kozeny equation [22]. It was assumed that the particles forming the sludge floc are spherical in shape. In reality however, characteristics of activated sludge floc viewed under the microscope show a varying difference in the particles' shape. Thus, this assumption induces a limitation to the derived model.

$$\mathrm{TMP}(t) = \mathrm{TMP}_0 . \frac{\left(R_m \cdot ((1+\beta \cdot Q_0 \cdot C_{MLSS} \cdot t_b)^2 - 1) + \varphi \cdot \left(\frac{180 \cdot (1-\varepsilon_c)^2}{{d_{pi}}^2 \cdot {\varepsilon_c}^3} \cdot \frac{C_d \cdot J_{m_o} \cdot t}{(1-\tau) \cdot \rho_b}\right) + R_{t0}\right)}{(1 - K_\alpha . Jm_o . t) . R_{t0}} \tag{22}$$

$$\mathrm{PT}(t) = -\frac{1}{4} \cdot \rho_f \cdot (k_\omega \cdot \omega \cdot r_o)^2 - \mu \cdot Jm_o \cdot e^{(K_\alpha \cdot J_{m_o} \cdot t)} . \left(R_m \cdot ((1+\beta \cdot Q_0 \cdot C_{MLSS} \cdot t_b)^2 - 1) + \varphi \cdot \left(\frac{180 . (1-\varepsilon_c)^2}{{d_{pi}}^2 \cdot {\varepsilon_c}^3} \cdot \frac{C_d \cdot J_{m_o} \cdot t}{(1-\tau) \cdot \rho_b}\right) + R_{t0}\right) \tag{23}$$

3. MATERIALS AND METHODS

3.1. Materials

The rotating MBR pilot unit used to generate short and medium term filtration data for testing of the fouling model consisted of a ultra-filtration (UF) module of 36 circular flat membrane sheets as shown on Figure 2 (FUV-185-A15R Flexidisks by Avanti Membrane Technology, Walnut, CA, USA). These circular membrane sheets were attached to a single shaft rotating via an electrical motor with an operational speed of 20 revolutions per minute (RPM). Each membrane sheet in disc form was composed of hydrophilic, low fouling PVDF (Polyvinylidene Fluoride) with the manifold that collected the permeate flow being located in the single shaft. TMP, dissolved oxygen levels, temperature, pH, permeate flux and air scouring flow rates were all measured and logged automatically by the pilot unit itself (RPU-185 Flexidisks MBR System by Avanti Membrane Technology, Walnut, CA, USA). The viscosity of the fluid was measured daily by the aid of rotating viscometers (Rotary-Viscometer ASTM by PCE Instruments UK Ltd, Southampton, UK and High Shear CAP-2000+ by Brookfield Viscometers Ltd, Essex, UK); while the MLSS concentration was constantly logged by a MLSS analyser (GE-138 MLSS Suspended Solids Sludge Concentration Meter Analyser Monitor by A. Yite Technology Group, Wanchai, Hong Kong).

Manufactured in Taiwan, this unique, bespoke pilot unit was designed as a research tool and included all data logging and measuring system interfaces. An anoxic tank was also included for de-nitrification experiments but this option was never used for the data sets used in this study. Figure 3 shows a partial picture and set-up of this research rig in operation.

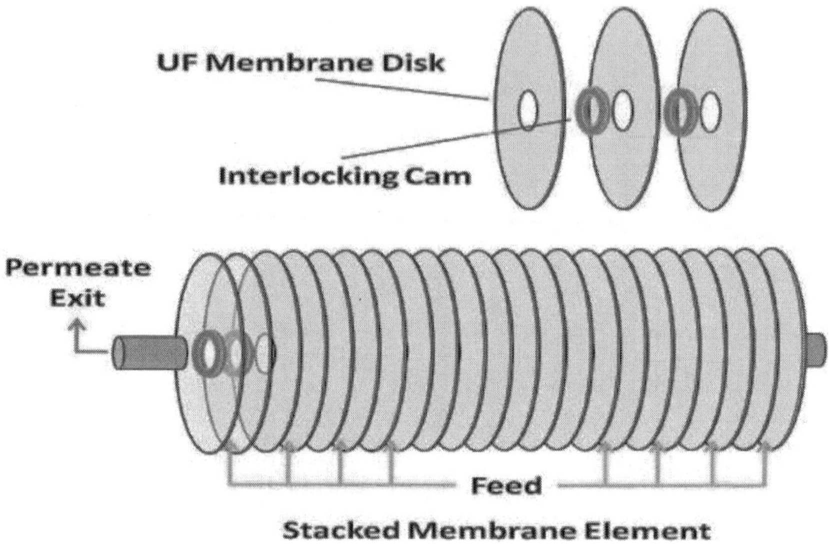

Figure 2. Rotating membrane module FUV-185-A15R manufactured by Avanti Membrane Technology, Walnut, CA, USA.

Figure 3. Partial picture and set-up of the rotating membrane bioreactor (MBR) system RPU-185 (Avanti Membrane Technology, Walnut, CA, USA) in operation. The membrane module is located in the batch tank for filtration purposes.

Table 1 shows this unit's membrane dimensioning and a general overview of the operating conditions of the MBR system as provided by the manufacturer.

Table 1. Dimensions and operating conditions of the FUV-185-A15R Flexidisks.

Description	Unit	Values
Membrane outer diameter	m	0.177
Membrane inner diameter	m	0.055
Membrane area	m^2	1.6006
Angular velocity	rad/s	2.094
Permeate flux	$L.m^2.H^{-1}$	Up to 50
TSS (Total suspended solids)	$g\ L^{-1}$	8–30
Transmembrane pressure	bar	≤ 2

3.2. Filtration Experiments

This MBR plant was initially seeded with activated sludge supplied by Thames Water (UK) and was semi-batch fed a synthetic wastewater made up using a standard recipe to mimic an influent source. MLSS concentrations were kept between the range of 3.34 and 4.26 g/L by periodic excess sludge wasting. The influent had an average pH of 8.2 and experiments were carried out at constant room temperature (23 °C).

3.2.1. Shear and Viscosity Experiments

Using the Brookfield rotating viscometer (mentioned in Section 3.1) which also acted as rheometer, measurements were taken following protocols in-line with Yang *et al.* [23] and Ratkovich *et al.* [24]. The readily designed software program for the apparatus was used for system control and collection of data. The sludge was tested at constant room temperature of 23 °C at MLSS of 4.26 g/L (although data points at MLSS range of 3.2–4.6 g/L were also analysed).

Additionally, the shear stress and viscosity were carefully tested in shear rate range of 10–350 s^{-1}. Although full on rheology tests were not carried on the activated sludge to ascertain its properties more precisely, the data collected appeared consistent. It should be noted that at MLSS of 3.34 g/L, the viscosity readings were largely similar to those measured at 4.26 g/L with a deviation of roughly 4% on the data. Thus, both yielded fairly similar *m* and *n* values which were kept constant during simulation and this was further confirmed via sensitivity analysis (data obtained is further discussed in Section 4).

3.2.2. Flux Steps Filtration Tests

Flux steps tests were carried out using standard protocols in-line with Le Clech *et al.* [25], with four flux steps being carried out for each variation in MLSS concentration. Flux steps up were carried out at constant TMPs of 15, 30, 45 and 58 kPa. The corresponding initial flow rates were respectively 1×10^{-5}, 1.83×10^{-5}, 2.25×10^{-5} and 2.75×10^{-5} m^3/s. Although data was constantly being logged, for the sake of simplicity and to keep model computation time down to a minimum, only the average data point for every 5 min of filtration time was actually used in the simulation study with the total filtration period being two hours. This meant a total of 25 data points were generated for each individual MLSS concentration. After each flux step testing, a chemical backwash was carried out with 125 mg/L worth of sodium hypochlorite solution and the membrane resistance was calculated to measure the extent of irreversible fouling. On unit start up, the clean membrane resistance was determined to be 6.26×10^{11} m^{-1}, while the cake water content, τ, was found to be 0.456 on average.

3.2.3. SMP Inclusion Experiments

In order to study the implications of foulants (*i.e.*, SMPs) and cake formation in relation to the MLSS concentration, after a filtration process, the total cake thickness was measured for desired bulk MLSS concentration used and was then divided by flux. This value was later referred to as cake thickness ratio. The MLSS concentrations used for cake thickness measurements varied from 1.2 to 4.3 g/L. The initial flow rate starting was 1×10^{-5} m^3/s and MBR was operated under constant TMP of 15 kPa.

3.2.4. Constant Flow Rate Experiments

The filtration process and ensuing experiments occurred under constant flow MBR operation. The flow rate was 8.67×10^{-6} m^3/s while the corresponding starting TMP was 12 kPa. In total, 25 TMP data points each averaged at 5 min interval for bulk MLSS concentrations at respectively 3.34 and 4.26 g/L were obtained and thus, plotted against the filtration time.

4. RESULTS AND DISCUSSION

4.1. Shear and Viscosity Relationship

A major parameter included in this model formulation was the combined shear due to both rotation and aeration. To that end, the viscosity of the MLSS at 4.26 g/L concentration was measured at different shear rates. The rotational speed of the spindle was 20 RPM and this equated to a shear rate of 26 s^{-1}. Results indicated that the fluid's viscosity had decreased much faster at higher shear rate (by almost 56%), which was expected since the calculated radial Reynolds number (Re_{NN}) showed that the flow was laminar. Furthermore, it should be noted that since activated sludge is a shear thinning fluid (as seen in literature), the rheological measurement must be kept in the laminar regime otherwise the outcome of the rheometer becomes increasingly hard to interpret.

Parameters m and n in Equation (1) which are the coefficients controlling the shear rate and viscosity respectively were determined by plotting logarithm of viscosity against logarithm of shear rate using a linear curve fitting process in Matlab.

Figure 4 shows the viscosity plotted against shear rate. The coefficient m was found to be 0.0113 whilst n gave a value of 0.761. The coefficient of determination for the linear fit process was 0.968 indicating a respectable model fit. A value of $n$less than one indicated that the fluid had deviated from Newtonian behaviour. The value

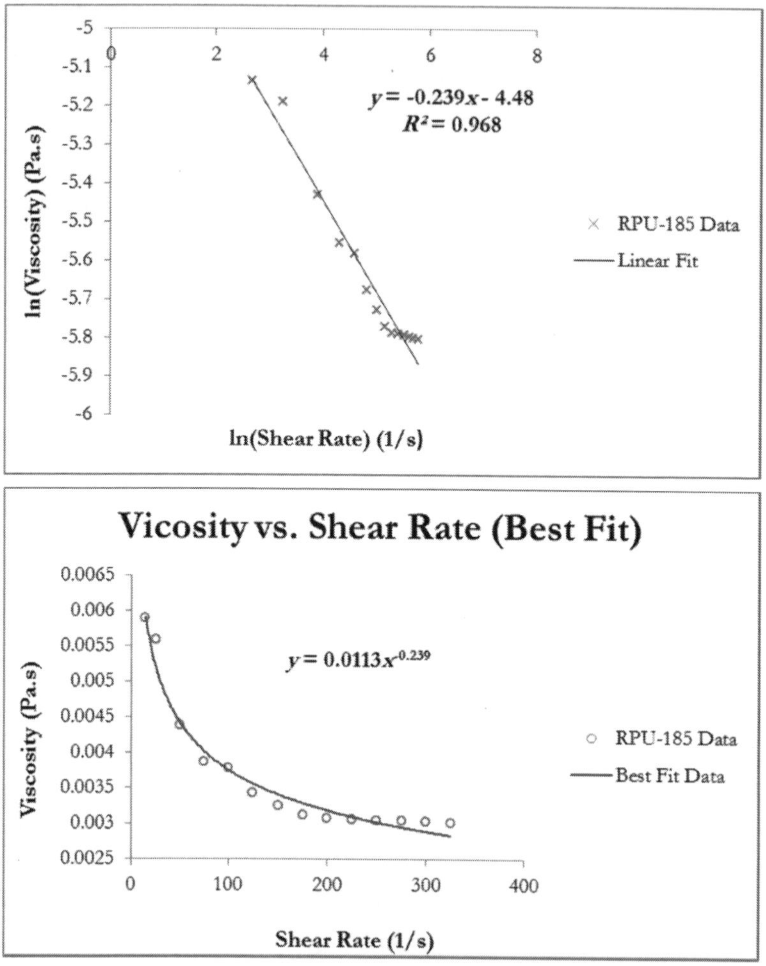

Figure 4. Viscosity plotted against shear rate for rotating MBR system (RPU-185).

of *m* was considered reasonable for this type of MBR operated at a relatively low MLSS of 4.26 g/L.

4.2. Model Validation-Hydrodynamic Regime

The earlier developed fouling model was tested for accuracy using the data generated from the unique hydrodynamic regime employed by this rotating MBR pilot unit. The bulk MLSS concentrations used for all the flux steps were 3.34 and 4.26 g/L. The flow regimes were laminar which were well within expectations since calculated Re_{NN} values were much less than 2×10^5.

The air scouring coefficient, α_v, and the resistance distribution, δ, were obtained via sensitivity analysis. The values found were respectively 0.0292 and 4.6×10^{-4} m^{-1} for α_v and δ. The air scouring flow rate of 3.55×10^{-4} m^3/s was also kept the same for all simulations. Due to varying fluxes the values of the term k_ω were also obtained via sensitivity analysis and are shown in Table 2. These aforementioned and determined values were used in all subsequent simulations to determine the best fit values for this model. To ensure validity, only the 6 most important parameters pertaining the three fouling mechanisms were used for data and curve fitting during simulations and these were $f'{\cdot}R'$, α, β, R_{bo}/R_m, g_o and k_{Ab}. These best fit simulation values were attained by minimising the sum of squared residuals between the model and the collected experimental data. This was used in conjunction with "Genetic Algorithm" function in the Matlab software package with an initial population large enough for the data set used to converge to the minimal possible error. The simulations were performed for each TMP at respectively 15, 30, 45 and 58 kPa for MLSS concentrations of 3.34 and 4.26 g/L. The term σ_a was calculated upon obtaining the fitting value of β since the membrane pore size was known. Table 2 summarises best fit values for all four flux steps for the rotating membrane FUV-185-A15R (Avanti Membrane Technology, Walnut, CA, USA).

At a constant TMP of 15 kPa and MLSS concentration of 4.26 g/L, after two hours of filtration time, the flux had declined at a steady rate and had gone down by 60%. A similar decrease was observed for MLSS concentration of 3.34 g/L. This gradual drop in flux is as expected and in-line with critical flux theory. At a constant TMP of 30 kPa, the flux increased from initial value 1×10^{-5} to 1.83×10^{-5} m^3/s. This was within expectations since flux increases with increasing TMP. After two hours of filtration of a MLSS concentration 4.26 g/L, the flux had declined by 48% from its original value. Again this gradual drop in flux is as expected although not as much as theory would predict.

Table 2. Best fit simulation values and key data used during simulations that includes hydrodynamics effects.

Parameter	Unit	15 kPa Flux Step	30 kPa Flux Step	45 kPa Flux Step	58 kPa Flux Step
		Best Fit Simulation Values			
g_o	–	21.792	3.178	70.628	35.6743
k_{Ab}	–	29.787	229.77	29.27	0.382
R_{bo}/R_m	–	0.174	0.867	0.239	0.390
$f'\cdot R'$	m/kg	489.04×10^9	435.88×10^9	490.67×10^9	65.72×10^9
α	m^2/kg	0.332	0.0579	4.929	0.670
β	kg	2.342	0.856	1.751	0.472
		Key Data Used During Simulations			
m	Pa s^n	0.0113 ± 0.01	0.0113 ± 0.01	0.0113 ± 0.01	0.0113 ± 0.01
n	–	0.761 ± 0.02	0.761 ± 0.02	0.761 ± 0.02	0.761 ± 0.02
α_v	–	0.0292	0.0292	0.0292	0.0292
δ	m^{-1}	4.6×10^{-4}	4.6×10^{-4}	4.6×10^{-4}	4.6×10^{-4}
k_ω	rad^{-1}	2.446×10^{-5}	4.484×10^{-5}	5.503×10^{-5}	6.725×10^{-5}
σ_a	kg m^3	1.788×10^{-16}	6.535×10^{-17}	1.336×10^{-16}	3.601×10^{-17}

Figure 5 shows the normalised volumetric flow rate and the total resistances ratios plotted against the filtration time at constant TMP of 15 kPa (flux step data), for MLSS concentrations of 3.34 and 4.26 g/L for the rotating membrane FUV-185-A15R; with the solid lines representing the best fit simulation data. The total resistance was calculated using Darcy's law. The resistances displayed a rather linear trend, suggesting fouling was caused by the combination of all three fouling mechanisms. A weak caking layer showcased by a relatively small R_{bo}, a big cake removal factor g_o and almost equally big blocked pores area constant k_{Ab}, suggested that fouling was dominated by pore constriction (as $\beta >> \alpha$).

Figure 6 shows the normalised volumetric flow rate and the total resistances ratios plotted *versus* the filtration time at constant TMP of 30 kPa (flux step data), for MLSS concentrations of 3.34 and 4.26 g/L for the rotating membrane FUV-185-A15R; with the solid lines representing the best fit simulation data. The resistance-time plot, again, seems to indicate that fouling could be attributed to the combined effect of all three mechanisms. A strong caking layer showcased by a relatively bigger R_{bo} and a small cake removal factor g_o, all seemingly implied that fouling was dominated by both cake filtration and pore blocking mechanisms.

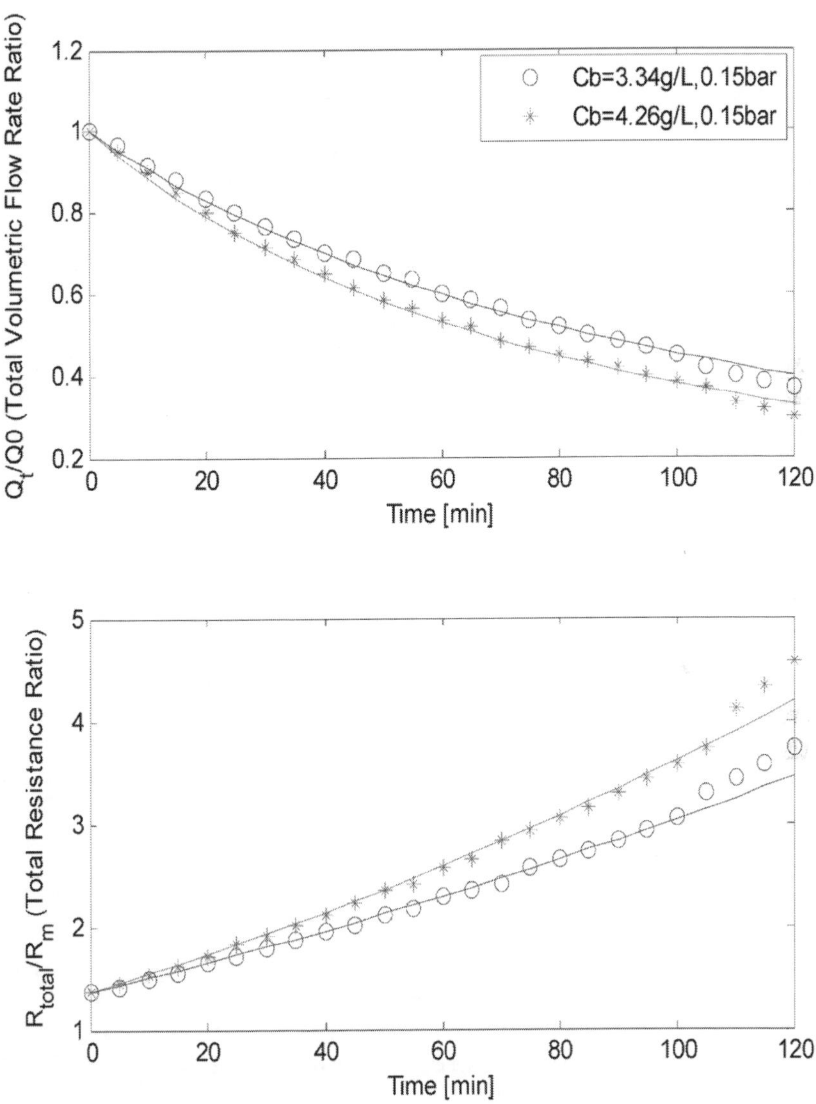

Figure 5. Flux decline and total resistance for flux step at trans-membrane pressure (TMP) 15 kPa for FUV-185-A15R.

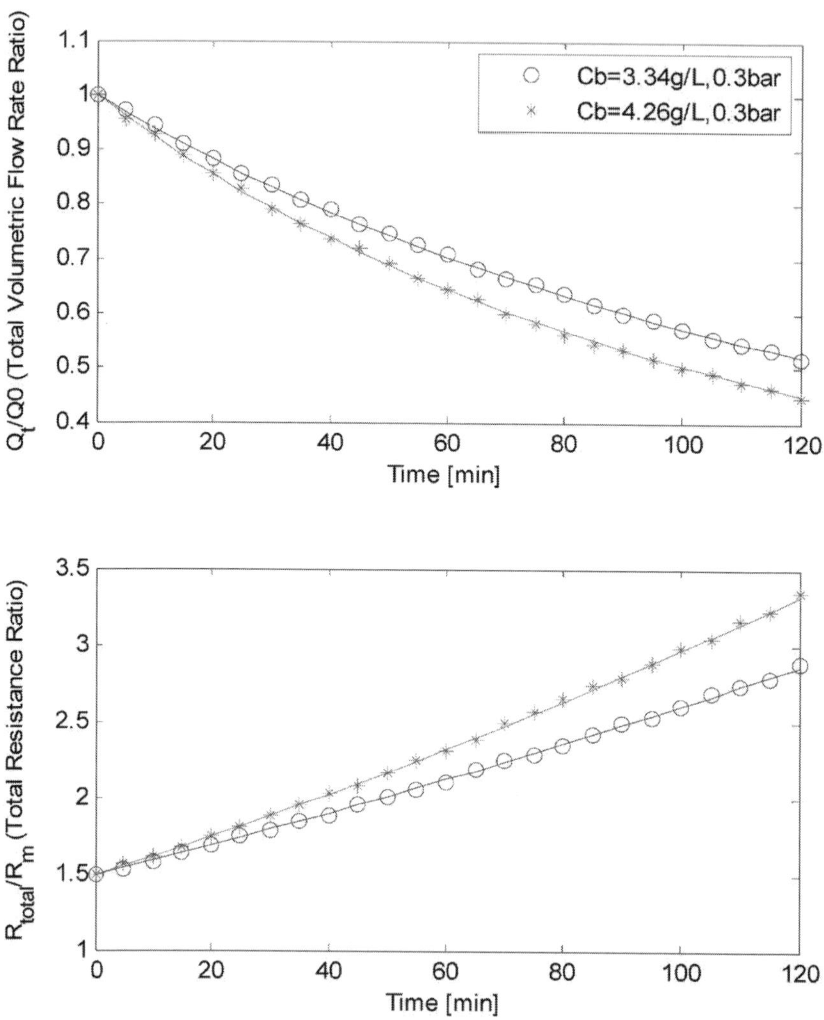

Figure 6. Flux decline and total resistance for flux step at TMP 30 kPa for FUV-185-A15R.

At a constant TMP of 45 kPa and MLSS concentration of 3.34 and 4.26 g/L, the initial flow rate was 2.25×10^{-5} m^3/s. After two hours of filtration time, at MLSS concentration of 4.26 g/L, the flux had decreased drastically and gone down by 85%. A similar reduction was detected at MLSS concentration of 3.34 g/L. As expected this meant that not only had the initial flux increased at higher TMPs, but also that the flux decline rate had increased with more pressure. These findings are in-line with theory since a membrane is likely to foul more quickly especially when approaching or exceeding critical flux. At a constant TMP of 58 kPa, the initial flow rate increased from 2.25 $\times 10^{-5}$ to 2.75 $\times 10^{-5}$ m^3/s. Results showed that at MLSS concentration of 4.26 g/L, the flux had still decreased considerably, and had gone down by only 62%; which is a consistent decline when compared with the 45 kPa TMP flux step data.

Figure 7 depicts the effects of the fouling behaviour of FUV-185-A15R, using both the normalised volumetric flow rate and total resistance ratios for MLSS concentrations of 3.34 and 4.26 g/L at a constant TMP of 45 kPa (with the solid lines representing the best fit simulation data). Due to a colossal drop in flux, the total resistance had also increased at an exponential rate. Although fouling may have been caused by the combined effect of all three fouling mechanisms, it can be argued that the fouling was mainly dominated by pore blocking. A weak caking layer showcased by a relatively small R_{b0}, a very big cake removal factor g_o and pore blocking parameter β being roughly four times that of the pore constriction, clearly suggested that fouling was dominated by the pore blocking mechanism.

Figure 8 depicts the fouling behaviour of FUV-185-A15R, by using both the normalised volumetric flow rate and total resistance ratios for MLSS concentrations of 3.34 and 4.26 g/L at constant TMP of 58 kPa. The solid lines represent the best fit data obtained from the simulation. The total resistance seemed to intrinsically increase linearly with filtration time, albeit at a much higher rate. This is arguably because fouling was caused by a combine effect of the three fouling mechanisms. Pore blocking factor α and pore constriction β are of almost equal value, suggesting neither of the two mechanisms was dominant. Furthermore, R_{b0} being almost half R_m and the somewhat small blocked pores area constantk_{Ab} suggested cake filtration also took place although to a lesser degree than the other fouling mechanisms.

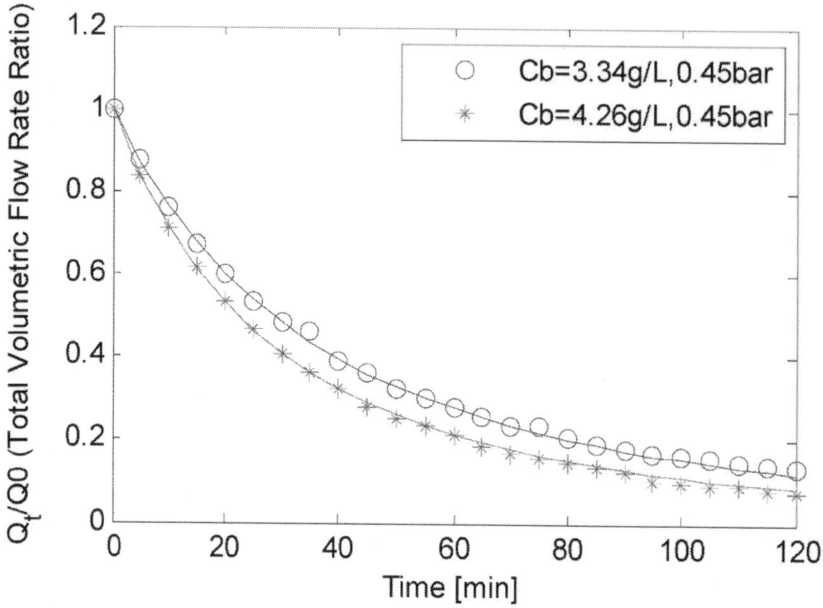

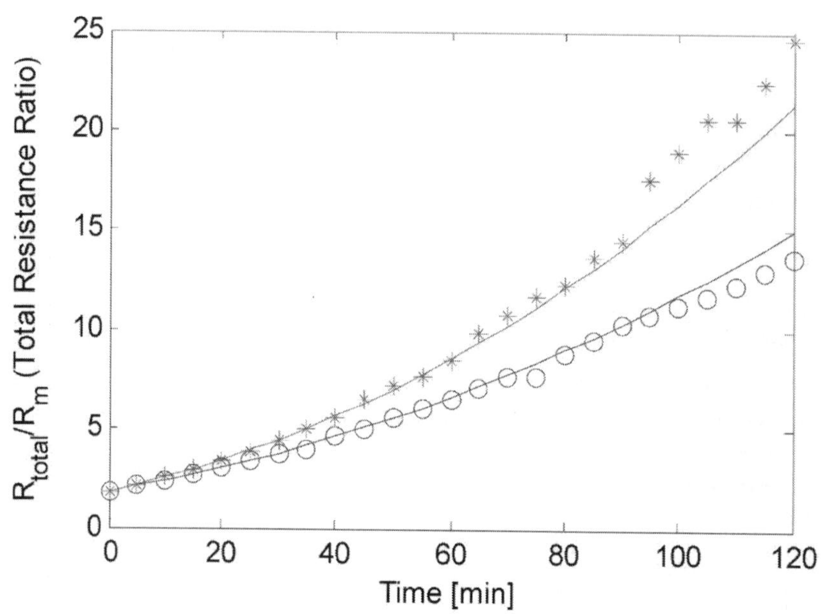

Figure 7. Flux decline and total resistance for flux step at TMP 45 kPa for FUV-185-A15R.

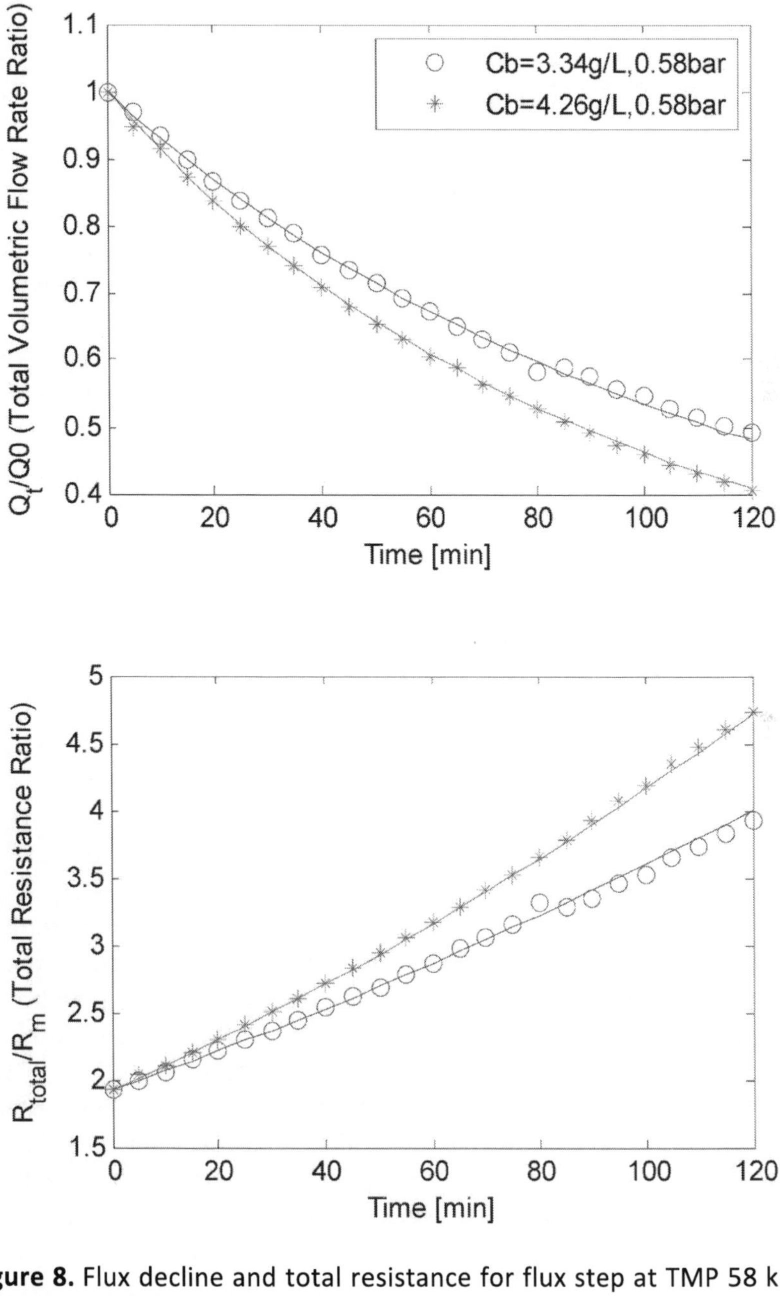

Figure 8. Flux decline and total resistance for flux step at TMP 58 kPa for FUV-185-A15R.

Overall, the modelling calculations are seemingly in reasonable agreement with the collected data, with a 25% deviation on the resistance curve at constant TMP of 45 kPa (*i.e.*, for MLSS concentration of 4.26 g/L) for the end data points. This could be attributed to a permeate restart needed before the flux stepping was carried out due to the low batch tank fluid levels.

As a short conclusion, it was noticed that viscosity indirectly affects fouling. A less viscous mixed liquor under the same operating conditions as those experienced by higher viscous mixed liquor will likely foul less (*i.e.*, flux likely to drop slower). This is because, generally, higher viscosities are associated to high MLSS concentrations.

4.3. SMP Inclusion

Using Equations (16) and (17), and then by plotting logarithm of MLSS concentration against cake thickness ratio whilst also doing a linear fit using Matlab's polyfit function, the k_i and $\epsilon_{SMP}\, C_b'$ values were obtained as shown in Figure 9; with solid line being best fit for a two hour filtration period. Simulation best fit value for $\epsilon_{SMP}.C_b'$ in g/L was found to be 1.054 while k_i in s^{-1} was 0.039 respectively. At first glance, the exponential fit appears to not accurately predict SMP concentration for MLSS concentrations of 2.82, 4.12 and 4.26 g/L respectively. This is likely because their corresponding cake thickness values were simply interpolated based on other experimentally measured cake thicknesses. However, upon closer inspection, the fit seems to succinctly describe the fouling behaviour of the membrane. Thus, the model predicts that for a bigger thickness cake to form, an exponentially bigger MLSS concentration is required and with it, a subsequent increase in SMP concentration on the membrane surface. This appears to explain why higher MLSS concentrations give rise to faster total flux decline whilst membrane resistances climb rapidly at the same rate. This finding is in-line with Yuan *et al.* [26] study.

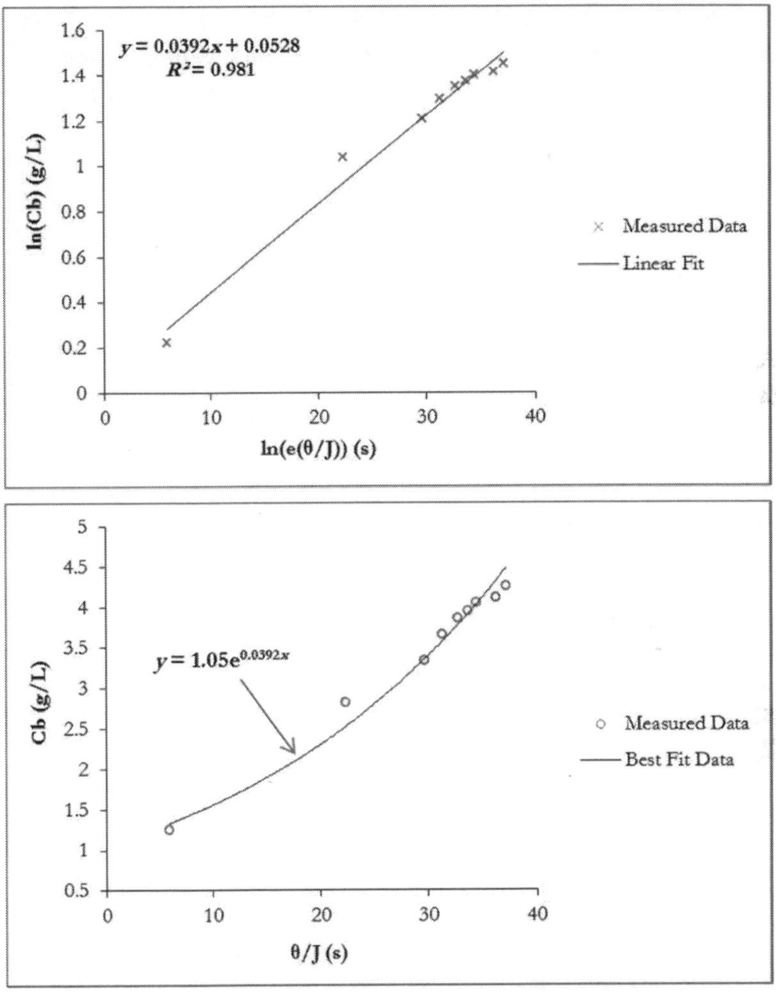

Figure 9. Mixed liquor suspended solids (MLSS) concentration plotted against cake thickness ratio for rotating MBR system.

4.4. Constant Flow Rate/Varying TMP Mode

The collected experimental data indicated that TMP had increased by almost 88% for MLSS of 4.26 g/L and 85% for MLSS of 3.34 g/L. An increase in TMP is a clear indication that the membrane had become progressively fouled. The fouling rate seemingly increased with bigger MLSS concentration values, as seen by higher TMP readings at MLSS concentrations. As already explained, this is likely due to the fact that at higher MLSS concentrations more caking is observed due to the higher solids content in the liquor, causing more clogging of the membrane and thus progressively increasing the TMP over time.

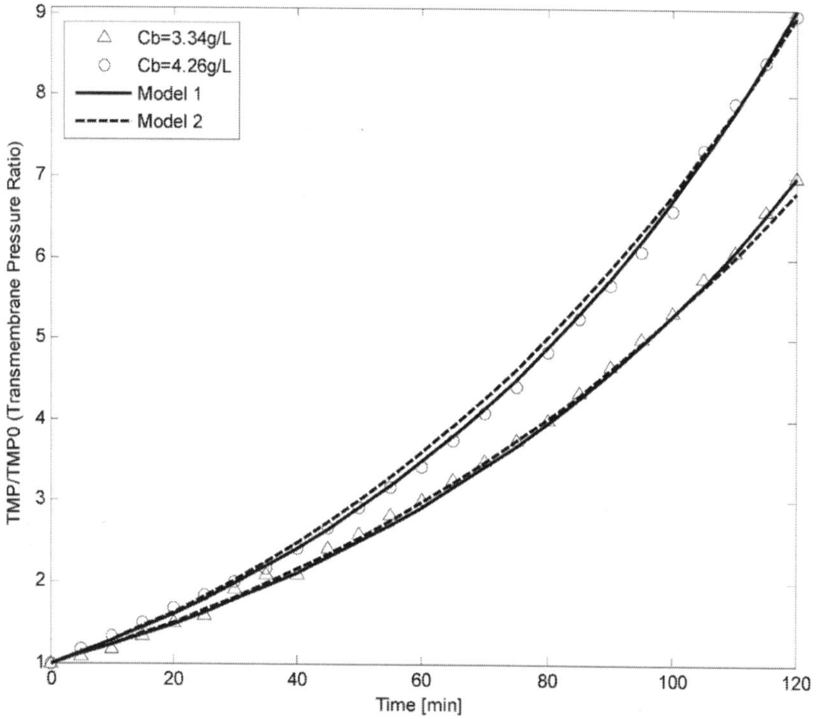

Figure 10. TMP plotted against filtration time at constant flow rate of 8.67×10^{-6} m^3/s for rotating MBR.

Figure 10 shows best fit solutions for two different models that depict constant flow rate/varying TMP operation. Model 1 is derived from Equation (18) whilst Model 2 is derived from Equation (19) which relies on the truncated Taylor's expansion. Between time intervals from 30 to 90 min for MLSS concentration of 4.26 g/L, Model 2 had an error deviation of 9% on simulated data when compared with Model 1. This is a direct consequence of the Taylor's expansion truncation error. Thus, Model 2 predicted the available remaining area to be much lower than expected and so it predicts higher TMP values than Model 1. This is reflected in parameter K_α where for Model 2 it had a value of 10.53 while for Model 1 it had a value of 9.975. The bigger this value the higher the predicted TMP will be with more subsequent fouling. The shape of the curve of TMP *versus* time indicates that fouling was likely caused by cake filtration although initially induced by the pore constriction effects, with β found to be 16.308 for Model 1 and 17.58 for Model 2 respectively. Once again, the best fit simulation parameters for these two models were attained by using Matlab's Genetic Algorithm function. It was found that for both models k_ω amounted to 1.4044×10^{-5} whilst ϕ was 0.0939 for Model 1 and 0.06 for Model 2 respectively.

5. CONCLUSIONS

In this study, a unique rotating MBR fouling model was formulated from prior extensive work produced by Duclos-Orsello *et al.* [18] and later by Paul [19]. It was tested using relevant data sets, and the rotation efficiency in terms of fouling prevention was estimated to be 12%. This suggests that prevention of cake build-up and fouling is mostly accomplished by air scouring. New parameters related to the shear hydrodynamics, especially those describing the rotational membrane effects, were determined for the first time and seemed reasonably realistic and consistent with good agreement achieved using experimental data. This work initially indicates this model gives a decent representation and description of the fouling mechanisms occurring within a rotating MBR system. To further develop this model, it needs to be calibrated using data sets generated by the rotating MBR RPU-185 for long term filtration. Furthermore, by turning-off the rotating terms and obtaining a linear model, it can be compared to a non-rotating MBR model and, thereby, the true extent of the rotation on fouling reduction can be measured for this pilot unit.

ACKNOWLEDGMENTS

The authors would like to acknowledge Avanti Technology (USA) for their technical contribution and The Royal Society (UK) for providing funding to allow this work to proceed.

AUTHOR CONTRIBUTIONS

The experimental work, data processing, and model development in this study were carried out by Franck Anderson Jones under the direction and supervision of Parneet Paul, and is based upon earlier work originally carried by Parneet Paul [19]. The first draft of the original manuscript was prepared by Franck Anderson Jones, and later versions were revised and edited extensively by Parneet Paul before publication. This included broadening the scope and nature of this study to be in-line with other researchers working in this field.

CONFLICTS OF INTEREST

The authors declare no conflict of interest.

REFERENCES

1. Bhattacharjee, C.; Bhattacharya, P.K. Ultrafiltration of black liquor using rotating disk membrane module. Sep. Purif. Technol. 2005, 49, 281–290.

2. Jaffrin, M.Y.; Ding, L.H.; Akoum, O.; Brou, A. A hydrodynamic comparison between rotating disk and vibratory dynamic filtration systems. J. Membr. Sci. 2004, 242, 155–167.

3. Al-Akoum, O.; Jaffrin, M.Y.; Ding, L.H.; Paullier, P.; Vanhoutte, C. An hydrodynamic investigation of microfiltration and ultrafiltration in a vibrating membrane module. J. Membr. Sci. 2002, 197, 37–52.

4. Bouzerar, R.; Paullier, P.; Jaffrin, M.Y. Concentration of mineral suspensions and industrial effluents using a rotating disk dynamic filtration module. Desalination 2003, 158, 79–85.

5. Frappart, M.; Jaffrin, M.Y.; Ding, L.H. Reverse osmosis of diluted skim milk: Comparison of results obtained from vibratory and rotating disk modules. Sep. Purif. Technol. 2008, 60, 321–329.

6. Sarkar, D.; Bhattacharjee, C. Modeling and analytical simulation of rotating disk ultra-filtration module. J. Membr. Sci.2008, 320, 344–355.

7. Sarkar, D.; Datta, D.; Sen, D.; Bhattacharjee, C. Simulation of continuous stirred rotating disk-membrane module: An approach based on surface renewal theory. Chem. Eng. Sci. 2011, 66, 2554–2567.

8. Torras, C.; Pallares, J.; Valls, R.G.; Jaffrin, M.Y. CFD simulation of a rotating disk flat membrane module. Desalination2006, 200, 453–455.

9. Bentzen, T.R.; Ratkovich, N.; Madsen, S.; Jensen, J.C.; Bak, S.N.; Rasmussen, M.R. Analytical and numerical modelling of Newtonian and non-Newtonian liquid in a rotational cross-flow MBR. Water Sci. Technol. 2012, 66, 2318–2327.

10. Engler, J.; Mark, R.W. Particle fouling of a rotating membrane disk. Water Res. 2000, 34, 557–565.

11. Jørgensen, M.K.; Malene, T.P.; Morten, L.C. Dependence of shear and concentration on fouling in a membrane bioreactor with rotating membrane discs. AIChE J. 2014, 60, 706–715.

12. Judd, S. The MBR Book: Principles and Applications of Membrane Bioreactors, 1st ed.; Elsevier: Amsterdam, the Netherlands, 2006.

13. Rosenberger, S.; Laabs, C.; Lesjean, B.; Gnirss, R.; Amy, G.; Jekel, M.; Schrotter, J.C. Impact of colloidal and soluble organic material on membrane performance in membrane bioreactors for municipal wastewater treatment. Water Res. 2006, 40, 710–720.

14. Ahn, Y.T.; Choi, Y.K.; Jeong, H.S.; Shin, S.R. Modeling of extracellular polymeric substances and soluble microbial products production in a submerged MBR at various SRTs. Water Sci. Technol. 2006, 53, 209–216.

15. Hermia, J. Constant pressure blocking filtration laws-application to power-law non-Newtonian fluids. Chem. Eng. Res. Des. 1982, 60a, 183–187.

16. Meng, F.; Zhang, H.; Li, Y.; Zhang, X.; Yang, F. Application of fractal permeation model to investigate membrane fouling in membrane bioreactor. J. Membr. Sci. 2005, 262, 107–116.

17. Liu, R.; Huang, X.; Sun, Y.F.; Qian, Y. Hydrodynamic effect on sludge accumulation over membrane surfaces in a submerged membrane bioreactor. Process Biochem. 2003, 39, 157–163.

18. Duclos-Orsello, C.; Li, W.; Hob, C.-C. A three mechanism model to describe fouling of microfiltration membranes. J. Membr. Sci. 2006, 280, 856–866.

19. Paul, P. Development and testing of a fully adaptable membrane bioreactor fouling model for a sidestream configuration system. Membranes 2013, 3, 24–43.

20. Jaffrin, M.Y. Dynamic shear-enhanced membrane filtration: A review of rotating disks, rotating membranes and vibrating systems. J. Membr. Sci. 2008, 324, 7–25.

21. Liang, S.; Song, L.; Tao, G.; Kekre, K.A.; Seah, H. A modeling study of fouling development in membrane bioreactors for wastewater treatment. Water Environ. Res. 2006, 78, 857–863.

22. Giraldo, E.; Le Chevallier, M. Dynamic mathematical modelling of membrane fouling in submerged membrane bioreactors. In Proceedings of the Water Environment Federation; Session 61 through Session 70. Water Environment Federation: Alexandria, VA, USA, 2006; Volume 19, pp. 4895–4913.

23. Yang, F.; Bick, A.; Shandalov, S.; Brenner, A.; Oron, G. Yield stress and rheological characteristics of activated sludge in an airlift membrane bioreactor. J. Membr. Sci. 2009, 334, 83–90.

24. Ratkovich, N.R.; Horn, W.; Helmus, F.; Rosenberger, S.; Naessens, W.; Nopens, I.; Bentzen, T.R. Activated Sludge Rheology: A critical review on data collection and modelling. Water Res. 2013, 47, 463–482.

25. Le Clech, P.; Jefferson, B.; Chang, I.S.; Judd, S.J. Critical flux determination by the flux-step method in a submerged membrane bioreactor. J. Membr. Sci. 2003, 227, 81–93.

26. Yuan, W.; Kocic, A.; Andrew, L.Z. Analysis of humic acid fouling during microfiltration using a pore blockage–cake filtration mode. J. Membr. Sci. 2002, 198, 51–62.

Chapter 6

Analysis of Gene Expression Signatures for Osteogenic 3D Perfusion-Bioreactor Cell Cultures Based on a Multifactorial DoE Approach

Ioannis Papantoniou [1,2], Maarten Sonnaert [1,3], Toon Lambrechts [1,4], Jean-Marie Aerts [1,4], Lies Geris [1,5], Frank P. Luyten [1,2] and Jan Schrooten [1,3,*]

[1] *Prometheus, Division of Skeletal Tissue Engineering, KU Leuven, Onderwijs en Navorsing 1 (+8), Herestraat 49-PB813, B-3000 Leuven, Belgium*

[2] *Skeletal Biology and Engineering Research Center, KU Leuven, Onderwijs en Navorsing 1 (+8), Herestraat 49-PB813, B-3000 Leuven, Belgium*

[3] *Department of Materials Engineering, KU Leuven, Kasteelpark Arenberg 44-PB 2450, B-3001 Heverlee, Belgium*

[4] *Division Measure, Model & Manage Bioresponses (M3-BIORES), KU Leuven, Kasteelpark Arenberg 30, B-3001 Leuven, Belgium*

[5] *Biomechanics Research Unit, Universite de Liege, Chemin des Chevreuils 1-BAT 52/3, B-4000 Liege, Belgium*

ABSTRACT

The use of multifactorial design of experiments (DoE) in tissue engineering bioprocess development will contribute to the robust manufacturing of tissue engineered constructs by linking their quality characteristics to bioprocess operating parameters. In this work, perfusion bioreactors were used for the *in vitro* culture and osteogenic differentiation of human periosteum-derived cells (hPDCs) seeded on three-dimensional titanium (Ti) alloy scaffolds. A CaP-supplemented medium was used to induce differentiation of the cultured hPDCs. A two-level, three-factor fractional factorial design was employed to evaluate a range of bioreactor operating conditions by changing the levels of the following parameters: flow rate (0.5–2 mL/min), cell culture duration (7–21 days) and cell seeding density (1.5×10^3–3×10^3 cells/cm^2). This approach allowed for evaluating the individual impact of the aforementioned process parameters upon a range of genes that are related to the osteogenic lineage, such as collagen type I, alkaline phosphatase, osterix, osteopontin and osteocalcin. Furthermore, by overlaying gene-specific response surfaces, an integrated operating process space was highlighted within which predetermined values of the six genes of interest (*i.e.*, gene signature) could be minimally met over the course of the bioreactor culture time.

Keywords: perfusion bioreactor; osteogenic differentiation; gene expression; DoE analysis; tissue engineering; biomanufacturing

1. INTRODUCTION

Bone tissue-engineering (TE) strategies aim at the *ex vivo* dynamic cultivation of human mesenchymal stem cells, seeded on appropriate three-dimensional (3D) biomaterials (scaffolds), and the use of bioactive factors within a bioreactor setup in order to create TE constructs with regenerative potential upon *in vivo* implantation [1]. Scaffolds allow cell attachment and proliferation within their pores, while at the same time providing the surface properties and porous structure that are required to permit cell growth in a setup that resembles more the native tissue than 2D culture conditions [2,3]. In order to support improved nutrient and oxygen mass transport to cells residing at the center and not only at the peripheral layers of the scaffold, while at the same time more actively controlling the cellular microenvironment, TE constructs are often cultured in (perfusion) bioreactors [4,5,6]. Furthermore, with the use of bioreactors for TE construct culture, critical culture parameters, such as dissolved oxygen concentration, pH and perfusion velocity, as well as the magnitude of the applied shear stress to the cells can be controlled [7].

However, currently, no quantitative relationships exist that link cell phenotype during bioreactor culture to operating bioprocess parameters [8]. The clinical translation of *in vitro* produced TE constructs as graft material requires that process parameters are determined and controlled in such a way that they enable cellular constructs to be robustly manufactured [9]. The selected process parameters will ultimately determine the type, quality and quantity of the produced tissue, which is typically assessed as a function of numerous output variables or performance endpoints (e.g., cell content and/or gene expression levels). In a subsequent phase, these process parameters could be used to actively steer the properties of the *in vitro*-developed TE construct to mimic those of the target tissue, which, in this study, is "bone" [10]. To this end, the design of experiment (DoE) approaches, with a track record in bioprocess optimization, have been introduced for stem cell [11,12,13] and tissue engineering [14,15] research. In these DoE studies, multiple-factor screening of stem cell/TE process parameters and their ranking in terms of significance were obtained. Furthermore, a better understanding was gained of the possible interactions of these process parameters, which, in turn, will help in deciphering the complex relationships that are entailed when stem cell populations interact with their culture environment [16].

A number of studies have shown that during bioreactor culture of osteoprogenitor cells, shear stress resulting from the perfusion of culture medium not only improves the spatial distribution of the cells in the scaffolds, but that it also promotes the mineralization of the secreted extracellular matrix [17,18]. Furthermore, shear stress induces cell differentiation towards the osteogenic lineage indicated by the increased expression of early osteogenic markers, such as, collagen type I (Col1), alkaline phosphatase (ALP), transcription factors like osterix (OSX) and late differentiation markers, such as osteopontin (OPN) and osteocalcin (OCN) [19,20,21]. However, it is expected that gene expression signatures under perfusion conditions might be application specific, as they are dependent on the presence of various bio-instructive factors in the culture medium, like, for example, Ca^{2+} and P_i ions [22]. In addition, certain culture parameters might be interdependent [16]; the cell seeding density influences the spatial distribution of cells [15], their subsequent 3D growth [23] and also their differentiation [24,25], but it also correlates to the amount of secreted growth factors in the medium and might therefore mediate the expression of osteogenic markers. This makes the interpretation of these gene expression signatures difficult and results in a limited understanding of the osteogenic differentiation process of cell-based constructs in perfusion culture. One of the key objectives in the field of bone TE will be to efficiently guide the osteogenic differentiation process of cultured mesenchymal stem cells towards a predefined gene expression signature that would ensure the clinical applicability of the produced TE constructs [26]. However, to date, there is minimal knowledge regarding the determination of those minimal requirements for *in vitro* produced TE constructs, in order to ensure a successful *in vivo* outcome. Hence, the systematic production of TE constructs in well-characterized bioprocesses is a prerequisite for compliance with regulatory guidelines and subsequently successful translation to the market.

In this work, the TE constructs of interest were human periosteum-derived cells (hPDCs) seeded on regular pore Ti6Al4V (Ti) scaffolds and cultured in an osteogenic medium. The aim of this study was to gain insight into the effect of standard culture process parameters, such as seeding density and perfusion flow rate, on the *in vitro* osteogenic cell differentiation as a function of culture time. Gene expression analysis of the hPDCs in TE constructs after osteogenic 3D perfusion culture was performed using a multifactorial DoE approach. This approach allowed the evaluation of multiple process parameters simultaneously in a cost and time efficient way, as opposed to the one-factor-a-time approach [27]. Based on the obtained data, a proof-of-concept was given that, for a dedicated TE construct process set-up, an integrated "window of operation" could be determined that resulted in a cell population with a given gene signature along the osteogenic differentiation pathway.

2. EXPERIMENTAL SECTION

2.1. Ti6Al4V Scaffolds

Porous Ti6Al4V scaffolds (Ø = 6 mm; *h* = 6 mm) with a highly regular design were produced by selective laser melting [28]. Based on micro-CT image analysis, the following scaffold characteristics were determined: 73% ± 1% porosity, 6.5 ± 0.2 cm^2 surface area, 245 ± 2 µm strut diameter and 755 ± 3 µm pore size. Scaffolds were cleaned in an ultrasonic bath consecutively in pure acetone, 70% ethanol and distilled water for 30 min in total. Subsequently, scaffolds were oxidized for 12 h in a 5 M sodium hydroxide solution at 60 °C, rinsed with distilled water and autoclaved. One day before cell seeding, scaffolds were pre-wetted with culture medium by vacuum impregnation, incubated for 2 h in an incubator at 95% humidity and dried overnight in a non-humidified incubator.

2.2. hPDC Culture

hPDCs were isolated from periost biopsies of different donors and pooled as described by Eyckmans *et al.* [29]. The ethics committee for Human Medical Research (KU Leuven) approved the procedure, and biopsies were taken from the patient after informed consent. The cells were cultured in a monolayer in growth medium consisting of high glucose Dulbecco's modified Eagle's medium (Invitrogen) supplemented with 10% fetal bovine serum (FBS; Lonza BioWhittaker, Basel, Switzerland), 1% sodium pyruvate and 1% antibiotic–antimycotic (100 units/mL penicillin, 100 mg/mL streptomycin and 0.25 mg/mL amphotericin B; Invitrogen). At 80%–90% confluence, the cells were trypsinized with Tryple Express (Invitrogen) and replated for up to 5 passages. At passage 6, the cells were trypsinized and seeded in the pre-wetted Ti scaffolds using static drop-seeding at a density of 10^5 or 2×10^5 cells per scaffold. The scaffolds were cultured simultaneously in an in-house-developed perfusion bioreactor, in which culture medium was pumped by a peristaltic pump (PC-24; Ismatec SA, Vancouver, BC, Canada) from a disposable medium reservoir (50-mL Falcon tubes; Franklin Lakes, NJ, USA) containing 10 mL of culture medium, through a scaffold that was fixed in the bioreactor chamber. TE constructs were cultured for up to 21 days in a bio-instructive medium, consisting of growth medium supplemented with 6 mM Ca^{2+}, 4 mM phosphate ions (P_i) and 0.05 ng/mL ascorbic acid [22].

2.3. qPCR

After 7, 14 and 21 days of culture in differentiation medium, the total RNA of each sample was isolated using an RNeasy mini kit (Qiagen, Venlo, The Netherlands) and quantified using a Nanodrop ND-1000 spectrophotometer (Thermo Scientific, Waltham, MA, USA). Complementary DNA was synthesized using the RevertAid H Minus First Strand complementary DNA synthesis kit (Fermentas, Burlington, ON, Canada). SYBR green quantitative polymerase chain reaction was performed for ALP, Sox9, Col1, OCN, OPN, OSX (OSX-F 5'-AGTGACCTTTCAGCCTCCAA-3', OSX-R 3'-GGGAAAAGGGAGGGTAATCA-5'; ALP-F 5'-GGACATGCAGTACGAGCTGA-3', ALP-R 3'-GTCAATTCTGCCTCCTTCCA-5'; Col1-F 5'-GACGAAGACATCCCACCAAT-3', Col1-R 3'-AGATCACGTCATCGCACAAC-5'; OCN-F 5'-GTGCAGCCTTTGTGTCCAA-3', OCN-R 3'-GCTCACACACCTCCCTCCT-5'; OPN-F 5'-ACTGATTTTCCCACGGACCT-3', OPN-R, 5'-TCAGGGTACTGGATGTCAGG-3'; OCN-F 5'-GTGCAGCCTTTGTGTCCAA-3') and compared to HPRT (HPRT-F, 5'-TGAGGATTTGGAAAGGGTGT-3', HPRT-R, 5'-GAGCACACAGAGGGCTACAA-3'). The PCR reaction was cycled in a Rotor-Gene sequence detector (Qiagen) as follows: 95 °C for 3 min, 40 cycles of 95 °C for 3 s and 60 °C for 60 s.

2.4. Multi-Factorial Analysis

A fractional factorial design with three factors (flow rate, culture time and cell-seeding density) and two levels was used. The factor levels were derived from the literature and previous experimental findings (Figure 1). The 0.5 mL/min to 2 mL/min flow rate range is deemed to be within the beneficial flow rate range for osteogenic differentiation [20]. hPDCs at 7 days of culture are considered to be in an early differentiation stage, while they will be expected to be fully differentiated after 21 days [30].

The low cell-seeding density of 10^5 cells per scaffold is the minimal amount of cells that [31] supports growth in the bioreactor. The high cell-seeding density of 2×10^5 cells per scaffold was chosen, since this is the maximum cell amount for this specific scaffold type that results in a similar cell-seeding efficiency compared to the low seeding level [15]. The gene expression response on these different factor levels was determined as an average value of triplicate measurements on constructs produced in three parallel bioreactor runs per condition. As a fractional factorial design (Resolution III, main factor effect aliased with second order interactions) is used in this study, linear behavior between process parameters and gene expression response is assumed for the process space under investigation. Gene expression results were analyzed by ANOVA, and the data was fitted to a general linear model with a statistical software package (JMP Software, version 9; SAS Institute: Cary, NC, USA). The statistical significance level was set at $p < 0.05$. Statistical models were accepted when there was no lack of fit and no correlation in the residual plots, and the residuals were normally distributed. General linear-model parameter estimation was performed by least-squares estimation. The main effects are included in the statistical model following,

$$Y = b_o + \sum_{i=1}^{n} b_i X_i + e \tag{1}$$

where: *Y* is the predicted response; *b* is the parameter estimate; *X* is the coded value of the factor levels; and *e* is the residual error.

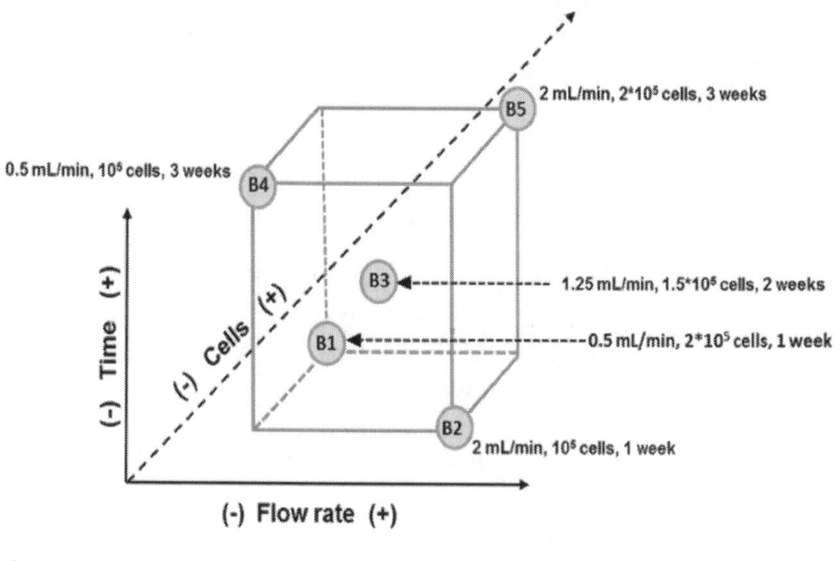

Figure 1. The three-factor, two-level fractional factorial design showing the process space investigated and the experimental conditions chosen for this work.

2.5. DNA Content Analysis

The DNA content of hPDCs on scaffolds was determined using a quantitative fluorometric DNA assay (Quant-iT™ dsDNA HS kit, Invitrogen, Carlsbad, CA, USA). Scaffold samples were rinsed with phosphate-buffered saline (PBS) and lysed in 350 µL RLT lysis buffer (Qiagen, Venlo, The Netherlands) supplemented with 3.5 µL β-mercaptoethanol (Sigma, St. Louis, MO, USA). Prior to analysis, the samples underwent a freeze-thaw cycle at −80 °C. After thawing, samples were vortexed vigorously for 1 min and spun down for 1 min at 13,000 rpm. For each sample, 10 µL of supernatant was diluted in 90 µL of Milli-Q water, after which, the DNA content was quantified with a Qubit® Fluorometer (Invitrogen), as described by Chen *et al.*, 2012 [32].

2.6. Live/Dead Assay

A Live/Dead viability/cytotoxicity kit (Invitrogen, Carlsbad, CA, USA) was used according to the manufacturer's instructions to qualitatively evaluate cell viability and distribution on the scaffolds. Prior to capturing images by fluorescence microscopy (Zeiss Fluorescence Stereo-Microscope, Oberkochen, Germany), the samples were rinsed with PBS and incubated at 37 °C in the fluorescent dye solution (0.5 µL calcein and 2 µL ethidium homodimer in 1 mL PBS) for 20 min.

2.7. Scanning Electron Microscopy Analysis

Cell morphology on scaffolds was assessed by scanning electron microscopy (SEM) imaging coupled with an energy dispersive X-ray (EDAX) analysis (FEI XL30 FEG, Hilsboro, OR, USA) at 10 kV. The following sample preparation was used: rinsing with PSB, fixing with 2.5% glutaraldehyde (in PBS) for 1 h and postfixing in 1% osmium tetroxide for 2 h before dehydration in 50%, 75%, 95% and 100% ethanol solutions. Finally, the samples were chemically dried with hexamethyldisilazane for 3 min and gold-sputtered before SEM analysis.

2.8. Picrosirius Red Collagen Assay

3D collagen matrix production on porous scaffolds was characterized by Picrosirius Red staining (1 mg/mL Sirius Red in saturated picric acid, $n = 3$). The stained samples were thoroughly washed with distilled water to remove unbound dye and dried at 37 °C before qualitative analysis by stereomicroscopy.

2.9. Alizarin Red Mineralization Assay

For each bioreactor condition, mineralization of the cell cultures was assessed by Alizarin Red staining (pH 4.2) after 7, 14 and 21 days of culture. Briefly, cell cultures were rinsed with PBS, followed by fixation in 4% formalin (in PBS) for 10 min and washed with distilled water before staining with the Alizarin Red solution for 1 min. Nonspecific staining was removed by thoroughly washing in distilled water over 24 h.

3. RESULTS AND DISCUSSION

3.1. Cell Proliferation

Figure 2 shows Ti6Al4V scaffolds used for cell seeding and subsequent cell culture. Cells started bridging strut junctions early on (Day 2) in the cell culture, thus initiating a 3D cell growth. Figure 3A,B shows live cells on a representative TE construct obtained after 21 days of perfusion bioreactor culture (B4 experimental condition; see Figure 3), indicating a homogeneous distribution of living cells and ECM throughout the whole scaffold. Cells seem to have filled the scaffold voids and branched out, creating a cell-ECM network in three dimensions. SEM images (Figure 2C,D) show the presence of cells in addition to CaP grains and ECM fibers in the TE construct. In static setups, 3D cell growth has been studied recently for hPDC cultures [33] and hBMSCs [34], and a two stage *in vitro* cell growth was described for MC3T3-E1 pre-osteoblast cells [35]. In both cases, the pore geometry was seen to play an important role on cell growth kinetics. This highlights the possibility to create 3D *in vitro* tissue-like structures where cells may grow independently of the initial scaffold

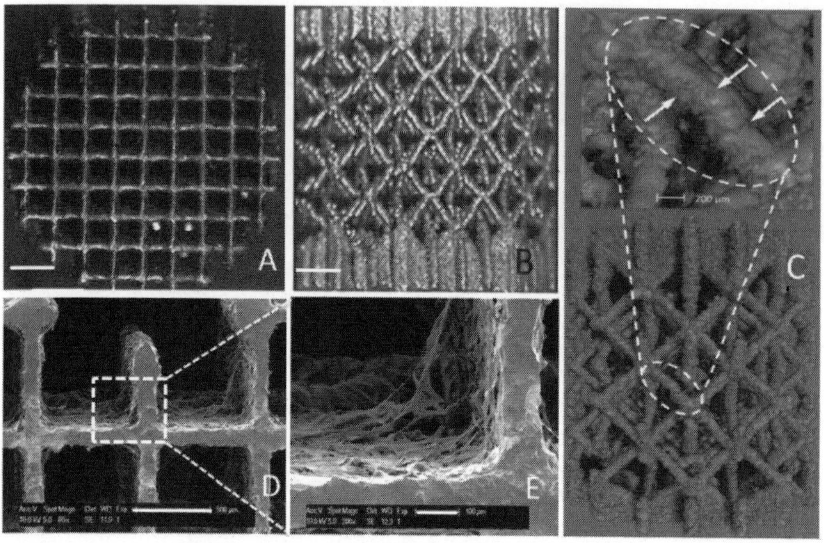

Figure 2. Ti6Al4V scaffolds used for cell seeding and subsequent cell culture: (**A**) scaffold top view (**B**) scaffold side view (scale bar (**A**) and (**B**): 1 mm); (**C**) micro-CT 3D visualization of scaffold and strut close-up from [36]; and (**D**,**E**) SEM images (scale bar: (**D**) 500 µm; (**E**) 100 µm).

geometry and where the interaction between the cells and their own ECM and culture environment may be studied independently.

Post-culture DNA content for the selected experimental conditions (as measured via DNA content analysis) is shown inTable 1. The Pareto chart of standardized effects shows that culture time and flow rate both significantly influenced hPDC proliferation (DNA content) during bioreactor culture, whereas the initial seeding density was not seen to have a significant effect on the final DNA content. For increasing culture times, a significant cell proliferation was observed, as expected for cell culture systems. Increasing flow rates, however, resulted in a slight decrease in final DNA content. In the setup used for this work, the number of cells seeded on the scaffold did not have a significant effect on the final cell number in the TE construct, as also observed elsewhere for hMSCs [37]. Similar observations showing a weak negative effect of flow rate on the DNA content have been recently reported for a 15-fold increase in flow rate [38], while significant negative effects have also been observed for increasing flow rates in other bioreactor systems [17]. McCoy *et al.* [39] have

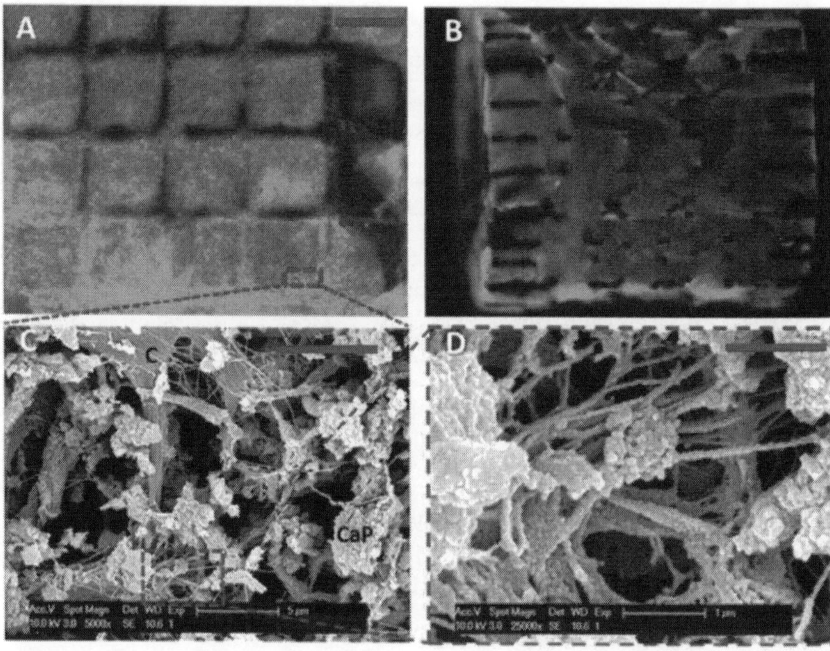

Figure 3. *In vitro*-engineered three-dimensional (3D) osteogenic tissue-engineering (TE) constructs using porous Ti6Al4V scaffolds in a perfusion bioreactor culture (Experimental Condition B4). (**A**) Close-up live/dead image (pore size: 800 μm); (**B**) live/dead image showing the distribution of cells throughout the construct (scale bar: 1 mm); (**C**) SEM micrograph, showing cell and extracellular matrix micromorphology at the void for a representative bioreactor condition (B4) (a magnification of 5000× was used; scale bar: 5 μm); (**D**) SEM micrograph showing mineralization of extracellular fibers. (SEM, scanning electron microscopy; C, cell; CaP, mineral grains; extracellular matrix fibers are also visible; scale bar: 5 μm, 14,000× (scale bar: 1 μm) magnification, respectively).

recently investigated the detachment of cells from scaffolds during perfusion culture, which was attributed to shear stress levels and to a bridged cell-scaffold attachment morphology. This phenomenon could also explain the negative effect of high flow rates observed in this work.

Table 1. (**A**) DNA content after perfusion bioreactor culture for all experimental conditions; (**B**) Pareto chart showing levels of significance of process parameters (inputs) on final DNA content (output) of *in vitro* cultured TE constructs.

Name	Experimental conditions	DNA content (ng/mL) (average, $n = 3$)
B1	0.5 mL/min, 2×10^5 cells, 7 days	10,000
B2	2 mL/min, 10^5 cells, 7 days	7,600
B3	1.25 mL/min, 1.5×10^5 cells, 14 days	14,000
B4	0.5 mL/min, 10^5 cells, 21 days	34,000
B5	2 mL/min, 2×10^5 cells, 21 days	28,200

3.2. Osteogenic Cell Differentiation: An Overview

Genes, such as Col1, ALP, OSX, OCN and OPN, have been used as markers for evaluating the specification of stem cell and osteochondro-progenitor cell types towards the osteogenic lineage [40,41]. As shown in Figure 4, the use of different culture process conditions (based on the multifactorial DoE approach) resulted in significant changes in gene expression of the aforementioned genes. Overall, it may be stated that early osteogenic markers of osteoprogenitor cells, like ALP and Col1, show a significant time-dependent decrease in expression from Day 7 to Day 21, as expected [40]. From Day 14 onwards, no changes were observed anymore between the different conditions for ALP. The downregulation of Col1 observed for later time points could be explained by the fact that cells become confluent within their 3D growth configuration, hence modulating the gene expression level due to less need for matrix synthesis in such a configuration. For the late osteogenic markers, such as OCN, OPN and the transcription factor, OSX, a clear time-dependent increase in gene expression was observed, as reported elsewhere for Ca^{2+} and P_i containing media for 2D cultures of hBMSCs [42] and during static 3D culture of hPDCs [22,30]. Osteogenic differentiation was also evidenced by collagen type I secretion and mineralization (Figure 5). However, due to the DoE approach used in this work, all process parameters were systematically changed simultaneously (as shown in Figure 1), making direct comparison of the experimental conditions meaningless; thus, an integrated analysis is further required, as described in the subsequent section.

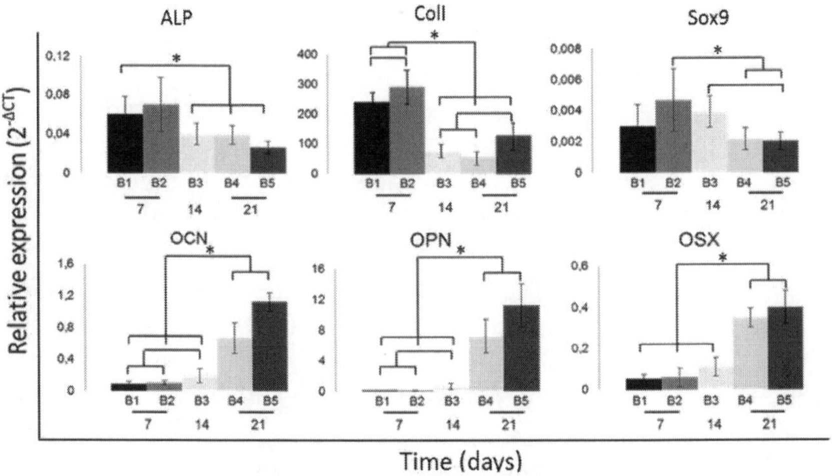

Figure 4. Gene expression data for hPDCs cultured in CaP-supplemented medium for all experimental conditions. Data shown are the relative expression of the gene of interest normalized to the HPRT1 housekeeping gene. This data set corresponds to the experimental design employed in this study, as shown in Table 1. Mean ± S.D. error of the mean (n = 3). Unpaired t-test (two-tailed): * $p < 0.05$. ALP, alkaline phosphatase; Col1, collagen type I; OCN, osteocalcin; OPN, osteopontin; OSX, osterix.

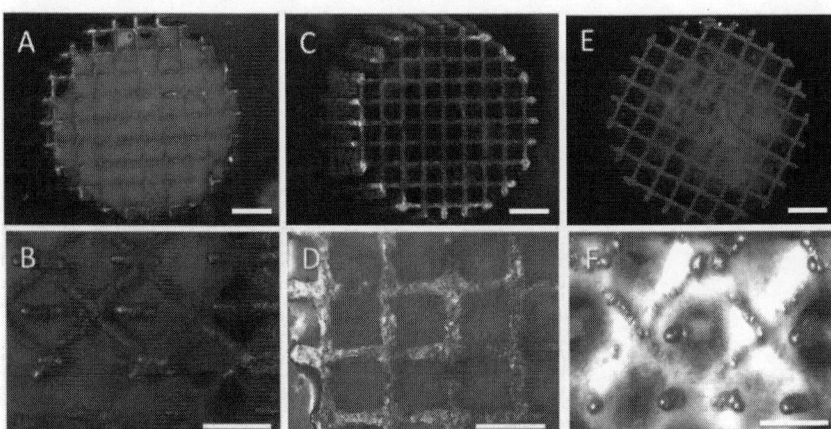

Figure 5. Representative images for the midpoint experimental time point (B3) showing collagen matrix content by positive Picrosirius Red staining (**A**,**B**) and mineral content by positive Alizarin Red staining (**C**,**D**), but also as evidenced by bright field images (**E**,**F**). Scale bar: 1 mm.

3.3. DoE Gene Expression Analysis: Flow Rate and Seeding Density Effect

In order to further interpret the influence of the selected process parameters on the gene expression levels, response surface models were created based on least-squares linear fits. The goodness-of-fit of the statistical models with the experimental data is shown in Figure 6. The strong upregulation of OSX, OPN and OCN was captured accurately, resulting in R^2 values above 0.8. The same was seen in the case of the downregulation of Col1 (R^2 = 0.79). However for the culture times evaluated in this study, both ALP and Sox9 were not clearly affected by the process conditions, resulting in R^2 values that were substantially lower (0.53 and 0.58, respectively). This demonstrates the limitation of a fractional factorial design (and least-squares linear fitting) in accurately capturing gene expression patterns that might fluctuate over the culture period of interest. However, in those cases where the u-regulation of genes was strong, the obtained fits were satisfactory.

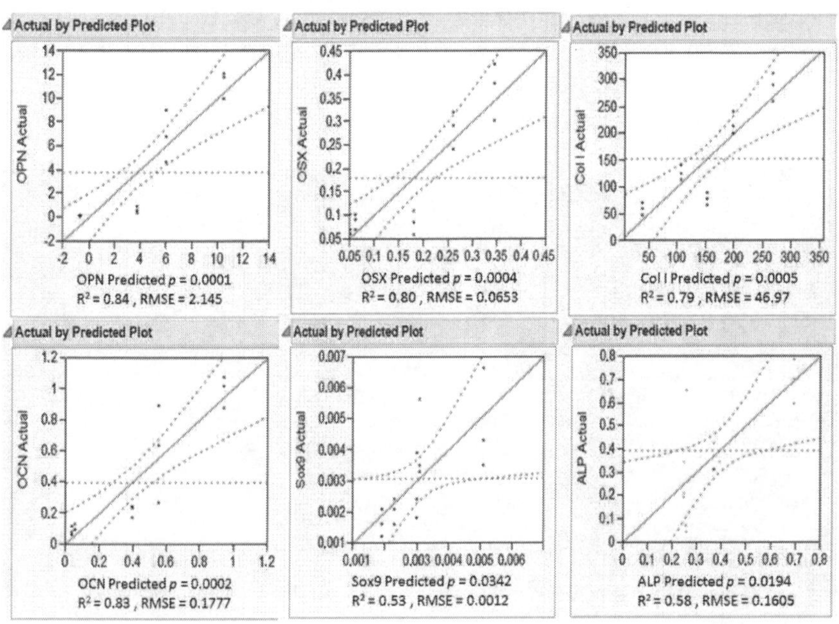

Figure 6. Goodness-of-fit between predicted values obtained via partial least-squares fitting and experimentally measured gene expression values, for the selected genes studied in this study. R^2 values are also given for all plots.

Figure 6 shows the positive effect of an increased seeding density and flow rate, which both resulted in a significant increase in the expression of the osteogenic markers, OSX (p = 0.02), OCN (p = 0.03) and OPN (p = 0.0008). Increased seeding densities may result in confluency at earlier time points, inducing osteogenic differentiation at earlier time points and, thus, enhancing the upregulation of these genes from early on in culture; hence, the positive correlation of seeding density with upregulation of these genes [25,43]. However, this positive correlation has been seen to level off after a critical value has been exceeded [44]. Shear stress has been linked with the upregulation of OSX, OCN and OPN during perfusion bioreactor culture [37,45,46,47], but only a limited number of studies used human mesenchymal cells in 3D setups [19,38,41,48]. Prior studies have shown that the expression of these markers increased in the presence of medium flow relative to static cultures [49], and other studies have correlated flow and/or shear stresses with an increased induction of osteogenic differentiation and tissue formation [18,50].

These findings agree with our results on the significant effect of flow on the aforementioned genes. However, we should note that, due to differences in scaffold material and design and the composition of osteogenic media, the extent and timing of osteogenic differentiation would be expected to vary across systems. Regarding ALP gene expression, our data show a negative correlation to flow rate magnitude (between seven and 21 days of culture), which has also been observed by other groups. Higher shear stress in a perfusion bioreactor decreased ALP expression after 14 days of culture [21], while a decrease in ALP specific activity from Day 7 to Day 21 was also observed during 3D culture of hMSCs [41]. Furthermore, a positive correlation between seeding density and ALP gene expression has been reported for human umbilical cord MSCs [44], in agreement with the effect observed in this work. Interestingly, hMSCs cultured in osteogenic differentiation medium under shear stress exposure in a 2D system became less responsive in the gene expression of alkaline phosphatase, possibly explaining the dose dependency observed in this study [51].

Col1 was seen not to be affected by the magnitude of flow, while it correlated positively with seeding density. Although collagen matrix synthesis has been reported in numerous studies to be positively affected by flow rate [6,50,52], a possible explanation for the lack of correlation between Col1 and fluid flow magnitude could be the fact that by Day 7, which is the initial time point studied in our work, Col1 expression was already downregulated. Similar Col1 temporal trends parallel to elevated alkaline phosphatase levels have, however, been observed in dynamic culture systems [53].

3.4. Highlighting Gene Expression Signature Windows via Response Surface Methodology

The overall aim of this study was to introduce a "windows of operation" methodology as a tool to allow instantaneous visualization of multiple gene expression data related to osteogenic differentiation, thereby aiding decision-making regarding the end-point properties of 3D TE constructs obtained in dynamic culture conditions. By mapping out operating spaces using a DoE approach, user-defined levels of process performance may be finally obtained by linking the effects of process parameters (factors) on pre-selected response variables, in this case, gene expression levels. By using gene specific response surfaces presented in Figure 7 and overlaying them as shown in Figure 8, a case study on the development of a gene expression signature over culture time (days) as a function of flow rate and cell seeding density. By gene expression signature, we refer to a combination of genes that will be expressed by cultured cells to predefined values, where minimum criteria or intermediate ones (between a set minimum and maximum value) may be met. Dashed lines (Figure 8) highlight the values of the two selected process parameters that are required in order to produce TE constructs containing cells that express the selected genes above a desired threshold value. As the culture progresses and the osteogenic differentiation process "matures" from Day 12 to Day 15, it may be seen that the gene expression signature target-values are obtained with a wider combination of culture process parameters, since this is a time-dependent biologic process. This ultimately means that based on the selection of the operating process parameters, TE cultures may be steered towards desired directions where the cell population may possess desirable phenotypic characteristics. Confidence intervals (95%), as seen in Figure 5 could be also incorporated in the outlining of a more restricted, but more reliable window of operation. Recently, a similar approach was used for highlighting "windows of operation" of perfusion bioreactors during early culture time points (up to three days of cell culture), by operating in minimal cell detachment and increased gene expression levels of COX2 and OPN [54].

We do realize, however, that the use of a fractional factorial, rather than full-factorial design, aliases (*i.e.*, does not decouple) the interactive effects of remaining factors to the main effect of a factor not making use of the full extent of the possibilities of such a strategy. However, the systematic investigation of the interplay between culture process parameters and neo-tissue quality attributes, such as cell phenotype, will give insights regarding TE bioprocess development and optimization. Overall, it should be stated that the use of multifactorial DoE approaches and response surface models for process optimization in TE applications has recently gained momentum [12,14,16,40,55]. These studies highlight the rising need for improved process understanding, in particular when dealing with inherently highly complex TE systems, meeting, at the same time, regulatory requirements.

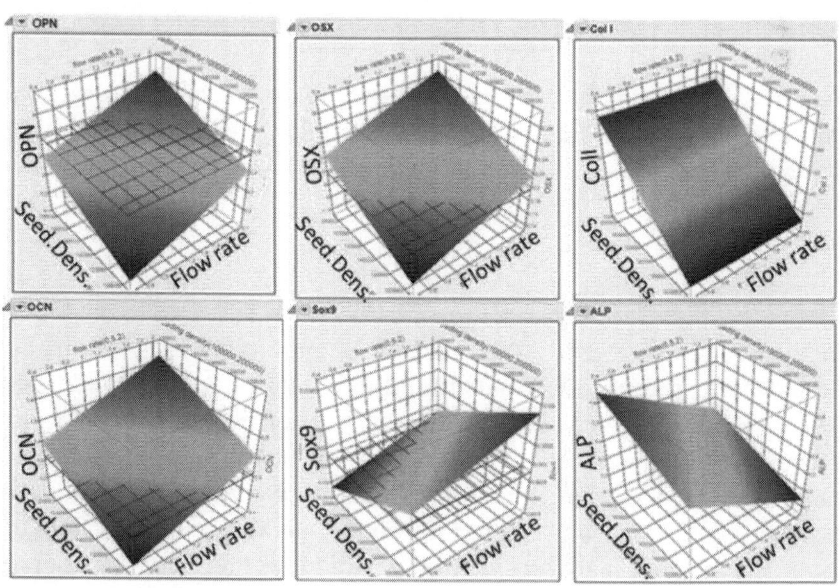

Figure 7. Response surface representations showing the effect of seeding density (Seed. Dens.) and flow rate on gene expression levels for all genes studied. Relative expression levels were used to plot the response surfaces shown. The data shown are indicative of Day 14.

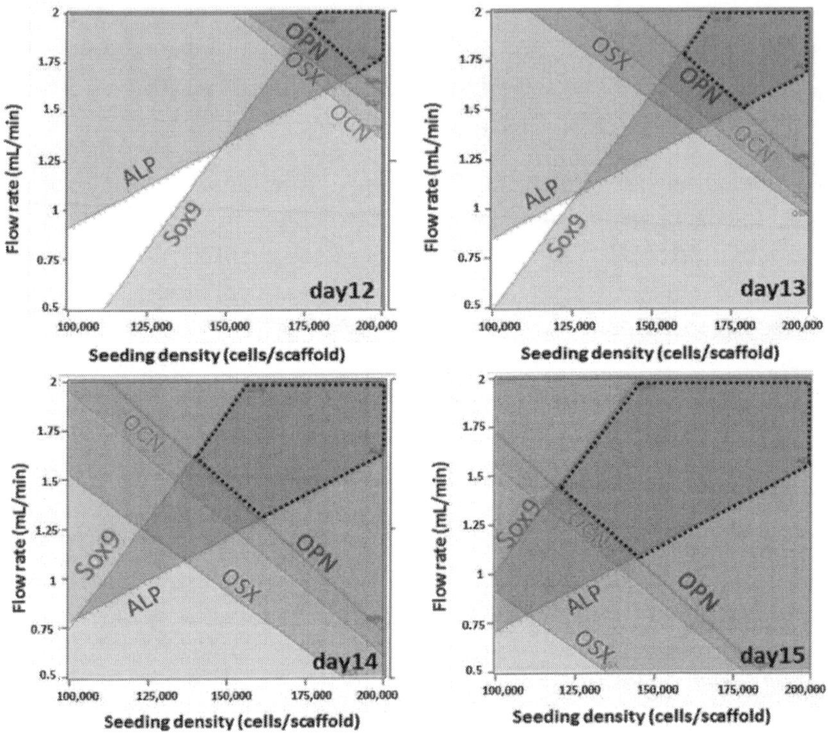

Figure 8. Development of a selected gene expression signature over culture time (as indicated by the dashed lines) in a perfusion bioreactor setup, as a function of flow rate and cell seeding efficiency.

4. CONCLUSIONS

In this work, we showed that the use of multifactorial DoE can be employed as a tool to link perfusion bioreactor operating conditions (process parameters, such as seeding density and flow rate) to osteogenic differentiation. Furthermore, by overlaying gene-specific response surfaces, an integrated operating process space was highlighted within which predetermined values of six genes of interest (*i.e.*, gene signature) could be minimally met over the course of a bioreactor culture period. Such an approach will enhance our understanding of the highly complex TE bioprocesses and allow the development of predictive models for *in vitro* cell behavior and, hopefully, *in vivo* outcomes. This strategy would thus facilitate the transition from bench to clinic and, ultimately, to the market.

ACKNOWLEDGMENTS

Ioannis Papantoniou is funded by the ENDEAVOUR Project G.0982.11N of the Research Foundation Flanders (Fonds Wetenschappelijk Onderzoek (FWO) Vlaanderen). Maarten Sonnaert is supported by a Ph.D. grant of the Agency for Innovation by Science and Technology (Innovatie door Wetenschap en Technologie (IWT)/111457). Toon Lambrechts is supported by the KU Leuven Concerted Research Actions (Geconcerteerde Onderzoeksacties (GOA)/13/016). Lies Geris acknowledges support by the European Research Council under the European Union's Seventh Framework Program (FP7/2007-2013)/European Research Council (ERC) Grant Agreement No. 279100. This work is part of Prometheus, the Leuven Research and Development Division of Skeletal Tissue Engineering of the KU Leuven:www.kuleuven.be/prometheus.

AUTHOR CONTRIBUTIONS

Ioannis Papantoniou designed and performed all cell culturing and bioreactor experiments, performed data analyses and modeling and wrote the manuscript. Maarten Sonnaert and Toon Lambrechts supported the writing of the manuscript and figure editing. Jean-Marie Aerts and Lies Geris edited and corrected the text. Frank Luyten supported this work from a translational and clinical point of view. Jan Schrooten was the overall supervisor. All authors read and approved the final manuscript.

CONFLICTS OF INTEREST

The authors declare no conflict of interest.

REFERENCES

1. Laurencin, C.T.; Ambrosio, A.M.A.; Borden, M.D.; Cooper, J.A. Tissue engineering: Orthopedic applications. Annu. Rev. Biomed. Eng. 1999, 1, 19–46.

2. Stevens, M.M. Biomaterials for bone tissue engineering. Mater. Today 2008, 11, 18–25.

3. Pampaloni, F.; Reynaud, E.G.; Stelzer, E.H.K. The third dimension bridges the gap between cell culture and live tissue. Nat. Rev. Mol. Cell Biol. 2007, 8, 839–845.

4. Bancroft, G.N.; Sikavitsas, V.I.; Mikos, A.G. Design of a flow perfusion bioreactor system for bone tissue-engineering applications. Tissue Eng. 2003, 9, 549–554.

5. Grayson, W.L.; Bhumiratana, S.; Cannizzaro, C.; Vunjak-Novakovic, G. Bioreactor cultivation of functional bone grafts. Methods Mol. Biol. 2011, 698, 231–241.

6. Datta, N.; Pham, Q.P.; Sharma, U.; Sikavitsas, V.I.; Jansen, J.A.; Mikos, A.G. In vitro generated extracellular matrix and fluid shear stress synergistically enhance 3D osteoblastic differentiation. Proc. Natl. Acad. Sci. USA 2006, 103, 2488–2493.

7. Yeatts, A.B.; Fisher, J.P. Bone tissue engineering bioreactors: Dynamic culture and the influence of shear stress. Bone2011, 48, 171–181.

8. Placzek, M.R.; Chung, I.M.; Macedo, H.M.; Ismail, S.; Blanco, T.M.; Lim, M.; Cha, J.M.; Fauzi, I.; Kang, Y.; Yeo, D.C.L.; Ma, C.Y.J.; et al. Stem cell bioprocessing: Fundamentals and principles. J. R. Soc. Interface 2009, 6, 209–232.

9. Ratcliffe, E.; Thomas, R.J.; Williams, D.J. Current understanding and challenges in bioprocessing of stem cell-based therapies for regenerative medicine. Br. Med. Bull. 2011, 100, 137–155.

10. Lenas, P.; Moos, M.; Luyten, F.P. Developmental engineering: A new paradigm for the design and manufacturing of cell-based products. Part I: From three-dimensional cell growth to biomimetics of in vivo development. Tissue Eng. Part B 2009, 15, 381–394.

11. Thomas, R.J.; Hourd, P.C.; Williams, D.J. Application of process quality engineering techniques to improve the understanding of the in vitro processing of stem cells for therapeutic use. J. Biotechnol. 2008, 136, 148–155.

12. Ratcliffe, E.; Hourd, P.; Guijarro-Leach, J.; Rayment, E.; Williams, D.J.; Thomas, R.J. Application of response surface methodology to maximize the productivity of scalable automated human embryonic stem cell manufacture. Regen. Med. 2013, 8, 39–48.

13. Lim, M.; Panoskaltsis, N.; Ye, H.; Mantalaris, A. Optimization of in vitro erythropoiesis from CD34+ cord blood cells using design of experiments (DOE). Biochem. Eng. J. 2011, 55, 154–161.

14. Papantoniou, I.I.; Chai, Y.C.; Luyten, F.P.; Schrooten, J.I. Process quality engineering for bioreactor-driven manufacturing of tissue-engineered constructs for bone regeneration. Tissue Eng. Part C 2013.

15. Chen, Y.; Bloemen, V.; Impens, S.; Moesen, M.; Luyten, F.P.; Schrooten, J. Characterization and optimization of cell seeding in scaffolds by factorial design: Quality by design approach for skeletal tissue engineering. Tissue Eng. Part C2011, 17, 1211–1221.

16. Hunt, M.M.; Meng, G.L.; Rancourt, D.E.; Gates, I.D.; Kallos, M.S. Factorial experimental design for the culture of human embryonic stem cells as aggregates in stirred suspension bioreactors reveals the potential for interaction effects between bioprocess parameters. Tissue Eng. Part C 2014, 20, 76–89.

17. Cartmell, S.H.; Porter, B.D.; Garcia, A.J.; Guldberg, R.E. Effects of medium perfusion rate on cell-seeded three-dimensional bone constructs in vitro. Tissue Eng. 2003, 9, 1197–1203.

18. Sikavitsas, V.I.; Bancroft, G.N.; Lemoine, J.J.; Liebschner, M.A.K.; Dauner, M.; Mikos, A.G. Flow perfusion enhances the calcified matrix deposition of marrow stromal cells in biodegradable nonwoven fiber mesh scaffolds. Ann. Biomed. Eng. 2005, 33, 63–70.

19. Bjerre, L.; Bunger, C.E.; Kassem, M.; Mygind, T. Flow perfusion culture of human mesenchymal stem cells on silicate-substituted tricalcium phosphate scaffolds. Biomaterials 2008, 29, 2616–2627.

20. McCoy, R.J.; O'Brien, F.J. Influence of shear stress in perfusion bioreactor cultures for the development of three-dimensional

bone tissue constructs: A review. Tissue Eng. Part B 2010, 16, 587–601.

21. Kim, J.; Ma, T. Perfusion regulation of hMSC microenvironment and osteogenic differentiation in 3D scaffold.Biotechnol. Bioeng. 2012, 109, 252–261.

22. Chai, Y.C.; Roberts, S.J.; van Bael, S.; Chen, Y.; Luyten, F.P.; Schrooten, J. Multi-level factorial analysis of Ca2+/Pisupplementation as bio-instructive media for in vitro biomimetic engineering of three-dimensional osteogenic hybrids. Tissue Eng. Part C 2012, 18, 90–103.

23. Bitar, M.; Brown, R.A.; Salih, V.; Kidane, A.G.; Knowles, J.C.; Nazhat, S.N. Effect of cell density on osteoblastic differentiation and matrix degradation of biomimetic dense collagen scaffolds. Biomacromolecules 2008, 9, 129–135.

24. Eyckmans, J.; Lin, G.L.; Chen, C.S. Adhesive and mechanical regulation of mesenchymal stem cell differentiation in human bone marrow and periosteum-derived progenitor cells. Biol. Open 2012, 1, 1058–1068.

25. Kim, K.; Dean, D.; Mikos, A.G.; Fisher, J.P. Effect of initial cell seeding density on early osteogenic signal expression of rat bone marrow stromal cells cultured on cross-linked poly(propylene fumarate) disks. Biomacromolecules 2009,10, 1810–1817.

26. Salter, E.; Goh, B.; Hung, B.; Hutton, D.; Ghone, N.; Grayson, W.L. Bone tissue engineering bioreactors: A role in the clinic? Tissue Eng. Part B 2012, 18, 62–75.

27. Lim, M.; Shunjie, C.; Panoskaltsis, N.; Mantalaris, A. Systematic experimental design for bioprocess characterization: Elucidating transient effects of multi-cytokine contributions on erythroid differentiation. Biotechnol. Bioproc. E 2012,17, 218–226.

28. Pyka, G.; Burakowski, A.; Kerckhofs, G.; Moesen, M.; van Bael, S.; Schrooten, J.; Wevers, M. Surface modification of Ti6Al4V open porous structures produced by additive manufacturing. Adv. Eng. Mater. 2012, 14, 363–370.

29. Eyckmans, J.; Luyten, F.P. Species specificity of ectopic bone formation using periosteum-derived mesenchymal progenitor cells. Tissue Eng. 2006, 12, 2203–2213.

30. Chai, Y.C.; Roberts, S.J.; Schrooten, J.; Luyten, F.P. Probing the osteoinductive effect of calcium phosphate by using anin vitro biomimetic model. Tissue Eng. Part A 2011, 17, 1083–1097.

31. Chai, Y.C.; Truscello, S.; Bael, S.V.; Luyten, F.P.; Vleugels, J.; Schrooten, J. Perfusion electrodeposition of calcium phosphate on additive manufactured titanium scaffolds for bone engineering. Acta Biomater. 2011, 7, 2310–2319.

32. Chen, Y.; Sonnaert, M.; Roberts, S.J.; Luyten, F.P.; Schrooten, J. Validation of a PicoGreen-based DNA quantification integrated in an RNA extraction method for two-dimensional and three-dimensional cell cultures. Tissue Eng. Part C2012, 18, 444–452.

33. Van Bael, S.; Chai, Y.C.; Truscello, S.; Moesen, M.; Kerckhofs, G.; van Oosterwyck, H.; Kruth, J.P.; Schrooten, J. The effect of pore geometry on the in vitro biological behavior of human periosteum-derived cells seeded on selective laser-melted Ti6Al4V bone scaffolds. Acta Biomater. 2012, 8, 2824–2834.

34. Zhao, F.; Pathi, P.; Grayson, W.; Xing, Q.; Locke, B.R.; Ma, T. Effects of oxygen transport on 3-d human mesenchymal stem cell metabolic activity in perfusion and static cultures: Experiments and mathematical model. Biotechnol. Prog.2005, 21, 1269–1280.

35. Kommareddy, K.P.; Lange, C.; Rumpler, M.; Dunlop, J.W.C.; Manjubala, I.; Cui, J.; Kratz, K.; Lendlein, A.; Fratzl, P. Two stages in three-dimensional in vitro growth of tissue generated by osteoblastlike cells. Biointerphases 2010, 5, 45–52.

36. Pyka, G.; Kerckhofs, G.; Papantoniou, I.; Speirs, M.; Schrooten, J.; Wevers, M. Surface roughness and morphology customization of additive manufactured open porous Ti6Al4V structures. Materials 2013, 6, 4737–4757.

37. Kreke, M.R.; Goldstein, A.S. Hydrodynamic shear stimulates osteocalcin expression but not proliferation of bone marrow stromal cells. Tissue Eng. 2004, 10, 780–788.

38. Grayson, W.L.; Marolt, D.; Bhumiratana, S.; Frohlich, M.; Guo, X.E.; Vunjak-Novakovic, G. Optimizing the medium perfusion rate in bone tissue engineering bioreactors. Biotechnol. Bioeng. 2011, 108, 1159–1170.

39. McCoy, R.J.; Jungreuthmayer, C.; O'Brien, F.J. Influence of flow rate and scaffold pore size on cell behavior during mechanical stimulation in a flow perfusion bioreactor. Biotechnol. Bioeng. 2012, 109, 1583–1594.

40. Roberts, S.J.; Chen, Y.; Moesen, M.; Schrooten, J.; Luyten, F.P. Enhancement of osteogenic gene expression for the differentiation of human periosteal derived cells. Stem. Cell Res. 2011, 7, 137–144.

41. Stiehler, M.; Bunger, C.; Baatrup, A.; Lind, M.; Kassem, M.; Mygind, T. Effect of dynamic 3-D culture on proliferation, distribution, and osteogenic differentiation of human mesenchymal stem cells. J. Biomed. Mater. Res. Part A 2009, 89A, 96–107.

42. Barradas, A.M.; Fernandes, H.A.; Groen, N.; Chai, Y.C.; Schrooten, J.; van de Peppel, J.; van Leeuwen, J.P.; van Blitterswijk, C.A.; de Boer, J. A calcium-induced signaling cascade leading to osteogenic differentiation of human bone marrow-derived mesenchymal stromal cells. Biomaterials 2012, 33, 3205–3215.

43. Vehof, J.W.M.; de Ruijter, A.E.; Spauwen, P.H.M.; Jansen, J.A. Influence of rhBMP-2 on rat bone marrow stromal cells cultured on titanium fiber mesh. Tissue Eng. 2001, 7, 373–383.

44. Zhou, H.Z.; Weir, M.D.; Xu, H.H.K. Effect of cell seeding density on proliferation and osteodifferentiation of umbilical cord stem cells on calcium phosphate cement-fiber scaffold. Tissue Eng. Part A 2011, 17, 2603–2613.

45. You, J.; Reilly, G.C.; Zhen, X.C.; Yellowley, C.E.; Chen, Q.; Donahue, H.J.; Jacobs, C.R. Osteopontin gene regulation by oscillatory fluid flow via intracellular calcium mobilization and activation of mitogen-activated protein kinase in MC3T3-E1 osteoblasts. J. Biol. Chem. 2001, 276, 13365–13371.

46. Kreke, M.R.; Huckle, W.R.; Goldstein, A.S. Fluid flow stimulates expression of osteopontin and bone sialoprotein by bone marrow stromal cells in a temporally dependent manner. Bone 2005, 36, 1047–1055.

47. Scaglione, S.; Wendt, D.; Miggino, S.; Papadimitropoulos, A.; Fato, M.; Quarto, R.; Martin, I. Effects of fluid flow and calcium phosphate coating on human bone marrow stromal cells cultured in a defined 2D model system. J. Biomed. Mater. Res. Part A 2008, 86A, 411–419.

48. Meinel, L.; Karageorgiou, V.; Hofmann, S.; Fajardo, R.; Snyder, B.; Li, C.; Zichner, L.; Langer, R.; Vunjak-Novakovic, G.; Kaplan, D.L. Engineering bone-like tissue in vitro using human bone marrow stem cells and silk scaffolds. J. Biomed. Mater. Res. Part A 2004, 71, 25–34.

49. Yu, X.J.; Botchwey, E.A.; Levine, E.M.; Pollack, S.R.; Laurencin, C.T. Bioreactor-based bone tissue engineering: The influence of dynamic flow on osteoblast phenotypic expression and matrix mineralization. Proc. Natl. Acad. Sci. USA2004, 101, 11203–11208.

50. Bancroft, G.N.; Sikavitsast, V.I.; van den Dolder, J.; Sheffield, T.L.; Ambrose, C.G.; Jansen, J.A.; Mikos, A.G. Fluid flow increases mineralized matrix deposition in 3D perfusion culture of marrow stromal osteloblasts in a dose-dependent manner. Proc. Natl. Acad. Sci. USA 2002, 99, 12600–12605.

51. Yourek, G.; McCormick, S.M.; Mao, J.J.; Reilly, G.C. Shear stress induces osteogenic differentiation of human mesenchymal stem cells. Regen. Med. 2010, 5, 713–724.

52. Sikavitsas, V.I.; Bancroft, G.N.; Holtorf, H.L.; Jansen, J.A.; Mikos, A.G. Mineralized matrix deposition by marrow stromal osteoblasts in 3D perfusion culture increases with increasing fluid shear forces. Proc. Natl. Acad. Sci. USA2003, 100, 14683–14688.

53. Grellier, M.; Bareille, R.; Bourget, C.; Amedee, J. Responsiveness of human bone marrow stromal cells to shear stress.J. Tissue Eng. Regen. Med. 2009, 3, 302–309.

54. McCoy, R.J.; O'Brien, F.J. Visualizing feasible operating ranges within tissue engineering systems using a "windows of operation" approach: A perfusion-scaffold bioreactor case study. Biotechnol. Bioeng. 2012, 109, 3161–3171.

55. Barbosa, H.S.C.; Fernandes, T.G.; Dias, T.P.; Diogo, M.M.; Cabral, J.M.S. New insights into the mechanisms of embryonic stem cell self-renewal under hypoxia: A multifactorial analysis approach. PLoS One 2012, 7.

Chapter 7

Syngas Biomethanation in a Semi-Continuous Reverse Membrane Bioreactor (RMBR)

Supansa Y. Westman*, Konstantinos Chandolias and Mohammad J. Taherzadeh

Swedish Centre for Resource Recovery, University of Borås, Borås 50190, Sweden

ABSTRACT

Syngas biomethanation is a potent bio-conversion route, utilizing microorganisms to assimilate intermediate gases to produce methane. However, since methanogens have a long doubling time, the reactor works best at a low dilution rate; otherwise, the cells can be washed out during the continuous fermentation process. In this study, the performance of a practical reverse membrane bioreactor (RMBR) with high cell density for rapid syngas biomethanation as well as a co-substrate of syngas and organic substances was examined in a long-term fermentation process of 154 days and compared with the reactors of the free cells (FCBR). The RMBR reached maximum capacities of H_2, CO, and CO_2 conversion of 7.0, 15.2, and 4.0 mmol/$L_{reactor}$.day, respectively, at the organic loading rate of 3.40 gCOD/L.day. The highest methane production rate from the RMBR was 186.0 mL/$L_{reactor}$.day on the 147th day, compared to the highest rate in the FCBR, 106.3 mL/$L_{reactor}$.day, on the

58th day. The RMBR had the ability to maintain a high methanation capacity by retaining the microbial cells, which were at a high risk for cell wash out. Consequently, the system was able to convert more syngas simultaneously with the organic compounds into methane compared to the FCBR.

Keywords: syngas fermentation; methane production; semi-continuous process; reverse membrane bioreactor; co-substrate; cell retention

1. INTRODUCTION

Biogas is a renewable energy source with several applications in heating, cooking, or electricity production. Biogas mainly consists of methane and carbon dioxide but may also contain minor impurities of other components [1]. It can also be upgraded to about 97% biomethane, which is used as a popular renewable form of energy such as car fuel.

Biogas or biomethane can be produced from waste resources that can be classified as easily degradable, difficult to degrade, and non-degradable wastes. To obtain biogas from easily degradable wastes such as food wastes, a biochemical approach called anaerobic digestion process is traditionally employed. In this process, complex polymers of organic substances are degraded easily by microorganisms through the different steps of the anaerobic fermentation process [2]. In the same way, difficult to degrade materials such as lignocelluloses from crop residues and agricultural residues can also be converted into methane by the performance of microorganisms in the anaerobic digestion process. However, the recalcitrance of these difficult to degrade biomass sources, such as the coverage of lignin or the crystallinity of cellulose, limits the access of the microorganisms and enzymes for efficient digestion [3]. The hydrolysis rate can be accelerated by pretreating the substrate with chemical, physical, or biological processes before feeding the substrate to the digester [4]. Nevertheless, the pre-treatment process has been found to be an expensive and rate limiting factor [5]. Thus, the biochemical process may face challenges in converting difficult to degrade wastes into methane. Non-degradable materials such as lignin or plastic wastes cannot be decomposed by microorganisms in an anaerobic digestion process. Consequently, it is common to incinerate this category of waste to energy.

On the other hand, it is possible to convert non-degradable wastes and lignocelluloses to biofuels via gasification to syngas and the fermentation routes. The biomass is first gasified into a gas mixture called syngas or synthesis gas. Syngas contains primarily CO, H_2, and CO_2. The syngas can be upgraded by methanization, either by using chemical catalysts (e.g., Fischer-Tropsch Synthesis) or through fermentation with microbial catalysts. The fermentation process offers several benefits over the chemical catalytic process, such as a more specific process, higher yields, lower energy consumption, being environmentally friendly, and having better robustness [6,7]. Syngas fermentation for methane production, *i.e.*, syngas biomethanation, is a relatively new technology and a good alternative to the first-generation biofuel.

The biomethanation of the syngas by microorganisms can be performed in two pathways [8]. The first one utilizes an acetate pathway as a methane precursor (Reactions 1 and 2). *Acetobacterium woodii* and *Enbacterium limosum*, for example, are microbial cells that perform this reaction. Thereafter, methanogenic microorganisms such as *Methanosarcina barkeri*convert acetate into methane (Reaction 3):

$$2CO_2 + 4H_2 \rightarrow CH_3COOH + 2H_2O \quad \text{Reaction 1}$$

$$4CO_2 + H_2O \rightarrow CH_3COOH + 2CO_2 \quad \text{Reaction 2}$$

$$CH_3COOH \rightarrow CH_4 + CO_2 \quad \text{Reaction 3}$$

The other pathway utilizes the H_2/CO_2 pathway. CO can be converted into CO_2 (Reaction 4) by microorganisms, for example, *Methanothermobacter thermoautotrophicus* and *Clostridium thermoaceticum* [9]. The H_2 and CO_2 produced by reaction 4 and initially present in the syngas are converted into methane by some microorganisms such as *Methanosarcina formicicum*(Reaction 5) [8]:

$$CO + H_2O \rightarrow CO_2 + H_2 \quad \text{Reaction 4}$$

$$4H_2 + CO_2 \rightarrow CH_4 + H_2O \quad \text{Reaction 5}$$

However, these microbial groups, especially, methane-producing microorganisms, require a long retention time in the digester, since their growth rate is very low. In addition, they are very sensitive to harsh conditions; hence, the cells can easily be washed out from the digester at high dilution rates in a continuous process. For these reasons, the population size of the microbial cells is easily reduced, resulting in a decreased methane production and low process efficiency. Moreover, fermentation processes with low cell density need long start-up periods, and larger digesters are required for proper function, which means that the capital cost is high. Retaining the microbial cells inside a compact bioreactor with a low chance of bio-fouling and abraded microorganisms might be a solution to overcome these problems.

Different bioreactor designs have been developed in order to enhance the process efficiency of the syngas fermentation [10,11,12,13,14,15]. For instance, continuous stirred tank reactors (CSTR) have been frequently employed for syngas fermentation. A high speed of agitation in the CSTR can be used to enhance the mass transfer efficiency. However, it has been observed to result in high shear stress on the cells and high-energy consumption [16,17].

In another study, a bioreactor for syngas fermentation was connected to a hollow fiber membrane module [16]. The system enhanced the gas-liquid mass transfer as well as allowed the microbial cells to be attached on the membrane layer [16]. However, a long start-up period for cell attachment to the outer membrane layer was crucial. The same authors also developed a novel bioreactor configuration, called a monolithic biofilm reactor, for the same purpose. The results revealed that the performance of the syngas fermentation process depended not only on the mass transfer efficiency, but the low efficiency was also related to bio-fouling and abrading of the microbial cells attached to the channel of the monolithic wall [18]. Liu *et al.* [19] used the membrane module for the cell retention system in continuous syngas fermentation for ethanol production. However, cell wash out still occurred, which was one of the reasons for low product formation.

From these results and the nature of methane-producing microorganisms, retaining a high microbial cell density in the bioreactor and preventing cell washout during the syngas continuous fermentation processes are important aspects to keep the process stable and increase the methane productivity [15].

The reverse membrane bioreactor (RMBR) is a configuration of a bioreactor for methane production. The RMBR system can be defined as a process that employs a fixed microbial growth system with the use of membranes. This bioreactor system was designed to enclose the cells completely in the permeable membrane filter, while substrates in the surrounding liquid are able to diffuse through the membrane to the cells. The fermentation products can thereafter diffuse out to the surrounding solution. Additional equipment for the cell recycle system is not necessary for this kind of process. This technique provided a high cell density; consequently, the process efficiency and productivity of the anaerobic digestion process for methane production were improved [20,21,22,23].

The current work focuses on applying the RMBR for syngas biomethanation under anaerobic semi-continuous mode in order to retain a high cell loading and consequently, improve the process performance. The simultaneous fermentation of syngas and organic compounds was also investigated. The performance of the system was evaluated under thermophilic anaerobic conditions and compared to the conventional system of free cells bioreactor (FCBR) under the same conditions.

2. MATERIALS AND METHODS

2.1. Anaerobic Culture, Medium, and Raw Syngas

An anaerobic culture was obtained from a 3000-m^3 municipal solid waste digester, operating under thermophilic (55 °C) conditions (Borås Energy and Environment AB, Borås, Sweden). The inoculum was incubated at 55 °C for 3 days to keep the bacteria active while consuming the carbon source provided by the inoculum. After incubation, the inoculum was filtered through a sieve (1-mm pore size) to remove the large particles. The digesting sludge was then centrifuged at 31,000× *g* for 15 min to separate the solid inoculum

(85 % Total solid (TS)) and the microorganisms, which were loaded into membrane sachets (Section 2.2). The synthetic medium solution contained acetate, propionate, butyrate with COD strength of 6.72 gCOD/L, and a vitamin solution (basal medium) with COD strength of 3.34 gCOD/L at a ratio of 3:1:1:1 [24]. The medium solution was buffered to pH 7.0 ± 0.2 with $NaHCO_3$ [25]. The artificial syngas containing CO (55% mol), H_2 (20% mol), and CO_2 (10% mol) [11] was provided by AGA gas AB (Borås, Sweden).

2.2. Cell Containment Procedure for the RMBR Configuration

The microbial cell encasement was performed following a previously described method [23]. Flat plain hydrophilic PVDF (polyvinylidene fluoride, Durapore®) membranes (Merch Millipore Ltd., Cork, Ireland) with a pore size, thickness, and diameter of 0.1 μm, 125 μm, and 90 mm, respectively, were used as supporting materials. The main physicochemical characteristics of the membranes are: air flow rate of 0.15 L/min.cm^2, 0.5% gravimetric extractables, 70% porosity, and water flow rate greater than 0.33 mL/min.cm^2. The membranes were cut into rectangular shapes of 6 × 6 cm^2 and folded to create membrane pockets of 3 × 6 cm^2. They were then heat-sealed (HPL 450 AS, Hawo, Obrigheim, Germany) on three sides with heating and cooling times of 4.5 and 4.5 s, leaving one side open for the insertion of the inoculum. Solid sludge inoculum (3 g per sachet) was then injected carefully into the synthetic membrane pockets, and the fourth side was subsequently sealed. The sachets containing the inoculum were used immediately for biomethanation of syngas.

2.3. Reactor Set up for Semi-Continuous Operation

The schematic illustration of the RMBR system is shown in Figure 1. The reactors used were serum glass bottles with 600-mL working volume, closed with rubber seals and an outlet for the biogas. The RMBR contained 15 sachets of encased inoculum (a total of 45 g) and 475 mL of synthetic medium. In parallel, the same amount of solid inoculum and medium was used in a reference reactor of free cells (FCBR) and performed under the same process conditions. The thermophilic temperature was maintained at 55 ± 1 °C throughout the process by placing the reactors in a water bath. The syngas amount was gradually increased by flushing fresh syngas at different gas pressures. Simultaneously, the OLR was gradually increased by increasing the concentrations of the medium fed (Table 1). During the fermentation process, the syngas was continuously bubbled through the reactors, from the bottom rising up to the top of the reactors, from where it was circulated to the bottom at different flow rates. Each co-substrate loading rate and gas circulation rate was maintained for different experiments (different periods of time), giving a total digestion process of 154 days.

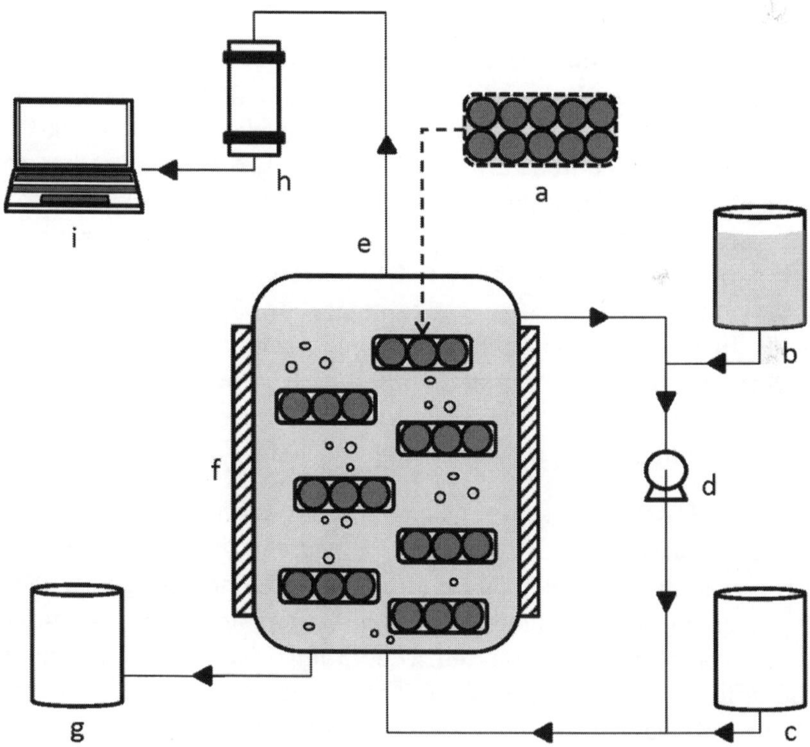

Figure 1. Schematic illustration of the reverse membrane bioreactor (RMBR) in the semi-continuous biomethanation process of syngas and organic substances. (**a**) Digesting sludge encased in PVDF membrane; (**b**) Organic and nutrient inlet; (**c**) Syngas inlet; (**d**) Peristaltic pump; (**e**) Product outlet; (**f**) Warm water bath; (**g**) Effluent outlet; (**h**) Gas sampling; and (**i**) Data analysis.

Table 1. Parameter profiles during the simultaneous semi-continuous biomethanation process.

Periods (Days)	Gas Circulation Rate (mL/min)	Organic Loading ($gCOD/L_{reactor}\cdot day$)	Syngas Amounts ($mmol/L_{reactor}\cdot day$)		
			H_2	CO	CO_2
I (0–16)	100	0.02	1.1	3.1	1.6
II (17–36)	200	0.02	2.2	6.1	1.7
III (37–58)	200	0.02	2.8	7.7	1.6
IV (59–87)	300	0.43	1.5	4.0	0.7
V (88–126)	300	0.86	1.7	4.7	1.0
VI (127–147)	300	1.70	3.8	9.4	1.9
VII (148–154)	300	3.40	7.0	15.2	4.0

The parameter profiles are shown in Table 1. At the beginning of the digestion (periods I, II, and III), the syngas amount added was gradually increased. The OLR was kept relatively low, according to a very low organic content in the basal medium that was used as the vitamins and minerals solution during these periods. This was done in order to allow the anaerobic culture to adapt to the environment with a low risk of cell washout and to investigate the ability of both systems to result in pure syngas fermentation. Then, from period IV to VII, the organic compounds containing acetate, propionate, and butyrate were added simultaneously with syngas. The OLR was doubled in order to investigate the efficiency of the systems under the harsh conditions at a shorter retention time.

For the adjustment of the syngas compounds inside the reactor, syngas was placed in a 1-L gas sampling bag and then the gas was fed to the reactor by a peristaltic pump. Inside the sampling bag, there was a known syngas volume that could be adjusted, and the content of each compound was analysed. Then, the gas was placed inside the reactor (with a known headspace), and the percentage of each syngas component was measured again. The ideal gas law was used for calculating the mole number:

$PV = nRT$, where:

P: 1 atm, adjusted with a needle after the syngas feeding; V: the headspace of the reactor (stable); R: the ideal gas law constant; T: the temperature of the reactor; n: the unknown mole value that was calculated.

2.4. Analytical Methods

The composition of the gas samples (methane, hydrogen, carbon monoxide, and carbon dioxide) was measured regularly, using a gas chromatograph (Perkin-Elmer, Norwalk, CT, USA), equipped with a packed column (CarboxenTM 1000, SUPELCO, 6′ × 1.8″ OD, 60/80 Mesh, Shelton, CT, USA) and a thermal conductivity detector (Perkin-Elmer) with an injection temperature of 200 °C. The carrier gas was nitrogen, with a flow rate of 30 mL/min at 75 °C. A 250-μL gas tight syringe (VICI, Precision Sampling Inc., Baton Rouge, LA, USA) was used for the gas sampling. The obtained peak area was compared with a standard gas, analyzed under the same conditions (STP, 273.15°K and 101.325 kPa). The volatile fatty acids (VFAs) were analyzed using a gas chromatograph (Auto System, Perkin-Elmer) equipped with a capillary column (Zebron ZB-WAXplus, Polyethylen glycol (PEG), 30 m × 0.25 mm × 0.25 μm, Shelton, CT, USA) and a flame ionized detector (Perkin-Elmer) with an injection and detection temperature of 250 and 300 °C, respectively. The carrier gas was nitrogen, with a flow rate of 2 mL/min at a pressure of 20 psi. The experiment was performed in duplicate, and the results were presented as the average ± standard deviation.

3. RESULTS AND DISCUSSION

Syngas biomethanation is a potent bio-conversion route, utilizing microorganisms to assimilate intermediate gases to produce methane. However, the cell density in continuous bioreactor operations plays an important role in the process efficiency. In this work, a novel application of the RMBR was investigated: rapid syngas biomethanation in a semi-continuous operation at high cell loading. The performance of the RMBR was compared to the performance of a reactor with free cells (FCBR) under otherwise identical conditions.

During the semi-continuous biomethanation process of 154 days, the performance of the RMBR and the FCBR was investigated under seven experimental conditions (seven periods). The conditions of each period are presented in Table 1.

3.1. Methane Production

Figure 2 and Table 2 show the trend of the methane production throughout the anaerobic process. Methane was produced from mainly pure syngas at the beginning of the process (Periods I–III), to thereafter be produced also from the co-substrates until the last day. The methane formed from these substrates was likely made by the acetic cleavage of acetate and the reduction of carbon dioxide. The microorganisms assimilating these substrates are mainly hydrogenotrophic methanogens and acetotrophic methanogens. It was observed that the methane production increased with the increasing concentration of gaseous and organic substrates fed, until the maximum conversion capacity was reached and the production decreased. This shows that the metabolism of the microorganisms occurred as expected.

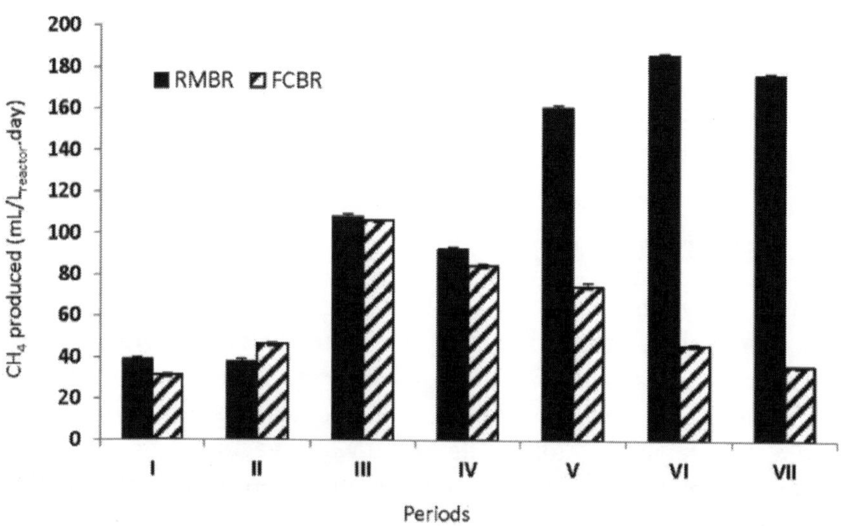

Figure 2. Comparison of the methane production in the reverse membrane bioreactor (RMBR) system and the free cell bioreactor (FCBR) during the semi-continuous biomethanation of syngas and organic substances.

Table 2. Investigated parameters during the semi-continuous biomethanation process of the co-substrates.

Periods	Methane Production (mL/$L_{reactor}$.day)		Total VFA (g/L)	
	RMBR *	FCBR **	RMBR *	FCBR **
I	39.1 ± 0.4	31.4 ± 0.5	0.4 ± 0.0	0.5 ± 0.0
II	38.0 ± 0.7	46.4 ± 0.5	0.4 ± 0.0	0.5 ± 0.0
III	108.9 ± 0.2	106.3 ± 0.2	0.4 ± 0.0	0.5 ± 0.0
IV	92.5 ± 1.5	84.4 ± 1.2	0.8 ± 0.3	1.0 ± 0.3
V	160.8 ± 1.1	74.5 ± 1.7	0.4 ± 0.3	1.2 ± 0.7
VI	186.0 ± 1.3	46.0 ± 0.6	4.4 ± 3.5	4.0 ± 3.0
VII	176.5 ± 0.3	36.2 ± 0.1	7.8 ± 0.8	9.4 ± 0.5

* The reverse membrane bioreactor. ** The free cells bioreactor.

In the beginning of the experiment, a total pure syngas amount of 5.8 mmol/L.day was added to the reactors. The amount was thereafter gradually increased throughout the operation of the reactors (Table 1). The basal medium with an organic content was fed at a low rate of 0.02 gCOD/L.day during the periods I, II, and III, and a similar methane production was observed in both reactors. The methane amount produced in the RMBR and the FCBR during these periods ranged between 38.0–108.9 mL/L.day and 31.4–106.3 mL/L.day, respectively. These results show that under a low risk of cell wash-out condition, the encased microorganisms in the RMBR displayed a similar methane production performance from syngas as the free microorganisms in the FCBR. The results also indicate that using PVDF membranes as a cell supporting material in the current reactor setup was not a major issue for the continuous syngas fermentation when it came to diffusion limitations. In addition, due to the practical design of the RMBR, the problematic issues of cell clogging and cell abrading are likely less severe.

During the periods IV, V, and VI, the organic compounds were introduced to both the reactors while the syngas amount added to the systems was decreased slightly in order to maintain a mild condition for microbial adaptation. From these experiments, the microorganisms retained in the RMBR could assimilate the co-substrate perfectly with maintained efficient performance, resulting in a corresponding increase of the methane production (Table 2 and Figure 2). The maximum methane productivity of the RMBR during these periods was 92.5, 160.8, and 186.0 mL/L.day, respectively. On the other hand, the wash-out of the microbial cells from the FCBR was clearly occurring during these periods, resulting in a substantially lower methane production from the FCBR than the RMBR during the periods V and VI (74.5 and 46.0 mL/L.day). In the RMBR, the microbial cells were still enclosed completely in the membrane sachets, and cell abrading was not visually occurring.

A better cell retention performance of the RMBR for syngas biomethanation in a semi-continuous process was clearly shown during period VII, when a higher syngas amount (26.2 mmol/L.day) was fed to both the reactors, while the organic loading was doubled in comparison to period VI. The methane production in the RMBR was higher than the production in the FCBR (176.5 and 36.2 mL/L.day, respectively). These results indicate that the RMBR had the ability to maintain a high methanation capacity, by retaining the microbial cells under the high risk of cell-wash out condition. Consequently, the system was able to convert more substrates into methane than the one with the free cells. This result stresses the importance of cell-retention inside anaerobic digestion as shown in other studies in which biofilm was used for high cell-density. However, with the method of cell-enclosure in the membranes, there is no danger of cell-detachment in contrast with the use of biofilm [26].

In the last period, the higher co-substrate concentration was fed to the systems in order to investigate if the product profiles changed. The results showed that the methane production in both the reactors was maintained at a low level, observed as a lower utilization of H_2 and CO (Figure 3a,b) and higher concentration of VFAs (Table 2). The co-substrate was not completely converted by the microbial cells in this period. This result indicates that the maximum conversion capacity of the systems had been reached. The lower methane production was probably because of the inhibitory effect of a high hydrogen partial pressure from the syngas, as well as the accumulation of the volatile fatty acids from the organic substances [2]. However, a higher amount of methane was still formed in the RMBR compared to the FCBR. This is an effect of the higher amount of microbial cells retained in the RMBR, still able to consume the co-substrates and convert them into methane.

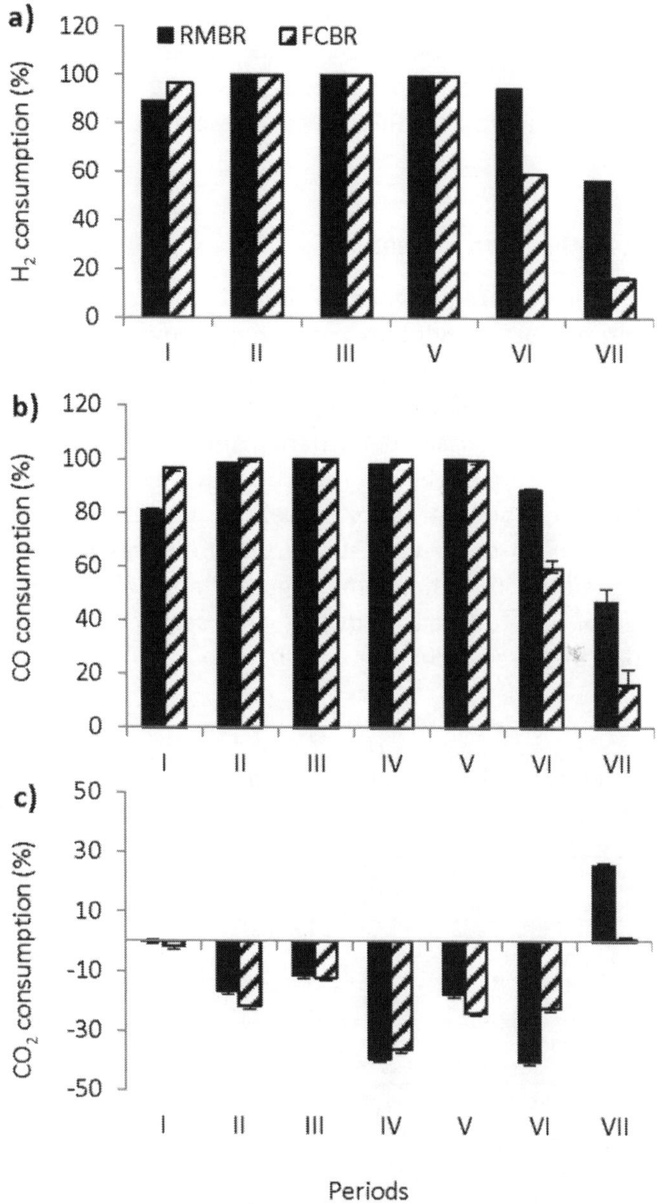

Figure 3. Comparison of the performance of the reverse membrane bioreactor (RMBR) system and the free cell bioreactor (FCBR) during the semi-continuous biomethanation of syngas and organic substances. The utilization of (**a**) Hydrogen; (**b**) Carbon monoxide; and (**c**) Carbon dioxide.

The above results indicate that during 154 days of syngas biomethanation, the RMBR system was an efficient and practical process in retaining the microbial cells, resulting in a high methane production under a semi-continuous process condition.

3.2. Syngas Utilization Efficiency

Periods I, II, and III were designed to allow the microbial cells to adapt to the environmental conditions in the beginning of the experiment. The artificial syngas fed was gradually increased, while the organic loading rate was controlled at a very low level (0.02 gCOD/L.day). The medium used only contained nutrients and vitamins during these periods. The flow rate of the gas recirculation was 100 mL/min in the first experiment, and thereafter increased to 200 mL/min during periods II and III in order to test the performances of the systems with shortened gas retention time. Figure 3 and Table 3 present the percentage of gas utilization during the semi-continuous syngas fermentation process of 154 days.

Table 3. Investigated parameters during the semi-continuous biomethanation process of the co-substrates.

Periods	Syngas Component Utilization (%) RMBR *			Syngas Component Utilization (%) FCBR **		
	H_2	CO	CO_2	H_2	CO	CO_2
I	88.9 ± 0.0	80.8 ± 0.4	−0.0 ± 0.5	96.5 ± 0.0	87.2 ± 0.2	−1.7 ± 0.0
II	100.0 ± 0.0	98.7 ± 0.0	−16.6 ± 0.1	100.0 ± 0.0	99.5 ± 0.0	−21.7 ± 0.0
III	100.0 ± 0.0	100.0 ± 0.0	−11.4 ± 0.2	100.0 ± 0.0	100.0 ± 0.0	−12.2 ± 0.1
IV	100.0 ± 0.0	98.2 ± 0.1	−39.3 ± 0.1	100.0 ± 0.0	99.8 ± 0.0	−36.3 ± 0.0
V	99.7 ± 0.0	100.0 ± 0.0	−17.6 ± 0.2	99.5 ± 0.0	100.0 ± 0.0	−23.8 ± 0.2
VI	94.7 ± 0.2	88.4 ± 0.7	−40.3 ± 0.1	59.3 ± 0.6	42.3 ± 3.3	−22.3 ± 0.1
VII	56.6 ± 0.2	46.8 ± 4.9	25.6 ± 0.7	16.4 ± 0.3	38.9 ± 5.7	0.8 ± 0.7

* The reverse membrane bioreactor. ** The free cells bioreactor.

The amount of H_2 in both the reactors remained at a very low level even when the H_2 (syngas) fed was increased from 1.1 to 2.8 mmol/L.day, and the gas circulation rate was increased from 100 to 200 mL/min. The percentage of H_2 consumed in the RMBR and the FCBR was close to 100 percent. This shows that the microbial cells in both the RMBR and the FCBR could convert the H_2 easily within 1 day. Similar to the conversion of H_2 in both the reactors during these periods, the microorganisms also converted all the CO, without any observed negative effects. The CO in the gas fed was increased from 3.1 to 7.7 mmol/L.day (Table 1), and it was utilized by the microbial cells in both the systems at almost the same rate (about 100 percent). The CO_2 amounts showed a different trend from the other gases. It increased during the first 3 days, and then stayed stable throughout periods I–III. It was observed that the CO_2 amounts in both the reactors increased rather than decreased during these periods (a CO_2 amount of 1.6–1.7 mmol/L.day was present in the syngas fed). This trend indicated that the microbial cells in both the reactors had performed as expected, with the CO_2 being both produced and consumed during the fermentations. Thus, even though CO_2 was supplemented together with the other compounds in the syngas, CO_2 was also produced, leading to a stable amount of CO_2 (Figure 3c). The most interesting conclusion that can be drawn from the results of these periods is that the gases transfer through the PVDF membrane used, as the cell encasing material was not a limiting factor during the semi-continuous fermentation process, since the amount of the different components of the syngas were at similar levels as in the free cell system. The encased cells in the RMBR could assimilate the syngas continuously for product formation.

During periods IV and V, the gas circulation rate was increased to 300 mL/min, reducing the gas retention time in the systems. The syngas amount was decreased slightly while higher organic loading rates with a medium containing acetic, propionic, and butyric acid was introduced. The results showed that the syngas conversion performance of both the reactors was maintained during the simultaneous co-substrate fermentation. The microorganisms in both of the systems utilized almost 100 percent of the H_2 and CO. However, CO_2 started accumulating during these periods, indicating that the microbial cells decomposed the organic acids.

During the last two periods, VI and VII, a higher concentration of co-substrates was provided to the reactors. The results showed that the syngas utilization showed a decreasing trend in both the reactors, despite a higher concentration being added to the reactors during period VII (Table 1). The higher gas amounts, especially of H_2, in the systems probably increased the partial pressure, thereby leading to a higher pH of the liquid solution (Figure 4b). Furthermore, additional organic substances, which resulted in the accumulated VFA, were present during these periods (Figure 4a). This resulted in a decreased performance of the microorganisms in the reactors. However, the RMBR still showed a better ability to utilize the high concentration of co-substrates than the FCBR during these periods, shown by a higher percentage of H_2 and CO utilization (Table 2). The percentage of H_2 utilization in the RMBR and the FCBR from period VI was 94.7 and 59.3, respectively. The CO utilization in the RMBR and the FCBR was 88.4 and 42.3 percent, respectively. CO_2 was accumulated, resulting in negative utilization values of −40.3 and −22.3 percent, respectively. These results revealed that the RMBR had a better capacity than the conventional system of the FCBR to convert higher syngas and co-substrate concentrations in a semi-continuous fermentation process. However, a positive CO_2 utilization in both the reactors was observed in period VII. This means that CO_2 was consumed at a higher rate than it was produced. In general, CO_2 is produced during the anaerobic digestion of organic compounds. In period VII, the VFAs were accumulated, meaning that the organic substances were not much used. This leads to less CO_2 production in both the RMBR and FCBR. Although a higher amount of $CO_2$was fed to the reactors (Table 1), CO_2 was likely utilized by the microbial cells, thus resulting in a positive CO_2 utilization. It can be concluded that retaining the microorganisms in the RMBR was a successful technique for improving the syngas biomethanation in the long-term fermentation process. Encased microbial cells in the RMBR showed a similar performance to assimilate the syngas in a semi-continuous biomethanation process as the system with the free cells at a low organic loading rate. Moreover, when higher syngas and organic loading rates were applied, a higher process efficiency of the RMBR, compared to the FCBR, was observed.

3.3. Volatile Fatty Acids and pH Profile

In this work, the performance of the bioreactors with cells degrading a mixture of two substrates in a semi-continuous process was investigated. Organic acids, including acetic, propionic, and butyric acid, were used as co-substrates to the syngas in the fermentations.

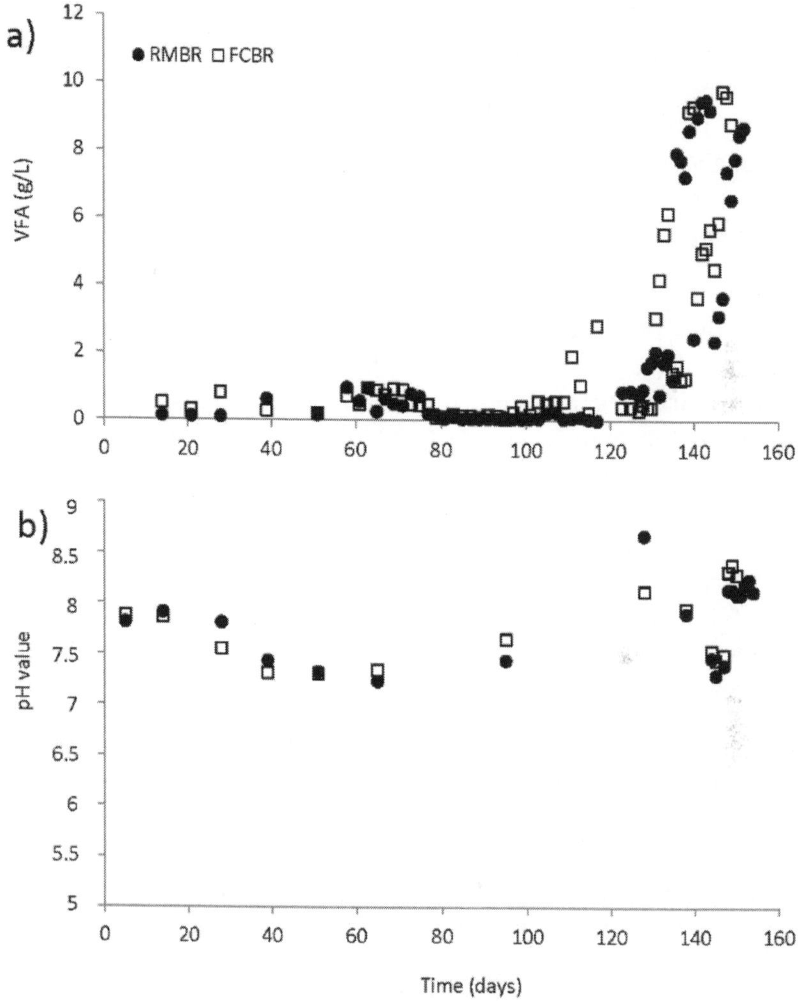

Figure 4. Accumulation of organic acids and pH during the semi-continuous biomethanation of co-substrates. (**a**) Volatile fatty acids; (**b**) pH.

The organic loading rate (OLR), in the form of the organic acids fed, was gradually increased in both the systems. The data of total volatile fatty acids (VFAs) in the effluents represented the organic acids utilization during the simultaneous fermentation process. The VFA value is also an indicator for monitoring the stability of the anaerobic digestion process [4]. In a previous work, repeated batch syngas biomethanation was examined [27]. All of the medium was removed, and the encased cells were reused in a new batch experiment. In that setup, the inhibiting substances probably disappeared, which is different from the continuous process of the present work, where most of the substrates remained in the reactors. Thus, the trend of the VFA content and the pH values were investigated in this experiment.

Figure 4 represents the total VFA concentration (a) and the pH values (b) in the effluents during the semi-continuous fermentation processes in the two investigated cell systems. The VFA amounts in both the reactors were close to zero during the periods I, II, III, and IV, even when the organic loading was increased from 0.02 to 0.43 g COD/L.day. This indicates that the microorganisms in both the reactors were able to convert the organic substances simultaneously with syngas, without any observed negative effect. However, the pH value decreased slightly when the organic acids were introduced to the system during these periods. The pH was in the range of 7.0–7.8, and the changes were not observed to affect the stability of the processes.

A low amount of VFAs in the reactors shows that the microorganisms are coping well with the process conditions. In the anaerobic digestion process, VFAs can be consumed by the methane-producing microorganisms. This reduction of VFAs increases the alkalinity of the surrounding medium. The pH in the anaerobic digester is significantly affected by the production of VFAs and the CO_2 content of the biogas.

In period V (days 88–126), there were substantially lower VFA concentrations measured in the effluent from the RMBR (around 0.2 g/L) compared to the free cell system FCBR (around 0.6 g/L), as the OLR was increased to 0.86 gCOD/L.day. However, the VFAs concentration still remained at a low level during this period. The VFAs concentration in the RMBR was totally consumed. The reason for this fact was probably the high active microbial cell density retained in the RMBR, while the cell wash out was visually occurring from the FCBR. During this experiment, the pH value of both the reactors started to ramp up slightly. This probably happened because of the high conversion rate of the VFAs to biogas (methane and CO_2), as well as the additional CO_2 fed contained in the syngas (Figure 4b). In particular, the value from the RMBR had lower residual VFAs content than the FCBR. The pH increased to 8.7 and 8.1 in the RMBR and the FCBR, respectively.

When the concentration of the organic acids and syngas were increased in the last period, the accumulation of the VFAs was even higher, while the pH dropped slightly. The VFA accumulation in the FCBR increased, reaching a maximum amount of 9.4 g/L, while the total VFAs in the RMBR were detected at 7.8 g/L, indicating that the cell encasement in the RMBR helped to maintain a higher ability to degrade the VFAs compared to the FCBR in a semi-continuous fermentation process. However, the recommended VFA concentrations during the anaerobic digestion, without negatively affecting the methane-producing microorganisms in the process, are under 4 g/L [1,2]. At the observed levels in the reactors, it was thus clear that the maximum process capacity had been reached in this condition.

These results indicated that the RMBR system performed efficiently during the semi-continuous syngas biomethanation with the addition of organic substances as a co-substrate. Organic acids were degraded simultaneously with the reduction of the syngas until too high amounts of substrates were fed to the systems.

4. CONCLUSIONS

The syngas biomethanation under simultaneous semi-continuous fermentation could be enhanced by retaining a high microbial cell density in a reverse membrane bioreactor (RMBR). No cell washout was visually observed from the RMBR during the process, running for 154 days. The performance of the RMBR for the simultaneous fermentation of syngas and the organic compounds was better than the conventional system of free cells (FCBR). The microorganisms in the RMBR were able to convert the syngas simultaneously with organic acids to methane at higher substrate concentrations and productivity than the FCBR system. The RMBR reached maximum capacities of H_2, CO, and CO_2 conversion of 7.0, 15.2, and 4.0 mmol/L.day, respectively, at the organic loading rate of 3.40 gCOD/L.day. The highest methane production rate from the RMBR was 186.0 mL/$L_{reactor}$.day on the 147th day, compared to the highest rate in the FCBR, 106.3 mL/$L_{reactor}$.day, on the 58th day.

ACKNOWLEDGMENTS

This work was financially supported by the Swedish Research Council. The authors would like to thank Johan Westman for the useful discussions.

AUTHOR CONTRIBUTIONS

All authors contributed to the conception and design of experiments; Supansa Y. Westman and Konstantinos Chandolias performed the experiments and analyzed the data; all authors contributed to writing the paper.

CONFLICTS OF INTEREST

The authors declare no conflict of interest.

REFERENCES

1. Deublein, D.; Steinhauser, A. Biogas from Waste and Renewable Resources; Wiley-VCH Verlag GmbH & Co.: Weinheim, Germany, 2008; pp. 49–50.

2. Gerardi, M.H. The Microbiology of Anaerobic Digesters; John Wiley & Sons: Hoboken, NJ, USA, 2003.

3. Nizami, A.-S.; Korres, N.E.; Murphy, J.D. Review of the integrated process for the production of grass biomethane.Environ. Sci. Technol. 2009, 43, 8496–8508.

4. Santosh, Y.; Sreekrishnan, T.R.; Kohli, S.; Rana, V. Enhancement of biogas production from solid substrates using different techniques—A review. Bioresour. Technol. 2004, 95, 1–10.

5. Daniell, J.; Köpke, M.; Simpson, S. Commercial biomass syngas fermentation. Energies 2012, 5, 5372–5417.

6. Mohammadi, M.; Najafpour, G.D.; Younesi, H.; Lahijani, P.; Uzir, M.H.; Mohamed, A.R. Bioconversion of synthesis gas to second

generation biofuels: A review. Renew. Sust. Energy Rev. 2011, 15, 4255–4273.

7. Munasinghe, P.C.; Khanal, S.K. Biomass-derived syngas fermentation into biofuels: Opportunities and challenges.Bioresour. Technol. 2010, 101, 5013–5022.

8. Kimmel, D.E.; Klasson, K.T.; Clausen, E.C.; Gaddy, J.L. Performance of trickle-bed bioreactors for converting synthesis gas to methane. Appl. Biochem. Micro. 1991, 28–29, 457–469.

9. Henstra, A.M.; Sipma, J.; Rinzema, A.; Stams, A.J.M. Microbiology of synthesis gas fermentation for biofuel production. Curr. Opin. Biotech. 2007, 18, 200–206.

10. Klasson, K.T.; Ackerson, M.D.; Clausen, E.C.; Gaddy, J.L. Bioconversion of synthesis gas into liquid or gaseous fuels.Enzym. Microb. Technol. 1992, 14, 602–608.

11. Klasson, K.T.; Elmore, B.B.; Vega, J.L.; Ackerson, M.D.; Clausen, E.C.; Gaddy, J.L. Biological production of liquid and gaseous fuels from synthesis gas. Appl. Biochem. Biotechnol. 1990, 24–25, 857–873.

12. Lee, P.-H.; Ni, S.-Q.; Chang, S.-Y.; Sung, S.; Kim, S.-H. Enhancement of carbon monoxide mass transfer using an innovative external hollow fiber membrane (HFM) diffuser for syngas fermentation: Experimental studies and model development. Chem. Eng. J. 2012, 184, 268–277.

13. Madigan, M.T.; Martinko, J.M.; Parker, J. Brock biology of Microorganisms; Prentice-Hall: Upper Saddle River, NJ, USA, 1997.

14. Orgill, J.J.; Atiyeh, H.K.; Devarapalli, M.; Phillips, J.R.; Lewis, R.S.; Huhnke, R.L. A comparison of mass transfer coefficients between trickle-bed, hollow fiber membrane and stirred tank reactors. Bioresour. Technol. 2013, 133, 340–346.

15. Younesi, H.; Najafpour, G.; Ku Ismail, K.S.; Mohamed, A.R.; Kamaruddin, A.H. Biohydrogen production in a continuous stirred tank bioreactor from synthesis gas by anaerobic

photosynthetic bacterium: Rhodopirillum rubrum. Bioresour. Technol. 2008, 99, 2612–2619.

16. Shen, Y.; Brown, R.; Wen, Z. Enhancing mass transfer and ethanol production in syngas fermentation of clostridium carboxidivorans p7 through a monolithic biofilm reactor. Appl. Energy 2014, 136, 68–76.

17. Bredwell, M.D.; Worden, R.M. Mass-transfer properties of microbubbles. 1. Experimental studies. Biotechnol. Prog.1998, 14, 31–38.

18. Shen, Y.; Brown, R.; Wen, Z. Syngas fermentation of clostridium carboxidivoran p7 in a hollow fiber membrane biofilm reactor: Evaluating the mass transfer coefficient and ethanol production performance. Biochem. Eng. J. 2014,85, 21–29.

19. Liu, K.; Atiyeh, H.K.; Stevenson, B.S.; Tanner, R.S.; Wilkins, M.R.; Huhnke, R.L. Continuous syngas fermentation for the production of ethanol, n-propanol and n-butanol. Bioresour. Technol. 2014, 151, 69–77.

20. Wikandari, R.; Youngsukkasem, S.; Millati, R.; Taherzadeh, M.J. Performance of semi-continuous membrane bioreactor in biogas production from toxic feedstock containing d-limonene. Bioresour. Technol. 2014, 170, 350–355.

21. Youngsukkasem, S.; Akinbomi, J.; Rakshit, S.K.; Taherzadeh, M.J. Biogas production by encased bacteria in synthetic membranes: Protective effects in toxic media and high loading rates. Environ. Technol. 2013, 34, 2077–2084.

22. Youngsukkasem, S.; Barghi, H.; Rakshit, S.; Taherzadeh, M. Rapid biogas production by compact multi-layer membrane bioreactor: Efficiency of synthetic polymeric membranes. Energies 2013, 6, 6211–6224.

23. Youngsukkasem, S.; Rakshit, K.S.; Taherzadeh, M.J. Biogas production by encapsulated methane producing bacteria.Bioresources 2012, 7, 56–65.

24. Osuna, M.B.; Zandvoort, M.H.; Iza, J.M.; Lettinga, G.; Lens, P.N. Effects of trace element addition on volatile fatty acid

conversions in anaerobic granular sludge reactors. Environ. Technol. 2003, 24, 573–587.

25. Isci, A.; Demirer, G.N. Biogas production potential from cotton wastes. Renew. Energy 2007, 32, 750–757.

26. Langer, S.; Schropp, D.; Bengelsdorf, F.R.; Othman, M.; Kazda, M. Dynamics of biofilm formation during anaerobic digestion of organic waste. Anaerobe 2014, 29, 44–51.

27. Youngsukkasem, S.; Chandolias, K.; Taherzadeh, M.J. Rapid bio-methanation of syngas in a reverse membrane bioreactor: Membrane encased microorganisms. Bioresour. Technol. 2015, 178, 334–340.

Chapter 8

Characterization and Application of a Disposable Rotating Bed Bioreactor for Mesenchymal Stem Cell Expansion

Anne Neumann [1,2,†], Antonina Lavrentieva [2,†], Alexandra Heilkenbrinker [2], Maren Loenne [2] and Cornelia Kasper [1,*]

[1]*Department for Biotechnology, University of Natural Resources and Life Sciences, Muthgasse 18, 1190 Vienna, Austria*

[2]*Institute for Technical Chemistry, Gottfried Wilhelm Leibniz University Hanover, Callinstrasse 5, 30167 Hanover, Germany*

ABSTRACT

Recruitment of mesenchymal stromal cells (MSC) into the field of tissue engineering is a promising development since these cells can be expanded *ex vivo* to clinically relevant numbers and, after expansion, retain their ability to differentiate into various cell lineages. Safety requirements and the necessity to obtain high cell numbers without frequent subcultivation of cells raised the question of the possibility of expanding MSC in one-way (single-use) disposable bioreactors. In this study, umbilical cord-derived MSC (UC-MSC) were expanded in a disposable Z®RP 2000 H bioreactor under dynamic conditions. Z®RP was characterized regarding residence time and mixing in order to evaluate the optimal bioreactor settings, enabling optimal mass transfer in the absence of shear stress, allowing an reproducible expansion of MSC, while maintaining their stemness properties. Culture of the UC-MSC in disposable Z®RP 2000 H bioreactor resulted in a reproducible 8-fold increase of cell numbers after 5 days. Cells were shown to maintain specific MSC surface marker expression as well as trilineage differentiation potential and lack stress-induced premature senescence.

Keywords: umbilical cord stem cells; MSC expansion; dynamic culture; bioreactor

1. INTRODUCTION

Almost four hundred clinical trials [1] recruiting mesenchymal stem cells (MSC) for the treatment of several diseases such as spinal cord injuries, burns, liver cirrhosis or failure, graft *versus* host disease, diabetes mellitus, progressive multiple sclerosis and cardiac ischemia are being carried out at the moment. For each treatment, millions of cells are required and optimal expansion methods can help in obtaining MSC of good quality within a short period of time, enhancing chances for treatment optimization and patient survival. The expansion of MSC in bioreactors is a promising development for the future application of MSC in cell-based therapies and tissue engineering. There are numerous types of bioreactors used to expand adherent anchorage-dependent cells including MSC (e.g., WAVE-bioreactor, GE Healthcare, PluriX^{TM} 3D bioreactor, Pluristem and Quantum bioreactor, TerumoBCT) [2,3,4,5]. Dynamic cultivation conditions have several advantages in comparison to static cell expansion. First of all, cultivation in a closed system without the need to manually change the culture medium in a clean bench significantly reduces the risk of possible contamination; Second, the control of all parameters of culture together with continuous documentation using IT systems makes it possible to assure the quality of cells and to avoid human errors; Third, dynamic cultivation systems like bioreactors provide active mass transfer, supplying MSC with gases and nutrients while removing toxic metabolites; Last but not least, there is the argument of production costs - which can be a major obstacle to the spread of MSC clinical applications [6,7,8]. MSC are anchorage-dependant cells, which cannot be expanded in suspension culture. Several techniques including cultivation on microcarriers, three-dimensional matrix and conventional cell culture plastic surfaces (cell factories) were developed over the past few years. These techniques may allow obtaining the necessary cell numbers without manual cultivation of MSC, reducing the risk of bacterial and fungal contamination as well as cross-contamination. Additionally, continuous on-line monitoring and control of important cultivation parameters like pH, temperature, oxygen, CO22 and metabolite concentrations help to provide the optimal growth conditions for the cells and assure reproducible cell expansion [9,10,11]. Many publications have been issued on that subject reporting a large number of reactor modifications, a wide variety of tissue function as well as biomaterial properties. Bioreactor systems target a reliable and efficient procedure, enabling highly reproducible, automated and controlled process compatible with good manufacturing practice (GMP) requirements [7,12,13]. A new approach in the expansion of adherent MSC is provided by Zellwerk GmbH (Oberkraemer, Germany), where cells are cultivated on rotating stalked polycarbonate cell carrier slides (Figure 1). The Z®RP 2000 H bioreactor is connected to the pH and pO22 sensor electrodes, which are integrated into the tubing system. Besides cell culture medium mixing via rotation, medium is also constantly circulating via a tubing system, where feed- and waste-flasks are connected, making it possible to culture cells in fed-batch or perfusion modus. Disposable Z®RP 2000 H bioreactor provides a surface of 2000 cm22 for cell growth, while Z®RP 8000 H offers 8000 cm22. Cultivation of cells is performed in a GMP-breeder under fully automated control with documentation. According to the manufacturers data, MSC in a Z®RP 8000 H system can be expanded in 9 days to 400 million cells [14].

Overcoming nutrient limitation is an important factor in all existing bioreactor systems. *In vivo* cells benefit from blood vessels being located in most tissues within a distance of 100–200 μm from capillaries. Furthermore, MSC are suggested to be associated with blood vessels *in vivo* [15,16], and consequently are not subjected to major nutrient limitation in their niche. Under conventional, static culture conditions mass transport is controlled by diffusion, being insufficient for high cell densities and high medium volumes [13]. On

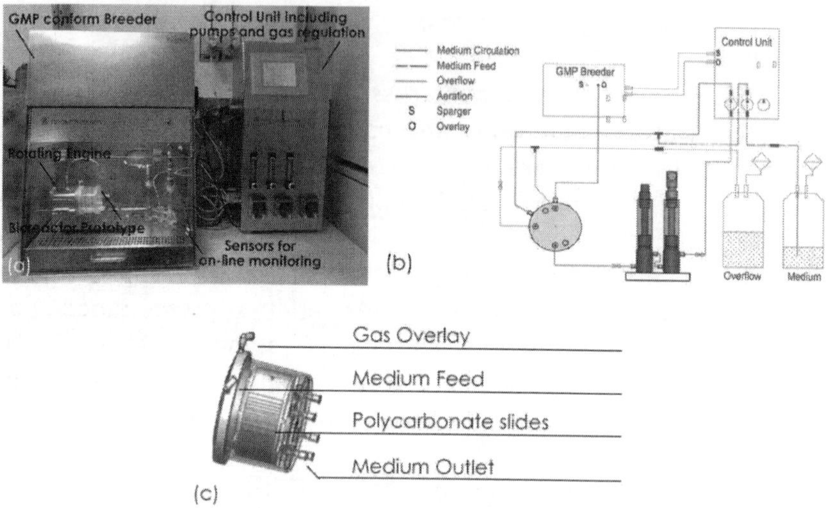

Figure 1. Z®RP 2000 H (Zellwerk GmbH, Oberkraemer) bioreactor system with breeder and control tower (**a**) and disposable bioreactor (**b**) set up and (**c**) rotating bed consisted of polycarbonate cell carrier slides (total surface area 2000 cm22, reactor size 8.8 × 4.6 cm) (drawings adopted and modified from manufacturers manual and [14]).

the other hand, fluid flow induces shear stress to which MSC are very sensitive, responding with biochemical cascades resulting in phenotype chances [17]. Thus, mechanical stimuli play a crucial role in differentiation of MSC, often targeted when bone or cartilage tissue constructs for implantation need to be obtained. On the contrary, these are undesired effects in MSC expansion when undifferentiated cells are requested. It is therefore important to estimate mixing profiles within the bioreactor and possible resulting shear stress prior to bioreactor approval. This work was aimed to characterize the ZRP 2000 H bioreactor as a first step towards comparability and a future scale-up system for MSC expansion *in vitro*.

We analyzed residence time distribution under different operation conditions, obtaining the Bodenstein number as a dimensional parameter, describing mixing properties within the system. Umbilical cord derived MSC (UC-MSC) were expanded over 5 days without subcultivation in the Z®RP 2000 H bioreactor, whereafter the yield and quality of the expanded cells were studied.

2. EXPERIMENTAL SECTION

2.1. Z®RP Platform

The Z®RP platform consists of the bioreactor, a GMP-conform breeder and an external control unit. The Z®RP 2000 H bioreactor (Figure 1c) is a disposable rotating bed bioreactor that is working in perfusion mode. The core of the bioreactor is the rotating bed, which consists of polycarbonate cell carrier slides with total surface area 2000 cm22. The polycarbonate slides are fixed to a vertical shaft, which is rotated by a non-contact magnetic drive. During culture, bioreactor was placed in a GMP conform breeder. The breeder was thermostated and working as a laminar flow hood allowing manipulations of the bioreactor in a sterile working environment. All process parameters including feeding rate, gassing and rotational speed were monitored and regulated by an external control unit. The temperature within the bioreactor and the breeder as well as the pH-value and oxygen content were controlled by sensor electrodes. pH-value was regulated by overlay gassing with carbon dioxide or air.

2.2. Residence Time Distribution

Residence time distribution was determined using an approximation of Dirac pulse. The Dirac pulse was approximated by adding the tracer substance methylene blue into the bioreactor in a time frame of 5 s, which results in a slope of about 2 × E(ϑ). The tracer substance was injected into the bioreactor through an upper injection port. At the beginning of the Dirac pulse the reactor bed disks were oriented horizontally to simulate conditions for residence time distribution like in cell expansion experiments. When starting reactor bed rotation during cell expansion, reactor bed disks were also oriented horizontally, due to cell seeding. Dirac pulse was performed with 200 μL methylene blue (15 mg/mL) for a filled and with 120 μL methylene blue for a half-filled bioreactor, respectively. During the measurement H22O was pumped through the bioreactor with a pump rate of 2 mL/min utilizing a peristaltic pump. The concentration gradient of the tracer was measured photometrically at 664 nm. Residence time distribution was determined for different reactor volumes (120 mL, 70 mL) and for different rotation speeds of the bioreactor bed (0.25 rotations per minute (rpm), 0.5 rpm, 1 rpm).

2.3. Cumulative Residence Time Function

Cumulative residence time function was determined performing a displacement measurement. The bioreactor was filled with H22O and the tracer substance methylene blue (25 μg/L) was pumped continuously through the bioreactor with a pump rate of 2 mL/min. The concentration gradient of the tracer was measured photometrically at 664 nm. Residence time distribution was determined for different reactor volumes (120 mL, 70 mL) and for different rotation speeds of the bioreactor bed (0.25 rpm, 0.5 rpm, 1 rpm).

2.4. Cell Culture

Human MSC were isolated from the umbilical cords of three different term-deliveries (38–40 weeks) by Cesarean section. All patients delivered their informed consent, as approved by the Institutional Review Board, project #3037 on 17 June 2006 and in an extended permission #443 on 26 February 2009. The isolated populations were extensively characterized as mesenchymal stem cells by surface marker analysis and functional properties [18]. MSC were expanded and cryopreserved until the start of the experiment as described. After thawing, the cells were expanded over two passages. Experiments were performed with cells of passages 3 to 7. Cells were cultivated in αMEM containing 1 g/L glucose (Biochrom, Berlin, Germany), 10% human serum (provided by the Division of Transfusion Medicine, Medical University Hanover, Hanover, Germany) and 50 μg/ml gentamicin (PAA Laboratories GmbH, Pasching, Germany) in a humidified atmosphere containing 5% CO22 and 21% O22 at 37 ∘C∘C (Incubators: Thermo scientific, Hanau, Germany).

2.5. Expansion of UC-MSC in the Z®RP 2000 H Bioreactor

For the expansion in the Z®RP 2000 H bioreactor, frozen UC-MSC were first revitalized and subsequently cultured over two passages in αMEM (Biochrom, Germany) supplemented with 10% human serum (Division of Transfusion Medicine, Medical University Hanover, Germany) and 0.5% gentamycin (PAA Laboratories GmbH, Pasching, Germany) in T-flasks and then seeded at cell density 1500 cells/cm22 (total cell number 3 × 1066 cells; 1.2 × 1044 cells/mL). Cells were seeded on both sides of polycarbonate cell carrier slides and incubated for 24 h for cell attachment on each side, respectively. For each seeding and attachment period, the rotation bed was stopped resulting in a horizontal position of the carrier slides. Afterwards, the bioreactor was filled with cell suspension (125 mL αMEM supplemented with 10% human serum and 0.5% gentamicin, 37 ∘C∘C). After attachment of the cells on both sides of the slides for 24 h, respectively, bed rotation and medium circulation were started. Medium circulation was set at 0.1 mL/min, bed rotation at 0.1 rpm. Feeding rate with fresh cell culture medium was set to the intermitted mode (starting with 2%) and increased each day depending on glucose consumption and lactate production. Breeder temperature was set at 37 ∘C∘C. The overlay gas mixture consisted of 95% air and 5% CO22. In total, three cultivations under the same conditions were performed. Cell culture media from the bioreactor was sampled once a day with the help of a syringe via a septum installed on the bioreactor.

2.6. Cell Number, Population Doublings and Doubling Time

After 5 days of expansion, cells were harvested by treatment with accutase (PAA Laboratories GmbH). First of all, the cell culture medium was removed from the bioreactor with the help of the pump, then the bioreactor was filled with warm (37 ∘C∘C) PBS, bed rotation was switched on and cells were washed for 5 min. After washing, PBS was removed, the bioreactor was filled with 80 mL accutase (37 ∘C∘C), and bed rotation was switched on for the next 20 min. After incubation with accutase, the harvested cells were collected in falcon-tubes and centrifuged for 15 min at 300× *g*. Cell pellets were resuspended in fresh αMEM and cell numbers were estimated by counting in a haemocytometer. Population doublings were calculated according to:

$$Nd = \frac{ln(\frac{x}{x0})}{ln2} \tag{1}$$

where NdNd is the number of population doublings during a ΔtΔt period of time, x0x0 is the number of living cells at time t=0t=0, and *x* is the number of living cells at time *t* (end of cultivation). Population doubling time TdTd was calculated according to:

$$Td = \frac{\Delta t}{Nd} \tag{2}$$

2.7. Cell Differentiation

After expansion in the Z®RP 2000 H bioreactor, UC-MSC were seeded on two-dimensional fibronectin surfaces (Corning, Berlin, Germany) with cell densities of about 3000 cell/cm22. Subsequently, UC-MSC were cultivated in DMEM containing 1 g/L glucose (Sigma-Aldrich, Munich, Germany), 10% human serum (provided by the Division of Transfusion Medicine, Medical University Hannover, Germany) and 50 µg/mL gentamicin (PAA Laboratories GmbH, Pasching, Germany) for 4 days. Afterwards UC-MSC were cultivated for three weeks in NH AdipoDiff Medium, NH ChondroDiff Medium and NH OsteoDiff Medium (Miltenyi Biotech, Bergisch Gladbach, Germany), supplemented with 50 µg/mL gentamicin. Medium was changed every second day.

2.8. Histological Stainings

Cell fixation: Cells were fixed with 600 µL paraformaldehyde (4% in PBS) for 30 min at 4 ∘C∘C. BODIPY staining: The fixed cell layer was covered with 300 µL of BODIPY solution (5 µM in PBS) (Invitrogen, Darmstadt, Germany). Samples were incubated for 5 min in the dark and thereafter staining solution removed. The fluorescence was detected at an excitation wavelength of 485 nm and an emission wavelength of 535 nm. Alcian Blue staining: The fixed cell layer was incubated for 3 min in 700 µL acidic acid (3%) and subsequently covered with 700 µL Alcianblue 8G solution (Sigma Aldrich, Munich, Germany). Samples were incubated for 30 min at room temperature and thereafter washed with acidic acid (3%). Pictures were taken at a light microscope (Olympus, Tokyo, Japan). Calcein staining: The fixed cell layer was covered with 500 µL of calcein solution (5 µg/mL in ddH22O) (Sigma Aldrich, Munich, Germany). Samples were incubated overnight at 4 ∘C∘C and thereafter washed extensively with distilled water. The fluorescence of the bounded calcein was detected at an excitation wavelength of 485 nm and an emission wavelength of 535 nm.

2.9. Glucose and Consumption and Lactate Production

The concentration of glucose and lactate in the medium was measured using an YSI 2700 SELECT analyzer (YSI Inc., Yellow Springs, OH, USA).

2.10. Senescence-Associated β-Galactosidase Staining

Cell senescence was estimated with the use of the Senescence *β*-Galactosidase Staining Kit (Cell Signaling Technology, Danvers, MA, USA) in accordance to the manufacturer's instructions. For the staining, harvested cells were seeded at a density of 6000 cells/cm22 for 48 h, then washed with PBS, fixed with the fixation solution from the kit. Senescence-associated *β*-galactosidase (SA-*β*-gal) staining was performed overnight at 37 ∘C∘C. Counterstaining was performed with DAPI (Roth GmbH & Co. KG, Karlsruhe, Germany).

2.11. Flow Cytometric Analysis of Surface Antigen Expression

UC-MSC were harvested by accutase treatment, washed twice in a cold blocking buffer and resuspended to a concentration of 1066 cells per mL. Specific antibody-staining was performed by adding 20 µL of prediluted staining solution (BD Biosciences, Heidelberg, Germany) to 100 µL of cell suspension as described earlier [19]. Cells stained with matched isotype control antibodies served as a negative control. After 20 min incubation at room temperature in the dark, 400 µL of blocking buffer were added and cells were analyzed in an EPICS XL/MCL flow cytometer (Beckman Coulter, Krefeld, Germany). At least, 10,000 gated events were acquired on a LOG fluorescence scale. Generated data were analyzed using the program WinMDI 2.8.

3. RESULTS AND DISCUSSION

3.1. Residence Time

Residence time is an important parameter, providing information about homogeneity of the liquid phase within the bioreactor. Residence time distribution (RTD) as well as average residence time were therefore considered. We characterized the RTD in the reactor by conducting a series of washout experiments (Dirac pulse experiments). We considered grade of filling of the bioreactor with liquid as well as rotation speed of the reactor bed to have an influence on the residence time and backmixing within the bioreactor. We therefore achieved characterization of a half-filled reactor (70 mL) and filled bioreactor (120 mL, which is nearly the maximum volume for Z®RP 2000H) (see Figure 2). Rotation was set at 0.25, 0.5 and 1 rpm since these rotation speeds were considered for the later cell culture. Data obtained were compared to the hydrodynamic residence time (τ) (indicating perfectly mixed phase, the ideal condition in case of continuous stirred tank reactor (CSTR)).

$$\tau = \frac{V_R}{Q} \tag{3}$$

where *VRR* is the reactor volume (medium volume) and *Q* the volume flow.

The RTD (E(t)) is obtained from these experimental data by normalization.

$$E(t) = \frac{C_t - C_0}{\int_0^{\infty} [C_t - C_0] dt} \tag{4}$$

where CtCt represents the concentration of the tracer, C0C0 the initial concentration of the tracer and *t* the time.

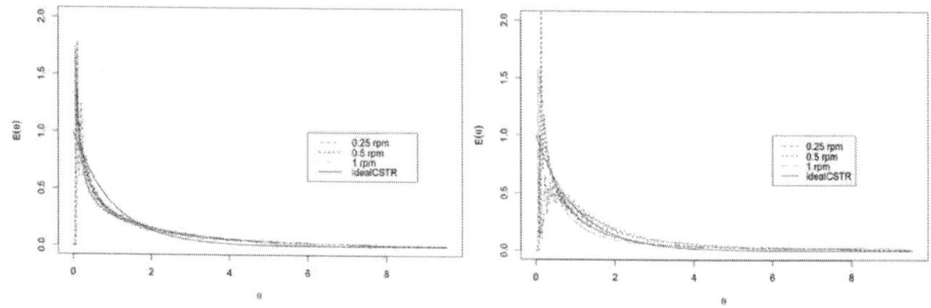

(a) 70 mL

(b) 120 mL

Figure 2. Residence time distribution (RTD) in Z®RP 2000H bioreactor depending on rotation speed of the reactor bed (0.25, 0.5, 1 rpm) and medium volume (**a**) 70 mL and (**b**) 120 mL; (n = 1). RTD for ideal CSTR is plotted for comparison reasons.

To obtain dimensionless functions the dimensionless time ϑ is used according to:

$$\theta = \frac{t}{\tau} \tag{5}$$

The mean residence time (tmtm) was calculated by integrating the RTD as follows:

$$t_m = \int_0^{\infty} tE(t)dt \tag{6}$$

The variance σ2σ2 of the standard deviation of the RTD is calculated using:

$$\sigma^2 = \int_0^\infty (t - t_m)^2 E(t) dt \tag{7}$$

The magnitude of this 2nd moment is an indication of the spread of the RTD.

RTD is integrated, resulting in the non-dimensional function F(t) from which mean residence time and the variance can also be deduced (see Figure 3). Additionally, step experiments (Heaviside) for the operation modes were achieved, showing the same results as obtained from integrated pulse response (data not shown).

Mean residence time tmtm obtained from the experimental data is plotted as a function of reactor bed rotation speed (rpm) for both reactor filling (volumes) in Figure 4. Hydrodynamic residence time τ was calculated according to Equation (3) and additionally plotted for comparison purposes. Hydrodynamic residence time represents the ideal back mixing in the CSTR, which is a desirable condition for cell culture. Regarding high filling volumes (120 mL) and low rotation speed, it is noticeable that the tmtm is higher than for the ideal reactor. Here we see that tmtm decreases with increasing rpm until a constant value is reached. tmtm obtained at higher rotation speeds more match the hydrodynamic values. This indicates a less complete mixing for low rotation speeds. There are no such effects visible for the half filled reactor (70 mL), indicating a more complete mixing at low rotation speeds. However, these data indicate a very uniform concentration distribution throughout the reactor and data match the ideal CSTR. Results from the washout experiments suggest that the liquid phase in the reactor could be considered homogeneous under normal operation conditions. For further analysis of the reactor the dissolved substrate/product concentrations in the liquid phase can hence be assumed to be uniform throughout the reactor.

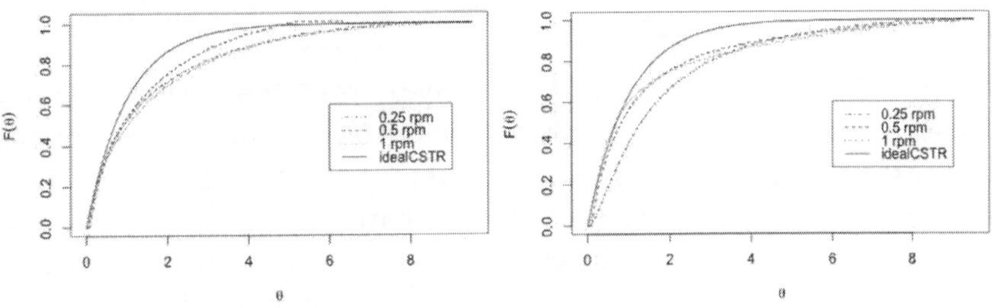

(a) 70 mL (b) 120 mL

Figure 3. Accumulated residence time of Z®RP 2000 H bioreactor for operation conditions of (**a**) 70 mL and (**b**) 120 mL volume depending on rotation speed of reactor bed (0.25, 0.5, 1 rpm), (*n* = 1). Accumulated residence time for ideal continuous stirred tank reactor (CSTR) is plotted for comparison reasons.

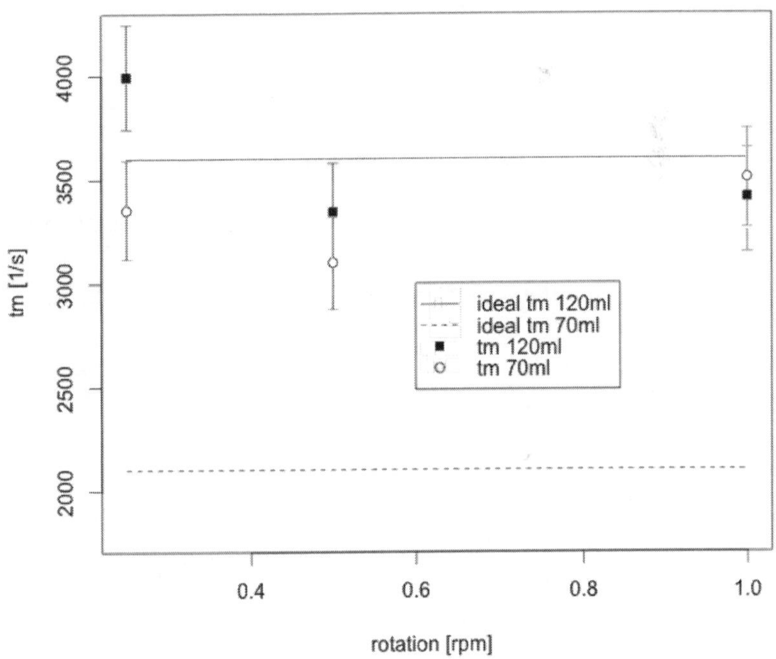

Figure 4. Mean residence time *vs.* rotation speed of bioreactor bed for different filling volumes (70 mL, 120 mL). Hydrostatic residence time plotted for comparision. Errorbars represent standard deviation.

3.2. Bodenstein Number

To further confirm the results obtained from the residence time analysis and examine back mixing properties within the bioreactor, Bodenstein number (Bo) was determined for the operation conditions. Bo is a parameter that measures the extent of axial dispersion. It is inversely proportional to the axial dispersion coefficient. When Bo approaches zero, there is an intense axial dispersion, then the mixed flow prevails. When Bo reaches infinity the flow has negligible axial dispersion, hence becomes plug flow. For MSC culture a low value for Bodenstein number is desirable since an appropriate back mixing is required for nutrient supply of the cells.

Bo was determined according to;

$$Bo = \sqrt{\frac{(1 + (8 \cdot \sigma_{\Theta}^2))}{\sigma_{\Theta}^2}} \tag{8}$$

$$\sigma_{\Theta}^2 = \frac{\sum (t - t_m)^2 \cdot E(t)dt}{\tau^2} \tag{9}$$

with σ non-dimensional variance of residence time distribution. Results are shown in Figure 5. For all examined operation conditions Bo is below 4, indicating a high back mixing within the bioreactor. The lower the filling volume and the higher the rotation speed, the higher the back mixing. A boundary value of 7 is used in practice to distinguish between CSTR and PFR type [20]. With Bo < 4 the ZRP 2000 H reactor can be classified as CSTR for all operation conditions. The CSTR type favorable over the PFR type for MSC culture, since it allows mass transfer and thus homogenous nutrient supply to the cells. The results obtained by Bodenstein number calculation revealed that even operating with a fully filled (120 mL) bioreactor at the lowest rotation speed (0.1 rpm) provides sufficient back mixing. Since MSC are sensitive to shear stress and can react to the mechanical stimulation with unwanted spontaneous differentiation, 120 mL filling volume and 0.1 rpm rotation speed were chosen for expansion experiments.

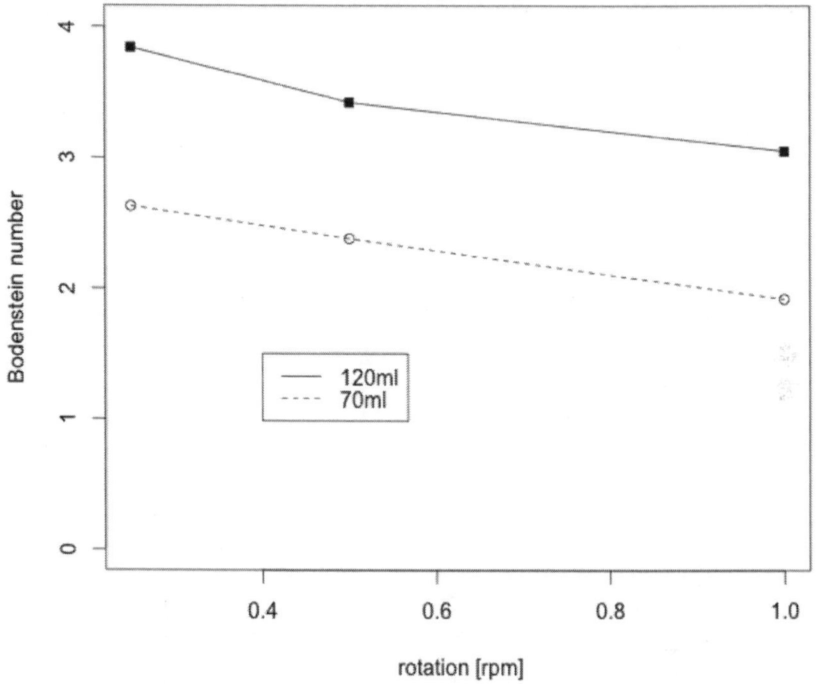

Figure 5. Bodenstein numbers of Z®RP 2000 H rotating bed bioreactor. Bodenstein number indicate a high backmixing within the bioreactor.

3.3. Cell Expansion in the Z®RP 2000 H Bioreactor

The total cell number at the end of the dynamic cultivation was 24.6 ± 2.4 × 1066 cells and 8.2 ± 0.8-fold expansion. Population doubling time was 39.6 ± 1.8 h (in static cultivation 31 h) and the total population doublings were 3.03 ± 0.14. Differentiation potential of UC-MSC was analyzed, after expansion in the Z®RP 2000 H bioreactor. Therefore, cells were cultured after expansion on a two-dimensional fibronectin surface. Collected UC-MSC retained their differentiation capacity towards chondrogenic, adipogenic and osteogenic lineages (see Figure 6). Total glucose consumption and lactate production was increased during cultivation, reaching 157.3 ± 40.7 mg per day for glucose and 133.0 ± 11.6 mg per day for lactate at day 5 (Figure 7).

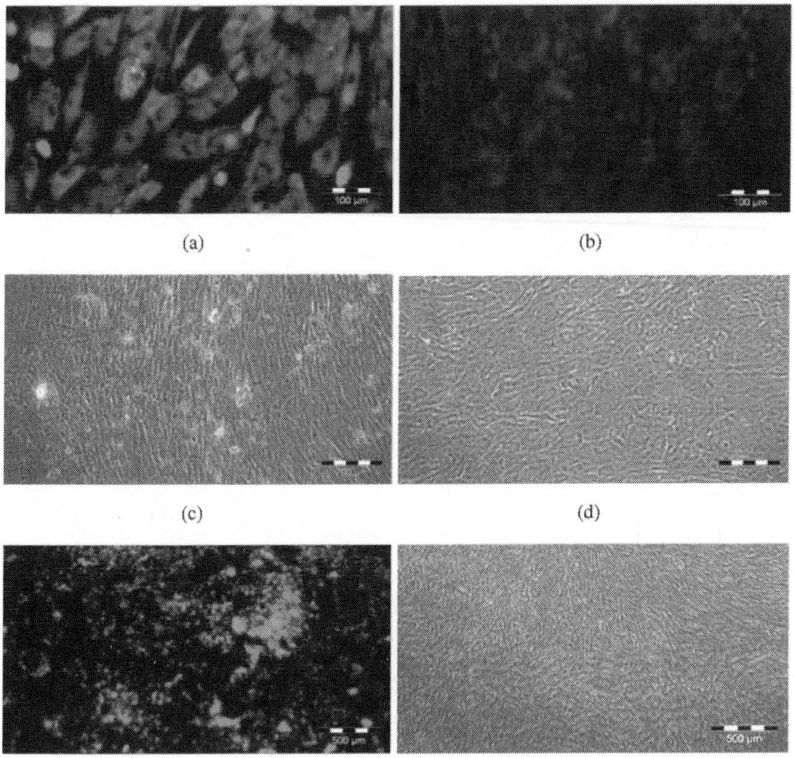

(a) (b) (c) (d) (e) (f)

Figure 6. Differentiation of umbilical cord-derived mesenchymal stromal cells (UC-MSC) cultured in the Z®RP 2000 H bioreactor. (**a**) Adipogenic differentiation (BODYPI staining) (cultured in NH AdipoDiff medium (Miltenyi Biotech) and 50 µg/mL gentamicin) (**b**) control (cultured in DMEM, 10% human serum and 50 µg/mL gentamicin); (**c**) chondrogenic differentiation (Alcian Blue staining) (cultured in NH ChondroDiff medium (Miltenyi Biotech) and 50 µg/mL gentamicin) (**d**) control (cultured in DMEM, 10% human serum and 50 µg/mL gentamicin); (**e**) osteogenic differentiation (Calcein staining) (cultured in NH OsteoDiff medium (Miltenyi Biotech) and 50 µg/mL gentamicin) (**f**) control (phase contrast) (cultured in DMEM, 10% human serum and 50 µg/mL gentamicin) after three weeks of cultivation. MSC retained their differentiation capacity towards chondrogenic, adipogenic and osteogenic lineages after cultivation in the Z®RP 2000 H bioreactor.

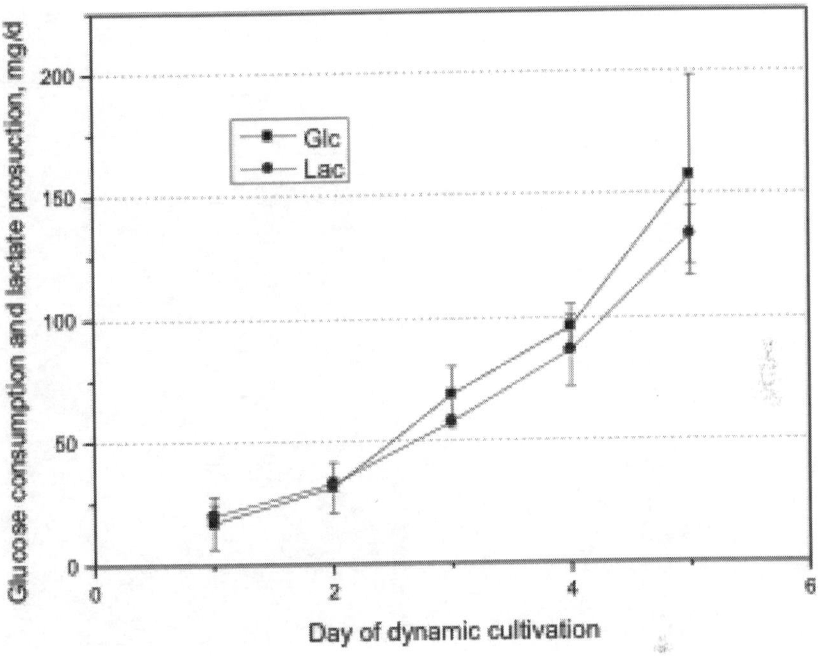

Figure 7. Total glucose consumption and lactate production of UC-MSC cultured in the Z®RP 2000 H bioreactor. Glucose consumption indicates cell proliferation throughout the cultivation process.

3.4. Cellular Senescence after Expansion in Z®RP 2000 H Bioreactor

The appearance of senescence during short-term expansion is a sign of non-optimal culture conditions, since senescence is one of the responses of the cells to stress (stress-induced premature senescence) [21]. No expression of *β*-galactosidase and, consequently, no cellular senescence was detected. Moreover, high proportions of cells undergoing cell division (arrows) could be observed, indicating that UC-MSC expanded in the bioreactor did not lose their mitotic activity (Figure 8).

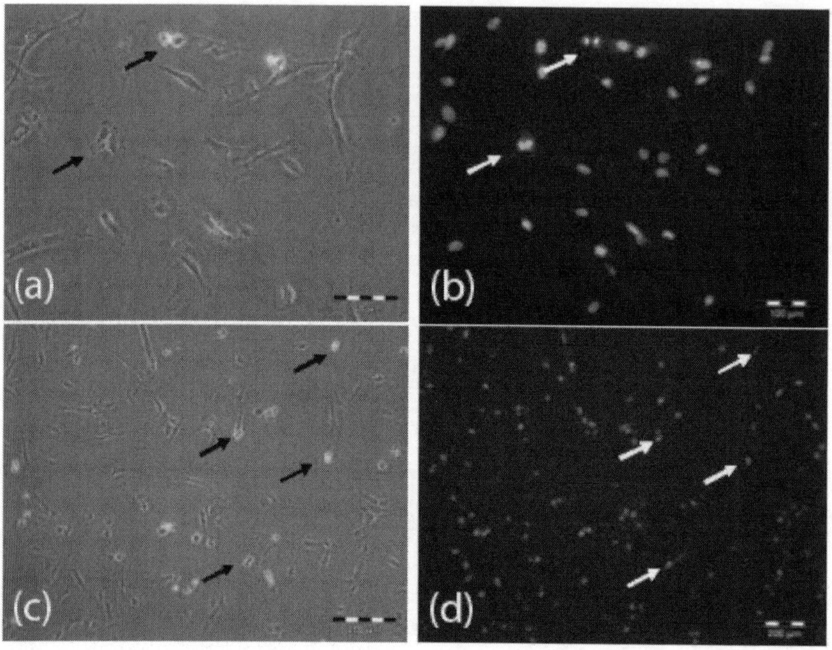

Figure 8. Senescence-associated β-galactosidase staining of UC-MSC cultured in the Z®RP 2000 H bioreactor: (**a**) β-galactosidase and (**b**) DAPI-staining, magnification ×50; (**c**) β-galactosidase and (**d**) DAPI-staining, magnification ×20. No β-galactosidase and consequently no stress-induced premature senescence could be detected. Cells demonstrate mitotic activity by cell division (arrows).

3.5. Surface Immunophenotype Characterization of UC-MSC after Expansion in the Z®RP 2000 H Bioreactor

After expansion in the Z®RP 2000 H bioreactor, UC-MSC were harvested and analyzed by flow cytometry after staining with FITC- or PE-conjugated antibodies against CD31, CD34, CD44, CD45, CD73, CD90, CD105 and isotype control immunoglobulins. Flow cytometric analysis of UC-MSC showed that they were negative for hematopoietic (CD34, CD45) and endothelial (CD31) markers and were strongly positive for specific immunophenotypic MSC markers (CD44, CD73, CD90 and CD105) (Table 1).

Table 1. Summarized surface antigen expression after dynamic cultivation in Z®RP 2000 H bioreactor. Cells lack hematopoetic and endothelial surface marker expression while expressing specific MSC immunophenotypic markers.

Marker	Expression
CD31	0.0%
CD34	0.3%
CD44	98.3%
CD45	0.3%
CD73	99.9%
CD90	98.1%
CD105	99.8%

4. CONCLUSIONS

Characterization of the Z®RP bioreactor 2000 H showed that for the purpose of shear stress reduced expansion of MSC it is optimal to cultivate with a completely filled bioreactor chamber and a slow rotation speed. The bioreactor provides properties, comparable to an ideal continuous stirred tank reactor offering beneficial mixing properties and therewith sufficient nutrient supply. The results demonstrate the dynamic cultivation of UC-MSC under these optimized conditions, showing that this system is suitable for UC-MSC expansion, providing high cell yields. Cells obtained from dynamic cultivation demonstrate high quality, maintaining MSC morphology, differentiation potential, mitotic activity as well as MSC surface marker expression. This reproducible cultivation process, offering a controllable environment, has high potential for MSC expansion for future clinical applications.

AUTHOR CONTRIBUTIONS

A.N. performed data analysis of the bioreactor characterization, contributed in writing and finalized the manuscript. A.L. achieved MSC expansion in the ZRP bioreactor and performed the flow cytometric analysis, proliferation studies as well as histological stainings and contributed in writing and finalized the manuscript. A.H. contributed to the bioreactor characterization and differentiation and histological stainings. M.L. was involved in MSC isolation and cultivation. C.K. designed the study and drafted the manuscript. All authors have read and approved the final manuscript.

CONFLICTS OF INTEREST

The authors declare no conflict of interest.

REFERENCES

1. ClinicalTrials.gov. Avaliable online: http://www.clinicaltrials.gov (accessed on 11 September 2014).

2. Raviv, L.; Karnieli, O. Cell therapies—The challenges and possible solutions for transferring cell therapy from the bench to the industry. Drug Dev. Deliv. 2014, 3.

3. Ramot, Y.; Meiron, M.; Toren, A.; Steiner, M.; Nyska, A. Safety and biodistribution profile of placental-derived mesenchymal stromal cells (PLX-PAD) following intramuscular delivery. Toxicol. Pathol. 2009, 37, 606–616.

4. Nold, P.; Brendel, C.; Neubauer, A.; Bein, G.; Hackstein, H. Good manufacturing practice-compliant animal-free expansion of human bone marrow derived mesenchymal stroma cells in a closed hollow-fiber-based bioreactor.Biochem. Biophys. Res. Commun. 2013, 430, 325–330.

5. Asnaghi, M.A.; Jungebluth, P.; Raimondi, M.T.; Dickinson, S.C.; Rees, L.E.; Go, T.; Cogan, T.A.; Dodson, A.; Parnigotto, P.P.; Hollander, A.P.; et al. A double-chamber rotating bioreactor for

the development of tissue-engineered hollow organs: From concept to clinical trial. Biomaterials 2009, 30, 5260–5269.

6. Martin, I.; Wendt, D.; Heberer, M. The role of bioreactors in tissue engineering. Trends Biotechnol. 2004, 22, 89–86.

7. Ratcliffe, A.; Niklason, L.E. Bioreactors and bioprocessing for tissue engineering. Ann. N. Y. Acad. Sci. 2002, 961, 210–215.

8. Hansmann, J.; Groeber, F.; Kahlig, A.; Kleinhans, C.; Walles, H. Bioreactors in tissue engineering—Principles, applications and commercial constraints. Biotechnol. J. 2013, 8, 298–307.

9. Glindkamp, A.; Riechers, D.; Rehbock, C.; Hitzmann, B.; Scheper, T.; Reardon, K.F. Sensors in disposable bioreactors status and trends. Adv. Biochem. Eng. Biotechnol. 2009, 115, 145–169.

10. Behr, L.; Joeris, K.; Burnett, M.; Scheper, T. A novel in situ probe for oxygen uptake rate measurement in mammalian cell cultures. Biotechnol. Prog. 2012, 28, 581–586.

11. Babitzky, A.; Lindner, P.; Scheper, T. Cell assessment by at-line microscopy. Methods Mol. Biol. 2014, 1104, 343–353.

12. Committee for Advanced Therapies. Reflection paper on stem cell-based medicinal products. EMA/CAT/571134/20092011, 1, 1–14.

13. Naughton, G.K. From lab bench to market: Critical issues in tissue engineering. Ann. N. Y. Acad. Sci. 2002, 961, 372–385.

14. Reichardt, A.; Polchow, P.; Shakibaei, M.; Henrich, W.; Hetzer, R.; Lueders, C. Large scale expansion of human umbilical cord cells in a rotating bed system bioreactor for cardiovascular tissue engineering applications. Open Biomed. Eng. J. 2013, 7, 50–61.

15. Bianco, P.; Riminucci, M.; Gronthos, S.; Robey, P.G. Bone marrow stromal stem cells: Nature, biology, and potential applications. Stem Cells 2001, 19, 180–192.

16. Crisan, M.; Yap, S.; Casteilla, L.; Chen, C.-W.; Corselli, M.; Park, T.-S.; Andriolo, G.; Sun, B.; Zheng, B.; Zhang, L.; et al. A

perivascular origin for mesenchymal stem cells in multiple human organs. Cell Stem Cell 2008, 3, 301–313.

17. Yeatts, A.B.; Fisher, J.B. Bone tissue engineering bioreactors: Dynamic culture and the influence of shear stress. Bone2011, 48, 171–181.

18. Majore, I.; Moretti, P.; Hass, R.; Kasper, C. Identification of subpopulations in mesenchymal stem cell-like cultures from human umbilical cord. Cell Commun. Signal. 2009, 7, 1–6.

19. Moretti, P. Establishment of Recombinant Cell Lines and Characterization of Primary Cells for Stem Cell Technology Applications. Ph.D. Thesis, Institute for Technical Chemistry, Leibniz University of Hanover, Hanover, Germany, 2010.

20. Hagen, J. Chemische Reaktionstechnik; VCH: Weinheim, Germany, 1992.

21. Toussaint, O.; Dumont, P.; Remacle, J.; Dierick, J.-F.; Pascal, T.; Frippiat, C.; Magalhaes, J.P.; Zdanov, S.; Chainiaux, F. Stress-induced premature senescence or stress-induced senescence-like phenotype: One in vivo reality, two possible definitions? Sci. World J. 2002, 2, 230–247.

Chapter 9

Co-Utilization of Glucose and Xylose for Enhanced Lignocellulosic Ethanol Production with Reverse Membrane Bioreactors

Mofoluwake M. Ishola [1,2,*], Päivi Ylitervo [1] and Mohammad J. Taherzadeh [1]

[1]*Swedish Centre for Resource Recovery, University of Borås, Allégatan 1, Borås 50190, Sweden*

[2]*Department of Chemical and Polymer Engineering, Faculty of Engineering, Lagos State University, PMB 1012 Epe, Lagos, Nigeria*

ABSTRACT

Integrated permeate channel (IPC) flat sheet membranes were examined for use as a reverse membrane bioreactor (rMBR) for lignocellulosic ethanol production. The fermenting organism, *Saccharomyces cerevisiae* (T0936), a genetically-modified strain with the ability to ferment xylose, was used inside the rMBR. The rMBR was evaluated for simultaneous glucose and xylose utilization as well as *in situ* detoxification of furfural and hydroxylmethyl furfural (HMF). The synthetic medium was investigated, after which the pretreated wheat straw was used as a xylose-rich lignocellulosic substrate. The IPC membrane panels were successfully used as the rMBR during the batch fermentations, which lasted for up to eight days without fouling. With the rMBR, complete glucose and xylose utilization, resulting in 86% of the theoretical ethanol yield, was observed with the synthetic medium. Its application with the pretreated wheat straw resulted in complete glucose consumption and 87% xylose utilization; a final ethanol concentration of 30.3 g/L was obtained, which corresponds to 83% of the theoretical yield. Moreover, complete *in situ*detoxification of furfural and HMF was obtained within 36 h and 60 h, respectively, with the rMBR. The use of the rMBR is a promising technology for large-scale lignocellulosic ethanol production, since it facilitates the co-utilization of glucose and xylose; moreover, the technology would also allow the reuse of the yeast for several batches.

Keywords: detoxification; lignocellulosic ethanol; reverse membrane bioreactor; *Saccharomyces cerevisiae*; xylose fermentation

1. INTRODUCTION

Ethanol production from lignocellulosic materials, such as woody biomass, forest, and agricultural residues, has the potential of reducing society's dependence on fossil fuels [1,2,3]. Lignocellulosic materials consist of three main structural components: cellulose, hemicellulose, and lignin [4,5,6]. The hemicellulose fraction of hardwoods and agricultural residues, e.g., wheat straw, is dominated by xylose; hence, xylose utilization is essential for the successful fermentation of all the sugars into ethanol. However, the wild-type of yeast, *Saccharomyces cerevisiae*, which is commonly used for the fermentation of sugar to ethanol, cannot utilize xylose. Thus, the use of genetically-engineered *S. cerevisiae* for xylose uptake for the fermentation of xylose-rich biomass for ethanol production is one of the options that have been widely investigated [7,8,9]. On the other hand, the genetically-modified strain prefers glucose in a mixture of glucose and xylose, leading to the sequential utilization of sugars and, consequently, incomplete sugar utilization [10,11,12].

The cell retention strategy denoted as encapsulation has been reported to improve the xylose utilization and aids the *in situ* detoxification of the bioconvertible inhibitors [9,13,14]. Previous reports [9,13,15] show that the encapsulation of genetically-modified strains creates a sugar concentration gradient inside the tight agglomeration of cells. The glucose is consumed by the cells closer to the membrane of the capsules, thereby lowering the glucose concentration, which the inner cells closer to the core of the capsules acquire. Consequently, this improves the xylose uptake, thereby facilitating simultaneous sugar utilization. The encapsulated cells are in a microenvironment provided by the membrane layer of the capsules, a similar concept to the rMBR technology. However, encapsulating the cells is a laborious and time consuming task, since the process takes about 48 h to accomplish [16,17]. In addition, the capsules can easily disintegrate during the process with agitation. Moreover, complete xylose utilization was not achieved with the encapsulated cells [9].

Over the last decade, membrane bioreactors (MBRs) have had a conventional application in water and wastewater treatment [16,18,19]. In recent years, the MBRs have gained a wider application including its use in ethanol production. The technology has been used to e.g., enhance *in situ* detoxification of furfural [20] and to make it possible to perform continuous cultivations at high acetic acid concentrations [21]. MBRs have also been applied to allow optimum conditions in the hydrolysis and fermentation reactors in a recently developed simultaneous saccharification, filtration and fermentation (SSFF) process for lignocellulosic ethanol production [22]. The use of flat sheet membranes to contain and retain the cells can be advantageous over other cell retention methods such as encapsulation. The membrane modules are commercially available for use and could, thus, be a means of successfully creating several agglomerations of cells inside the panels, which will create the desired sugar concentration gradient in the agglomerates of the cells and eventually facilitate simultaneous utilization of both glucose and xylose. It will also facilitate *in situ* detoxification of the available lignocellulosic inhibitors in the medium to their less toxic derivatives and also create a possibility of instant cell reuse for several fermentation batches, even in substrates which contain particles. To our knowledge, the application of the flat sheet membranes in a reverse manner, wherein the yeast *S. cerevisiae* is inside the membrane panels for ethanol production, has not been reported in the literature.

This study investigated the use of integrated permeate channels (IPC) membranes in a reverse manner for lignocellulosic ethanol production, a technology referred to as rMBR. Simultaneous utilization of glucose and xylose was first investigated with the rMBR in a synthetic media. The rMBR was later evaluated in xylose-rich pretreated lignocellulosic material for sugar co-utilization and detoxification of the bioconvertible inhibitors.

2. RESULTS AND DISCUSSION

The reverse membrane bioreactor (rMBR) provides a microenvironment for the yeast cells through the agglomeration of the yeast cells inside the membrane panels. The technology could facilitate a similar concentration gradient of sugars and inhibitors, as observed with the encapsulated cells [13] through the agglomerates of cells inside the inner matrix of the membrane panels. The agglomeration of cells will consequently facilitate the simultaneous utilization of glucose and xylose as well as *in situ* detoxification of the bioconvertible inhibitors. Moreover, the limitations of encapsulation such as long processing time, disintegration of capsules, and incomplete sugar utilization [9,16,17] necessitate the use of an improved technology, such as rMBR. The commercial availability of the membranes, as well as the ease of its application, makes the rMBR a preferred technology over encapsulation. The rMBR technology was investigated for simultaneous utilization of both glucose and xylose, as well as *in situ* detoxification of inhibitors in this study.

2.1. Performance of the Integrated Permeate Channel (IPC) Flat Sheet Membrane as rMBRs for Ethanol Production

The IPC membranes were used in a novel way as rMBR with the genetically-modified yeast inside the membrane panels (Figure 1). The membranes performed well during their use, as the yeast inside the rMBR were able to ferment the available sugars to ethanol. Fouling is a major challenge in membrane applications [16,18]. However, the IPC membranes were successfully used for batch fermentations of the synthetic medium as well as the liquid fraction of the lignocellulosic hydrolyzate for up to eight days without fouling. The membranes were found to be reusable after the fermentation. The yeast cells inside the rMBR were also found to be metabolically active after the fermentation, as the cells were able to form colonies when plated. However, it was observed that after the panels had been used for two consecutive batch fermentations, there was a need for chemical cleaning and back-washing in order to get rid of all the cells entrapped inside the matrix of the membrane panels. This indicates that the rMBR can be used for a prolonged fermentation of lignocellulosic medium without any significant effect on the membranes or the cells.

2.2. Simultaneous Utilization of Glucose and Xylose in a Synthetic Medium with the rMBR

In order to obtain a good ethanol yield and productivity during the fermentation of the xylose-rich lignocellulosic medium, it is important that the fermenting organism has an efficient uptake of xylose and conversion to ethanol. Xylose utilization by genetically-modified yeast strains has been previously reported to be dependent on glucose concentration, as low glucose concentration can facilitate xylose uptake [8]. Creating a sugar concentration gradient within the cell agglomeration has been reported to facilitate a controlled glucose supply to the different layers of the cell agglomerates which will, thus, facilitate the xylose uptake [13]. During the fermentation with the synthetic medium, it was observed that both the glucose and the xylose concentrations of 6 g/L and 21 g/L, respectively, decreased simultaneously (Figure 2), which indicates that there was a simultaneous uptake of both sugars during the fermentation. This shows that the inner fabric cross layer of the IPC membrane panels, which contained the genetically-modified yeast created the required agglomeration for the cells. Thus, there was a concentration gradient of sugars inside the cell agglomerates (Figure 1), which facilitated the xylose metabolism. Interestingly, after 96 h of fermentation, both the glucose and the xylose concentrations were completely consumed, and an ethanol concentration of 12 g/L was observed (Figure 2), which corresponds to 85.7% of the theoretical yield.

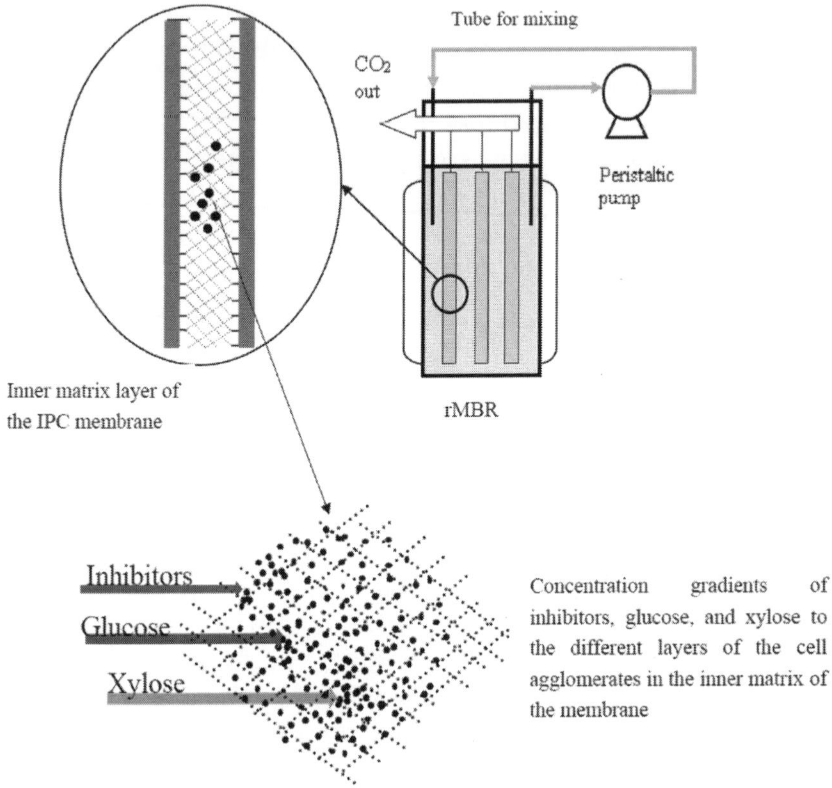

Figure 1. Schematic representation of the rMBR system configuration showing the IPC membrane panels' inner matrix layers and the concentration gradient of glucose, xylose, and inhibitors into different layers of the yeast cell's agglomerates inside the panels.

The synthesis of glycerol during the yeast fermentations plays a significant role for its growth; glycerol maintains the intracellular redox balance as well as the osmoregulation with the cell's external environment [23,24]. The glycerol concentration was observed to be very low during the fermentation, an indication that the cells inside the rMBR were able to maintain their metabolic activities throughout the fermentation, with very low glycerol formation and without having a significant effect on the ethanol yield. The highest glycerol concentration was 1.4 g/L during the fermentation, which lasted for 96 h (Figure 3); similar observation of low glycerol production with the specific strain has been reported [9]. Lactic acid concentration of approximately 0.2 g/L was measured at the end of the fermentation (Figure 3). This suggests that the chemical cleaning procedure used as a means of sterilizing and disinfecting the membrane panels in the reactor is effective in keeping contamination under control throughout the fermentation. It also indicates that the rMBR can successfully be used for prolonged fermentation without any contamination effect. Acetic acid is an inhibitor that is strongly pH dependent; it can be present in the medium as well as be a product of the fermentation [25]. Acetic acid concentration of only 0.5 g/L was produced by the end of the fermentation (Figure 3), which suggests that the acid was also produced during the fermentation with no direct effect on the fermentation process.

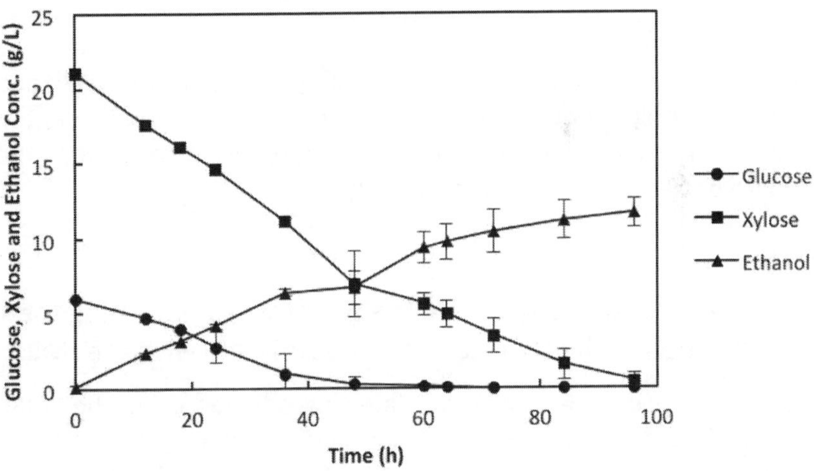

Figure 2. Concentration (g/L) profiles of glucose, xylose, and ethanol during the use of rMBR in the synthetic medium. The values presented are mean values of the two experiments, with error bars as the standard deviation between the two values.

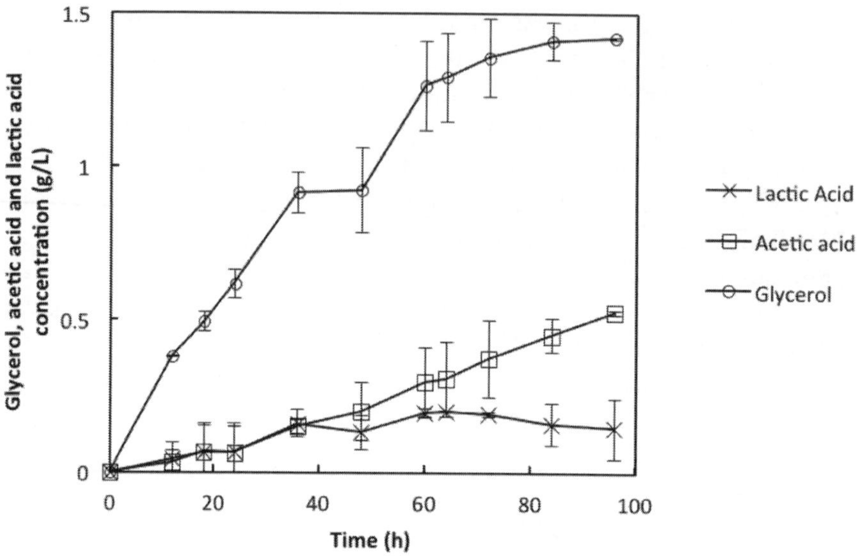

Figure 3. Concentration (g/L) profiles of glycerol, acetic acid, and lactic acid during the use of rMBR in the synthetic medium. Presented values are average values of two experiments, with error bars as the standard deviation between the two values.

2.3. Co-Utilization of Sugars and In Situ Detoxification Using the Liquid Fraction of the Lignocellulosic Hydrolyzate with the rMBR

The performance of the rMBR was later investigated using the liquid fraction of the hydrolyzed wheat straw slurry. This was done in order to evaluate the performance of the rMBR in the real lignocellulosic medium. The supplied slurry of 14.9% SS was diluted to 10% SS with deionized water after which it was hydrolyzed. The 24 h enzymatic hydrolysis was performed at a temperature of 50 °C and a pH of 5.0. This increased the glucose concentration from 6.0 g/L up to 50.6 g/L, which indicates that the Cellic® Ctec2 enzyme cocktail used was very effective for the cellulose hydrolysis. It was also observed that operating the enzymatic hydrolysis at optimum conditions is profitable for the lignocellulosic ethanol production, which is in agreement with a previous report on the benefits of performing the hydrolysis and fermentations at separate optimum conditions [22].

During the fermentation with the rMBR, despite the presence of the inhibitors; e.g., acetic acid, HMF, and furfural in the medium, the co-utilization of glucose and xylose was observed (Figure 4). The glucose was consumed faster than the xylose, as the 50.1 g/L glucose was completely depleted within 132 h while 2.6 g/L of the xylose remained, out of the initial concentration of 21.2 g/L after the fermentation that lasted for 180 h (Figure 4). This corresponds to 87.7% xylose utilization. It was observed that the xylose uptake by the genetically-modified yeast encased in the membrane panels was not affected by the high initial glucose concentration of 50.1 g/L. This suggests that the rMBR resulted in a higher xylose uptake compared to the study performed by the encapsulated yeast used in a SSFF process, where a 80% xylose uptake was reported at an initial glucose concentration of 36 g/L, while only 36% xylose uptake was reported at an initial glucose concentration of 53.5 g/L due to catabolite repression [9].

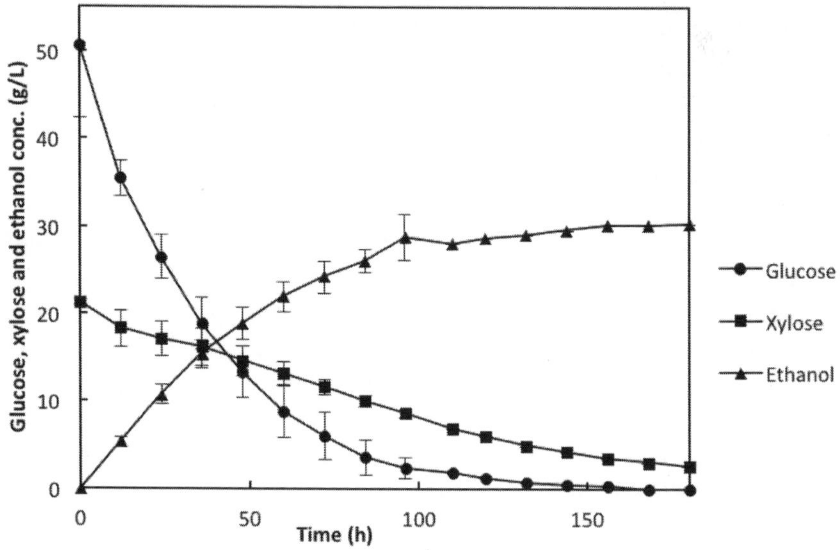

Figure 4. Concentration (g/L) profiles of glucose, xylose, and ethanol during the use of rMBR in the liquid fraction of the prehydrolyzed pretreated wheat straw used as xylose-rich lignocellulosic material. The values presented are mean values of two experiments, with error bars as the standard deviation between the two values.

The observations from this study indicate that a high initial glucose concentration in the medium does not really affect the xylose uptake by the genetically-modified strain as much as the fermentation process used does. Creating a microenvironment for the cells by having the cells inside the IPC membranes facilitated the co-utilization and higher xylose uptake despite the initial glucose concentration. The possibility of achieving the desired concentration gradient due to the agglomeration of cells in the panels facilitated the improved xylose uptake.

In situ detoxification of furfural and HMF was also observed. Within 36 h of fermentation, the initial furfural concentration of 4.5 g/L was completely converted (Figure 5), while the initial HMF concentration of 0.6 g/L was completely converted within 60 h (Figure 5). Although HMF has a lesser inhibitory effect compared to furfural, its rate of conversion has been reported to be slower than that of furfural [26,27] as observed in this study. This observation suggests that the agglomeration of cells in the panels, which created the concentration gradient of the streams reaching the cells, does not only facilitate the co-utilization of the glucose and xylose but also helps with the *in situ* detoxification. The cells close to the outer layer of the agglomerates detoxified the inhibitors, hence, improving the rate of their conversion (Figure 1). This observation is in agreement with a previous report on *in situ* detoxification of the bioconvertible inhibitors [14]. The rate of the *in situ* detoxification with the rMBR was much faster than an earlier reported rate with the particular strain when encapsulation was used with the SSFF process. It was reported that it took up to 72 h for both HMF and furfural to be completely converted even though a cell concentration of 6 g/L was used [9]. With the use of the rMBR in this study, the ethanol concentration of 30.3 g/L was observed at the end of the fermentation, which lasted for 180 h (Figure 4). This corresponds to 83% of the theoretical ethanol yield. It can, thus, be stated that the rMBR with the IPC membrane panels is beneficial for the co-utilization of glucose and xylose utilization as well as for the *in situ* detoxification of the bioconvertible inhibitors, which are important factors for an efficient and successful lignocellulosic ethanol production.

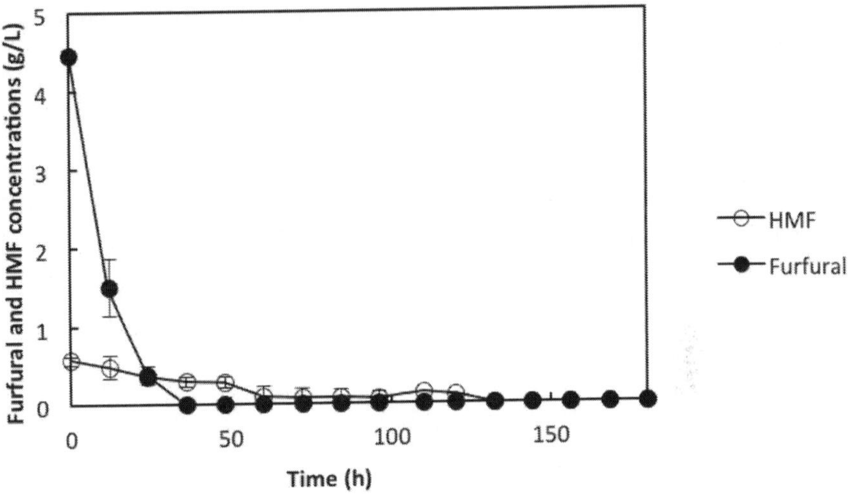

Figure 5. Concentration (g/L) profiles of furfural and HMF during the use of rMBR in the liquid fraction of prehydrolyzed pretreated wheat straw used as xylose-rich lignocellulosic material. Presented values are average values of two experiments, with error bars as the standard deviation between the two values.

3. EXPERIMENTAL SECTION

3.1. Lignocellulosic Material

Wheat straw, an agricultural residue from a Swedish farm was used in the experiments. It is a xylose-rich lignocellulosic biomass. The biomass was chemically pretreated with dilute H_2SO_4 (0.3%–0.5%) at 185 °C for 8 min at SEKAB E-Technology (Örnsköldsvik, Sweden). It was supplied as a pretreated slurry with pH of 1.9, 14.9% suspended solids (SS), and 22.2% total solids. The slurry was stored in a cold room at 5 °C until use. The composition of the liquid fraction of the slurry was analyzed by the high-performance liquid chromatography (HPLC) and presented in Table 1. The solid fraction of the slurry was characterized according to the NREL protocols [28]; it contained 43.6% ± 0.5% cellulose, 34.8% ± 0.1% acid insoluble lignin (AIL), 5.1% ± 0.1% acid soluble lignin (ASL), and 39.9% ± 0.2% total lignin. The hemicellulose fraction was completely fractionated into monomeric sugars during the pretreatment. The theoretical ethanol yield was calculated based on 0.51 g/g of the glucose and xylose available in the liquid fraction of the enzymatically-hydrolyzed slurry.

Table 1. Composition of the liquid fraction of the supplied pretreated wheat straw (slurry), used as xylose-rich lignocellulosic biomass with 14.9% suspended solids.

Component		Concentration (g/L)
Monomeric sugars	Xylose	33.4
	Glucose	8.5
	Mannose	1.5
	Arabinose	4.9
	Galactose	3.1
Inhibitors	Acetic acid	8.9
	HMF	1.1
	Furfural	9.2

3.2. Enzymes and Yeast Strain

The Cellulase Cellic® Ctec2 enzyme (Novozymes, Bagsvaerd, Denmark) was used for the enzymatic hydrolysis. The enzymatic activity was measured as 185 FPU/mL activity and was determined according to the NREL method [29]. A genetically-engineered strain of *Saccharomyces cerevisiae* (T0936) was used in all the experiments. The yeast was maintained at 4 °C on yeast extract, peptone, and dextrose (YPD) agar plates, containing 20 g/L agar, 10 g/L D-glucose, 10 g/L D-xylose, 10 g/L yeast extract, and 20 g/L peptone. Prior to the fermentations, 200 mL yeast pre-culture in the YPD growth medium, containing 25 g/L D-glucose, 25 g/L xylose, 20 g/L peptone, and 10 g/L yeast extract was prepared by cultivations performed in two 250 mL Erlenmeyer flasks with 100 ml medium in each. The flasks were incubated in a shake-bath (Grant OLS 200, Grant Instrument Ltd., Royston, UK) at 121 rpm and 30 °C for 48 h.

3.3. Cell Cultivation for the rMBR

In order to achieve a high cell concentration inside the membrane panels, the 200 mL pre-culture was inoculated into a 2.5 L bioreactor (Infors AG107504, Minifors, Bottmingen, Switzerland) at 30 °C and pH 5.0, using a YPD growth medium consisting of 17 g/L D-glucose, 33 g/L D-xylose, 20 g/L peptone, and 10 g/L yeast extract. Silicone antifoam (1 g/L) and 3.5 g/L KH_2PO_4 were added. The cultivation was aerated at 4.0 vvm for 42 h to produce a cell concentration of 5 g/L per intended fermentation volume of 3 L. After the cell cultivation, the cells were harvested by centrifugation at 4500 rpm for 5 min and concentrated into 150 mL, thus, making a cell concentration of 100 g/L per membrane volume of 150 mL

3.4. Flat Sheet Integrated Permeate Channels (IPC) as the rMBR

The IPC membrane panels were developed and produced by the Flemish Institute for Technological Research (Vito NV, Boeretang, Mol, Belgium). The polymeric membrane panels consist of double membrane layers that consist of an integrated permeate channels, interposed to the two membrane layers. The IPC membrane was manufactured of PES/PVP with a pore size of 0.3 μm. The IPC membranes are unique for their sturdiness and ability to withstand high pressure differences during the filtration and backwashing [30]; this property qualifies the membrane for application as rMBR. Each membrane panel had a total membrane area of 0.0252 m^2, which was available for the filtration and can take a volume of about 50 mL Three membrane panels were placed in parallel inside a 4.0 L bioreactor (Webant BE0076, Belach Bioteknik AB, Skogås, Sweden).

The membrane panels cannot be sterilized by autoclavation; hence, they were chemically cleaned and disinfected according to the following procedures before each fermentation run. First, the membrane panels were immersed in a two percent NaOH solution at 50–80 °C for 30 min, after which they were rinsed with deionized water. Then, 1% phosphoric acid solution was applied to the panels for 30 min and then rinsed with deionized water. Thereafter, the panels were disinfected with 200 ppm NaOCl solution and rinsed with sterile deionized water before the fermentation run. Finally, the concentrated cultivated cells described earlier were aseptically transferred into the membrane panels, resulting in 5 g/L dry weight of the yeast cells that were added to the rMBR.

3.5. Configuration of the Reverse Membrane Bioreactor (rMBR)

The schematic configuration of the rMBR is shown in Figure 1. The genetically-modified yeasts cells were added inside the membrane panels, which were submerged in the medium inside the reactor (Figure 1). The inner matrix layer of the membrane panels created a microenvironment for the yeast cells and resulted in several agglomerations of the cells. The yeast cells inside the panels acquired substrate and nutrients when the medium diffuses through the membrane panel. The metabolites also diffuse through the membrane panels into the medium.

3.6. Synthetic Medium Fermentation with the rMBR

The performance of the genetically-modified yeast cell inside the rMBR was first investigated in 3 L synthetic medium containing glucose and xylose, equivalent to that present in the 10% suspended solids (SS), corresponding to 6 g/L glucose and 21 g/L xylose. The medium was supplemented with 2 g/L $(NH_4)_2SO_4$, 0.35 g/L KH_2PO_4, and 1 g/L yeast extract; 0.6 g/L silicone antifoam was also added. The three membrane panels containing the yeast cells were submerged in the fermentation medium inside the bioreactor. The fermentation was performed anaerobically at a temperature of 30 °C and a pH of 5.0. A marprene process tube (internal diameter 8.0 mm, thickness 2.4 mm and outer diameter 12.6 mm, 902.0080.24, Watson Marlow, Falmouth, England) was used for circulating the liquid inside the bioreactor with a peristaltic pump (323DU/D Watson Marlow, Falmouth, England) at a flow rate of 0.6 L/min and thereby mixing the medium. Fermentation was carried out for 96 h, and samples were taken every 12 h from the medium to monitor the sugar consumption and the metabolite production.

3.7. Fermentation of the Liquid Fraction of the Hydrolyzed Pretreated Wheat Straw with the rMBR

Enzymatic hydrolysis of the pretreated wheat straw was carried out at a temperature of 50 °C, pH of 5.0, and agitation of 700 rpm for 24 h. Substrate and enzyme loading of 10% SS and 12 FPU/g SS, respectively, was used. Thereafter, the hydrolyzate was centrifuged aseptically (5000 rpm, 5 min) in order to separate the liquid fraction from the solid residue. The liquid fraction containing the sugars and the inhibitors was later used for the fermentation, in a similar way as the synthetic medium described above, with freshly cultivated genetically-modified yeast inside the membrane panels. All of the experiments were performed in duplicates, with error bars showing the standard deviation.

3.8. Analytical Methods

Cellulose, hemicellulose and lignin contents of the solid fraction of the slurry was determined according to the NREL protocols [28]. The solid and liquid fractions of the slurry were separated with a centrifuge at 4000 × *g* for 5 min. The solid fraction was washed with 40 mL deionized water to a neutral pH and then freeze-dried (Labconco, Kansas City, MO, USA) at −52 °C until its moisture content was less than 10%. Two steps hydrolysis was later performed on the dried solid fraction: first with 72% H_2SO_4 in a shaker water bath at 30 °C for 60 min, and later with 4% H_2SO_4 in an autoclave at 121 °C for 60 min. The ASL was determined on the liquid portion of the hydrolyzate with a UV spectrophotometer (Libra S60, Biochrom, Cambridge, UK) at 283 nm. The AIL was gravimetrically determined as the residual solid after the hydrolysis, corrected with the ash content. The ash content was determined in the muffle furnace at 575 °C overnight. The hydrolysis liquid was analyzed by HPLC for the monomeric sugars.

The sugars and the metabolic products were analyzed using a HPLC (Walters 2695, Walters Corporation, Milford, CT, USA). A hydrogen-based column (Aminex HPX-87H, Bio-Rad, Hercules, CA, USA) at 60 °C and 0.6 mL/min 5 mM H_2SO_4as eluent was used for the glucose, furans, carboxylic acids, ethanol, lactic acid, and glycerol. Mannose, glucose, galactose, xylose, and arabinose were analyzed using the Aminex HPX-87P column (Bio-Rad) at 85 °C and 0.6 mL/min ultrapure water as an eluent. A UV absorbance detector (Walters 2487), operating at 210 nm wavelength, was used in a series with a refractive index (RI) detector (Walters 2414).

4. CONCLUSIONS

Integrated permeate channel (IPC) flat sheet membranes were examined as a reverse membrane reactor (rMBR) for lignocellulosic ethanol production. The rMBR was investigated for co-utilization of glucose and xylose utilization as well as for *in situ* detoxification of inhibitors. The synthetic medium was initially investigated, followed by using the liquid fraction of the enzymatically hydrolyzed pretreated wheat straw as a xylose-rich media. The IPC membrane panels containing the yeast cells were successfully used for the batch fermentation lasting for up to eight days without fouling. With the rMBR, complete xylose utilization, together with 86% of the theoretical ethanol yield, was observed when the synthetic medium was used. Its usage with the pretreated wheat straw resulted in 87% xylose utilization and complete *in situ* detoxification of furfural and HMF within 36 h and 60 h, respectively; a final ethanol concentration of 30.3 g/L equivalent to an ethanol yield of 83% of the theoretical value was obtained. The use of the rMBR with the yeast cells inside the membranes could be a promising technology in the future for large-scale lignocellulosic ethanol production.

ACKNOWLEDGMENTS

This work was financially supported by the Swedish Energy Agency. The authors are grateful to SEKAB E-Technology (Sweden) for supplying the wheat straw slurry as well as Novozymes (Denmark) for supplying the enzymes.

AUTHOR CONTRIBUTIONS

Mofoluwake M. Ishola: Carried out all the experimental work and wrote the first draft of the manuscript. Päivi Ylitervo: Assisted Mofoluwake M. Ishola in the experimental set up and analysis of the result. Mohammad J. Taherzadeh: Supervised the project. All authors contributed to the writing of the article.

CONFLICTS OF INTEREST

The authors declare no conflict of interest.

REFERENCES

1. Farrell, A.E.; Plevin, R.J.; Turner, B.T.; Jones, A.D.; O'Hare, M.; Kammen, D.M. Ethanol can contribute to energy and environmental goals. Science 2006, 311, 506–508.

2. Olofsson, K.; Bertilsson, M.; Liden, G. A short review on SSF—An interesting process option for ethanol production from lignocellulosic feedstocks. Biotechnol. Biofuels 2008, 1.

3. Ishola, M.M.; Babapour, A.B.; Gavitar, M.N.; Brandberg, T.; Taherzadeh, M.J. Effect of high solids loading on bacterial contamination in lignocellulosic ethanol production. Bioresources 2013, 8, 4429–4439.

4. Klinke, H.B.; Thomsen, A.B.; Ahring, B.K. Inhibition of ethanol-producing yeast and bacteria by degradation products produced during pre-treatment of biomass. Appl. Microbiol. Biotechnol. 2004, 66, 10–26.

5. Aslanzadeh, S.; Ishola, M.M.; Richards, T.; Taherzadeh, M.J. An overview of existing individual unit operations. InBiorefineries: Integrated Biochemical Processes for Liquid Biofuels, 1st ed.; Qureshi, N., Hodge, D., Vertes, A.A., Eds.; Elsevier: Cambridge, UK, 2014; pp. 3–36.

6. Ishola, M.M.; Taherzadeh, M.J. Effect of fungal and phosphoric acid pretreatment on ethanol production from oil palm empty fruit bunches (OPEFB). Bioresour. Technol. 2014, 165, 9–12.

7. Zaldivar, J.; Nielsen, J.; Olsson, L. Fuel ethanol production from lignocellulose: A challenge for metabolic engineering and

process integration. Appl. Microbiol. Biotechnol. 2001, 56, 17–34.

8. Bertilsson, M.; Olofsson, K.; Liden, G. Prefermentation improves xylose utilization in simultaneous saccharification and co-fermentation of pretreated spruce. Biotechnol. Biofuels 2009, 2.

9. Ishola, M.M.; Branbdberg, T.; Taherzadeh, M.J. Simultaneous glucose and xylose utilization for improved ethanol production from lignocellulosic biomass through SSFF with encapsulated yeast. Biomass Bioenergy 2015, 77, 192–199.

10. Kotter, P.; Ciriacy, M. Xylose fermentation by Saccharomyces cerevisiae. Appl. Microbiol. Biotechnol. 1993, 38, 776–783.

11. Hahn-Hägerdal, B.; Karhumaa, K.; Fonseca, C.; Spencer-Martins, I.; Gorwa-Grauslund, M.F. Towards industrial pentose-fermenting yeast strains. Appl. Microbiol. Biotechnol. 2007, 74, 937–953.

12. Kim, S.R.; Park, YC.; Jin, YS.; Seo, J.H. Strain engineering of Saccharomyces cerevisiae for enhanced xylose metabolism. Biotechnol. Adv. 2013, 31, 51–861.

13. Westman, J.; Bonander, N.; Taherzadeh, M.; Franzen, C. Improved sugar co-utilisation by encapsulation of a recombinant Saccharomyces cerevisiae strain in alginate-chitosan capsules. Biotechnol. Biofuels 2014, 7.

14. Westman, J.O.; Manikondu, R.B.; Franzén, C.J.; Taherzadeh, M.J. Encapsulation-induced stress helps saccharomyces cerevisiae resist convertible lignocellulose derived inhibitors. Int. J. Mol. Sci. 2012, 13, 11881–11894.

15. Westman, J.O. Ethanol Production from Lignocellulose Using High Local Cell Density Yeast Cultures. Investigations of Flocculation and encapsulated Saccharomyces cerevisiae. Ph.D. Thesis, Chalmers University of Technology, Gothenburg, Sweden, 19 February 2014.

16. Ishola, M.M. Novel Application of Membrane Bioreactors in Lignocellulosic Ethanol Production: Simultaneous

Saccharification, Filtration and Fermentation (SSFF). Ph.D. Thesis, University of Borås, Borås, Sweden, 31 October 2014.

17. Ylitervo, P.; Franzén, C.J.; Taherzadeh, M.J. Ethanol production at elevated temperatures using encapsulation of yeast. J. Biotechnol. 2011, 156, 22–29.

18. Judd, S.; Judd, C. The MBR book. In Principles and Applications of Membrane Bioreactors for Water and Wastewater Treatment, 2nd ed.; Butterworth-Heinemann: Oxford, UK, 2011.

19. Guglielmi, G.; Andreottola, G. Selection and Design of Membrane Bioreactors in Environmental Bioengineering. InEnvironmental Biotechnology; Wang, L.K., Ivanov, V., Tay, J.H., Eds.; Humana Press: New York, NY, USA, 2010; Volume 10, pp. 439–516.

20. Ylitervo, P.; Franzen, C.J.; Taherzadeh, M.J. Impact of furfural on rapid ethanol production using a membrane bioreactor. Energies 2013, 6, 1604–1617.

21. Ylitervo, P.; Franzen, J.C.; Taherzadeh, M.J. Continuous ethanol production with a membrane bioreactor at high acetic acid concentration. Membranes 2014, 4, 372–387.

22. Ishola, M.M.; Jahandideh, A.; Haidarian, B.; Brandberg, T.; Taherzadeh, M.J. Simultaneous saccharification, filtration and fermentation (SSFF): A novel method for bioethanol production from lignocellulosic biomass. Bioresour. Technol.2013, 133, 68–73.

23. Luyten, K.; Albertyn, J.; Skibbe, W.F.; Prior, B.A.; Ramos, J.; Thevelein, J.M.; Hohmann, S. Fps1, a yeast member of the MIP family of channel proteins, is a facilitator for glycerol uptake and efflux and is inactive under osmotic stress.EMBO J. 1995, 14, 1360–1371.

24. Wang, Z.; Zhuge, J.; Fang, H.; Prior, B.A. Glycerol production by microbial fermentation: A review. Biotechnol. Adv.2001, 19, 201–223.

25. Taherzadeh, M.J.; Niklasson, C.; Liden, G. Acetic acid—Friend or foe in anaerobic batch conversion of glucose to ethanol by

Saccharomyces cerevisiae? Chem. Eng. Sci. 1997, 52, 2653–2659.

26. Larsson, S.; Palmqvist, E.; Hahn-Hägerdal, B.; Tengborg, C.; Stenberg, K.; Zacchi, G.; Nilvebrant, N.O. The generation of fermentation inhibitors during dilute acid hydrolysis of softwood. Enzym. Microb. Technol. 1999, 24, 151–159.

27. Taherzadeh, M.J. Ethanol from Lignocellulose: Physiological Effects of Inhibitors and Fermentation Strategies. Ph.D. Thesis, Chalmers University of Technology, Göteborg, Sweden, 28 May 1999.

28. Sluiter, A.; Hames, B.; Ruiz, R.; Scarlata, C.; Sluiter, J.; Templeton, D.; Crocker, D. Determination of structural carbohydrates and lignin in biomass. In Laboratory Analytical Procedure; National Renewable Energy Laboratory: Golden, CO, USA, 2011.

29. Adney, B.; Baker, J. Measurement of Cellulase Activities. In Laboratory Analytical Procedure; National Renewable Energy Laboratory: Golden, CO, USA, 2008.

30. Doyen, W.; Mues, W.; Molenberghs, B.; Cobben, B. Spacer fabric supported flat sheet membranes: A new era of flat-sheet membrane technology. Desalination 2010, 250, 1078–1082.

Chapter 10

Optimization of Culture Conditions of *Talinum paniculatum* Gaertn. Adventitious Roots in Balloon Type Bubble Bioreactor Using Aeration Rate and Initial Inoculum Density

Y.S.W. Manuhara, A.N. Kristanti and **E.S.W. Utami**

[1]*Department of Biology, Faculty of Science and Technology, Airlangga University, Surabaya, 60115, Indonesia*
[2]*Department of Chemistry, Faculty of Science and Technology, Airlangga University, Surabaya, 60115, Indonesia*

ABSTRACT

Optimization of culture conditions of Talinum paniculatum Gaertn. adventitious roots in the balloon type bubble bioreactor have been done in order to increase its production of adventitious roots and saponin content. Culture conditions were used in this research were combination of aeration rate (0.25, 0.5 and 0.75 vvm) and initial inoculum density (0.5, 1, 2 g/400 mL). Bioreactor with a volume of 1000 mL was filled with 400 mL of liquid MS medium supplemented with IBA 2 mg L-1 were then given sterile air through a microfilter (0.2 μm) with different air flow rates. Into each bioreactor were added of different inoculum density of adventitious roots that had previously been induced from leaf explants of T. paniculatum on solid MS medium supplemented with IBA 2 mg L-1. Cultures were maintained for 14 days and sampling was done for every two days to determine the sugar content, conductivity and pH of the medium. The results showed that the combination of aeration rate of 0.5 vvm and inoculum density of 1 g/400 mL was the best treatment that can increase biomass of adventitious roots, whereas the combination of aeration rate of 0.75 vvm and inoculum density of 2 g/400 mL was the best treatment that can be increased of saponin content.

INTRODUCTION

Talinum paniculatum Gaertn which is in Indonesia also called java ginseng, has a bulging shape of the roots like *Panax ginseng* root and use as synchronized with *Panax ginseng*, especially its potential in increasing testosterone levels at the low testosterone condition, increasing number and motility of sperm (cell differentiation inductor (induce of sperm viability) and protection of human body from pathogen). In Indonesia, this plant usually was used as traditional medicine. One of the chemical content of the roots of this plant is saponins that are used as aphrodisiac. There are many kind of saponin, like saponin glycoside from *Gynostema penthaphyllum* known as gypnoside that are responsible for its pharmacological activities and ginsenoside from *Panax ginseng* (Yin *et al.*, 2014). Since, saponin ginsenoside are the well-known biologically active constituents in Korean ginseng, *T. paniculatum* has also received considerable attention. But java ginseng roots grow very slowly in their natural habitat which is about 2-3 years to get more than 100 g of roots per plant. In addition, it is known that levels of saponins of java ginseng root age of 3 months was lower than the java ginseng roots grown**in vitro** for 28 days. Because of the necessary compounds in *T. paniculatum* was accumulated in root organ, the root culture technology is essential for the preservation of these plants developed in order to awake and efficacious compounds, especially saponin compounds that was accumulated in the root organs can be improved.

In many decades, adventitious root cultures have been used to produce many kind of secondary metabolites which have naturally in root. The advantages of adventitious root culture are the root not influenced by geotropism, growth of root branch fast and had a genetic stability. Many researches have been conducted to increase biomass and secondary metabolite by adventitious roots in bioreactor, for examples, producing whitanolide-A in adventitious root of *Whitania somnifera* (Praveen and Murthy, 2010; Sivanandhan *et al.*, 2012), increasing biomass and secondary metabolite of *Glycyrrhiza uralensis* Fisch (Yin *et al.*, 2014), increasing bioreactor capacity to produce biomass and cafeic acid derivatives in adventitious root culture of *Echinacea angustifolia* (Cui *et al.*, 2013), production of adventitious root biomass of *Podophyllum hexandrum* Royle (Rajesh *et al.*, 2014), *Astragalus membranaceus* (Wu *et al.*, 2011), *Stevia reboudiana* Bertoni (Reis *et al.*, 2011) and *Panax ginseng* (Wang *et al.*, 2013).

Inducing the formation of adventitious roots of *T. paniculatum* using hypocotyls, epicotyls and leaves explants have been succeeded in solid and semisolid MS (Murashige and Skoog, 1962) medium supplemented with IBA 2 mg L^{-1}. But the growth in semi-solid media is limited by the availability of oxygen and culture space. This can be overcome by moving it into a liquid medium in a larger vessel such as flasks or bioreactors. Some of the advantages of liquid culture method in the bioreactor is oxygen demand that can be done by agitation or aeration, the culture space limitations can be overcome by using of the flask or bioreactor and nutrients can be accessed by all parts of the organ cultured. But growth in the bioreactor is influenced by many factors, such as shear stress, oxygen supply and gas composition (Kanokwaree and Doran, 1997).

Gas exchange between the gas and liquid phase is one of the factors that influence the cell and organ culture of plants in a liquid medium. In the bioreactor, strong aeration necessary for the supply of **dissolved oxygen** and increase the homogeneity of the liquid. Leeet *al.* (1998) reported that the concentration of **dissolved oxygen** through the aeration was beneficial for root growth and alkaloid production (tropan) in roots cultured of *Atropa belladonna*. In addition to aeration, inoculum density was also reported to affect the performance of cell suspension cultures and increased production of secondary metabolites. If the initial inoculum density was low, the cell growth was also low (Kanokwaree and Doran, 1997). But, if the initial inoculum density is high, the lag phase in cell culture does not occur because of the direct growth to be in the exponential phase. This suggests that increased secondary metabolites along with increased number of cells (Van Gulik *et al.*, 1994; Sakurai *et al.*, 1996). So, this experiment was conducted to optimization of the culture conditions of *T.*

paniculatum Gaertn. adventitious roots in balloon type bubble bioreactor with the treatment of various aeration rate dan initial inoculum density.

MATERIALS AND METHODS

Materials: *Talinum paniculatum* Gaertn. was obtained from the Botanical Garden Purwodadi, Pasuruan, East Java Indonesia which further was nurtured in polybag with mix of soil and organic fertilizer (50:50%) and incubated at room temperature (28-31°C). Adventitious root was obtained from leaf explants of *T. paniculatum* Gaertn.

Induction and proliferation of adventitious roots: Leaves were washed with detergent and then rinsed thoroughly with tap water. Explants were sterilized with clorox 10% (v/v) and soaked for 10 min while gently agitated. After that, clorox solution discarded and rinse 3 times with sterile distilled water. Explants were placed in sterile filter paper in the petridishes and cut 1 cm^2 and then planted in MS medium supplemented with IBA 2 mg L^{-1}, 30 g L^{-1} sucrose and 7 g L^{-1} agar. Cultures were maintained in room culture at 25°C in the dark conditions. After 4 weeks, adventitious root were used for the next stage.

Adventitious root culture in balloon type bubble bioreactor: Adventitious roots obtained from the previous stage were used as inoculum. Balloon Type Bubble Bioreactor (BTBB) was designed by Gupta and Ibaraki (2008). Bioreactor with a capacity of 1 L was filled with 0.4 L of liquid MS medium supplemented with IBA 2 mg L^{-1}, 30 g L^{-1} sucrose and sterilized by autoclaving at 121°C for 20 min. The experiment consisted of 9 cultures that received the combinations of treatment aeration rate: 0.25, 0.5 and 0.75 vvm (volumes of gas per volume of liquid per minute) and the initial inoculum density: 0.5, 1.0 and 2 g/400 mL. The cultures were incubated at room temperature for 14 days and each treatment has 3 replications. Fresh weight and dry weight of adventitious roots and saponin content were analyzed at the end of the cultivation period. To determine the growth of adventitious roots, pH, total sugar content and conductivity of the medium were done. Measurements were done every two days by taking 1 mL of culture medium. Measurement of pH was done using a pH meter (Boeco, BT-600), the total sugar content was measured using a hand refractometer (Atago), while the conductivity was measured using conductometer (Ezdo, Cond5021).

Extraction and analysis of saponins: Saponins contained in adventitious roots were analyzed qualitatively using thin layer chromatography and quantitatively using HPLC. Adventitious roots were dried at 50°C for 5 days and then were grinded used mortar. A 100 mg powder of adventitious roots were immersed in 10 mL of ethanol and then heated 80°C in water bath for 30 min. The extract was then concentrated in 80°C for 3 h until a volume of 0.2 mL was obtained. Extracts and saponins standard (Calbiochem) were spotted on silica gel GF254 and eluted using propanol: water (14:3). Spot were detected by spraying with a mixture of anisaldehyde 0.5 mL, acetic acid glacial 10 mL, ethanol 85 mL, sul**furic acid** 5 mL and then heated at 110°C for 6-10 min. Saponin standard gave the dark green colour. Quantitatively measurement of saponin was done using HPLC system (Agilent Q-TOF 6530 L) equipped with c18 columns. The mobile phase was a mixture of reagent 0.1% **formic acid** in water grade and acetonitrile (40:60, v/v) and the volume inject were 0.2 µL. The detection wavelength was set at 299 nm.

RESULTS

Effect of combinations of treatment of initial inoculum density and aeration rate on adventitious root biomass: Combinations of treatment of initial inoculum density and aeration rate affect the growth of adventitious roots. Growth ratio of adventitious root indicated by root fresh weight at the end of the culture reduced the initial fresh weight (Fig. 1).

The growth of adventitious roots of ginseng java were highest in the combinations of treatment aeration rate 0.5 vvm and initial inoculum density 1 g/400 mL (0.635 g), where as the combinations of treatment aeration rate 0.25 vvm and initial inoculum density 0.5, 1 and 2 g/400 mL also showed high growth (Fig. 1). This is supported by the data of conductivity, sugar content and pH in culture medium for 14 days (Fig. 2).

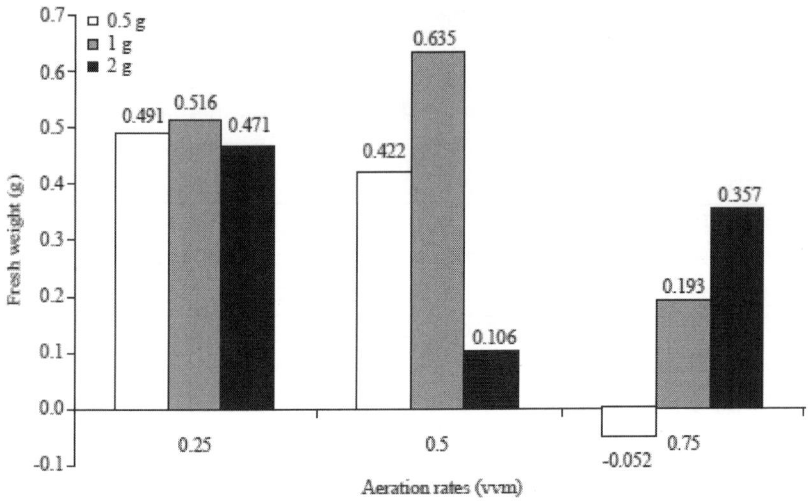

Figure 1. Growth ratio of adventitious roots on combination of aeration rate and initial inoculum density on 14 days culture

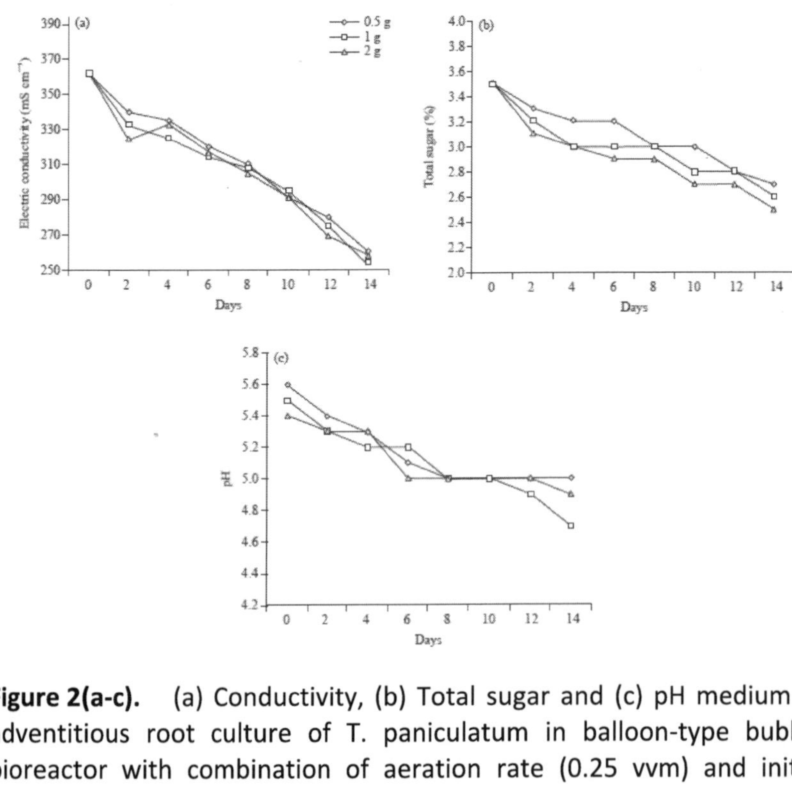

Figure 2(a-c). (a) Conductivity, (b) Total sugar and (c) pH medium of adventitious root culture of T. paniculatum in balloon-type bubble bioreactor with combination of aeration rate (0.25 vvm) and initial inoculum density 0.5, 1 and 2 g/400 mL

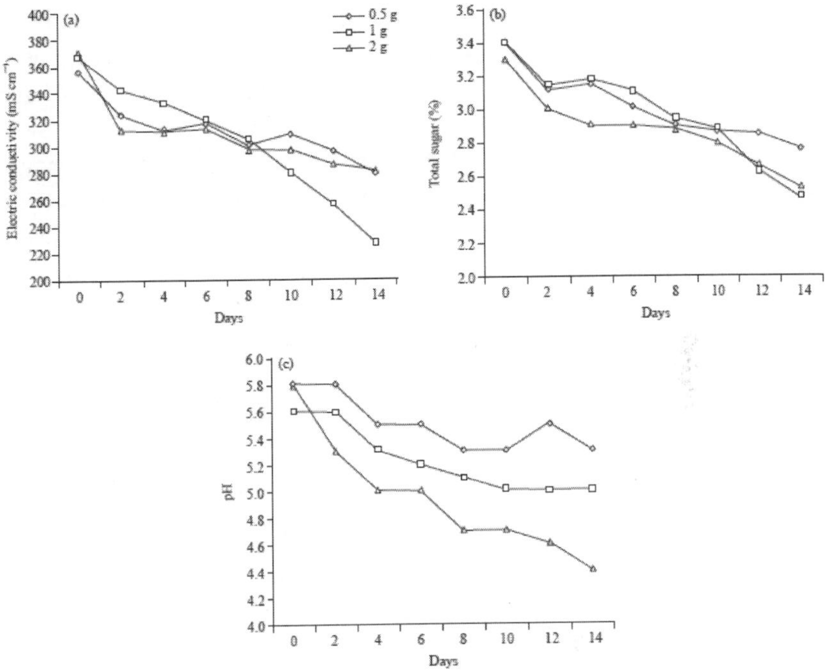

Figure 3(a-c): (a) Conductivity, (b) Total sugar and (c) pH medium of adventitious root culture of T. paniculatum in balloon-type bubble bioreactor with combination of aeration rate (0.5 vvm) and initial inoculum density 0.5, 1 and 2 g/400 mL

Combination of treatment aeration rate 0.5 vvm and initial inoculum density 0,5 1 and 2 g have highest biomass at the treatment of 0.5 vvm and 1 g. Growth of the adventitious roots in that treatment were support of the medium condition include the conductivity, total sugar and pH medium during culture (Fig. 3). Final conductivity at the combinations of treatment 0.5 vvm and 1 g/400 mL was lower than two other combinations of treatment. It was indicate the maximum absorption of nutrient from medium. The same condition also happen in the absorption of sugar which were showed of concentration of total sugar at 14 days also lowest, whereas pH medium during culture were constant at 5-5.3. This condition induced the growth of adventitious root cells, so the biomass of adventitious root increased.

Combinations of treatment aeration rate 0.75 vvm and initial inoculum density 0.5, 1, 2 g/400 mL showed the negative growth at treatment

0.75 vvm and 0.5 g (Fig. 2). It was seen from the data of conductivity, total sugar and pH medium showed that condition not different with another treatment (Fig. 4). At the combination of aeration rate 0.75 vvm and initial inoculum density 1 g/400 mL and 2 g mL–1 have a positive growth, same as aeration rate 0.25 and 0.5 vvm, although the growth rate were lower. Negatively growth rate of the adventitious root at that treatment were caused by shear stress, so the adventitious root became cut to small pieces and growth of root branch were rare, it can be seen in Fig. 5c and e.

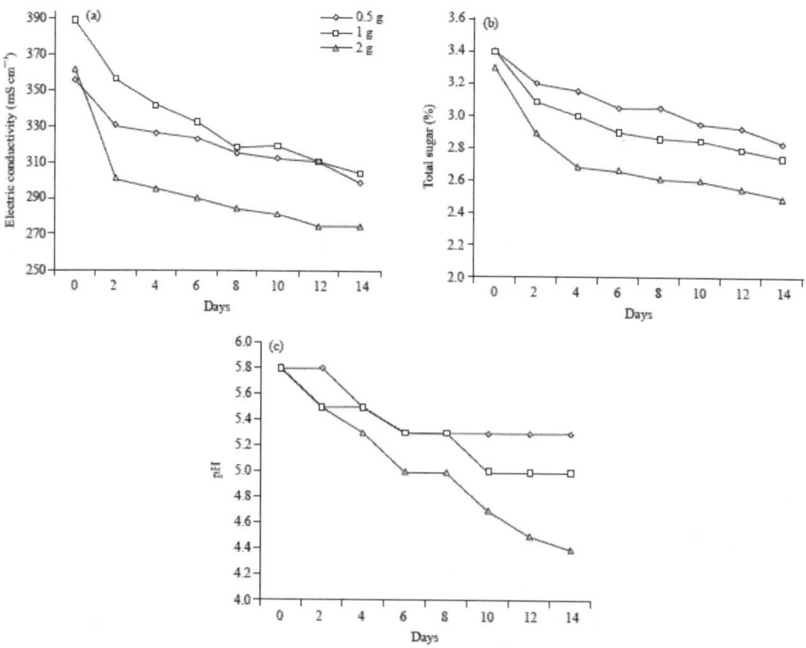

Figure 4(a-c). (a) Conductivity, (b) Total sugar and (c) pH medium of adventitious root culture of T. paniculatum in balloon-type bauble bioreactor with combination of aeration rate (0.75 vvm) and initial inoculum density 0.5, 1 and 2 (g mL–1)

But at the combinations of treatment aeration rate 0.5 vvm and initial inoculum density 1 g/400 mL were the best condition of culture. It was indicated by highest of biomass and growth of root branches much more than other combinations of treatment (Fig. 5b and d). At the

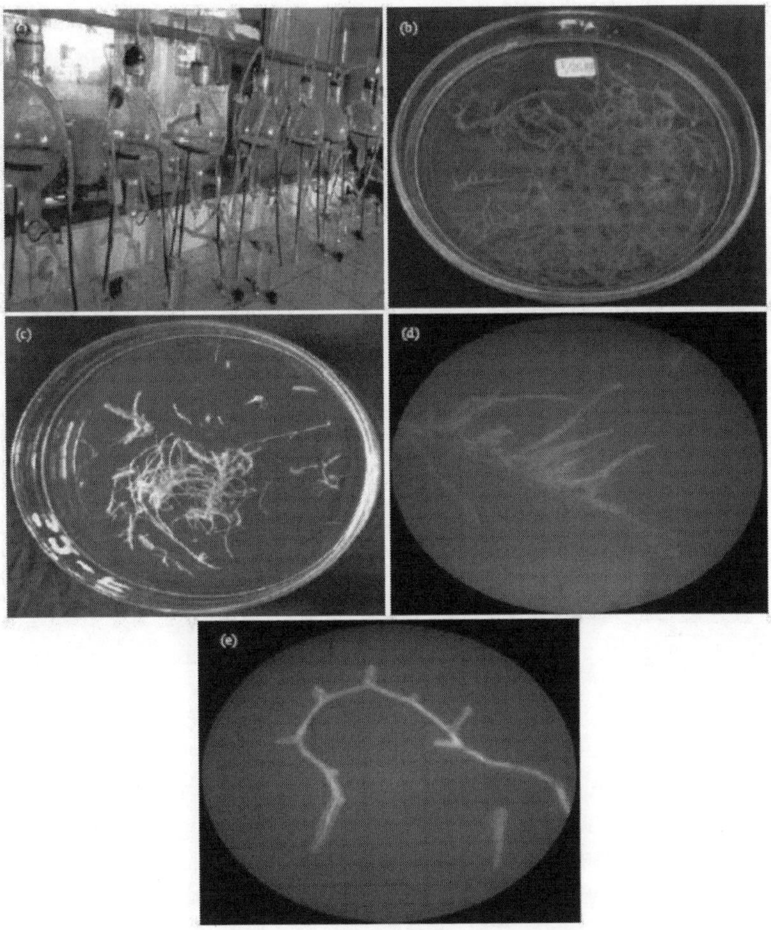

Figure 5(a-e) (a) Adventitious root cultures of T. paniculatum in balloon type bubble bioreactor, (b, d) Macroscopic and microcopies (40x) pictures of adventitious root at the combinations of treatment of aeration rate and initial inoculum density: 0.5 vvm, 1 g/400 mL and (c, e) 0.75 vvm, 0.5 g/400 mL

aeration rate 0.75 vvm adventitious root culture will get the shear stress caused by produce of size and number of bubble. When aeration rate increase, produce of bubble will be increased, so it can inhibit the growth of adventitious root. It also happened in hairy root culture of T.

panicultum which got the shear stress in treatment of aeration rate 0.75 vvm (Manuhara et al., 2012).

Effect of combinations of treatment of initial inoculum density and aeration rate on saponin content of adventitious root: Qualitative analyzed of saponin at adventitious root showed that all of the adventitious roots of java ginseng in all combination of treatment were posit if in thin layer chromatography which indicate of dark green color and Rf value same as standard saponin (data not shown). Result of saponin content used high performance liquid chromatography were showed at Table 1.

Table 1. Saponin content (ppm/g dry weight) of adventitious roots of T. paniculatum at various aeration rate and initial inoculum density

	Aeration rate (vvm)		
Initial inoculum density (g/400 mL)	0.25	0.5	0.75
0.5	n.d	3.790	1.1500
1.0	1.070	6.390	2.2100
2.0	2.400	16450	25.500

n.d: Not detected

The highest saponin was gotten at the combinations of treatment of aeration rate 0.75 vvm and initial inoculum density 2 g/400 mL whereas, at the aeration rate 0.25 vvm and initial inoculum density 0.5 g/400 mL saponin content was not detected, although in the qualitat if test showed the posit if result. Its maybe caused the saponin content was very low. At combinations of treatment of aeration rate 0.5 vvm and initial inoculum density (0.5, 1 and 2 g/400 mL) showed saponin content increased, although its content lower than combinations of treatment of aeration rate 0.75 vvm and initial inoculum density 2 g/400 mL.

DISCUSSION

The conductivity and sugar levels during the culture medium decreased. Its showed that absorption of inorganic compound and sucrose by adventitious root are effectively, so the growth of cell increase and it cause the biomass of adventitious root also increase. Beside that, decreasing of pH medium from 5.8-4.5-5.2 at the 14th day did not inhibit absorption of inorganic compound in the medium. Its also happened in hairy root culture of *Arachis hypogaea* in agitated liquid medium. Until 9 days culture, pH medium was decreased from 5.5-4.8 (Bolivar *et al.*, 2007). In the cell suspension culture of *Elaeis guineensis* Jacq. decreased of pH medium from 5.6-4 was take place very fast during 9 days culture (Gorret *et al.*, 2004), whereas hairy root culture of *Talinum paniculatum* Gaertn in balloon-type bubble bioreactor at the first week pH of culture was decreased from 6-4 (Manuhara *et al.*, 2012). Vani (1996) also reported that decreasing of pH during culture of *Catharanthus roseus* hairy root in the circulated bioreactor was take place at 10-15 days culture. Decreasing pH of MS medium during hairy root culture was caused by MS medium consist of ammonium. Source of ammonium in MS medium was ammonium nitrate that necessary as a buffer and source of nitrogen. When cell need nitrogen, cell uptake the ammonium and release H^+. Releasing of H^+into the medium caused acid condition.

Conductivity was used as indirect method to biomass estimated in the cell culture at bioprocess technology with efficient and accurate result. Conductivity was reflected of uptake inorganic compound by the cell during cultivation which was showed by the decrease of it's concentration and on the contrary the cell population or biomass increased (Thanh *et al.*, 2006). Carbon source of MS medium is sucrose, which in the beginning of culture have been hydrolyzed to glucose and fructose. Cell consumed its sugar during cultivation, so measurement of total sugar also reflected growth of the cell (Gorret *et al.*, 2004).

The lower growth of adventitious root in combinations of treatment of aeration rate 0.5 vvm and initial inoculum density 2 g were supported by the value of conductivity which was still high and the low of pH medium at the end of cultivation (Fig. 3). The high conductivity of medium showed that the adventitious root unavailable to absorb inorganic compound from medium. These conditions were also supported by the decreased pH of medium at the end of cultivation. Decreasing pH of medium can cause the low ability of cell to absorb inorganic compound from the medium. At the normal condition, organic compound will be absorbed at pH 5-6.

The highest saponin content in this research was achieved at aeration 0.75 vvm and initial inoculum density 2 g/400 mL. The same result was obtained in hairy root culture of *T. paniculatum* that showed the increasing of initial inoculum density can cause increasing of saponin content (Manuhara *et al.*, 2012). According to Van Gulik *et al.* (1994), the high of initial inoculum density can eliminated lag phase of growth curve, so specific growth rate became maximum. The high of growth rate indicated that the culture have long of exponential phase. At the end of culture was assumed that content of sucrose in the culture medium still support to growth acceleration, so culture still in exponential phase. Culture with initial inoculum density 2 g/400 mL was assumed have lag and exponential phase shorter because sucrose in medium not enough to support growth acceleration. At the end of cultivation, culture was on the early stationer phase, so saponin accumulation higher than other culture. Bhojwani and Razdan (1996) stated that production of secondary metabolite generally happened at early to the end of stationer phase of growth curve, when the source of nutrient limited. Sakurai *et al.* (1996) also state that increasing production of secondary metabolite and change of profile product was carried out by increasing inoculum density or modification of medium. Inoculums density was also reported that would significant influence on cell growth, saponin and polysaccharide production in cell culture of *Panax notoginseng* (Zhang and Zhong, 1997). In this study, the highest saponin content in adventitious root of*T. paniculatum* was achieved at aeration rate 0.75 vvm but in hairy root culture of *T. paniculatum*, the highest of saponin content was achieved at aeration rate 0.25 vvm (Manuhara *et al.*, 2012). It's maybe caused by supply of oxygen in culture medium can support cell to produce secondary metabolite, so saponin content in adventitious root of *T. paniculatum* was increased.

CONCLUSION

Based on nine combinations of treatments of aeration rate and initial inoculum density, the best combination to produce biomass of adventitious root of *T. paniculatum* in balloon-type bubble bioreactor was aeration rate 0.5 vvm and initial inoculum density 1 g/400 mL, whereas, the best treatment to produce saponin was aeration rate 0.75 vvm and initial inoculum density 2 g/400 mL. This result could be used as base to improve large scale of adventitious root of *T. paniculatum* in balloon-type bubble bioreactor.

ACKNOWLEDGMENTS

This research was supported by Grant from Universitas Airlangga, Surabaya, Indonesia with grant number 6091/UN3/KR/2013.

REFERENCES

1. Bhojwani, S.S. and N.K. Razdan, 1996. Plant Tissue Culture: Theory and Practice. Vol. 5, Elsevier Science, USA., ISBN-13: 9780444816238, Pages: 767.

2. Bolivar, F.M., J. Condori, A.M. Rimando, J. Hubstenberger and K. Shelton *et al.*, 2007. Production and secretion of resveratrol in hairy root cultures of *Pueraria lobata* (Willd). J. Environ. Biol., 28: 321-326.

3. Cui, H.Y., A. Baque, E.J. Lee and K.Y. Paek, 2013. Scale-up of adventitious root cultures of *Echinacea angustifolia* in a pilot-scale bioreactor for the production of biomass and caffeic acid derivatives. Plant Biotechnol. Rep., 7: 297-308.

4. Gorret, N., S.K.B. Rosli, S.F. Oppenheim, L.B. Willis, P.A. Lessard, C.K. Rha and A.J. Sinskey, 2004. Bioreactor culture of oil palm (*Elaeis guineensis*) and effects of nitrogen source, inoculum size and conditioned medium on biomass production. J. Biotechnol., 108: 253-263.

5. Gupta, D.S. and Y. Ibaraki, 2008. Plant Tissue Culture Engineering. Springer, New York, USA., pp: 83-92.

6. Kanokwaree, K. and P.M. Doran, 1997. Effect of inoculum size on growth of *Atropa belladonna* hairy roots in shake flasks. J. Ferment. Bioeng., 84: 378-381.

7. Lee, K.T., T. Yamakawa, T. Kodama, Y. Igarashi and K. Shimomura, 1998. Effects of aeration on tropane alkaloid production by transformed root of *Atropa belladonna* in flask cultures. J. Ferment. Bioeng., 86: 614-616.

8. Manuhara, Y.S.W., A. Yachya and A.N. Kristanti, 2012. Effect of aeration and inoculum density on biomass and saponin content

of*Talinum paniculatum* gaertn. Hairy roots in balloon-type bubble bioreactor. J. Pharm. Biomed. Sci., 2: 47-52.

9. Murashige, T. and F. Skoog, 1962. A revised medium for rapid growth and bio assays with tobacco tissue cultures. Physiologia Plantarum, 15: 473-497.

10. Praveen, N. and H.N. Murthy, 2010. Production of withanolide-a from adventitious root cultures of *Withania somnifera*. Acta Physiol. Plant., 32: 1017-1022.

11. Rajesh, M., G. Sivanandhan, M. Arun, V. Vasudevan and J. Theboral *et al.*, 2014. Factors influencing podophyllotoxin production in adventitious root culture of *Podophyllum hexandrum* royle. Acta Physiol. Plant., 36: 1009-1021.

12. Reis, R.V., A.P.P.L. Borges, T.P.C. Chierrito, E.R. de Souto and L.M. de Souza *et al.*, 2011. Establishment of adventitious root culture of<="" i="" style="color: rgb(70, 68, 61); font-family: Verdana, Arial, Helvetica, sans-serif; font-size: 13px; font-style: normal; font-variant-ligatures: normal; font-variant-caps: normal; font-weight: normal; letter-spacing: normal; orphans: 2; text-align: start; text-indent: 0px; text-transform: none; white-space: normal; widows: 2; word-spacing: 0px; -webkit-text-stroke-width: 0px; background-color: rgb(255, 255, 255);">Bertoni in a roller bottle system. Plant Cell Tiss Organ Cult., 106: 329-335.

13. Sakurai, M., T. Mori, M. Seki and S. Furusaki, 1996. Changes of anthocyanin composition by conditioned medium and cell inoculum size using strawberry suspension culture. Biotechnol. Lett., 18: 1149-1154.

14. Sivanandhan, G., M. Arun, S. Mayavan, M. Rajesh and M. Jeyaraj *et al.*, 2012. Optimization of elicitation conditions with methyl jasmonate and salicylic acid to improve the productivity of withanolides in the adventitious root culture of *Withania somnifera* (L.) dunal. Applied Biochem. Biotechnol., 168: 681-696.

15. Thanh, N.T., H.N. Murthy, K. Yu, C.S. Jeong, E. Hahn and K.Y. Paek, 2006. Effect of oxygen supply on cell growth and saponin

production in bioreactor cultures of *Panax ginseng*. J. Plant Physiol., 163: 1337-1341.

16. Van Gulik, W.M., A.M. Nuutila, K.L. Vinke, H.J.G. ten Hoppen and J.J. Heijnen, 1994. Effects of carbon dioxide, air flow rate and inoculation density on the batch growth of *Catharanthus roseus* cell suspensions in stirred fermentors. Biotechnol. Prog., 10: 335-339.

17. Vani, S.N., 1996. Bioreactor design for scaleup of *Catharanthus roseus* hairy root culture for production of indole alkaloids. Ph.D. Thesis, Rice University, Texas.

18. Wang, J., W. Gao, Q. Wang, S. Man and L. Zhang, 2013. Influence of step-wise aeration treatment on biomass and bioactive compounds of *Panax ginseng* adventitious root in balloon-type bubble bioreactor. Res. Chem. Intermed., 41: 623-629.

19. Wu, S.Q., M.L. Lian, R. Gao, S.Y. Park and X.C. Piao, 2011. Bioreactor application on adventitious root culture of *Astragalus membranaceus*. *In Vitro* Cell. Dev. Biol., 47: 719-724.

20. Yin, S., Y. Zhang, W. Gao, J. Wang, S. Man and H. Liu, 2014. Effects of nitrogen source and phosphate concentration on biomass and metabolites accumulation in adventitious root culture of *Glycyrrhiza uralensis* Fisch. Acta Physiol. Plant., 36: 915-921.

21. Zhang, Y.H. and J.J. Zhong, 1997. Hyperproduction of ginseng saponin and polysaccharide by high density cultivation of *Panax notoginseng* cells. Enzym Microb. Technol., 2: 59-63.

Chapter 11

Hydrogen Production by Green Alga GAF99 in Sea Water Bioreactor: II Modeling the Effect of Temperature

Farqad F.M. Saeed and Mohammed A. Ibrahim

Royal Scientific Society, Amman, Jordan

Princess Sumaya University of Technology, Amman, Jordan

ABSTRACT

The aim of this study is to ascertain the influence of temperature on the bio-hydrogen productivity of marine green algae Chaetomorpha sp. GAF99 in sea water bioreactor system by utilizing multiple regression analysis. The biohydrogen production by green alga cultures was measured periodically at different incubation temperatures of active biohydrogen production phase to generate a model as well as surface response. The generated model {P = 26.81015e (-0.1[(Te-22.6)2+(Tm-24.7)2])} relates production of H2 (mL) as a function of temperature at two daily measurements (i.e., Tm, Te). The results revealed that the model can give significant correlation ship between biohydrogen production and temperature of incubation according to ANOVA statistical analysis based on F and p tests. The model and surface response curve obtained in this study showed clearly that the optimum biohydrogen production was recorded at the dark period at 23.2°C.

INTRODUCTION

Algae are the fastest growing plants on the planet and have great potential to produce various forms of energy (Demirbas and Demirbas, 2010). They have been shown as an important source of **renewable energy**; these include biohydrogen (Chader *et al.*, 2009; Beer *et al.*, 2009), biogas (Vergara-Fernandez *et al.*, 2008), bioethanol (Goh and Lee, 2010; Eshaq *et al.*, 2010), biodiesel (Miao and Wu, 2004; Wiley *et al.*, 2011; Pfromm *et al.*, 2011) and bioelectricity (Rosenbaum *et al.*, 2010). Moreover these photosynthetic organisms have been known for their other important economical products which are used in cosmetics, bioactive functional compounds, pigments, food and feed (Plaza *et al.*, 2010; Spolaore *et al.*, 2006; Del-Campo *et al.*, 2007; Ming *et al.*, 2012).

Biohydrogen production by algae is one of the promising potential biofuel in the future and is a hopeful approach for solving environmental problems associated with fossil fuels. It is viewed as an attractive energy source for transportation by virtue of the fact that it is renewable, considered friendly to environment since it does not produce the CO_2 in combustion and as a consequence reduces air pollution (Balat, 2008; Nazlina *et al.*, 2009; Vijayaraghavan *et al.*, 2010). One important aspect of hydrogen production is the economic cost for production and the required process for utilization of hydrogen which are extremely high per unit of energy when compared to fossil fuel energy sources such as natural gas or gasoline. These issues require consideration in long term plans for high excellence research and development of hydrogen production. The reported results of research work and studies in this field have shown that the production of biohydrogen and other biofuels by biological systems and in particular by algae is an area of promising applications providing optimizing the cultural conditions for higher yield of biohydrogen (Benemann, 1997; Lindblad, 1999; Levin *et al.*, 2004; Kotay and Das, 2008). Early studies on the ability of bacteria (Stephenson and Stickland, 1931) and algae (Gaffron and Rubin, 1942) to produce biohydrogen had been mostly a biological curiosity. Subsequently research activities in this subject have shown that biohydrogen can be produced by various genera of blue-green (Ghirardi *et al.*, 2000; Dutta *et al.*, 2005) and green algae (Guana *et al.*, 2004; Markov *et al.*, 2006). In this context, green algae or Chlorophyta are the largest phylum of algae can live in diverse habitats, including fresh and sea water (Sandgreen, 1991; Anderson, 2005; Norris, 2010). Recently, the authors were able to isolate and characterize marine green alga*Chaetomorpha* sp. GAF99 from Gulf of Aqaba which produces biohydrogen under anaerobic and dark conditions in seawater bioreactor (Ibrahim and Saeed, 2012). The study indicated the importance of light/dark periods, anaerobic condition and temperature of incubations on hydrogen productivity of *Chaetomorpha* sp. GAF99. The role of temperature was found critical in the process of biohydrogen production. Production was shown to drop drastically during production phase at higher incubation temperature 33°C. Thus for an efficient process of hydrogen production in seawater bioreactor requires generating mathematical kinetic model of the process. Such studies will provide useful information on optimization of critical factors for the process effectiveness of biohydrogen production (Palazzi*et al.*, 2002; Akande *et al.*, 2006). The main argument of present investigation is to provide the required information on the effect of temperature which will assist the simulation and design of future seawater bioreactor for bio-hydrogen production by marine green alga*Chaetomorpha* sp. GAF99.

MATERIALS AND METHODS

Marine alga *Chaetomorpha* sp. GAF99: Marine green alga *Chaetomorpha* sp. GAF99 which was isolated originally in February 2008 from various shallow water niches (1-2 m deep) of Gulf of Aqaba shore (Ibrahim and Saeed, 2012) was used in present investigation. The cultures were maintained at room temperature in two liters flasks containing one liter sea water, the pH value of sea water is 8.3.

Biohydrogen production: Biohydrogen production by the marine green alga *Chaetomorpha* sp. GAF99 was followed according to reported method (Ibrahim and Saeed, 2012). Bio-hydrogen production was measured twice daily at 8.30 am (T_m) and at 17.30 pm (T_e) to determine the influence of temperature on productivity at various temperatures. The volume of the generated gas from algal culture incubated in 2 L flask was collected in the graduated glass cylinders and was measured directly by water displacement. The measurements of the composition of produced gases were performed qualitatively by detection instrument CD100/Kane-May/Kane International Ltd. (EN61000-6-3) and quantitatively by GC-2014/Shimadzu.

Model generation: Regression analysis was used to develop a model for the collected data of biohydrogen produced during active production phase at various temperatures. The values of biohydrogen produced in active production phase were subjected to various**mathematical models** by using MATLAB software package to find the optimum model that defines the behavior of algae as a function to two temperatures. The statistical analysis based on ANOVA test (Montgomery and Runger, 2007) was used to show the significance of the model based on F and T tests and p-values with 95% confidence limit.

RESULTS

Effect of temperature on biohydrogen production: Biohydrogen production by *Chaetomorpha* sp. GAF99 in sea water bioreactor under anaerobic and dark conditions starts after a period of 10±2 days of adaptation period. The production phase, which continues for another 10±2 days, is influenced greatly by temperature of incubation. The higher incubation temperature (33°C) was found not favorable for hydrogen production. In order to find the optimum correlation that represents the production of biohydrogen (P) as function of temperatures, a statistical analysis was conducted to find an optimum model to show the role of temperatures on biohydrogen production by *Chaetomorpha* sp. GAF99.

Model generation: The model was generated as a function of two temperatures measured at 8:30 AM (T_m) and at 5:30 PM (T_e). The regression model statistics was utilized based on ANOVA test. The numerical estimates of the regression model coefficients were based on 95% confidence limit (significance level (α) = 1-0.95 = 0.05). The significance normally assessed using the t-test statistics (significance F or p-values) which must be $<\alpha = 0.05$ to be significant. The results which are shown in Table 1-3 indicated that the coefficient of determination (R^2 = 78.47%) is acceptable.

Table 1. Regression model statistics

Regression	Statistics
Multiple R	0.885871
R^2	0.784767
Adjusted R^2	0.684767
Standard error	9.848025
Observations	11

Table 2. Adopted model of hydrogen production as a function of two temperatures (Teand Tm)

SOV	df	Sum of square	Mean of square	F-value	Significance
Regression	1	3536.154	3536.154	36.46136	0.000193
Residual	10	969.836	96.9836		
Total	11	4505.99			

Table 3. Numerical estimates of the regression model coefficients based on p-value with 95% confidence limit

					CI 95%	
	Coefficients	SE	t-value	p-value	Lower	Upper
Slope (β)	26.81015	4.439998	6.038324	0.000126	16.91722	36.70308

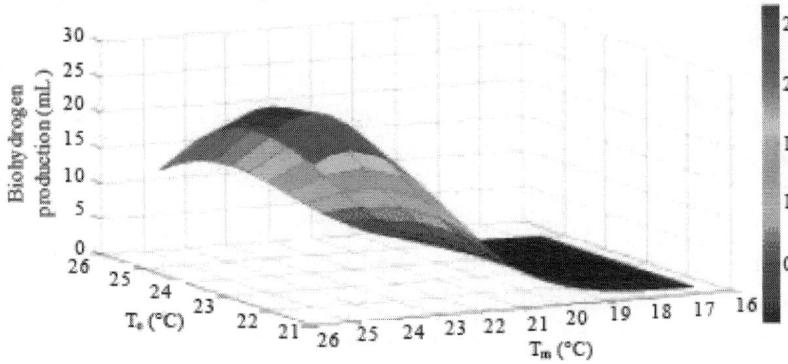

Figure 1. Three dimensional plot showing the surface response of biohydrogen production as a function of two temperatures Te and Tm as in Eq. 1

The obtained results also show the significance F value = 0.000193 which is <0.05 and the p value = 0.000126 which is also <0.05. Therefore the overall model given in Eq. 1 is significant.

Equation 1 represents an exponential form for the relation of biohydrogen production (P) as a function of two temperatures (T_e and T_m).

$$P = 26.81015\, e\, (-0.1[(T_e-22.6)^2+(T_m-24.7)^2]) \quad (1)$$

Furthermore, three dimensional mapping of the surface response (Fig. 1) of Eq. 1 shows clearly that the highest biohydrogen production was recorded at the morning [8:30 a.m.] (T_m) and the least production was recorded at the evening temperature (T_e) which was measured at 5:30 p.m. In other word the main production of biohydrogen production is occurring during dark period at T_m. The statistical analysis showed that the optimum temperature for biohydrogen production is 23.2°C.

DISCUSSION

Ever since the discovery that the green alga *Scenedesmus* was able to produce hydrogen during anaerobic conditions (Gaffron and Rubin, 1942), efforts have been made to investigate the influence of various **environmental factors** on hydrogen production. Temperature is one of important **environmental factors** which have critical effect on biohydrogen production by various tested organisms. It had shown that biohydrogen production by *Anabaena* was highest at 27°C (Prabina and Kumar, 2010). Whereas other study investigated production by*Chlamydomonas* sp. MGA161, a marine green alga, when cultivated at a high CO_2 concentration (15% CO_2) and low temperature (15°C), under these conditions the total productivity was significantly improved (Miura *et al.*, 1993). On the other hand, hydrogen production was studied using immobilized green alga *Chlorella* sp., the rate of hydrogen evolution was increased as temperature increased from 37-40°C (Song *et al.*, 2011). In this context, our previous study (Ibrahim and Saeed, 2012) showed that production of hydrogen is almost ceased at 33°C. As part of our efforts to understand the role of **environmental factors** in biohydrogen production by *Chaetomorpha* sp. GAF99 culture, the collected data of biohydrogen produced at various temperatures during production phase were subjected to regression analysis to generate the model shown in Eq. 1 (see the result section) which represents the biohydrogen productivity of *Chaetomorpha*sp. GAF 99 population for various periods during 2010 and 2011. It was possible to demonstrate in the present investigation the correlation between hydrogen productivity of *Chaetomorpha* sp. GAF 99 in sea water bioreactor and incubation temperature. The given relationship in Eq. 1 showed a significant behavior of biohydrogen production in relation with the given data of T_e and T_m. This was demonstrated by the R square value which is equivalent to 78.4767% (Table 1) and the p value which is equal to 0.000126 and was less than alpha value (α) of 0.05.

It is worth to mention that our study gave further support to utilize sea water for biohydrogen production. In addition and in contrast to the widely used freshwater green algae, the goal of our research was to ascertain utilization of marine green algae-based bioreactor system for biohydrogen production by developing a **mathematical model** to correlate biohydrogen production with incubation temperature. It is presumed that generating such system will demonstrate the cost feasibility effectiveness for sustained H_2 photo-production. Thus by utilizing seawater as the substrate and solar light as the source of energy and right temperature beside other environmental conditions it might be possible to develop economically feasible system for biohydrogen production. The specific objectives of this study could be met by developing such **mathematical model**s. These include higher production at lower cost in sustainable manner.

The results of this study and our other two studies (Ibrahim and Saeed, 2012; Saeed and Ibrahim, 2012) and those reported by other investigators (Palazzi *et al.*, 2002; Prabina and Kumar, 2010; Song *et al.*, 2011) show the importance of more standardized careful study which requires modeling and statistical analysis to define the effect of temperature as a crucial environmental factor in addition to other environmental factor (i.e., pH) in the production of biohydrogen by marine green alga *Chaetomorpha* sp. GAF99. Furthermore and taking in the account the influence of temperature on the activity of hydrogenases, key enzymes for biohydrogen production by green algae (Saeed and Ibrahim, 2012), it is possible to suggest designing improved hydrogenases for efficient production of biohydrogen at higher temperature by utilizing new molecular technologies (Ibrahim, 2012).

CONCLUSION

Marine green algae have been shown as promising candidates for future biohydrogen production. In this study Chaetomorpha sp. GAF99 was found dominant species in specimens obtained from habitats of Gulf of Aqaba. The green alga produced biohydrogen in bioreactor contained natural sea water and showed an interesting response to temperature. The study revealed the critical role of temperature on the amounts of biohydrogen produced during active production phase. The model and surface response curve obtained in this study showed clearly that the optimum biohydrogen production was recorded at the dark period at 23.2°C.

ACKNOWLEDGMENTS

The authors would like to thank the Ministry of Higher Education of Jordan/Scientific Research Support Fund (SRSF) and the Royal Scientific Society (RSS) for funding this work. The support of the Princess Sumaya University for Technology (PSUT) is highly appreciated. Special acknowledgment to Eng. Amani N. Abdulhadi and Eng. Sarah R. Al Weissi for their technical assistance.

REFERENCES

1. Akande, A., A. Aboudheir, R. Idem and A. Dalai, 2006. Kinetic modeling of hydrogen production by the catalytic reforming of crude ethanol over a co-precipitated Ni-Al2O3 catalyst in a packed bed tubular reactor. Int. J. Hydrogen Energy, 31: 1707-1715.

2. Anderson, R.A., 2005. Algal Culturing Techniques. Elsevier Academic Press, New York.

3. Balat, M., 2008. Potential importance of hydrogen as a future solution to environmental and transportation problems. Int. J. Hydrogen Energy, 33: 4013-4029.

4. Beer, L.L., E.S. Boyd, J.W. Peters and M.C. Posewitz, 2009. Engineering algae for biohydrogen and biofuel production. Curr. Opin. Biotech., 20: 264-271.

5. Benemann, J.R., 1997. Feasibility analysis of photobiological hydrogen production. Int. J. Hydrogen Energy, 22: 979-987.

6. Chader, S., H. Hacene and S.N. Agathos, 2009. Study of hydrogen production by three strains of Chlorella isolated from the soil in the Algerian Sahara. Int. J. Hydrogen Energy, 34: 4941-4946.

7. Del-Campo, J.A., M. Garcia-Gonzalez and M.G. Guerrero, 2007. Outdoor cultivation of microalgae for carotenoid production: Current state and perspectives. Applied Microbiol. Biotechnol., 74: 1163-1174.

8. Demirbas, A. and M.F. Demirbas, 2010. Green Energy and Technology: Algae Energy. Springer-Verlag, London..

9. Dutta, D., D. De, S. Chaudhuri and S.K. Bhattacharya, 2005. Hydrogen production by Cyanobacteria. Microb. Cell Fact., Vol. 4. 10.1186/1475-2859-4-36

10. Eshaq, F.S., M.N. Ali and M.K. Mohd, 2010. Spirogyra biomass a renewable source for biofuel (bioethanol) production. Int. J. Eng. Sci. Tech., 2: 7045-7054.

11. Gaffron, H. and J. Rubin, 1942. Fermentative and photochemical production of hydrogen in algae. J. Gen. Physiol., 26: 219-240.

12. Ghirardi, M.L., L. Zhang, J.W. Lee, T. Flynn, M. Seibert, E. Greenbaum and A. Melis, 2000. Microalgae: A green source of renewable H2. Trends Biotechnol., 18: 506-511.

13. Goh, C.S. and K.T. Lee, 2010. A visionary and conceptual macroalgae-based third-generation bioethanol (TGB) biorefinery in Sabah, Malaysia as an underlay for renewable and sustainable development. Renew. Sust. Energ. Rev., 14: 842-848.

14. Guana, Y., M. Denga, X. Yu and W. Zhang, 2004. Two-stage photo-biological production of hydrogen by marine green alga Platymonas subcordiformis. Biochem. Eng. J., 19: 69-73.

15. Ibrahim, M.A. and F.M. Saeed, 2012. Biohydrogen production by Green Alga Chaetomorpha sp. GAF99 from Gulf of Aqaba: 1 isolation and characterization of Alga. Biotechnology, (In Press).

16. Ibrahim, M.A., 2012. An insight into the use of genome, methylome and gethylome in synthetic biology. Asian J. Applied Sci., 5: 67-73.

17. Kotay, S.M. and D. Das, 2008. Biohydrogen as a renewable energy resource-prospects and potentials. Int. J. Hydrogen Energy, 33: 258-263.

18. Levin, D., L. Pitt and M. Love, 2004. Biohydrogen production: Prospects and limitations to practical application. Int. J. Hydrogen Energy, 29: 173-185.

19. Lindblad, P., 1999. Cyanobacterial H2 metabolism: knowledge and potential/strategies for a photobiotechnological production of H2. Biotecnol. Aplicada, 16: 141-144.

20. Markov, S.A., E.R. Eivazova and J. Greenwood, 2006. Photostimulation of hydrogen production in the green alga Chlamydomonas reinhardtii upon photoinhibition of its oxygen evolving system. Int. J. Hydrogen Energy, 31: 1314-1317.

21. Miao, X. and Q. Wu, 2004. High yield bio-oil production from fast pyrolysis by metabolic controlling of Chlorella protothecoides. J. Biotechnol., 110: 85-93.

22. Ming, L.C., R. Nurliyana, A.B. Syah, M.N. Azizah, H.L. Sim and M.Y. Hirzun, 2012. Identification and biochemical composition of a green microalgae. Asian J. Biotechnol., 4: 38-45.

23. Miura, Y., W. Yamada, K. Hirata, K. Miyamoto and M. Kiyohara, 1993. Stimulation of hydrogen production in algal cells grown under high CO2 concentration and low temperature. Applied Biochem. Biotecgnol., 39-40: 753-761.

24. Montgomery, D.C. and G.C. Runger, 2007. Applied Statistics and Probability for Engineers. 4th Edn., John Wiley and Sons, New York, ISBN-13: 978-0470067215.

25. Nazlina, H.M.Y., A.R. Nor Aini, F. Ismail, M.Z.M. Yusof and M.A. Hassan, 2009. Effect of different temperature, initial ph and substrate composition on biohydrogen production from food waste in batch fermentation. Asian J. Biotechnol., 1: 42-50.

26. Norris, J.N., 2010. Marine Algae of the Northern Gulf of California: Chlorophyta and Phaeophyceae. Smithsonian Institution Scholarly Press, Washington, DC, USA., pp: 50-51.

27. Palazzi, E., P. Perego and B. Fabiano, 2002. Mathematical modelling and optimization of hydrogen continuous production in a fixed bed bioreactor. Chem. Eng. Sci., 57: 3819-3830.

28. Pfromm, P.H., V. Amanor-Boadu and R. Nelson, 2011. Sustainability of algae derived biodiesel: A mass balance approach. Bioresoure Technol., 102: 1185-1193.

29. Plaza, M., S. Santoyo, L. Jaime, G.G.B. Reina, M. Herrero, F.J. Senorans and E. Ibanez, 2010. Screening for bioactive compounds from algae. J. Pharm. Biomed. Anal., 51: 450-455.

30. Prabina, B.J. and K. Kumar, 2010. Studies on the optimization of cultural conditions for maximum hydrogen production by selected cyanobacteria. ARPN J. Agric. Biol. Sci., 5: 22-31.

31. Rosenbaum, M., Z. He and L.T. Angenent, 2010. Light energy to bioelectricity: Photosynthetic microbial fuel cells. Curr. Opin. Biotech., 21: 259-264.

32. Saeed, F.F.M. and M.A. Ibrahim. 2012. Biohydrogen production by Green Alga Chaetomorpha sp. GAF99 from Gulf of Aqaba: III. Use of modeling and three dimensional plot to investigate critical influence of pH. Biotechnology, (In Press).

33. Sandgreen, G.D., 1991. Growth and Reproductive Strategies of Freshwater Phytoplankton. Cambridge University Press, Cambridge..

34. Song, W., N. Rashid, W. Choi and K. Lee, 2011. Biohydrogen production by immobilized Chlorella sp using cycles of oxygenic photosynthesis and anaerobiosis. Bioresource Technol., 102: 8676-8681.

35. Spolaore, P., C. Joannis-Cassan, E. Duran and A. Isambert, 2006. Commercial applications of microalgae. J. Biosci. Bioeng., 101: 87-96.

36. Stephenson, M. and L.H. Stickland, 1931. Hydrogenase: A bacterial enzyme activating molecular hydrogen. Biochem. J., 25: 205-214.

37. Vergara-Fernandez, A., G. Vargas, N. Alarcon and A. Velasco, 2008. Evaluation of marine algae as a source of biogas in a two-stage anaerobic reactor system. Biomass Bioenergy, 32: 338-344.

38. Vijayaraghavan, K., R. Karthik and S.P.K. Nalini, 2010. Hydrogen generation from algae: A review. J. Plant Sci., 5: 1-19.

39. Wiley, P.E., J.E. Campbell and B. McKuin, 2011. Production of biodiesel and biogas from algae: A review of process train options. Water Environ. Res., 83: 326-338.

Index